DMU 0629648 01 3

AF744644

WITHDRAWN
DE MONTFORT UNIVERSITY
LIBRARY

HUMAN RIGHTS BROUGHT HOME: SOCIO-LEGAL PERSPECTIVES ON HUMAN RIGHTS IN THE NATIONAL CONTEXT

What practical impact does the incorporation of international human rights standards into domestic law have? This collection of essays explores human rights in domestic legal systems. The enactment of the Human Rights Act in 1998, ushering the European Convention on Human Rights fully into UK law, represented a landmark in the UK constitutional order. Other European states similarly have elevated the status of human rights in their domestic legal systems. However, while much has been written about doctrinal legal developments, little is yet known about the empirical effects of bringing rights home. This collection of essays, written by a range of distinguished socio-legal scholars, seeks to fill this gap in knowledge. The essays, presenting new empirical research, begin their enquiry where many studies in human rights finish. The contributors do not stop at the recognition of international law and norms by states, but penetrate the internal workings of domestic legal systems to see the law in action — as it is developed, contested, manipulated, or even ignored by actors such as judges, lawyers, civil servants, interest groups, and others. This distinctly socio-legal approach offers a unique contribution to the literature on human rights, exploring human rights law-in-action in developed countries. In doing so, it demonstrates the importance of looking beyond grand generalities and the hopes of international human rights law in order to understand the impact of the global human rights movement.

Volume 3 in the Series, Human Rights Law in Perspective

Human Rights Law in Perspective
General Editor: Colin Harvey

The language of human rights figures prominently in legal and political debates at the national, regional and international levels. In the UK the Human Rights Act 1998 has generated considerable interest in the law of human rights. It will continue to provoke much debate in the legal community, and the search for original insights and new materials will intensify.

The aim of this series is to provide a forum for scholarly reflection on all aspects of the law of human rights. The series will encourage work that engages with the theoretical, comparative and international dimensions of human rights law. The primary aim is to publish over time books which offer an insight into human rights law in its contextual setting. The objective is to promote an understanding of the nature and impact of human rights law. The series is inclusive, in the sense that all perspectives in legal scholarship are welcome. It will incorporate the work of new and established scholars.

Human Rights Law in Perspective is not confined to consideration of the UK. It will strive to reflect comparative, regional and international perspectives. Work that focuses on human rights law in other states will therefore be included in this series. The intention is to offer an inclusive intellectual home for significant scholarly contributions to human rights law.

Volume 1 Importing the Law in Post-Communist Transitions
Catherine Dupré

Volume 2 The Development of the Positive Obligations Under the European Convention on Human Rights by the European Court of Human Rights
Alastair Mowbray

Volume 3 Human Rights Brought Home: Socio-Legal Perspectives on Human Rights in the National Context
edited by Simon Halliday and Patrick Schmidt

Volume 4 Corporations and Transnational Human Rights Litigation
Sarah Joseph

Human Rights Brought Home:
Socio-Legal Perspectives on Human Rights in the National Context

Edited by

Simon Halliday
Nicholas de B Katzenbach Research Fellow
Centre for Socio-Legal Studies, Oxford University

and

Patrick Schmidt
Assistant Professor in the Department of Political Science
Southern Methodist University, Dallas

•HART•
PUBLISHING

OXFORD AND PORTLAND OREGON
2004

Published in North America (US and Canada) by
Hart Publishing
c/o International Specialized Book Services
5804 NE Hassalo Street
Portland, Oregon
97213-3644
USA

© The editors and contributors severally 2004

The editors and contributors have asserted their right under the Copyright, Designs and Patents Act 1988, to be identified as the authors of this work.

Hart Publishing is a specialist legal publisher based in Oxford, England.
To order further copies of this book or to request a list of other publications please write to:

Hart Publishing, Salters Boatyard, Folly Bridge, Abingdon Rd, Oxford, OX1 4LB Telephone: +44 (0)1865 245533 Fax: +44 (0) 1865 794882
email: mail@hartpub.co.uk
WEBSITE: http//:www.hartpub.co.uk

British Library Cataloguing in Publication Data
Data Available

ISBN 1-84113-388-4 (hardback)

Typeset by Olympus Infotech Pvt Ltd, India, Sabon 10/12 pt
Printed and bound in Great Britain by
TJ International, Padstow, Cornwall

For Mark and Mary

— S H

For Lea Anne

— P S

Preface

This edited collection is a welcome and timely addition to the Series. As the editors suggest, there are unavoidable socio-legal questions raised by the presence of human rights standards in national legal systems. Evidence is, for example, required to assess the claims made for human rights at the national level and to measure impact in precise terms. The editors highlight a gap and with this collection hope to begin to fill it. They have gathered together a sample of socio-legal work, raising several pressing questions and offering an agenda for further research. The editors correctly stress the many research questions addressed in, and raised by, this collection.

The socio-legal research presented here complements existing doctrinal work and is a useful contribution to the literature on human rights. Not everyone will agree with the approaches adopted or conclusions reached. Disagreement continues, and the evidence gathered will not necessarily tell us what *should* be done. It does, however, provide a more secure basis for assessment of past and current practices and for future reform. The editors are surely right to encourage more socio-legal research on human rights.

This collection presents a challenge to those who genuinely believe that a culture of respect for human rights is worth striving for. How might this be achieved within diverse and complex national legal systems? This book provides some answers and presents options for further research.

Colin Harvey
June 2004

Acknowledgements

This collection of essays emerged out of a seminar series during Trinity term 2003 at the Centre for Socio-Legal Studies, Oxford University (where, at the time, we were both fellows). We would like to thank Denis Galligan and the Centre's fellows for sponsoring the series, and for providing a friendly and stimulating environment in which to develop this project. Since the inception of the project, Patrick Schmidt has taken up a post in the Department of Political Science at Southern Methodist University, and he similarly thanks the department and his new colleagues for their support.

We are grateful to all who gave papers in the original seminar series and to everyone who attended and contributed to the ongoing interesting debate. Many of the papers from the series have now been developed into chapters, and others were added later from outside the series. Special thanks are due to our authors for taking part in the project and making this volume possible. We are additionally very grateful to Oisin Tansey for his excellent research assistance and to Scarlet McBarnet for formatting the text with speed and thoroughness. We owe a debt of gratitude to the Law Faculty of Oxford University for funding this work. We shared ideas and discussions with many of our colleagues, and called upon some of them to read part drafts of the text. For the latter we thank in particular Valerie Hunt and Jim Hollifield. Finally, many thanks are owed to Richard Hart for his immediate enthusiasm for the idea of this book, and to April Boffin and the rest of the team at Hart for their help in bringing it to fruition.

Simon Halliday, Oxford
Patrick Schmidt, Dallas
January 2004

Contents

List of Contributors

Reza Banakar is a Reader at the School of Law, Westminster University, UK

Luke Clements is a Solicitor and Senior Research Fellow at Cardiff Law School, University of Wales, UK

Denis Galligan is Professor of Socio-Legal Studies and Director of the Centre for Socio-Legal Studies at Oxford University, UK

Anne Griffiths is a Reader in the School of Law, Edinburgh University, UK

Simon Halliday is the Nicholas de B Katzenbach Research Fellow at the Centre for Socio-Legal Studies, Oxford University, UK

Jacqueline Hodgson is a Senior Lecturer in the Law School at Warwick University, UK

Randy Frances Kandel is an Adjunct Associate Professor at John Jay College of Criminal Justice, City University of New York, USA

Stephen Livingstone is a Professor in the Law School of Queen's University Belfast, UK

Mikael Rask Madsen is a Doctoral Researcher at L'École des Hautes Études en Sciences Sociales, Centre de la Sociologie Européenne, Paris, France

Richard J Maiman is a Professor in the Department of Political Science, University of Southern Maine, USA, and a Visiting Fellow at the Human Rights Centre of the University of Essex, UK

Rachel Morris is a Research Associate at Cardiff Law School, University of Wales, UK

Rachel Murray is a Reader in the Law Department of Bristol University, UK

John Raine is a Professor in the School of Public Policy at the University of Birmingham, UK

Deborah Sandler is the Fay Millson Research Fellow at the Centre for Socio-Legal Studies, and a Fellow of St Catherine's College, Oxford University, UK

Patrick Schmidt is an Assistant Professor in the Department of Political Science at Southern Methodist University, Dallas, Texas, USA

Clive Walker is a Professor in the Law School of Leeds University, UK

1

Introduction: Socio-Legal Perspectives on Human Rights in the National Context

PATRICK SCHMIDT AND SIMON HALLIDAY

Stephen Gough, a 44-year-old former soldier nicknamed the 'Naked Rambler', was arrested numerous times while promoting naturism by walking naked over the length of Britain. Charged with a breach of the peace and jailed in Inverness, Scotland, while in the final stages of his Land's End to John O'Groats walk, he promised, 'I am going to continue with my naked walk and the campaign for naturists and human rights.'[1]

In the summer of 2002, Warwick University banned students from flying the English flag during football's World Cup. Challenging the university's claim that flag-flying causes racial tension, one student complained to the media that this act breached his 'human right to fly the national flag of my country.'[2]

After the UK Highways Agency failed to live up on a promise to resurface part of the A34 highway in Oxfordshire, in late 2003 the Gosford Village Committee moved to bring their complaint to the European Court of Human Rights, arguing that noise from the busy highway breached their human rights.[3]

EVEN IF YOU happened to miss Mr Gough on his nationwide trek, it would have been difficult to fail to notice that the landscape of law has been much changed by the language of rights. In the

[1] 'Bailed rambler vows to complete naturist trek', *The Guardian*, 27 August 2003, http://www.guardian.co.uk/silly/story/0,10821,102994,00.html (last accessed on 8 January 2004).
[2] 'University bans England flag', *The Telegraph*, 18 May 2002, http://news.telegraph.co.uk/news/main.jhtml?xml=/news/2002/05/18/nflag18.xml (last accessed on 8 January 2004).
[3] 'Noise "breaching human rights" ', BBC News, 30 November 2003, http://news.bbc.co.uk/go/pr/fr/-/1/hi/England/oxfordshire/3251494.stm (last accessed on 8 January 2004).

United Kingdom, the passage of the Human Rights Act 1998 (HRA), bringing the European Convention on Human Rights (ECHR) more fully within the UK's domestic legal system, hearkened a new era in which individuals could call on the protection of international human rights norms in the domestic courts as part of domestic law. As seen in Inverness, Warwick, and Gosford, some individuals and groups swiftly took hold of these legal tools in order to advance their claims — either rhetorically or legally — for protection from government encroachment or for affirmative government action for their social welfare.

At the end of the twentieth century one of the most striking features of the human rights field was the extent to which the law of human rights had become entrenched in the developed legal systems of the West. This is striking because the origins of human rights and its earliest applications have been expressed by the international community in international arenas. The Nuremberg war trials and subsequent international criminal courts typify the historical image of human rights, articulated against gross violations of rights such as torture and genocide. Further, though human rights earlier had largely been the province of international lawyers, in the twenty-first century it has become an instrument of domestic law across the common law and civil law world alike. Although human rights retains considerable vitality as an aspect of international law, with recent applications from Rwanda to Yugoslavia, this transformation has brought the concept more completely within complex and advanced legal systems, some of which have recognised some notions of civil and political rights for centuries.

In addition to its history in international law and politics, its influence on popular consciousness, and its place in a number of intellectual disciplines, then, 'human rights' has now become a concept of domestic law and may be explored and analysed within this framework. This has had a clear impact on legal research. Even before the full blossoming of domestic human rights adjudication in the UK, we witnessed the start of the now-explosion of legal scholarship exploring the implications of human rights for various areas of domestic law. As parties have raised human rights claims and judges have begun to develop a domestic human rights jurisprudence, the significance of human rights to domestic law and policy making has been all the more obvious. However, just as the reception of international human rights norms into domestic law raises a host of doctrinal questions, so too it raises unavoidable socio-legal questions in the national context. In the wake of such a seismic shift in the legal and constitutional landscape, a full and pressing socio-legal research agenda emerges. However, socio-legal work on human rights in the national context has failed to match the pace and enthusiasm of doctrinal work, particularly in terms of the empirical socio-legal evidence necessary to assess the claims made for human rights as legal practice. Michael Freeman has observed that, relative to law, the social sciences have traditionally neglected the study of human rights.[4] This observation, it is suggested, applies equally to the empirical study of human rights within the legal academy. Socio-legal analysis is the weaker party to doctrinal analysis.

Human rights, of course, have been the subjects of extensive study prior to their legal domestication. This scholarship has its origins in the study of international politics and law. A research agenda based in socio-legal studies has much to offer as a complement to such work. The dominant force of established research on human rights combines, we believe, to leave a gap in need of redress. That gap is in seeking focused empirical study of human rights implementation at the domestic level of developed nations, where that includes an interest in institutional and individual behaviour deeper than legislatures and constitutional courts.

Research on human rights, reflecting in part the concerns of international lawyers, has been slow to probe deeply into national systems to acquire empirical evidence about the dynamics of compliance with human rights norms. To be sure, there exists a wide recognition across disciplines that however international law is structured, as Richard Falk writes,

> unless internalisation by citizens of countries actually takes place, the impact of international standards is likely to be uneven and sporadic, both domestically and globally. One needs a continuing political struggle on the ground to realize human rights.[5]

This has encouraged an approach to research that is essentially comparative, rather than international in scope.[6] Yet, scholars of international law in particular have not generally employed a methodological apparatus that moves significantly beyond the structural elements of the judicial system or the legal decision-making of judges.[7]

International relations scholars have offered more searching empirical projects. Most notable in this regard has been the work of Risse, Sikkink, and others, demonstrating the importance of networks of actors (connecting domestic and transnational spheres) for the internalisation of norms.[8] In order to show the significance of transnational actors, their

[4] M Freeman, *Human Rights* (Cambridge, Polity Press, 2002).

[5] R Falk, *Human Rights Horizons: The Pursuit of Justice in a Globalizing World* (London, Routledge, 2000), 61.

[6] J Donnelly, *Universal Human Rights in Theory and Practice* (Ithaca, NY, Cornell University Press 2003).

[7] For a suggestive sample of work see the contributing authors in P Alston and J Crawford (eds), *The Future of UN Human Rights Treaty Monitoring* (Cambridge, Cambridge University Press, 2000), and P Alston (ed), *Promoting Human Rights Through Bills of Rights: Comparative Perspectives* (Oxford, Oxford University Press, 1999).

[8] Eg, T Rissee-Kappen, *Bringing Transnational Relations Back In* (Cambridge, Cambridge University Press, 1995); ME Keck and K Sikkink, *Activists Beyond Borders: Advocacy Networks in International Politics* (Ithaca, NY, Cornell University Press, 1998); T Risse,

case studies have examined the linkages in domestic contexts that support the acceptance of international norms. Other research has looked at national human rights institutions (the focus of Livingstone and Murray in chapter 6 of this volume) from the perspective of the development of a global order.[9] Some lines of inquiry remain largely at the level of international or transnational politics by asking, for example, what forces of the international system produce compliance with human rights norms, and what elements of political systems correlate most strongly with outward compliance. Multi-state comparisons help to generate one level of findings, though once beyond a handful of comparison countries, the quantitative measures necessary limit the depth of focus.[10] In overview, then, while scholars of international relations provide an empirical approach that heads in much of the same direction that we would seek, an underlying difference of approach stops short of inquiry that reaches inside national institutions and agencies for a thorough accounting of 'internalisation of norms' in practice. That job has often fallen to political scientists, whose contributions are well appreciated by the authors in this volume.[11] That is, the theoretical and empirical concern has centred on transnational organisations and actors, not to the exclusion of state actors, but without the depth of attention to 'sub-national' forces implementing human rights norms.

A related observation urging further socio-legal research on human rights is the particular need to distinguish the study of human rights implementation in advanced legal systems from human rights in more politically unstable nations. A healthy portion of work in international law and international relations naturally turns to the 'trouble spots' for compliance — problem cases among the former Communist-bloc countries, the new

SC Ropp and K Sikkink (eds), *The Power of Human Rights: International Norms and Domestic Change* (Cambridge, Cambridge University Press, 1999).

[9] S Cardenas, 'Transgovernmental Activism: Canada's Role in Promoting National Human Rights Commissions', (2003) 25 *Human Rights Quarterly* 775–90; S Cardenas, 'Emerging Global Actors: The United Nations and National Human Rights Institutions', (2003) 9 *Global Governance* 23ff.

[10] As leading examples see, L Camp Keith, 'The United Nations International Covenant on Civil and Political Rights: Does It Make a Difference in Human Rights Behavior?' (1999) 36 *Journal of Peace Research* 95–118; OA Hathaway, 'Do Human Rights Treaties Make a Difference?' (2002) 111 *Yale Law Journal* 1935ff; but for greater depth with impressive breadth, see C Heyns and F Viljoen, *The Impact of the United National Human Rights Treaties on the Domestic Level* (The Hague/London/New York, Kluwer Law International, 2002).

[11] H Tolley Jr, 'Interest Group Litigation to Enforce Human Rights' (1990) 105 *Political Science Quarterly* 617–38; CR Epp, *The Rights Revolution: Lawyers, Activists, and Supreme Courts in Comparative Perspective* (Chicago, The University of Chicago Press, 1998); A Stone Sweet, *Governing With Judges: Constitutional Politics in Europe* (Oxford, Oxford University Press, 2000).

democracies of Latin America, the states of Asia, or the failed states of central and western Africa. These nations have in common a higher likelihood of egregious violations of human rights, which allows for study free from serious questions about the universality of the norms being implemented. These nations also tend to share an institutional setting (particularly regarding legal traditions) that is less mature than the developed nations of Western Europe and North America. Undoubtedly, human rights deserves attention in countries where a radical breakdown of social order has resulted in large-scale violations of rights. Nevertheless, a collective contribution of the chapters in this volume is to suggest that the domestic politics in mature legal-political systems must be approached differently both because the institutional setting is different — where, for example, we can hypothesise that the internalisation of norms should be easier to achieve — and because the substance of rights discourse in systems free of genocide and torture are those about which disagreement is strong. Indeed, where human rights have been received into domestic law, the role of defining human rights abuses falls to the domestic courts rather than the international community and institutions. Even among the nations of Europe there remain sharp divisions over the meaning and scope of affirmative political and social rights. Thus, there is an interaction effect between the setting and the rights for investigation that makes further study of these systems necessary. The chapters in this volume suggest, even, that future scholars may wish to test a hypothesis regarding the prospect of internalising norms that would seem paradoxical from international relations treatments of human rights. It may be that mature domestic systems have a strong overall capacity for internalisation of international norms — especially, as Mikael Madsen points out in chapter 3, because these norms were first exported by these states to the nascent international order — but that in practice we find ambivalence or antagonism over human rights in mature states because the cutting-edge struggles working their way through the system concern claims of civil and political rights with less claim to universality as human rights.

As a collection, then, the chapters in this volume help to fill gaps left by other disciplines, and in doing so, they raise important questions about the nature of human rights regimes. Perhaps most importantly, the domestic legal politics of human rights suggests how cultural relativity is more vital than ever — that we must understand the national setting more closely than has been appreciated. The aim of this book is to use the tools of social science to analyse the operations of the domestic legal concept of human rights. It has collected new and largely empirical research on the subject of human rights in the national context. By gathering this work together within a single volume, we hope to offer a snapshot of current socio-legal work which illustrates the kind of research questions which must be pursued, and we also offer some further issues which may be explored.

ANALYTICAL FRAMEWORK FOR THE BOOK

In this section we set out a very general analytical framework which embraces the themes of the chapters in the book and which we believe is helpful for approaching the socio-legal study of human rights in the national context. It would be foolish, however, (and, indeed, against the spirit of social enquiry) to pretend that the framework suggests anything like a definitive list of socio-legal approaches. Similarly, it would be a wasted enterprise to try to set out a definitive list of specific questions to be asked in socio-legal research. Our aims are much more modest. We offer here a very broad sense of the settled terrain of socio-legal work which may be usefully applied to the study of human rights law in the domestic context. We might, then, suggest a 'map' of this terrain which has heuristic potential, though is not intended to be interpreted restrictively.

The chapters address a range of specific socio-legal questions. We believe these questions can be usefully conceived of as belonging to one (or more) of a number of fields of well-established socio-legal inquiry: the creation of law, its implementation, and the reach of law. This ordering of themes has an attractive simplicity about it given the fact that current political and legal debate poses international law as an instrument to be implemented into national law. 'Top-down' questions about implementation and impact easily follow such a conceptualisation of human rights law. However, before elaborating further on these themes, it is important to note that by suggesting them we do not mean to impose or restrict ourselves to a top-down model of law in society. The well rehearsed criticisms of top-down socio-legal scholarship have great merit, and it is important to explore the indirect and constitutive effects of law in society.[12] However, top-down questions are still worthy of enquiry, it is suggested, so long as it is recognised that they do not exhaust the range of socio-legal questions that may be pursued. Further, to ask top-down questions does not preclude an interpretivist or 'bottom-up' methodological approach.[13] Indeed, many of the authors in this collection point out the ways that human rights law has its sources or is shaped by bottom-up processes. The traditions of top-down

[12] See, eg S Silbey, 'Cultural Analyses of Law' (1992) 17(1), *Law and Social Inquiry* 39–48; M McCann, 'Reform Litigation on Trial' (1992) 17, *Law and Social Inquiry* 715ff; A Sarat and T Kearns, 'Beyond the great divide: forms of legal scholarship and everyday life' in A Sarat and T Kearns (eds), *Law in Everyday Life* (Ann Arbor, University of Michigan Press, 1993); P Ewick and S Silbey, *The Common Place of Law: Stories from Everyday Life* (Chicago, University of Chicago Press, 1998); D Engel and Frank Munger, *Rights of Inclusion: Law and Identity in the Life Stories of Americans with Disabilities* (Chicago, University of Chicago Press, 2003).

[13] M Hertogh and S Halliday, 'Judicial Review and Bureaucratic Impact in Future Research' in M Hertogh and S Halliday (eds), *Judicial Review and Bureaucratic Impact: International and Interdisciplinary Perspectives* (Cambridge, Cambridge University Press, 2004).

and bottom up approaches need not be mutually exclusive within a project as broad as the study of human rights. Rather, they may complement each other and display the range of socio-legal contributions across an array of more specific settings.

Creation of Law

Scholars in the social sciences have informed the understanding of how 'law on the books' is created. At one level, socio-legal studies has sought to expose the ways that law embodies the conflicts and differences of power and status in society. Reacting to visions of law as 'natural' or rational expressions of legislative wisdom, an alternative version pointed out the ways in which law is subject to contestation before legislatures, administrative bodies, courts or other bodies. At the most structural level, research in socio-legal studies has been influenced by Marxist or other critical perspectives that look for a privileged position in the workings of law making. Commentary on the international law of human rights frequently reflects such criticism, such as in the assertion that human rights norms have been the creation of Western developed nations and as such are a hegemonic and culturally biased force when other nations are held to the same standard. Less structurally, an important contribution from social science inquiry into law has been a focus on the judicialisation of politics, whereby law makers operate within the context of the courts' powers to review legislative content. This vein of research has particular significance for the study of human rights in the national context given their heightened constitutional significance. Another important contribution of socio-legal studies to our understanding of the creation of law has been the study of social and political forces in law-making. Owing much to political science, socio-legal scholars have long been interested in the mobilisation of social movements and interest groups, for example. Law-making institutions set agendas and make decisions influenced by the structure of interest participation. Wider social forces shape the options and choices of decision-makers, resulting in law that bears the marks of those struggles.

Implementation of Law

The earliest socio-legal research commonly pointed to the 'gap' between the assumed meaning of law 'on the books' and the meaning of law 'in practice'. This early research revealed an interplay of ideas and interests which reframed and shaped the content of law being applied. Socio-legal studies now assumes that an inevitable gap exists between black letter law and law-in-action. However, research in this tradition holds an abiding concern with analysing the discretion inherent in the process of applying general law in specific cases, amplified in practice by the problems of multi-level governance and governance that crosses communities and cultures. Research into the effectiveness of regulatory rulemaking and enforcement is the case *par excellence* of how empirical research has unpacked a complex configuration of pressures surrounding lower-level decision-making, revealing in the process apparent anomalies such as law creation-through-interpretation and non-compliance with legal norms. The position of human rights might be seen as particularly precarious in light of this prior research, as they seek to flow from 'universal' norms through layers of national and sub-national institutions, in the course of which human rights law is subjected to strong desires for local adaptation in discretionary decision-making.

The Reach of Law

Following immediately upon (and somewhat overlapping with) the study of legal implementation, social scientists have trained their sights to subjects further afield from the conceptual centre of formal law, where we might observe the ultimate impact of law. Taking an instrumental view of law, many socio-legal scholars have been interested in how the law — shaped as it is through the process of interpretation — affects the behaviours it was intended to address, with its actual effects being measured against its intended impact. This concern with the reach of law includes an interest in the way that law affects the consciousness of people — people's senses of fairness, grievance, identity, potential, and so forth — and the social actions that emerge from their consciousnesses. An interest in consciousness is pertinent for the study of human rights law given, for example, the UK government's stated goal of promoting a human rights culture. Importantly, of course, socio-legal studies has not ignored the reflexive influence of consciousness on law — that the creative process of the law takes as its source the norms and cultures that produce the law. Similarly, it has explored legal consciousness as a way both of highlighting the difference between formal and street-level perceptions of law and legal values, and of exploring experiences and perceptions of law in everyday life. The vignettes opening this chapter suggest that similar work about the reach of human rights into everyday experiences would be equally fruitful.

EMERGING QUESTIONS

The preceding section suggested a map of the settled terrain of socio-legal scholarship that may be usefully turned to the study of human rights in the national context. Before setting out synopses of the chapters in this volume, we build on this analytical sketch by briefly exploring some important questions for socio-legal research that emerge from the chapters.

'Domesticating' Human Rights

The title of this collection, 'Human Rights Brought Home', makes reference to the intention of the UK government to develop a human rights culture by incorporating the ECHR into domestic UK law.[14] In this sense, this book is an examination of the domestication of human rights law. There is another sense in which human rights may have been 'domesticated' by being received into national law. One of the themes to emerge from a number of the chapters is that the impact of bringing rights home has been more like a 'damp squib' than the fireworks anticipated. Human rights, then, or at least certain aspects of human rights, may have been 'domesticated' — in the sense of being tamed — by its entry into national legal systems. In other disciplines, such as international relations or politics, human rights may gain its strength as an idea precisely because it stands outside of law and thereby permits a critique of law in addition to political action.[15] The chapters of Raine and Walker and Clements and Morris suggest that human rights may lose some of its power as an idea by being transformed into a domestic legal concept. By becoming 'merely law' human rights becomes subject to the same limitations, qualifications, mundanities and technical operations as other aspects of domestic law. As they explain, those who witnessed this transformation first hand seemed to express some disappointment (or perhaps relief) at the reality of human rights law. To adapt Stuart Scheingold's phrase,[16] incorporation measures such as the HRA may simply have heralded the myth of human rights. For, despite Francesca Klug's suggestion that human rights constitute 'values for a godless age',[17] it may be that human rights cease to be sacred and become profane — or at least an uncomfortable and uncertain combination of the two — by being dragged down to the level of domestic law. The risk is higher when the domestic legal culture, like UK law, is not traditionally rights-based, when there is greater comfort with deference to Parliament and government,[18] or where human rights are interpreted as adding little to existing protections.

[14] Labour Party, *Bringing Rights Home: Labour's Plans to Incorporate the European Convention on Human Rights into UK Law* (London, Labour Party, 1996).
[15] M Freeman, *Human Rights* 8–12.
[16] S Scheingold, *The Politics of Rights: Lawyers, Public Policy, and Political Change* (New Haven, Yale University Press, 1974).
[17] F Klug, *Values for a Godless Age: The Story of the United Kingdom's New Bill of Rights* (London, Penguin Books, 2000).
[18] See M Hunt 'The Human Rights Act and Legal Culture: The Judiciary and the Legal Profession' (1999) 26(1), *Journal of Law and Society* 86–102; L Lazarus, *Contrasting Prisoners' Rights* (Oxford, Oxford University Press, 2004).

Should this prove to be the case, it raises the important question of who benefits from the domestication of human rights. There may be greater benefits for politicians and/or lawyers than there are for citizens.

These questions raise the need to focus on legal culture in assessing the effects and significance of constitutional developments such as the HRA. As Banakar observes in this collection, legal culture comprises both the legal consciousness of the judiciary and ordinary citizens. There is clearly a relation between the two. If the judiciary develops a jurisprudence of human rights based on deference or existing protections, the demands made on actors such as bureaucrats or the police are less exacting or special than they might otherwise be. Similarly, the popular consciousness of those who come into contact with the reality of human rights jurisprudence may be one of disappointment. In other words, human rights may become something of a 'non-event' in the perceptions both of those charged within implementing legal provisions and of the ordinary citizens.

Rights and Consciousness

Some important themes may arise as a counter point to the above discussion. First, socio-legal studies in the US has long had a debate about the role of courts in producing social change, which has sparked some interesting and important work on the power of rights in the face of the limited impact of the courts.[19] Much of the 'bottom-up' socio-legal work in this field has demonstrated that rights retain power as a concept despite their apparent lack of 'impact' when viewed from a 'top-down' perspective. Notions of fundamental rights may nevertheless inspire the imagination of individuals and social movement actors, provide rallying points for activists, and offer a sense of hope for social change. This literature, which is surveyed and discussed by Richard Maiman in his chapter, focuses our attention on the human rights consciousness of a range of actors.

The full range of actors may be more expansive than one might think at first. It is tempting to imagine that only the traditional 'victims' of society would mobilise around the concept of human rights. However, human rights may simultaneously fire the imaginations of corporate lawyers. Powerful corporations may also cast themselves as victims of rights abuses and litigate accordingly,[20] as for instance in the case of media corporations

[19] See, eg G Rosenberg, *The Hollow Hope: Can Courts Bring About Social Change?* (London, University of Chicago Press, 1991); M McCann, *Rights at Work: Pay Equity Reform and the Politics of Legal Mobilization* (London, University of Chicago Press, 1994); D Schulz (ed), *Leveraging the Law: Using the Courts to Achieve Social Change* (New York, Peter Lang, 1998).

[20] See, eg MJ Gibney, 'Introduction' in MJ Gibney (ed), *Globalizing Rights* (Oxford, Oxford University Press, 2003).

claiming the right of free speech.[21] The particular question raised in a constitutional context like that of the UK is whether something special about human rights — as opposed to other domestic legal rights — captures the hearts of citizens, or fires the imagination of social movement or interest groups. Do human rights rise above the limitations imposed on other legal rights in a constitution founded on parliamentary sovereignty? This is a question which has exercised doctrinal scholars, but it is also an important question about legal consciousness for socio-legal scholars.

Diversity of Human Rights

The second point to be made in response to the question of human rights' 'domestication' is that it is important not to treat human rights as a monolithic concept. As Galligan and Sandler point out in the next chapter, human rights are often categorised into three groups: civil and political rights, social and economic rights, and collective rights. Some authors trace an overlapping historical development of human rights, setting out three 'generations' of rights — from 'negative' liberties, to positive social and economic rights, to environmental rights — though others prefer the metaphor of 'waves' of human rights.[22] Human rights are many and varied. The chapters in this book focus principally on the human rights expressed in the European Convention, and so consider civil and political rights in the main. Nevertheless, it is still important to recognise that there is diversity even within this group. Returning to our earlier discussion, not all rights have equal pertinence for a society like the UK, though all are important in the event of breach. It may be that some human rights are regarded as being more of a damp squib than others. Such a view is certainly merited politically (and legally), and it may be that this is also reflected in public consciousness — or it may be so in time. Some human rights may be more inspirational or provide a greater rallying point than others. In other words, in engaging in socio-legal analysis we may have to be sensitive to different social processes that revolve around or emerge from particular human rights as they are played out in domestic society.

Explaining Successful/Failed Implementation

As we noted earlier, scholars in the fields of both international relations and international law recognise the importance of the national context for

[21] Sir S Sedley 'Human Rights: a Twenty-First Century Agenda' (1995) *Public Law* 386–400.
[22] F Klug, *Values for a Godless Age: The Story of the United Kingdoms' New Bill of Rights* 9.

the implementation of human rights norms. However, international law scholarship has focused too exclusively, perhaps, on the role of national institutions in understanding cross-national variations of implementation. International relations scholarship has shown greater diversity in the development of explanatory frameworks for analysing implementation. The debate within international relations can be characterised, broadly speaking, as being between realist and social constructivist explanations.[23] The realist school focuses on economic or military conditions as determining the impact of international human rights norms on domestic politics.[24] National compliance is explained in terms of material enforcement from one state to another. The social constructivist school, on the other hand, stresses the additional role of ideas and norm internalisation in explaining national compliance with human rights standards.[25] This debate about the significance of norms to behaviour, of course, is writ large across the social sciences. It is no surprise, then, that these perspectives are reflected in the chapters of this volume, particularly those of Banakar, Hodgson, and Clements and Morris. Banakar and Hodgson stress the cultural dimension of the implementation process. Both essays highlight the importance of the values and norms of various actors to implementation outcomes. Where clashes arise between human rights norms and the norms of street-level actors, the implementation process will be stifled or skewed. The chapter by Clements and Morris, on the other hand, focuses on the role of external constraints in understanding implementation. They account for the failure of the human rights implementation process by comparing the dynamics of human rights as a regulatory regime with those of other accountability regimes. Human rights as a regulatory regime, they suggest, is less prescriptive and imposing than other regulatory regimes which apply to local government action.

It should be noted, however, that each of these chapters are more subtle and sophisticated than these characterisations permit, and none of them would seek to explain general implementation exclusively in terms of either external constraints or internal norms. By highlighting the differing emphases, these chapters point us to the importance of intimately exploring particular contexts in understanding the success or failures of human rights regulatory regimes. The regulatory enforcement literature

[23] See T Risse and K Sikkink, 'The Socialization of International Human Rights Norms into Domestic Practices: Introduction' in T Risse, S Roppe and K Sikkink (eds), *The Power of Human Rights: International Norms and Domestic Change.*

[24] See SD Krasner, 'Sovereignty, Regimes and Human Rights' in V Rittberger and P Mayer (eds), *Regime Theory and International Relations* (Oxford, Oxford University Press, 1993).

[25] ME Keck and K Sikkink, *Activists Beyond Borders: Advocacy Networks in International Politics;* T Risse and S Ropp, 'International Human Rights Norms and Domestic Change: Conclusions' in T Risse, S Roppe and K Sikkink (eds), *The Power of Human Rights: International Norms and Domestic Change.*

shares the debate about the significance of external constraints as opposed to internal attitudes and values to compliance,[26] sometime referred to the difference between 'punishing' and 'persuading'. However, as a number of scholars have noted,[27] in terms of effectiveness, the important question is not whether to punish or persuade, but when to punish and when to persuade. Indeed, the theory of responsive regulation is premised on a flexible enforcement strategy which will permit a regulator to switch between punishment and persuasion in various degrees according to the behaviour, competence and attitude of the regulatee.[28] This insight demonstrates that to understand the success or failure of human rights as a regulatory regime we must investigate particular settings in order to discern the relative significance of internal and external factors to compliance. The socio-legal study of compliance with human rights law in the domestic setting, then, must be an incremental process where researchers build on the work of others and slowly construct an intimate picture of implementation. The research agenda is, accordingly, both broad and demanding.

SYNOPSES OF CHAPTERS

The contributors to this volume take up many of these themes and address many of the above questions, though the possible directions for ongoing inquiry seem limitless. As we have already indicated, the chapters in this volume offer only a snapshot of recent work and an illustration of possible socio-legal perspectives on human rights in the national context. We believe the chapters raise as many questions as they answer, and we hope, accordingly, that this book will provoke further socio-legal enquiry. We conclude this introduction with a summary of the chapters in this volume.

The first contribution begins on an analytical note. Denis Galligan and Deborah Sandler offer us a wide ranging consideration of the problem underlying many of the following chapters: namely, what is so distinctive about human rights as a regulatory regime? Socio-legal studies has devoted substantial effort to understanding the possibilities and limits of regulation

[26] See, eg K Hawkins, 'Compliance Strategy, Prosecution Policy and Aunt Sally' (1990) 30 *British Journal of Criminology* 444ff; and F Pearce and S Tombs, 'Ideology, Hegemony, and Empiricism: Compliance Theories of Regulation' (1990) 30 *British Journal of Criminology* 423ff.
[27] See, eg J Braithwaite, *To Punish or Persuade: Enforcement of Coal Mine Safety* (Albany, State University of New York Press, 1985); R Kagan and J Scholz, 'The "Criminology of the Corporation" and Regulatory Enforcement Strategies' in K Hawkins and J Thomas (eds), *Enforcing Regulation* (Boston, Mass, Kluwer-Nijhoff, 1984).
[28] I Ayres and J Braithwaite, *Responsive Regulation: Transcending the Deregulation Debate* (Oxford, Oxford University Press, 1992).

as a form of social control, and in some ways human rights would seem to be an evolutionary step taken to the level of international norms. Yet, as Galligan and Sandler note, the 'partnership' between the international and national presents difficult conceptual and practical problems. Not least of them is the problem of origins and definition: where do these rights come from and how are they defined? As rights, human rights may seem universal in character but they are also subjected to interpretation and adaptation in national contexts. In single domestic contexts observers may be comfortable with limiting assumptions made about the scope of human rights — such as whether they include economic and social rights in addition to civil and political rights — but taken internationally there are serious challenges made to the authority of human rights as norms for governance. In an important move, the authors recognise the dependence of the international on the national context. Thus, they map out the course of human rights from international treaties to constitutionalism and, ultimately, consider the significance of administrative processes to the protection of human rights. This tour emphasises the wide scope and breadth of the problem facing human rights implementation, for we are reminded that human rights must pass from a contested international order through layers of governance and layers of norms. Yet, while reminding us of the idiosyncratic nature of human rights, Galligan and Sandler frame the chapters to follow by directing us to seek out the patterns and variables affecting the regulatory effectiveness of human rights norms.

The remaining chapters present new empirical data to explore the subject of human rights in the domestic context. The first of these chapters examines the historical development of human rights law. Mikael Rask Madsen offers a richly textured account of the emergence of the field of human rights in the second half of the twentieth century. His structural account of the development of human rights takes as its focus the forces in France and the UK that worked to export national norms into the international sphere, and then he lets readers look on as many of the same individuals and institutions play a part in re-importing those norms into the French and British legal systems. With classic socio-legal sensitivities, Madsen provides a 'bottom-up' perspective on the construction of human rights as a new field of legal development. Laying out the two national cases in parallel, the author locates the motivation for human rights, in part, in the uncertain status of the legal profession in the post-War era. Undermined by wartime collaboration in France and the rise of the welfare state in both countries, it appeared that law could be revitalised and lawyers could regain status as engineers of this revolution. Madsen's research involved scores of interviews with key figures in both countries' human rights movements, and shows with compelling detail the interaction of individuals, interest groups, and the state as human rights rose from its nascent form to a significant legal tool. The reforms within the domestic system, though gradual, interacted with the developments at the regional and international level, with the European Convention on Human Rights beginning to test the domestic commitment. Thus, Madsen uncovers a central irony: that the new international field created out of domestic systems could focus back on its origins and challenge those very domestic systems. Though this dual quality of human rights — both domestic in origin but still external to national systems — allows for further inquiry into governmental efforts at compliance, it also invites consideration of how non-state actors are invested in the very fabric of law-making. This latter theme is picked up in the following chapter.

Richard Maiman continues the focus on the development of human rights law, though not from an historical perspective. Maiman looks at the role of interest groups in the development of human rights jurisprudence in the courts. He presents a case study of Liberty, a leading human rights interest group in the UK. Maiman offers us a close study of how Liberty has adapted to the new legal environment following the passage of the Human Rights Act 1998. Maiman's inquiry is well-grounded in the scholarly literature examining interest group advocacy for rights in the US. The language of 'human rights' remains somewhat foreign to the American ear, but the difference in name belies a common concern with rights that make the American experience a valuable intellectual resource for socio-legal research in other contexts. Much of this literature seemed to suggest that the UK was inhospitable to rights movements, but the transformation of the constitutional foundations through the full acceptance of the European Convention into UK law changes the conditions. Indeed, Maiman finds that Liberty, once the leading advocacy group for human rights, now must adapt to a burgeoning human rights movement that features more cases being raised and more organisations seeking to influence the direction of human rights law. The overall significance of interest groups to the effective meaning of human rights in national contexts cannot be doubted, but the author highlights a great need to understand both how the mobilisation of interests depends on the domestic setting and how variations lodged within those systems affect the kind of tool that 'human rights' law becomes. Far from a constitutional system that — now in place — is a self-propelled machine, the window provided by Liberty in the UK suggests that the trajectory of human rights implementation in national contexts will depend in part on idiosyncratic strategic choices made by legal actors motivated by a range of factors from policy goals to organisational maintenance. Maiman's foray into the UK context thus presents a path that socio-legal scholars in Europe must follow if they are to understand the landscape of human rights.

John Raine and Clive Walker continue the focus on courts, focusing on the impact of the Human Rights Act on the routine operations of a number of courts in England — the Crown Court, the county court and the magistrates' court. In the subtitle to their chapter, Raine and Walker raise the question that might be seen as a challenge to academic commentators as well as a synthesis of their empirical findings: could the adoption of international human rights norms into domestic legal practice be nothing more than a 'damp squib'? Their study, amply supported by qualitative and quantitative data from the courts, compares the expectations and the reality of human rights implementation as experienced by the courts. As the European Convention on Human Rights was fully incorporated into English courts, many people reasonably anticipated that courts would face the brunt of the onslaught, in the form of new appeals based on the newly-available legal tool. Asked by the Lord Chancellor's Department to study the implementation, Raine and Walker found mixed results. Perhaps their most noteworthy finding is that the volume of cases involving human rights issues appeared little more than a trickle, especially relative to overall case loads. The effect on other possible concerns, such as reason-giving by magistrates and a corresponding fear of longer case-processing times, appeared muted. These findings might challenge supporters and critics of the Human Rights Act alike, those who seek human rights as a revolutionary development and those who see human rights as a threat to the sovereignty of law. The authors note intriguingly that the impact on the consciousness of the courts may be far more significant, and the high level of preparation for the Act's implementation may account for the readiness and heightened expectations of a human rights flood. Indeed, Raine and Walker make note of the changes to internal court practices, evidencing how human rights can be received into an advanced legal system. Ultimately, then, the authors' challenge may be to push readers to seek out the impact of human rights in the subtleties of legal interactions and consciousness, where human rights may blend into the system without revolutionary effect.

In the wake of the reception of international human rights norms into domestic law, domestic courts become an important and central legal institution for the supervision and enforcement of human rights law. However, the courts are not the only such institution. In the next two chapters other institutions are examined. First, Stephen Livingstone and Rachel Murray examine the Northern Ireland Human Rights Commission in order to address the broader question of what makes national human rights institutions effective. Livingstone and Murray set out three aims for their chapter. First, they develop criteria for evaluating the effectiveness of national human rights institutions, looking especially at how a national human rights institution has used the powers and resources given to it and what impact this had on the promotion and protection of human rights. Secondly, they apply those criteria principally to the operations of the Northern Ireland Human Rights Commission (though consideration is also given to the South African Human Rights Commission). Thirdly, they draw upon the critical analysis of the Northern Irish and South African Commissions in order to make recommendations with regard to the composition, powers, resources and operation of human rights commissions, with particular reference to other potential commissions in the United Kingdom. The authors' analytical work is as important as their empirical assessment of the Northern Ireland Human Rights Commission's effectiveness. They develop eighteen benchmarks for assessing the effectiveness of national human rights institutions, each grouped within one of three categories: capacity (referring to the powers, resources, composition and the context within which the commission operates); performance (looking at how powers are exercised); and legitimacy (considering the commission's standing and relationships). Livingstone and Murray draw on a range of data when applying these criteria to the Northern Ireland Human Rights Commission. Notably, in considering the impact of the Commission, the authors draw on a series of semi-structured interviews with government, parliamentarians, NGOs, civil society, religious organisations, trade unions, and those who had used the Commission's services. The authors carefully analyse their data and set out the conclusion that the Northern Ireland Human Rights Commission to date has not proved as effective as many hoped it would and is struggling to make a significant impact on the promotion and particularly the protection of human rights. They conclude their chapter with a series of recommendations, both for the Northern Irish Commission, and for commissions in general.

Reza Banakar continues the focus on supervisory institutions in examining the role of the ombudsman in Sweden. His chapter is also the first of three which look empirically at the implementation of human rights law, exploring the conditions which mediate the effectiveness of the legal provisions. Banakar argues that the effective implementation of human rights and freedoms requires a multi-layered institutional infrastructure for legal decision-making, such as a hierarchy of courts and public authorities. Significantly, however, it also requires a legal culture — comprising both the legal consciousness of the judiciary and ordinary citizens — which is committed to upholding the underlying values of human rights and freedoms. Whereas an institutional infrastructure may be constructed fairly quickly (albeit dependent on sufficient political will and material resources), a legal culture cannot be introduced from above by a political elite or the state administration. This means that the reception and effectiveness of laws which try to introduce new values and behavioural patterns can be fundamentally different from laws whose values are already entrenched in the custom and mores of some sections of the society. Banakar's thesis is demonstrated by his case study of the operations of two Swedish ombudsmen monitoring and enforcing different aspects of anti-discrimination law — the right to sexual equality on the one hand, and the right to racial equality on the other. By looking at various data including the flow of cases considered by the ombudsmen and the disposals of these cases, Banakar argues that the law against sex discrimination has been far more effective. He explains this in terms of contemporary Swedish cultural values. The author argues that sexual equality has been an ingrained value in Swedish culture for a long time. The anti-discrimination law is best regarded, he suggests, as a continuation of a long struggle for equality by the women's movement, spanning over a century. Race equality, however, is a less prevalent cultural value. The anti-discrimination law arose after pressure from the international community and was not the culmination of a bottom-up political struggle. Thus, the two Swedish anti-discrimination laws and their corresponding rights to equal treatment produce different results not because they operate differently from a point of view internal to the law, nor because they prescribe different sanctions and employ different procedures, nor because one is enforced more rigorously than the other, but because they constitute two different forms of legislation, the one emerging from below as a result of an ongoing rights discourse and acting bottom-up, and the other being imposed from above to introduce a rights discourse and acting top-down.

Jacqueline Hodgson's chapter builds on that of Banakar in analysing the cultural barriers to the implementation of ECHR norms in the French criminal justice system. Her focus on France provides a very interesting point of comparison when thinking about the UK's reception of the ECHR via the Human Rights Act 1998. Unlike the UK, France has a monist constitutional system and so, in theory at least, the mechanism of incorporation is total and free from the shackles of parliamentary sovereignty. Additionally, France ratified the ECHR in 1974 and the right to individual petition was granted in 1981. Her case study, then, is able to contemplate, at least in comparison to the UK, a reasonably long history of incorporation and this adds weight to her analysis. Hodgson assesses the process of incorporation at both a macro and micro level. She argues that despite its monist system, France has displayed considerable anxiety in relation to the protection of judicial autonomy and national sovereignty from international legal norms. She describes the relationship between French political and legal culture and paints a picture of considerable resistance to what are regarded as alien legal norms. Legal values associated with adversarialism are regarded as inimical to France's mixed/inquisitorial system and a threat to French legal culture. At the micro level, Hodgson draws on her ethnographic data to reveal, similarly, the strength of inquisitorial values in the routine operation of the prosecution process. She focuses extensively on pre-trial defence rights offered through the ECHR and observes how they are interpreted negatively as undermining the existing structure of legal protections effected through a prevailing model of judicial supervision of the pre-trial process. Although police investigations are judicially supervised, the relationship between judge and police is marked by trust.

She observes that judicial supervision is unable to offer any real guarantees as to the treatment of the suspect and the process of her investigation and interrogation. Hodgson concludes that the reception of the ECHR into the French criminal justice process has been distorted by structural, systemic and cultural barriers and has fallen short of the shifts which ECHR jurisprudence demands.

Luke Clements and Rachel Morris explore the implementation of the Human Rights Act on local government behaviour. They conducted a survey of local authority responses to the Human Rights Act three years after it received the Royal Assent and one year after it came into force. The survey explored general issues of training, human rights awareness and perceptions about the likely impact of the Act on routine operations. Additionally, it focused specifically on local government operations in relation to travelling people. Clements and Morris paint a picture of some apathy, both in terms of local authorities' perceptions about the Act's import and in terms of their responses to the Act to date. A significant proportion of their respondents regarded the Act as being a non-event, echoing a theme of Raine and Walker's chapter above. This finding was particularly strong in relation to specific questions about the implications for the position of travelling people. Such a finding stands in great contrast to the constitutional implications of the Human Rights Act, and to the predictions concerning its impact for local authorities. In relation to training, Clements and Morris found that most local authorities did not fully utilise the two-year period between the Royal Assent and the Act's commencement. Rather they concentrated their training programmes into the period immediately before or in the year after its commencement and for more than half of their respondent local authorities, the training comprised a one-off event. The authors further found that only 61 per cent of respondent local authorities had undertaken a general review of their policies to assess their compliance with the 1998 Act, and only 36 per cent in relation to their policies relating to Travelling People. They point to the importance of accountability programmes to help explain local authority responses to the Human Rights Act. They note that the Act is only one of a number of accountability regimes which have been imposed upon local government in recent years. They focus in particular on the 'Best Value' regime and argue that it has been far more compelling for local government than the Human Rights Act. It is highly prescriptive, requires the development by the local authority of detailed plans and is accompanied by an array of performance targets, voluminous guidance and a rigorous auditing regime. The local authority imperative of developing and maintaining internal systems so as to meet these external targets and not fail the highly public auditing process means that legislation of this type is far more likely to concentrate the minds of local councils than open textured rights based 'stand alone' legislation.

So far the chapters in this volume have examined a number of arenas of socio-legal enquiry in relation to human rights in the national context: the formal reception of international human rights norms into the domestic sphere; human rights adjudication and the development of human rights jurisprudence; the role of human rights institutions; and the street-level implementation process. Anne Griffiths and Randy Kandel complete this collection by looking at a final arena of enquiry — the perspectives and consciousness of the bearers of human rights. They explore the experiences of young people who have come before the children's hearings system in Scotland. These proceedings have become the focus of human rights concerns in relation to due process, particularly under Article 6 of the ECHR. Griffiths and Kandel use their ethnographic data about children's experiences to highlight the differences between legal, institutional and children's approaches to the values which underpin the human right to fair proceedings. They set out the domestic jurisprudence about the implications of Article 6 for the children's hearing system, noting that the law solves the problem of ineffective participation on the part of the children by requiring legal representation. This approach can be contrasted with the institutional ethos of the children's panel system itself which marked a conscious shift towards an informal system of justice where children are encouraged to participate in proceedings by dispensing with the kind of legal formalities associated with courts. Significantly also, the authors examine the children's experiences of panel proceedings, exploring their understandings of the process, their senses of participation and their attitudes towards assistance from third parties and legal representation. Their data suggests that even when the children know their participation may be impaired, many of them preferred to speak for themselves. While, from the perspective of the legal system, legal representation might seem the obvious, if incomplete, remedy, most of the children interviewed did not understand it that way. A number of them preferred to represent themselves rather than cede control to another person, especially an adult, over what is presented in their name. Autonomy as well as narrative authenticity was important to them. Even where they acknowledged the value of assistance, they were concerned with having choice, and at pains to establish that this should not be at the expense of appropriating the young person's voice or view of proceedings. Griffiths and Kandel's work is important, not just because it explores the viewpoints of the bearers of the human right (a perspective which has been under-explored in socio-legal research on human rights), but because their data raises questions about what effective participation entails. It raises issues about whether children necessarily acquire a better understanding of the process through legal representation and whether they in fact have more power to make their voices heard and acted upon. And as the authors note, these issues must be more cogently addressed if international human rights for children are to have any meaning.

CONCLUSION

No single collection of essays can capture the nuances of a rapidly evolving phenomenon such as human rights, even if the scope is limited to a single country or policy area. Indeed, as the chapters in this volume cross borders and policy areas, the authors drive home the need to recognise and embrace the complexity of what we mean by 'compliance' with human rights law. We hope lasting contributions will flow in other ways from the examples of these pieces of scholarship. First, specific to the interdisciplinary effort to understand the zeitgeist that gives human rights regimes such prominence, the domestic guts of mature legal systems need deeper comparison among themselves and against developing states. Human rights is a global phenomenon, but one with deep tensions and differences within the countries where it does its work. Secondly, with the insights of these socio-legal projects as inspiration, a flowering of empirical inquiry along these lines should continue to probe the promises of the international system. Though Stephen Gough and others undoubtedly will remind us of the raw popularity of human rights discourse, without more study from the approaches taken by the authors here we will be unable to appreciate whether, when, how, and why human rights have been brought home.

2

Implementing Human Rights

DENIS GALLIGAN AND DEBORAH SANDLER[1]

INTRODUCTION

HUMAN RIGHTS HAVE become one of the great ideologies of the age. As an ideology, it sprang into life halfway through a century regarded by some as the worst on record for the levels of mass cruelty and killings, rape and torture, deportation and genocide.[2] Following the atrocities of the Second World War, on old and crumbling enlightenment foundations, new edifices were built to express human rights in numerous international treaties for the benefit and protection of all. Together with liberty, democracy, free markets, and the rule of law, human rights have become a fundamental ideology in modern societies, not only in the West where some levels of effectiveness have been achieved, but in other parts where it is held up as a goal to which to aspire. International standards have been stated, and societies, wherever they are, are judged according to them. At their foundation, human rights are a set of moral principles about how people should treat each other, particularly how people should be treated by state authorities. They are at the same time much more than moral principles; they have become so embedded in a global consciousness as to be able to influence the conduct of international and national affairs. All sorts of international benefits — aid, investment, security — may depend on a good human rights record, while a poor record may lead to isolation, poverty, and even conquest.

Some human rights are new to the international scene, while many have their roots in older civilisations and have been long recognised. The tendency

[1] The authors wish to acknowledge the very considerable contribution that Ms Ingrid Barnsley has made to the research supporting this essay and the valuable insights into numerous issues.
[2] Isaiah Berlin, for one, is said to have had this view: see M Ignatief, *Isaiah Berlin: A Life* (London, Chatto & Winden, 1998).

to put so much in human rights terms has its drawbacks, but, overall, it must surely be good to have a set of principles, claiming universality, enshrined in international law and state constitutions, and permeating large tracts of legislation, judicial decisions, and administrative action. Gradually and slowly over time the hope is that the standards will be widely internalised, becoming part of the fabric binding societies together and governing the citizen-state relationship. There are signs in some countries of this process taking place, while in others it has hardly begun.[3] There is certainly no reason for expecting a gradual, global progression towards better protection for human rights; it is just as likely to be spasmodic, uneven, and often retrogressive. Protection depends ultimately on the actions of states and their governments, and is closely connected to other aspects of a country's stage of development, in such matters as economic structure, governance and law, and civil society. Countries that are stable, peaceful, democratic, and tolerant are likely to offer better levels of protection than those lacking these qualities.[4]

Whatever the stage of a country's development, there is another general obstacle to the protection of human rights: no matter how compelling human rights standards are, they pull against the swell of human affairs. In the day-to-day conduct of government and administration, human rights standards are outsiders looking in; they are not natural partners in social organisations and must compete with the powerful forces and currents that are. In this respect, they are similar to notions of justice, due process, and equal treatment, all of which are against the dominant currents within social, and especially governmental, organisations.[5] Moreover, human rights standards do not take effect quietly and effortlessly; nor do they apply automatically upon being agreed or enacted. On the contrary, they

[3] According to the Danish Government's Country and Regional Database of Human Rights Indicators, set up in 2000, most world regions are fairly advanced in terms of formal commitment to human rights standards, evidenced through commitment to international human rights agreements and incorporation of relevant standards into national law. Many countries in the following regions continue to have low commitment in terms of the protection of civil, political, economic, social and or womens' rights: West Africa, the Mediterranean region, Russia and the western CIS region, the Caucasian, Central Asian, and East and South East Asia. H and L Lindholt, *Human Rights Indicators. Country and Regional Database* (Copenhagen, Danish Institute for Human Rights, 2000).

[4] The best known empirical study of the correlation between democratic governance and human rights protection is S C Poe and C N Tate, 'Repression of Human Rights to Personal Integrity in the 1980s: A Global Analysis' (1994) 88 (4) *American Political Science Review* 853–72. See also: C W Henderson, 'Conditions Affecting the Use of Political Repression' (1991) 35 (1) *The Journal of Conflict Resolution* 120–42 and UNDP, *Human Development Report 2002*. The latter illustrates the link between democracy, and economic development and poverty alleviation.

[5] For analysis of this idea in relation to administrative justice, see DJ Galligan, 'Authoritarianism in Law and Government: The Promise of Administrative Justice' (2001) 54 *Current Legal Problems* 79–102.

need the positive aid of government and administration, of corporations and organisations. They need the commitment of officials whose natural instincts are often to the contrary; they also need the persistent advocacy and vigilance of the institutions of civil society. The effectiveness of human rights standards depends ultimately on the actions of government and administration, and yet, and here is the paradox, they are the very bodies whose actions are most likely to be in violation.

The study of human rights may take any of several directions. Much analysis and discussion has been devoted to the legal aspects, that is, the formulation of legal standards in international law, in national constitutions, and in local legislation, followed by questions concerning their interpretation by courts and other bodies. It has been suggested, indeed, that the main impetus for the human rights revolution was legal, with lawyers and legal academics occupying the centre ground.[6] There is also an extensive philosophical literature on the nature and basis of human rights, although the social and political sciences for their part, until recently, have been minor characters. We need not consider here the reasons for this neglect, and anyhow it is changing, with a growing literature analysing the political conditions that affect levels of compliance with human rights. Similarly, while both sociology and anthropology are late-comers to the study of human rights, each has much to offer in understanding the social processes that have elevated human rights to the prominent position they hold in the contemporary world. The two disciplines could also advance our understanding of compliance by identifying the interrelationship between human rights and other social forces.[7]

The charge of neglect may be made also against socio-legal analysis, which does not begin to compete with the level of interest or refinement of legal analysis. Although there is little in the socio-legal literature specifically about human rights,[8] it should have much to offer: in understanding the process by which social issues become human rights issues for incorporation into legal standards; in identifying the factors influencing the interpretation of those standards; and in their compliance, implementation, and enforcement at the international and national levels. The last of these categories is especially familiar socio-legal territory: if the administration and implementation of human rights standards are understood as part of a particular type of regulatory regime, then the socio-legal issues for human rights research are broadly similar to those for other areas of legal regulation.

[6] See the chapter by Madsen in this volume, and M Freeman, *Human Rights* 77ff.
[7] For an up-to-date review of the literature, see Freeman, *ibid*, ch 5.
[8] See, eg A An-Naim, *Human Rights in Cross-Cultural Perspectives — A Quest for Consensus* (Philadelphia, University of Pennsylvania Press, 1992); M-L Bartolomei and H Hyden (eds), *The Implementation of Human Rights in a Global World, Lund Studies in Sociology of Law* (Lund, Lund Studies in Sociology of Law, 1999).

The object of this chapter is to examine the implementation of human rights standards. By implementation is meant putting those standards into effect. This concerns the laws, institutions, and procedures for converting normative ideals into practical realities; it highlights the attitudes of officials and the populace at large in support of rights. Taking up the idea mentioned above of human rights protection as a type of regulatory regime, the approach here is to explore its elements. In the space available, this is necessarily somewhat schematic, but it may provide the structure for further, more detailed analysis of its specific features. The question we ask ourselves is: what are the distinctive features of the human rights regime, considering such matters as, the character of human rights standards, the interrelationship between the international and national legal orders, the effects of globalisation, whether a distinct global order is emerging, the nature of the institutions dedicated to implementation at the two levels, and the mechanisms and processes used to secure implementation. A subsidiary question that we little more than touch on is how does the human rights regime differ from national regulatory regimes. The emphasis throughout the chapter is on compliance with human rights by government and administration; that of course is only part of the story, since private organisations, corporations and non-governmental institutions also need to respect human rights. That aspect, although of clear importance, must be the subject of another study.

HUMAN RIGHTS AS A REGULATORY REGIME

By a regulatory regime is meant a system of standards, institutions, and processes that are designed to control the actions of those involved in certain activities in order to achieve certain goals. Human rights protection constitutes a regulatory regime: standards are formulated at international law and then adopted at the national level; new institutions at both levels are created or existing ones utilised in order to give effect to the standards; while various mechanisms and processes are devised to assist in the endeavour. The actions sought to be controlled are those of all branches of government — judicial, legislative and executive — as well as the actions of private citizens to the extent that they impact upon other citizens, such as discrimination in the workplace. The goals are the protection of the human rights as stated in international law. Both positive and negative rights fit within the regulatory regime. In its elemental form, a human rights regime is similar to any other regulatory regime. But there are also important differences, the identification of which provides us with the outline of its main features.

1 The first outstanding difference is that a human rights regime has the added factor of international law and the institutions

and processes that go with it. Standards are formulated at the international level, but depend in the main for implementation on the national level. The significance is that the regulatory system, instead of being the exclusive concern of a national order, is shared between the international and the national.

2 This leads to a second distinctive feature: the international level influences implementation at the national level but has little capacity to enforce its standards. The international order's contribution to implementation then necessarily depends primarily on the weaker processes of encouraging, facilitating, and cajoling, with rare cases of direct intervention.

3 Where international institutions are created to assist states in implementation, they do not have the enforcement powers usually given to national regulatory bodies. Even in the national context, enforcement is a measure of last resort, although its presence as a last resort is an important factor in shaping the inevitable informal processes between regulator and regulatee.[9] The absence of a last resort colours and weakens the implementation process.

4 Individual persons or groups do not normally have remedies at international law. International law imposes duties on states to respect, protect, and promote the rights of their citizens and others within their jurisdiction.[10] But the failure of a state to do so generally leaves the person affected without a remedy, with important exceptions.

5 Human rights standards tend to originate from outside a national system (with many exceptions), and as a result they may lack the fuller legitimacy that normally attaches to standards generated internally. The commitment on the part of national institutions to implement the standards is likely then to be relatively weak. Where the standards would not be adopted internally but for outside pressure, they come into competition with strong internal attitudes, practices, and standards that tend to be difficult to change.[11]

6 Human rights standards are themselves often open-ended, leaving each national state with discretion as to what they mean and,

[9] The importance of enforcement as the last resort is borne out in empirical studies, the classic being R H Mnookin, 'Bargaining in the Shadow of the Law: The case of divorce' (1979) 88 *Yale LJ* 950.

[10] It has been pointed out that international agreements giving birth to human rights standards rarely refer to states' duties: H J Steiner and P Alston, *International Human Rights in Context: Law, Politics, Morals* (2nd edn, Oxford, Oxford, University Press, 2000) 180.

[11] For discussion of this point, see J Donnelly, *Universal Human Rights in Theory and Practice* 13 ff.

more importantly, what constitutes adequate compliance. This is especially the case with economic and social rights, but may apply also to civil and political rights. The common inclusion of escape clauses in human rights standards augments the discretion. This is not a defect awaiting remedy; on the contrary, the idea that national states must decide for themselves how international standards apply in the local context is fundamental to the human rights regime.[12] That is the compromise between the universalist claims of human rights and the imperatives of local culture.

7 A related difference is that the international order does not normally have the institutions to provide authoritative rulings on the interpretation and scope of such standards. In the national context this is provided normally by superior courts, which at the international level are scarce. The notable exceptions are regional bodies, such as, of the European Court of Human Rights and the European Court of Justice, although they have few counterparts elsewhere.[13] The absence of clear rulings by international courts or similar bodies tends to weaken the capacity of international administrative bodies to monitor and advance the levels of implementation.

Here we have the rudimentary elements of the human rights regulatory regime as it presently exists. Despite signs of change at the international level, obvious and deep-rooted tensions manifest themselves as the international system and the various national systems attempt to come together for implementation purposes. The tensions are systemic and structural, since each of the two orders,[14] the national and the international, is based on a distinct set of assumptions, has its own internal logic and world view. Each has its own *autopoeisis* which defines and limits its actions; it also defines and limits the capacity of each to connect and interrelate with the other. An appreciation of the autopoeitic character of the two orders, and of the consequential incompatibilities when brought together, is the first stage in understanding the implementation process and its obstacles. It should not be concluded, however, that the obstacles are immutable and nothing can be done. That conclusion is tempting, but should be resisted.[15] Systemic coherence and rationality can be powerful

[12] A Cassesse makes this point well in his book, *Human Rights in a Changing World* (Cambridge, Polity Press, 1990) 50 ff.

[13] It may seem unorthodox to include the European Court of Justice as a human rights court; but it clearly is for member states, especially since the incorporation of the European Convention on Human Rights into the Treaty of Maastricht in 1992.

[14] While we speak here of 'two orders', clearly there are multiple national orders, each of which has its own unique features.

[15] See G Teubner (ed), *Autopoietic law : a new approach to law and society* (Berlin, Walter de Gruyter, 1988); G Teubner and A Febbrajo (eds), *State, law, and economy as autopoietic*

forces, but they are the product of social forces and can themselves be changed by social forces. They should be the grounds for understanding, on the basis of which plans and strategies for change can be based, not for inaction or despondency.

Against this background, we now move to examine some of the distinctive features of the human rights regulatory regime. This is a large undertaking that warrants more than an introductory essay; but at least we can begin the process.

IMPLEMENTATION: THE GENERAL ISSUE

By implementation is meant the process by which standards are made effective in the actions and decisions of those to whom they apply. Since we are limiting ourselves here to governmental bodies, their behaviour is the object of implementation. The test of success in implementation is whether the human rights standards are accepted as authoritative by national institutions and officials in such manner that their practical actions and decisions are in compliance with them. (National institutions and officials also have responsibilities to ensure compliance by non-governmental bodies, such as firms and corporations, but that discussion is outside our present purposes.) Standards can be regarded as more or less authoritative; similarly compliance can be greater or lesser. The ideal position is the internalisation of standards by officials so that they become central to their cognitive and normative understandings.[16] Peter Winch has noted that 'all behaviour which is meaningful (therefore all specifically human behaviour) is ipso facto rule-governed.'[17] Talcott Parsons had earlier concluded that the normative attitudes of persons are the basic unit of social analysis,[18] while the same idea is conveyed in HLA Hart's internal point of view in relation to rules.[19] And just as the acceptance of human rights standards is the test of successful implementation, the competition with existing understandings and norms within the institutions of government and administration is its main obstacle. At its very

systems : regulation and autonomy in a new perspective (Milano, Giuffrè, 1992); N Luhmann, *A sociological theory of law*; translated by E King and M Albrow, ed M Albrow (London, Routledge & Kegan Paul, 1985), N Luhmann, *Closure and openness: on reality in the world of law* (Florence, European University Institute, 1986).

[16] For discussion of internalisation of norms, see A Etzioni, 'Social Norms: Internalization, Persuasion and History' (2000) 34 *Law and Society Review* 157–78.

[17] P Winch, *The Idea of a Social Science and its Relation to Philosophy* (2nd edn, London, Routledge, 1990).

[18] T Parsons, *Action theory and the human condition* (New York, Free Press, 1978); T Parsons, *Social systems and the evolution of action theory* (New York, London, Free Press; Collier Macmillan, 1977).

[19] H L A Hart, *The Concept of Law* (Oxford, Clarendon, 1961).

core, implementation involves the replacement of those competing norms or at least the evolution of existing norms to allow for the incorporation of human rights standards, and the cognitive understandings that accompany them. That is the object of the practical strategies of implementation, a point to which we return later.

A major practical obstacle to implementation, as noted earlier, is that human rights standards derive from the international order but apply within national systems. Implementation then depends on a partnership of the two. The partnership, however, is deeply unequal. Where a country is committed to human rights and has the institutions to make them effective, the international order is likely to have a relatively small role, confining itself to seeking improvements at the margins. In the opposite case, where a country has only a weak commitment to human rights and inadequate institutions, the international order will be more active in encouraging and facilitating implementation, although its influence in such cases is likely to be minor. The position any country occupies between these two extremes will determine the respective roles of the international and national orders. But wherever a country is placed on this test, it bears the primary responsibility for implementation, while the capacity of the international order is in general severely limited.

Although the partnership is unequal, the international order is becoming more active and can contribute to the implementation process. How significant its institutions and strategies are, is a matter of empirical investigation which to date hardly exists. We are limited, therefore, to sketching the international approach, leaving open questions as to how effective it is. At the national level, implementation of human rights standards depends on the normal constitutional, legislative, administrative, and judicial institutions. Special human rights institutions are sometimes created, but their effectiveness is closely linked to and in a sense parasitic on the activities of the normal institutions. A human rights commission, for instance, will depend to a substantial degree on cooperation from government, administrative bodies, and the courts. Again we can do little more in this chapter than sketch the main elements in implementation at the national level. Before considering these matters, mention should be made of several factors particular to human rights and relevant to implementation.

THE CONCEPT AND CONTEXT OF HUMAN RIGHTS

The Concept

We begin by considering the concept of human rights and the context in which it occurs. There are various ways of defining or describing human rights, some idealistic others more practical and prosaic; there are also different kinds of human rights. Here we work on a fairly simple idea of a right: for a person to have a right, whether within a system of legal or other kinds of rules, is to have an interest that is given a special status and protection within the rules.[20] In other words, the interest is guaranteed within the social organisation. The elements of a right may be expressed more formally in this way: a right-holder has an interest (the object of the right) which is given expression within and protection by the rules of the society.

A right is socially guaranteed when effective arrangements are in place to ensure that the right-holder may enjoy the object of the right. Such processes usually require a public or private actor to take positive action to create the conditions in which the right can be enjoyed, such as the provision of welfare or the restraint of others from interference with free speech. Alternatively, the process of protection may require forbearance from actions which would interfere with a right.

Human rights fit within the general concept of a right. Human rights mean that some interests are so tied to the very idea of being human that they warrant a special status and protection within a society. The recognition of human rights is said to be justified by an appeal to human nature, while their practical expression is a matter for international law. The Universal Declaration of Human Rights of 1948 begins by recognising 'the inherent dignity and the equal and inalienable rights of all members of the human family'. Since human rights are accepted as integral to being human, they must be universal in some sense and stand beyond any particular community or culture. Whether the claim of universality is compatible with cultural diversity is a matter of controversy.[21]

Universal Character and Cultural Relativity

The potential conflict between the universalist character of human rights and the cultural relativity of different societies has both normative and empirical aspects. The normative aspect concerns the relationship between the universal claims of human rights and their compatibility with particular religions, value systems, or ways of life. While this issue and the extensive literature it has produced is beyond our present concerns, several aspects of the debate are relevant to the question of implementation. First, the universalist claim, although often asserted,[22] is itself somewhat problematic.

[20] See J Raz, 'On the Nature of Rights' (1984) 93 *Mind* 194–214.

[21] For instance K Christie, 'Regime Change and Human Rights in Southeast Asia' (1995) 43 *Political Studies* 204–18 and D A Bell, D Brown, K Jayasuriya and D M Jones, *Towards Illiberal Democracy in Pacific Asia* (New York, St Martin's Press, 1995).

[22] Eg it is reasserted by both the Bangkok Declaration 1993 (Regional Meeting for Asia of the World Conference on Human Rights) and the Vienna Declaration and Plan of Action 1993.

Human rights standards are often expressed in general or abstract terms, allowing extensive discretion as to the nature of the right and its application in practice. As Cassese has noted, human rights standards themselves often allow large scope for local variation, with each country deciding what institutional arrangements to employ in implementing such rights. In reality, the human rights regime demands only that certain minimum standards be protected.[23]

A second and related point is that this system of implementation provides ample opportunity for states to tailor abstract human rights standards to local values, social structures and institutional capacities. The high degree of state autonomy is important; it derives partly from the fact that implementation is a state matter and partly from the fact that international oversight is usually weak. On this point, the implementation of international standards differs from that of domestic standards, since in the latter case there are normally institutions and mechanisms for ensuring implementation, if necessary with legal and judicial support. Even then, implementation is uneven and imperfect, but by comparison, the capacity of international institutions is greatly inferior.[24]

Thirdly, whether there is a deep incompatibility between human rights standards and different cultural or religious traditions can be assessed only on close analysis of specific situations. For instance, the notion that the precepts of Islam are incompatible with human rights is more a matter of emphasis and language than substance. According to Soroush, a leading scholar of Islam, the emphasis of the Koran on duties does not preclude a restatement of the same ideas in terms of rights generally and human rights in particular.[25]

Not all interests that gain international recognition as human rights have the same importance, and arguably some should be open to greater local variation than others.[26] At the same time, human rights standards, like any legal standards, soon develop a core of settled meaning, while allowing that variation may occur on peripheral matters. To suggest that human rights standards are wholly subject to local interpretation is untenable. We suggest that these matters should be understood as part of the process of implementation rather than signs of deep incompatibility between the universal and the local. Once the relationship between universal standards and particular conditions is seen in terms of implementation, attention can be

[23] See A Cassesse, *Human Rights in a Changing World.*
[24] There are numerous studies of implementation at the national level; a notable example being G Richardson, *Policing Pollution* (Oxford, Clarendon Press, 1983).
[25] A Soroush, *Reason, Freedom, and Democracy in Islam: Essential Writings of Abd Al-Karim Surush*, M Sadri (trans), A Sadri (ed) (Oxford, Oxford University Press, 2000).
[26] For further discussion, see J Donnelly, *Universal Human Rights in Theory and Practice* and M Freeman, *Human Rights.*

paid to identifying the obstacles to it and devising practical measures to overcome them. Such a perspective may also reveal how the cultural relativity claim can be employed to hide the inability or reluctance of governments to implement human rights standards. There may be good reasons for this; a government may be loath to impose its authority on powerful groups and interests, a stance in which the international community, through its inadequate monitoring practices, may be complicit.

Categories of Human Rights

Human rights are usually grouped in three categories. Civil and political rights are the most extensive and include rights to life, liberty, and security; rights against slavery, torture, and cruel punishment; rights not to be unfairly detained and to a fair trial, rights to freedom of thought, expression and religion, privacy and property.[27] Economic and social rights include, as to the first, the right to property, to work, and to social security, while the second include rights necessary for an adequate standard of living, the main elements of which are food and shelter, education and health care.[28] The third category may be referred to as collective rights, meaning primarily the rights of nations or peoples to self-determination.[29] The definition of these rights is found in a range of international law instruments, such as the *Universal Declaration of Human Rights*, the *European Convention on Human Rights*, and the *Convention Against Torture*.

The full realisation of such a list, which is ever expanding as new rights are adopted, would be a huge agenda. Since the list above is not complete and many rights have various parts, the sheer number of rights is overwhelming. In order to make the task of implementation more manageable, a line is often drawn among the categories, emphasising the primacy of civil and political rights as most fundamental and depending on forbearance by the state rather than positive action. Economic and social rights, on the other hand, generally require positive state action and the provision of resources. The practical attractions of this distinction are sometimes linked

[27] Civil and political rights are expressed in a number of international instruments, the most important being the Universal Declaration of Human Rights, the International Covenant on Civil and Political Rights, the Convention on the Elimination of Discrimination Against Women, the Convention Against Torture, and the International Convention on the Rights of the Child.

[28] Economic and social rights are stated in several international instruments including the Universal Declaration of Human Rights, the Convention on the Rights of the Child and the International Covenant on Economic, Social and Cultural Rights. For reasons of space, little is added in this chapter concerning collective rights, although in principle they fit within the general analysis.

[29] Art 1, International Covenant on Civil and Political Rights; Part I, International Covenant on Economic, Social and Cultural Rights.

to a theoretical claim that the state should be concerned only with civil and political rights, leaving economic and social considerations to a combination of individual endeavour and private benevolence.[30] In addition, it may be argued that to the extent that issues of an economic and social nature are the concern of governments, they are nonetheless not 'rights' in the way that those of a civil and political nature are.

Without entering into the theoretical debate, nor into the fact that different cultural traditions emphasise different aspects of human rights, we shall concentrate on the practical case. Simply put, the argument is that civil and political rights are easier to implement than economic and social rights. It is not at all clear, however, that such a case can be supported. One limb of the argument is that civil and political rights, such as the rights to a fair trial or to be free of torture, have a hard core definition which is unlikely to be disputed, while economic and social rights, such as the right to housing or health care, are soft and open-ended. However, a strong argument can be made in response that it is no more difficult to define acceptable levels of entitlement with respect to food, shelter, and medical care than it is for the right to a fair trial or the right to be free from torture. If open-ended civil rights such as free speech or privacy are chosen, then the distinction between the two categories is even less persuasive.

Another part of the argument is that civil and political rights generally depend on state forbearance, which is of low cost, while economic and social rights need positive, often extensive resources. Again the attraction of the argument is superficial. The demand for resources to support economic and social rights — to build houses or hospitals — is obvious, while the right not to be tortured, for example, appears to be satisfied by inaction. A moment's reflection, however, reveals the weakness of the argument in that significant resources are required to ensure that the police, military and other state organs are run in such a way as to protect citizens from torture. Forbearance by state officials from tendencies, such as oppressive policing, is not cost-free inaction; on the contrary, it requires a well-developed system in which natural tendencies are curbed through extensive forms of accountability and control. If this is the case for supposedly negative civil rights, it is even more so for others which are positive civil rights, such as the right to participate in free elections or to a fair trial. These are made possible only by a system of government and administration of a very particular kind.

Again these ideas may be linked to implementation. Even from this brief account it can be seen that generalisations depending on sharp divisions between different kinds of rights have little merit. All human rights

[30] A recent restatement of the case against economic and social rights is A Neier, *Taking Liberties* (New York, Public Affairs, 2003).

normally require some level of action and resources on the part of the state. That there could be occasional exceptions is largely irrelevant. The issue for implementation is always what actions and resources are necessary to make any set of human rights effective in a particular social setting. The costs may be more or less direct or indirect, with some rights requiring an explicit allocation of resources, others depending on a developed system of government and administration. Under the ICESCR, each state is obligated to do the best it can, considering its level of development and its resources. Criteria have been devised by the UN Development Programme for determining such levels.[31] The fact that a country is less developed is not an excuse for inaction, since the relevant standard is 'the maximum of its available resources.'[32] The main issue for implementation is how to get states to comply with that obligation, an issue that pertains to all areas of human rights, whether civil and political or economic and social.

A final observation on the two areas of rights is that it may be more difficult to achieve compliance with civil and political rights than with economic and social. Whether there is evidence to support this is not clear, but it is not unusual to find together reasonable protection of economic and social rights and a low level of civil rights protection, as in some of the former communist countries of Eastern Europe. The fairly obvious conclusion may be drawn that various cultural and historical factors influence implementation in different countries. China, for instance, is enthusiastic about economic and social rights, but declines to sign international treaties on political and civil rights. Another small but telling example is the difference in attitudes between Europe and the US towards economic and social rights, the former generally favouring them, the latter not, and yet both enjoying comparable levels of economic prosperity. Further study of these issues is needed, in particular the social, political and economic conditions that are conducive to the protection of different kinds of human rights.

THE INTERNATIONAL DIMENSION

The International Order

The international order in its many forms is a major element in the human rights regime. According to classical theories of international law, states are the main participants in the international legal order. Historically, the

[31] The UN Development Programme has developed criteria over a number of years of basic economic and social rights; its work is published in the annual *Human Development Report*.
[32] For extended discussion of the ICESCR, see W F Felice, *The Global New Deal: Economic and Social Human Rights in World Politics* (Maryland, Rowman Littlefield, 2003).

recognition of the rights of individuals was the exclusive domain of states, so that a government's treatment of individual persons was generally beyond the reach of international law. States could enter into treaties and offer protection to groups or nationalities, but generally no specific duty was owed to the individual in international law and, of equal importance, the individual person had no redress in the international forum. Rights were created in individuals only if international obligations were incorporated into national law when the usual procedures and remedies would then become available.

As the international order develops and matures, the classical position is changing. States are still the main 'participants' in the international legal order, but the individual (and other non-state actors) are slowly becoming 'subjects' under international law. Through its many avenues of cooperation, the international order has a central role in organising states collectively to deal with a wide range of matters, including human rights, the environment, and world trade. Since the Second World War, the international order has brought states to agreement on numerous treaties concerning human rights. Indeed, the international order is the main source of human rights standards. A country might independently develop human rights standards in its own constitutional and legal order, but for most the incentive to do so stems from international initiatives, and often the substance of such rights is derived from internationally recognised principles. Treaties, memoranda, and other forms of international agreements are often accompanied by the creation of institutions, some charged with generating policy, others with implementation.

These developments make the international order look more like a genuine legal order, with legislative processes supported by executive and administrative institutions, together sometimes with judicial bodies. Nevertheless, it remains weak in its capacity to implement its own standards, for no matter how active the international order is, the fact remains that the primary responsibility is with states. Against this background, the international order has two main avenues open to it. The traditional, and more indirect one, is to encourage and facilitate states to implement human rights standards. The more recent approach is to create forms of direct implementation at international law. Here the emphasis is put on the international order as a distinct legal system with its own laws, institutions, and procedures. Before discussing these two different approaches to implementation, we turn to a consideration of the social function and formulation of international human rights standards.

The Social Function Of Standards

The usual practice is that human rights standards are agreed at the international level and then adopted at the national. The declaration of standards at the international level is the first step in the regulatory process. Standards create obligations in states with respect to human rights, and so become the basis for evaluating, persuading, and criticising them and their institutions. Standards are important in forming the social context in which actions are taken, explained, and justified. But what exactly does this mean? What in other words is the social role of legal standards?

The first part of the answer is that legal standards create expectations that states, agencies, and officials will behave in certain ways. Standards become the basis for evaluation, criticism, and justification.[33] The second part of the answer attempts to show how this happens: human rights standards enter into the *cognitive* and *normative* world of states. By cognitive is meant that standards enter into the understandings of those to whom they are addressed. They may not necessarily be complied with, but they cannot just be ignored. Like the unwanted piece of furniture in the room, one's intention might be no more than to avoid running into it; similarly with legal standards: even if one's intention is to avoid the law, it has to be taken account of at least to the extent necessary to be able to do so. Examples of this minimal social view of law abound in the new democracies of eastern Europe. In a recent study of the relationship between law and social norms in eastern Europe, Kurkchiyan has shown that in Russia, for instance, where attitudes to law often verge on contempt and where avoiding law is a major industry, even there the law cannot be ignored. It has to be taken into account even if the intention is to avoid, manipulate, or negotiate around it. Law still enters into and shapes and influences the cognitive world of citizens and officials.[34] Where attitudes are more positive towards law, its place in the cognitive world of officials and citizens is likely to be more secure and have greater influence over practical actions and decisions.

Recent research expresses this idea in terms of a legal environment and a legal consciousness.[35] Legal standards create as part of the social world a legal environment and an accompanying legal consciousness. By legal consciousness it meant 'the broader set of legal principles, norms, and ideals that surround the formal legal system.'[36] Over time and with the aid of

[33] See HLA Hart's analysis of social rules in *The Concept of Law* ch 7, 'Formalism and Rule-Scepticism'.

[34] D Galligan and M Kurkchiyan (eds), *Law and Informal Practices: The Post-Communist Experience* (Oxford, Oxford University Press, 2003).

[35] See in particular, L Edelman, 'Legal Environments and Organisational Governance: The Expansion of Due Process in the American Workplace' (1990) 95 *American Journal of Sociology* 1401ff; B Garth and A Sarat (eds), *How Does Law Matter?* (Evanston, IL, Northeastern University Press, American Bar Association, 1998); B Garth and A Sarat (eds), *Justice and power in sociolegal studies* (Evanston, IL, Northwestern University Press, American Bar Foundation, 1998).

[36] S Riggs Fuller, L Edelman, SF Matusik, 'Legal readings: Employee interpretation and mobilization of law' (2000) (25)(1) *The Academy of Management Review* 200–16.

various pressures, from the international community for instance, legal standards may begin to generate normative expectations within a specific social sphere. This may mean no more initially than being a basis for criticism; but standards can be tenacious, eventually giving rise to expectations. Writing about standards against discrimination in employment, Edelman expresses it well: 'law influences the legal environment by changing public expectations about employees' civil rights and providing a basis for criticising well-ingrained patterns of governance.'[37] Where legal standards have a basis of legitimacy, because made by an elected parliament, say, or because the state has signed a treaty on the matter, those subject to them come under pressure to demonstrate compliance. This is the first step in the internalisation process, that is to say, the process by which legal standards are accepted as authoritative and binding.

At the same time, as noted earlier, legal standards usually encounter and have to compete with social norms that have become entrenched in the department or agency. In the human rights context, standards created under international law often conflict with existing expectations, practices, and norms, some created by national law, others derived from convention and informal norms. The practical task then is to devise ways of resolving the competition, so that the legal standards prevail. That is a difficult process requiring plans and strategies, where the level of success is likely, at best, to be moderate.

The Formation and Character of Human Rights Standards

Human rights standards within the international order normally result from a process of deliberation and discussion among states, within the framework of the international order and with the assistance of international institutions. This process is fundamental to the character and content of international treaties and the additional agreements and rules made under them.[38] It also has consequences for implementation. The final form a standard takes is bound to be a compromise among competing views, while the degree to which a country has to compromise may affect its attitude to the standard itself. Similarly, the inequality of negotiating power may mean that some countries feel their interests have not been considered adequately, and this again is likely to affect their attitude to the resulting standards.[39] Further, some countries may sign a treaty and agree to its standards for a

[37] Edelman, *ibid*, at 1408.
[38] A recent study is M Byers, *Custom, power and the power of rules: international relations and customary international law* (Cambridge, Cambridge University Press, 1999).
[39] Is it worth noting that international HR standards are also developed via customary international law, which by its nature is not necessarily agreed to by nation states per se.

range of reasons without intending to implement them; for example, economic or other incentives may be conditional on signing. In general, it is well known that the legitimacy of laws, and the attitudes of governments, officials, and the populace towards them, is influenced by the process by which they come into being.[40] That is surely equally true in the international context.

The process by which human rights standards are made is also conducive to their being abstract and open-textured, leaving room for widely different interpretations. International instruments contribute to the level of discretion vested in states in implementing human rights by using expressions such as 'as far as possible', 'achieving progressively the full realisation', and 'to the extent allowed by available resources'. Although such expressions are often found in relation to economic and social rights, they are not unknown in other areas. Considering that such standards have to be agreed and implemented by countries with widely different cultures and interests, these features are to a large degree inevitable.[41] The consequence of this structural feature of the human rights regime is that implementation becomes more variable and, in the face of widely different approaches, even problematic. We should be careful not to overstate the point; measures are taken at the international level to develop core conceptions of particular rights and of the minimum action necessary to constitute implementation.[42] Reporting and monitoring procedures and the investigation of complaints, conducted by international institutions help in that process; similarly non-governmental bodies contribute through various strategies, including the formulation of criteria and indicators of compliance.[43]

The way rights are expressed in international instruments is likely also to detract from the effectiveness of international institutions. Most international human rights instruments provide for their own institutional system of supervision. Additionally, many international human rights instruments do not necessarily incorporate the whole body of international human rights law, but focus on particular issues such as racial discrimination or

[40] For a recent case study, see S Newton, 'Transplantation and Transition: Legality and Legitimacy in the Kazakhstani Legislation Process' in D Galligan and M Kurkchiyan (eds), *Law and Informal Practices: the Post-Communist Experience* (Oxford, Oxford University Press, 2003).

[41] The fact that the content and scope of rights allows discretion does not justify a state's doing nothing; on the contrary, even in relation to economic and social rights, states have a duty to implement the rights: see, eg the International Convention on Social and Economic Rights Art 2. For discussion in the context of health, see L Gostin, *Human Rights and Public Health in the Aids Pandemic* (Oxford, Oxford University Press, 1997).

[42] Examples of regional attempts to clarify the content of rights can be seen in the International Covenant on Civil and Political Rights, Art 12.2 and the European Social Charter, Art 11.

[43] The Danish Institute of Human Rights, for instance, has established a Country and Regional Database of Human Rights Indicators, its object being to assess compliance by countries: H and L Lindholt, *Human Rights Indicators. Country and Regional Database.*

the rights of the child. As such, the institution charged with overseeing a particular human rights instrument may have authority to draw only from the principles contained within that particular instrument. The existence of multiple systems of supervision gives rise to problems of coordination and overlapping in areas of finance, administration and even the authority to supervise implementation in the first place.[44]

International Institutions and their Processes

The formulation of international standards, while difficult enough in itself to achieve, is only one aspect of the regulatory role of the international order; another is the creation of institutions. Institutions can be of various kinds, each with a range of purposes, and they do not always match those more familiar in national legal systems. Some are best characterised as administrative bodies whose main task is to facilitate the implementation by states of international standards. Within the UN human rights regime, there are two main types of administrative bodies, the six committees created under treaties, referred to as treaty bodies,[45] and those with a direct mandate under the UN Charter, which includes the Human Rights Commission (known as charter bodies).[46]

Both sets of bodies typically have no powers of enforcement, or at most very limited ones, but rely on other mechanisms, both formal and informal, for encouraging compliance by states. The Human Rights Commission is a good example: it investigates and monitors digressions and reports on them; it enters into discussion with offending states and offers advice; it devises a range of informal ways of raising awareness of human rights issues and encouraging the development of good practices.[47] The treaty bodies, such as the Human Rights Committee, also typically have a range of functions. They receive and investigate complaints from individuals concerning violation of treaty standards.[48] They investigate, report, and make

[44] For discussion of this, see T Meron, 'Norm Making and Supervision in International Human Rights: Reflections on Institutional Order' (1982) 76(4) *American Journal of International Law* 754–78.

[45] Human Rights Committee, Committee on the Elimination of Discrimination Against Women, Committee Against Torture, Committee of the Rights of the Child, Committee on Economic, Social, and Cultural Rights, and the Committee on the Elimination of Racial Discrimination.

[46] For a full description, see Steiner and Alston, *International Human Rights in Context: Law, Politics, Morals* (2nd edn, Oxford, Oxford University Press, 2000) 601.

[47] Steiner and Alston give a full account of the various institutions created under the UN Human Rights regime: Steiner and Alston, *ibid,* at 601.

[48] This power is available to three of the treaty bodies: the Human Rights Committee, the Committee Against Torture, and the Committee on the Elimination of Racial Discrimination. It is only available if a state agrees by ratification or declaration.

recommendations to the offending state as to future actions. They receive reports from states on issues of compliance and may enter into 'constructive dialogue' with them. Treaty bodies are said to be more independent of governments than the Human Rights Commission, and in the performance of their functions veer towards a more legal approach, while stopping short of real powers of enforcement. In addition to their more clearly stated functions, both treaty and charter bodies may develop other more informal mechanisms and procedures to encourage compliance by states.

At the regional level, while the same emphasis is laid on administrative-type institutions, attempts have been made also to insert courts or judicial type bodies into the implementation process. The European Convention on Human Rights (ECHR) with its mechanisms and judicial institutions applies to forty-four European countries, while their broad equivalents can be seen in Africa and the American continent under the African Charter and the Inter-American Convention. The European Court of Human Rights is a good example of the role that an international court can have: it is an active jurisdiction which receives and adjudicates individual complaints from the great majority of European countries; it is generally considered successful in providing recourse for individual violations and also in establishing the importance of the ECHR principles.[49]

Direct Implementation by the International Order: Legal Processes

The capacity of the international order to implement human rights standards directly in a country is severely limited. Three general approaches are open to it: one is through the processes of international law, the second is direct intervention, while the third is the exercise of indirect influence on member states. As to the first, the international order is still in the early stages of development with respect to two fundamental attributes of a legal system: the capacity to enforce judgments of an international court against states, and the availability of remedies to individual persons whose rights are violated.

According to the classic approach, a state in breach of its obligations under a treaty is in breach of international law and may be brought to account by the relevant international institution. This may be by way of a

[49] For analysis of the European Court of Human Rights, see JF Hartman, 'Derogation from Human Rights Treaties in Public Emergencies: A Critique of Implementation by the European Commission and Court of Human Rights and the Human Rights Committee of the United Nations' (1981) 22(1) *Harvard Journal of International Law*; ME Villiger, 'The European Court of Human Rights' (2000) 95 *American Society of International Legal Proceedings* 79ff.

process before the international court, in which case the remedies are limited and, enforcement in the usual legal manner is absent. That is not to say that a judgment in the international court is without value, since it is the basis on which other, less-directly-legal means of enforcement are invoked.

With respect to remedies for individuals, the international order has very limited authority. Since states, not persons, are traditionally the subjects of international law, it is only recently, and very much a result of the human rights revolution, that persons are beginning to have rights and duties. Rights require remedies; if these remedies are available only in national law, then the tension between the two orders over implementation reappears. The creation of rights and duties under international law would help to ease it. There are signs that the logic of this approach is beginning to unfold. Those who violate human rights may face prosecution before international criminal courts created to deal with specific events, such as in Rwanda, Bosnia, and Kosovo, while a permanent international criminal court, although of limited jurisdiction, is now a reality.[50]

For the victims of human rights abuses, parallel developments of equal importance are taking place. The creation of the European Court of Human Rights in 1959, with jurisdiction over those European countries that signed the European Convention on Human rights, is the outstanding example of judicial protection of human rights at international law. As we noted earlier, the Court hears cases brought by individual persons from the great majority of European countries on any issue of human rights arising under the Convention. The number of cases before the Court has grown steadily since 1980. While the Court heard seven cases in 1981, in 1997 it heard 119.[51] Additionally, since the individual complaints mechanism became compulsory for all state parties to the Convention for the Protection of Human Rights and Fundamental Freedoms in 1998, the Court's work has increased exponentially. The number of individual complaints received by the Court rose by 130 per cent in the three years to 2001.[52] The Court hears cases across the full range of human rights expressed in the Convention for the Protection of Human Rights and Fundamental Freedoms. These include cases on a wide range of rights.

[50] For consideration of the International Criminal Court see: W Allmand, 'The International Criminal Court and the Human Rights Revolution' (2000–01) 46 *McGill Law Journal* 263ff; A Cassese, P Gaeta, JRWD Jones (eds), *The Rome Statute of the International Criminal Court: A Commentary* (Oxford, Oxford University Press, 2002); P Kirsch, 'Negotiating an Institution for the Twenty-First Century: Multilateral Diplomacy and the International Criminal Court' (2000–01) 46 *McGill Law Journal* 1141ff.

[51] Council of Europe, 'European Court of Human Rights: Survey of Activities 2002', [http://www.echr.coe.int/Eng/EDocs/2002SURVEY.pdf], (Accessed on 12/07/03).

[52] Council of Europe, [http://www.echr.coe.int/Eng/EDocs/HistoricalBackground.htm#I.%20 HISTORICAL%20BACKGROUND], (Accessed on 11/05/03).

The Court's role is important in two ways: first, it adjudicates directly on the issues before it and, secondly, through its reasoned decisions, it influences national courts, most of which are required under their respective constitutions also to give effect to the Convention. Where remedies for breach of the Convention are not available in the national courts, as was the case in the UK until 1999, the European Court of Human Rights has a direct and significant role in ruling on human rights issues. The British experience up to 1999 shows how important the Court was in exposing various abuses, especially of prisoners, and in inducing the government to change certain practices.[53] Analogous experiences can be seen in other regional courts or court-like bodies, particularly the Inter-American Court and the African Commission on Human and Peoples' Rights.[54]

While the opening up of international courts to personal actions is an advance in the implementation of human rights, the process still falls short of being a complete judicial remedy. International courts, such as the European Court of Human Rights, address their judgments to national states whose actions are required in order to secure implementation. The prisoners' rights cases in Britain depended on the Home Office making the necessary changes to the Prison Rules, and, while the UK was conscientious in implementing the judgments of the Court, the same cannot be said of all European countries. It may appear that the same contingency applies to the judgments of national courts which depend on state institutions for enforcement, and in that sense the procedures of international courts are similar to their state counterparts. By way of counter argument, however, it would seem generally to be the case that a judgment of a national court, addressed to an institution of government or administration, has a better chance of being implemented than a similar judgment from an international court, addressed to the state *qua* state. It may be, however, that where the national courts are strong and the institutions of state mature, the natural progression is towards national courts having primary responsibility for adjudicating human rights cases, with the European Court of Human Rights a final resort.

[53] See: S Farran, *The UK before the European Court of Human Rights: Case Law and Commentary* (London, Blackstone, 1996); S Marks, 'Civil liberties at the margin: The UK derogation and the European Court of Human Rights' (1995) 15(1) *Oxford Journal of Legal Studies* 69–95; G Slapper, 'Impact on the legal system of the European Court of Human Rights' (1997) 20 *Student Law Review* 24.

[54] See: S Davidson, *The Inter-American Human Rights System* (Aldershot, UK, Ashgate Publishing Company, 1997); C Medina, 'The Inter-American Commission on Human Rights and the Inter-American Court of Human Rights: Reflections on a joint venture' (1990) 12 *Human Rights Quarterly* 439ff; GW Mugwanya, 'Realizing Universal Human Rights Norms Through Regional Human Rights Mechanisms: Reinvigorating the African System' (1999) 10(1) *Indiana International and Comparative Law Review* 38–50; C Odinkalu, 'The Individual Complaints Procedures of the African Commission on Human and Peoples' Rights: A Preliminary Assessment' (1998) 8 *Transnational Law and Contemporary Problems* 359ff.

Apart from judicial procedures, the international order has also made progress in devising complaints procedures by which individuals may have alleged human rights violations investigated by international bodies, such as the Human Rights Committee, the Committee against Torture and the Committee on the Elimination of Racial Discrimination. Each committee is empowered to receive, consider and issue views on communications received from individuals by way of complaint. This function is significant, providing a mechanism by which individuals can approach a United Nations body and allege that their human rights have been violated by a state, including their own.[55]

The availability of judicial procedures for the implementation of human rights standards, together with an increasing range of complaints procedures, are signs of a maturing international order. Such procedures are also important, but limited, elements in the implementation process. They are limited, firstly, because few human rights violations lead to action in court. Courts are not populist institutions offering justice to the masses; instead they respond to the select number of cases where the victim has the energy and resources to mount an action, or when the relevant government sees fit to run an appropriate prosecution. Complaints procedures are often more easily brought than judicial procedures and have proved popular in many countries, not least in the new democracies of eastern Europe. They are, however, weak enforcement mechanisms because they typically result in recommendations rather than remedies. A second even more important limitation on judicial and complaints procedures is that they deal with specific, individual cases and are likely to have little influence of a more systemic and structural kind. A judicial decision on a matter of great importance exerts some influence on a state or one or other of its institutions, but it is bound to be at best occasional and highly variable.[56]

Direct Implementation by the International Order: Direct Intervention

Another tangible sign of the capacity of the international order to implement directly human rights standards is the emergence of the doctrine of humanitarian intervention. This refers to the armed infringement of a

[55] The Human Rights Committee was empowered to receive individual complaints under the Optional Protocol to the ICCPR. Of the 189 member states of the United Nations, 149 states are party to the ICCPR and 104 States to the Optional Protocol. Office of the United Nations High Commissioner for Human Rights, *Status of Ratifications of the Principal International Human Rights Treaties*, 2 May 2003, [http://www.unhchr.ch/pdf/report.pdf] visited 10 May 2003.

[56] Studies of the effect of judicial rulings on government and administration abound; see for instance: S Halliday, 'The Influence of Judicial Review on Bureaucratic Decision-Making' [2000] *Public Law* 110–22; S Halliday, *Judicial Review and Compliance with Administrative*

state's sovereignty in order to prevent massive and grave violations of human rights or humanitarian law. The complexity and controversial nature of this form of implementation is apparent upon reflection on the NATO military action in Kosovo, under the Operation Allied Force 1999. The complexities of direct implementation require a study of their own which is beyond our present scope, it being enough to mention here the importance of direct implementation as it emerges through customary international law.

Indirect Implementation: Influencing States

Once human rights standards have been set, the international order and its institutions marshal their resources to encourage states to comply. This indirect approach is arguably, to date, the one more likely to produce positive and lasting results. The strategy is to devise ways of influencing states at the international level with the object of getting them to give effect to the standards within their national systems. The process has two parts: one is for the states to adopt the standards by ratifying the international treaty and incorporating it into domestic law; the other is to induce states to give substantive effect to the law. These are the 'formal' and 'substantive' components of implementation.

International authorities are apt to focus too much on the process of states signing treaties on human rights. The number of states that sign international human rights treaties is often impressive, but it is not unusual for signing to be accompanied by a catalogue of reservations or a refusal to ratify for one reason or another.[57] It is also often the case that after ratification little more is done to give effect to the treaty.[58] The obstacles to doing so are considerable. Once an international rule enters the domestic arena, there is inevitable competition with other rules, norms, values, and practices that have to change, sometimes drastically. The existing state order is already deeply embedded in the plans and commitments of domestic governments and in domestic administrative practices and structures, financial arrangements, and technical expertise. International standards, moreover, are handicapped in the competition;

Law (Oxford, Hart Publishing, 2004) G Richardson and D Machin, 'Judicial Review and Tribunal Decision-Making' [2000] *Public Law* 494.

[57] This is widely acknowledged as a major obstacle to implementation. See AF Bafesky, 'Making the Human Rights Treaties Work' in L Henkin and J Holgrove (eds), *Human Rights: An Agenda for the Century* (Washington DC, American Society of International Law, 1994).

[58] This is acknowledged as a major obstacle to implementation, see: AF Bafesky, *ibid*, G Robertson, *Crimes Against Humanity* (London, Penguin Books, 1999) 73.

they emanate from an external source and may not have the cultural support or the political legitimacy to secure their internalisation. The process of internalisation depends on how receptive the internal conditions are, a matter which naturally varies from state to state, according to the stage of development of attitudes, ideas and institutions.

The international order has various strategies at its disposal for assisting and encouraging the internalisation process. The imposition of sanctions on a recalcitrant state is generally not a realistic option, except in limited and exceptional circumstances. The internalisation of international norms must normally be achieved by other means, usually involving negotiation, persuasion, and accommodation.[59] One simple and standard device is to require regular reporting by member states to an international agency. The record of reporting, however, is poor, with most states not reporting most of the time. Reports that are filed are notoriously late, insufficient, politically doctored, and unreliable. For example, in 1999, the Human Rights Committee noted that 138 initial or periodic state reports were overdue. This included overdue reports from more than half of the state parties to the ICCPR.[60] For their part, international agencies usually have limited powers and resources, combined with low determination, to follow up and demand adequate reports from states. Even if states do report satisfactorily, the agencies do not always have the resources to receive and make productive use of the information they contain.[61]

Developing the role of international agencies is another approach to encouraging implementation by states. We noted earlier the range and character of such bodies under the human rights regime. Building on the experience in other areas of international regulation, we may characterise such agencies, in a slightly attenuated sense, as comprising the international equivalent of government departments and agencies within a state; as such they can be instrumental in encouraging the reception of human rights standards into national contexts. Although they lack the powers of their national counterparts, international agencies often have a range of significant powers which are greater and more effective than imagined. Often they are simply not used. One of the authors has recently conducted research which shows that, in addition to their formal powers, international institutions are able to utilise informal administrative authority and discretions, and to develop relationships with states and their officials, within which

[59] See A Chayes and AH Chayes, *The new sovereignty: compliance with international regulatory agreements* (Cambridge, Mass, Harvard University Press, 1995).

[60] Human Rights Committee. *Annual Report to the UN General Assembly* (A/54/40, 21 October 1999).

[61] See: P Alston and J Crawford (eds), *The Future of UN Human Rights Treaty Monitoring;* I Boerefijn, *The Reporting Procedure under the Covenant on Civil and Political Rights: Practice and Procedures of the Human Rights Committee* (Oxford, Hart Publishing, 1999).

processes, mechanisms, and structures are created to facilitate a continuing internalisation of international standards and norms.[62] International institutions set agendas, propose standards, assess state actions, disseminate information, control the flow of knowledge, and recruit experts. They have the quiet capacity to work with national officials and institutions to create extensive networks of governmental and non-governmental officials to foster conditions within society for the positive adoption of international norms and standards.

A different approach, as shown in a recent set of studies, is to portray internalisation as a process of *socialisation.*[63] Actors and agencies must be socialised into accepting international norms 'as collective expectations about proper behaviour'.[64] Socialisation in turn refers to three different mechanisms: processes of instrumental adaptation and strategic bargaining; processes of moral consciousness raising; and processes of institutionalisation and habitualisation. The first of these refers to the tendency of states to respond to external pressures in order to advance their interests and preferences. But this is only one mode of social change. The authors claim that 'actors identities can be reshaped through discursive processes of argumentation and persuasion.' Governments violating human rights standards are often engaged in an argumentative process with international institutions or advocacy groups, and within that engagement 'truth claims have to be justified and moral convictions are challenged.'[65] The third stage is the creation of state institutions within which compliance with human rights norms becomes a habit. Internalisation through socialisation is illustrated with studies of recent events in countries such as Chile, Turkey, the former Czechoslavakia and other Eastern European countries. In an illuminating study of Czechoslavakia and Poland, the authors show how the Helsinki Accords became internalised through the gradual replacement of repression with a spiral of social mobilisation, and trans-networking by various internal and external groups; followed by regime denial of the applicability of international norms; followed then by tactical concessions; and then by expanded mobilisation and trans-national pressure, until the regime accepted the normative validity of the human rights norms, embedded them in its rhetoric and institutions; concluding with their implementation through consistent practices.[66]

[62] For development of this administrative model of international institutions in the environmental context, see D Sandler, *International Treaty Institutions And State Compliance: Rules Processes And Practices* (forthcoming); DJ Sandler et al (eds), *Protecting the Gulf of Aqaba: A regional environmental challenge* (Washington, DC, Environmental Law Institute, 1993).
[63] T Risse, S Kopp, and K Sikkink (eds), *The Power of Human Rights: International Norms and Domestic Change* (Cambridge, Cambridge University Press, 1999).
[64] *Ibid,* at 236.
[65] *Ibid.*
[66] *Ibid,* at 206.

THE NATIONAL DIMENSION

The Role of the State

While the nation state is the greatest threat to human rights it is equally true that an effective system of protection depends on it. As to the first part, the role of the state, through its institutions and officials, in abusing or failing to protect human rights, is clear to see. As to the second, it is also the case, for reasons we have seen, that the state has to be the main instrument for curbing and preventing abuses. The involvement of the international order is important, and its capacity for direct implementation seems set to increase, although change is a slow and arduous process. It is not just a question of time; the international order is limited systemically in the ways we have already discussed, so that, in the absence of major shifts in its nature and in that of the nation state, the state must remain the principal party in implementation.

Another general point concerns the conditions within a state that are conducive to human rights. This has two aspects. One is that administrative and legal institutions are only part of those social conditions, indeed they might be said to be the product of those conditions, without which institutions would not be effective. Among the conditions are, for instance, a vigorous civil society and certain stages of economic prosperity.[67] While the underlying social conditions undoubtedly affect implementation, at the same time the study of law and institutions as central to a regulatory regime has its own issues which are our present concern. The other aspect of this general point is that legal and administrative institutions and processes are not themselves neutral or unproblematic. They are themselves involved in power relationships and may reflect an official version of human rights from which certain rights are excluded. Institutionalisation may also make it more difficult for other mechanisms, such as low-level democratic processes, to generate rights. And finally, institutional processes at the state level do not necessarily provide better protection than other, less formal processes.[68] Again these points should be acknowledged, and again they reinforce the close relationship between the various elements in making human rights effective.

What then are the conditions at the state level that are conducive to protecting human rights? Since there is little empirical research directed

[67] In fact there is little agreement as to what social conditions are necessary for human rights protection: compare by way of example J Donnelly, *International Human Rights in Theory and Practice,* whose 'trade-off theory' suggests a correlation between human rights and economic prosperity, and TR Gurr, *Peoples Versus States: Minorities at Risk in the New Century* (Washington, DC, US Institute of Peace Press, 2000).

[68] For an argument on these lines: N Stammers, 'Social Movements and the Social Construction of Human Rights' (1999) 21 *Human Rights Quarterly* 980ff.

specifically at human rights implementation, the answer is somewhat speculative; we draw on standard ideas from implementation research, while trying at the same time to identify features particular to human rights. Several issues arise. First, human rights standards that are given constitutional status are likely to have a greater chance of implementation than those that remain simply obligations at international law. Secondly, administrative institutions and processes play a role in recognising and respecting human rights, while a third concerns the usefulness of special bodies created to encourage that process. Finally, it is important to consider the remedies available within national systems.

The Reception of Human Rights Standards

The signing of a treaty is just the first step towards implementation. The actions taken by a state after signing an international treaty significantly impact upon whether the standards are given effect.[69] The way a state chooses to incorporate international standards depends partly upon whether it is 'monist' or 'dualist'. In the case of monist countries, such as The Netherlands, ratification of a treaty automatically gives rise to rights within that national jurisdiction. This is because in such countries the sources of national law may stem from either international or domestic instruments. In the case of dualist countries, an act of the legislature is required to ensure the rights are enforceable under national law. Some countries, such as the United States, are of a hybrid nature, where some international treaties are 'self-executing', while others require incorporation via an act of the legislature.

In the case of dualist countries, two approaches are open after the signing of an international treaty: the standards of the treaty may be left as obligations on the state at international law, or they may be adopted into the domestic legal system. The first approach, is not necessarily, but in practice often is, an indication of proposed inaction. Incorporation into the domestic legal system, whether by general provision, or by stating the standards in the constitution or other national laws, does suggest a more positive approach to implementation. How the standards are stated is itself another variable, which allows the state to adapt the treaty provisions to fit its own circumstances; this will in turn influence the interpretation and application by other state bodies, including the courts.

[69] For an empirical study of the relationship between ratification of international human rights treaties and the protection of human rights, see: L Camp Keith, 'The United Nations International Covenant on Civil and Political Rights: Does It Make a Difference in Human Rights Behavior?' 95ff; OA Hathaway, 'Do Human Rights Treaties Make a Difference?' (2002) 111 *Yale Law Journal* 1935ff.

Treaties dealing with human rights do not always make clear precisely what obligations are thereby imposed on states; indeed, they may be deeply equivocal. The duty may be simply not to interfere, or to provide the institutional machinery for their realisation, or to take positive action to ensure protection, or, as in the case of social and economic rights, to make resources available.[70] Arguably the statement of a general duty to protect and respect a right carries with it the duty to provide the mechanisms and resources necessary for that purpose. The trouble is that states themselves have to decide the extent of their duties and have varying degrees of discretion in doing so, despite efforts at the international level to provide guidance and consistency. The expression of rights in constitutions is in turn instructive in judging how states understand their duties and how serious they will be in giving protection. The mode of expression varies greatly. The Constitution of South Africa imposes duties on the state to 'respect, protect, promote and fulfil the rights in the Bill of Rights.'[71] It also expressly provides for a wide range of persons who may seek judicial remedies for violation. In the United States, particular rights are protected by way of amendments to the Constitution. While a number of constitutions on the African continent such as the Ugandan and South African Constitutions contain reference to economic and social rights, such rights are not referred to in the Constitution of the United States.

Human Rights and Constitutionalism

The way human rights are expressed in the constitution of a country is part of a wider issue concerning their relationship to other features of *constitutionalism*. By constitutionalism is meant that certain values of respect for persons, democracy, the rule of law, and related ideas, are recognised and broadly respected within a country; and that institutions and mechanisms exist for upholding them.[72] This usually means an institutional structure that reflects the values in a general way and provides mechanisms for their protection in particular cases. While we do not know with any certainty the interrelationship among the various values or the conditions that make their realisation possible, experience suggests that they do tend to go together and that only in very particular social and economic circumstances are they successful. In other words, to take examples, a country that is not

[70] Steiner and Alston provide a good account of the various levels of obligation: Steiner and Alston, *International Human Rights in Context* 181ff.
[71] 1996 Constitution, ch 2, s 7.2.
[72] Constitutionalisation is not achieved simply by inserting values in a constitution; it requires a supporting set of ideas, attitudes, and processes.

democratic is unlikely to show high respect for persons;[73] similarly a country without a governmental structure that diffuses power among different institutions is unlikely to have the mechanisms necessary to commit to the values noted.[74] Other examples could be given.

The implications for human rights protection are clear. The levels of protection in a country will be a factor of its general commitment to constitutionalism. It is not then surprising that countries with well-developed constitutionalism tend to have a better record on human rights protection than those low in the stakes. This is borne out in the new democracies of eastern Europe, the human rights record of each over the last twelve or so years being broadly in accordance with its record in relation to constitutionalism generally. At the same time, western European countries and beyond, with longer and more developed notions of constitutionalism, have better human rights records.[75] The explanation for these correlations should be understood in terms of competing cognitive and normative systems, as explained earlier. Those countries with a good record of constitutionalism have accepted a view of government and political power of a very particular kind, which includes the absorption of matching norms; that they have done so is manifested in the creation of institutions and processes which are both premised on and reinforce their cognitive and normative world.[76]

Human Rights in the Administrative Process

If, as appears to be the case, most human rights violations are perpetrated by the state, then it is in the exercise of administrative power that they mainly occur. The real test of the levels of violation are in police stations, prisons, mental health institutions, social security and welfare offices, schools, and the like. Again it is not difficult to see why: the internal view of officials within each set of institutions is prone to be heavily influenced by cognitive and normative considerations that, for example, pertain to the

[73] It does not follow that a democratic country necessarily provides a high level of protection of human rights: see further J Donnelly, *Universal Human Rights in Theory and Practice.*

[74] Some would single out an independent judiciary as an institutional necessity, and much constitutional reform is premised on that assumption. Whether it is warranted is not clear and it may be that other institutional mechanisms may be just as if not more important. See further: EG Jensen and TC Heller, *Beyond Common Knowledge: Empirical Approaches to the Rule of Law* (Palo Alto, Stanford University Press, forthcoming).

[75] Constitutionalisation implies respect for certain values: the entrenchment of a Bill of Rights in a written constitution is one instrument towards consitutionalisation, but countries may be highly consitutionalised without a bill of rights, Australia for example, or without a written constitution, the United Kingdom for example.

[76] See further: RD Putman, with R Leonardi and RY Nanetti, *Making Democracy Work: civic traditions in modern Italy* (Princeton, Princeton University Press, 1993).

nature of the task, the professional assumptions around it, and peer-group pressures that prevail. As one of the present authors has described elsewhere, each administrative body is characterised by a certain inner rationality and a degree of autonomy from external influences. There the issue was the inherent resistance to notions of administrative justice;[77] a similar resistance should be expected to human rights standards.

The implementation of human rights standards depends crucially on their penetrating the internal world of administrative institutions and their officials. Since they are generally weak norms compared with those naturally prevailing, internalisation is likely to be difficult to achieve. The building of institutions or the modification of existing ones is a subject in itself which we cannot enter into here beyond a few brief comments. Many different factors are influential. The very statement of clear standards as binding on administrators is an obvious first step. Restatement from time to time by authoritative institutions, such as courts or an ombudsman, may add to the strength of the standards, although the direct impact on administrative behaviour of isolated judicial rulings, even from the highest courts and on the most important issues, is probably small.[78] Court decisions provide a remedy in the particular case, but rarely influence the structure of the administrative body. Other external factors such as investigations of complaints, disciplinary processes, reports, and monitoring all exert some influence on internal administrative behaviour. Pressures from the international order may also be present, a good example being the Council of Europe and, even more particularly, the European Union, which has provided substantial incentives for potential member states to modify the behaviour of their administration.

Perhaps the most important variable among many in the behaviour of administrative institutions and officials towards human rights standards is the stage of development of the system of government and administration. The point can be illustrated by reference to eastern Europe where strong, authoritarian states were replaced, in general, with weak and ineffective (and in some cases still authoritarian) states.[79] Their administrative institutions tend to be poorly developed and display internal cultures often hostile to human rights. Strong administrative institutions are not necessarily good

[77] DJ Galligan, 'Authoritarianism in Government and Administration: The Promise of Administrative Justice', note 5, and Machin, Note 56, 79–102.

[78] See the discussion of this issue in BG Garth and A Sarat, *How Does Law Matter?* Also G Richardson; S Halliday, 'The Influence of Judicial Review on Bureaucratic Decision-Making' 110–22; S Halliday, *Judicial Review and Compliance with Administrative Law* (Oxford, Hart Publishing, 2004).

[79] See DJ Galligan, 'Public Administration and the Tendency to Authoritarianism' in A Sajo (ed), *Out of and Into Authoritarian Laws* (The Hague, Kluwer, 2002).

at protecting rights, but arguably being strong is a pre-condition, since being strong suggests the capacity to moderate its internal world and to bring it into line with external standards. It is also arguable that the strength of administrative bodies derives in part at least from the existence of an environment of other strong institutions, such as parliaments, courts, and various other balancing and supervising bodies. Perhaps this is to say nothing more than repeat the conventional view that human rights depend on there being strong states with well-developed legal and administrative cultures.[80]

It is useful to distinguish between primary institutions that make day-to-day decisions having human rights aspects and other institutions dedicated to their supervision. Courts are the classic supervisory body, although their powers of review of administration and their influence are limited. The ombudsman is another with powers to investigate complaints in a range of matters. Other institutions are often created to add a level of protection specifically for human rights. The new democracies of Eastern Europe are, for instance, replete with human rights commissions, ombudsman institutions for human rights, parliamentary committees, and other dedicated institutions. These should be included in a full account of the implementation process, although again empirical research concerning their contribution to effective implementation remains to be done.

Our suggestion so far has been that unless administrative bodies have reached a certain level of internal development and are subject to a network of external checks and controls, the prospects for human rights within them are low. This is not to suggest that human rights standards are automatically or easily received into well-developed administrative systems. A recent study of the clash between the professional, clinical world of psychiatrists and statutory standards protecting patients' rights shows just how resistant the former were to the latter, even though individual doctors would undoubtedly see themselves as respecters of rights.[81] If that is the case in the specialised environment of mental health tribunals, it is likely to be true generally across the whole administration.

However, human rights standards are not doomed to remain aliens within the administrative process; on the contrary, a range of strategies can be used to encourage and facilitate their internalisation. Naturally there is no blueprint, no master plan; an assessment has to be made of each administrative context to ascertain the forms of quality control that are most likely to have influence both in individual cases and structurally.

[80] See S Holmes, 'Constitutionalism, Democracy, and State Decay' in H Koh and R Slye (eds), *Deliberative Democracy and Human Rights* (London, Yale University Press, 1999)

[81] N Eastman and J Peay (eds), *Law Without Enforcement: Integrating mental health and justice* (Oxford, Hart, 1999).

We conclude with an example: how to introduce standards into policing, in particular, the treatment of suspects, a matter notoriously difficult. Closed institutions like the police station are the hardest to bring under external influence. In 1984, the UK Parliament tackled the matter in a statutory code of police powers and suspects' rights, first by stating the standards to be observed, and then devising institutions and mechanisms to encourage their internalisation by the police. The key to a reasonably successful venture was to identify the risks and then devise practical measures for reducing them. This consisted of devices such as: a division of labour in relation to a suspect; extensive recording of each step taken in the holding and questioning of suspects, and the reasons; the scrutiny of one officer by another; and the right of the suspect to have a lawyer in the police station, together with practical steps to ensure the right was meaningful.

The police at first resisted the system and campaigned against it. It seemed to interfere with their efficiency; it imposed new duties of recording and reporting; it involved cumbersome procedures; and it appeared to favour the suspect. However, in time, the police attitudes changed; they came to view the new regulatory regime as protecting them as well as the suspect. Allegations of mistreatment or impropriety could be met with detailed records made at the time and subject to cross-checking. The code came to be seen as a shield for the police, and attitudes towards it began to change; initial hostility gave way to acceptance of it as binding and legitimate. The point of the example is to show that an apparently intractable situation can be structured through institutions and processes in order to bring about change of attitudes and practice. Other situations can be subjected to the same analysis and structuring, whether it is the mistreatment of gypsies or ethnic minorities by the police, or the behaviour of officials in welfare agencies, schools, or prisons.

CONCLUSION

Human rights are often referred to in a generic and sweeping way, as if they presented to all countries one set of common issues. The reality is very different; countries are at different stages in their acceptance of human rights standards. In stable, democratic, and prosperous societies, where the standards are accepted and suitable institutions for implementation are in place, the issue is often how to improve or refine an already tolerable record. By way of example, the UK's recent enactment of the Human Rights Act 1998, and thereby incorporation of the European Convention on Human Rights into UK law, may be expected to make marginal rather than fundamental improvements in the level of respect for rights by the government and administration. The UK is one of a group whose members generally have developed a reasonable and stable standard of acceptance and protection.

In other countries, such as the new democracies of eastern Europe, where stability and democracy are less secure, where institutions are in place but their operation is less reliable, and where official attitudes are more equivocal, naturally the obstacles to human rights protection are greater, and serious shortcomings persist. Further along the spectrum is a raft of other countries in which concern for human rights has hardly been aroused and in which institutional protection barely exists. And finally at the far end are those cases where violations, whether through torture, genocide, or forced migration, are so gross that external force has to be applied.

Many contingencies and variables, from right to right and country to country, are relevant to the implementation of human rights standards: the local, the particular, and the cultural relativities all have to be accommodated in any attempt to make rights effective. At the same time, debilitation by the particular is not the whole story: patterns of a general kind can be detected, strategies and techniques have been tried and tested; some are more effective than others. The matter of making law effective in a variety of social contexts is an old campaign about which quite a lot is known, and while human rights present their own issues, they are not different in any dimensional sense. The present chapter is no more than a brief introduction to some of these issues.

3

France, the UK, and the 'Boomerang' of the Internationalisation of Human Rights (1945–2000)

MIKAEL RASK MADSEN

INTRODUCTION

IT MIGHT BE considered an irony of history that the demise of French and British imperial power coincided with the internationalisation of one of the greatest accomplishments of their political and democratic culture: human rights. Coincidental as well as a by-product of century long exportation of their respective ideas of liberal democracy and republicanism, the double-shift occurred as part of a structural transformation of the international field. In the immediate postwar period, the two wounded imperial powers self-confidently projected themselves as the true authors of the concept of human rights and unquestionably put their fingerprints on the two most central texts of the new international regime, the Universal Declaration of Human Rights (UDHR) and the European Convention on Human Rights (ECHR). Yet, their activism at the international level was soon overshadowed by the Cold War and the politics of decolonisation. While the development of human rights on the international level thus was brought to a deadlock, this new area of law gained distinctive importance on the European level under the auspices of the Council of Europe. In this new legal arena less exposed to the constraints of the Cold War and decolonisation, France and the UK could pursue key roles, comfortably assuming that the ECHR constituted merely a Europeanisation of their own particular national practices of civil rights and 'libertés publiques'. The subsequent development of an increasingly autonomous European regime of human rights saw the UK and France become the two most regular customers before the Court and Commission in Strasbourg. This implied a nationalisation of an evolutionary European doctrine of human rights that — after a series of high profile legal and political controversies — eventually transcended national institutions and raison d'État. What essentially had been regarded as an external measure for an external threat and altogether a means to help bring future peace to Europe was to become one of the key challenges to the national conceptualisations of law and justice as they had developed under the French and British 'new deal' economics of the postwar welfare states.

This chapter focuses on the structural history of this process of reconstructing the empires in relation to the increasing European, international and, eventually, national importance of human rights thus being an analysis of the transformation of state, law and the idea of human rights over the last fifty years in France and the UK. In broad theme, the chapter compares an initial period marked by exteriorisation and exportation of human rights with a subsequent period, beginning around the early 1970s, that witnessed an increased nationalisation of the international accomplishments, as well as a resurrection of the national political interests in the area. Obviously, the line cannot be drawn sharply: the initial international activism was produced by a number of local agents, to some extent implying that local battles were being projected internationally and vice versa.[1] However, the prevailing distinction of the time that human rights were essentially international and, thus, dealt with by experts of diplomacy and international law while the national developments in area fell under different categories — typically civil rights or *libertés publiques* — provides a good analytical starting-point even if it is potentially an exaggerated categorisation. This corresponds with the fact that the fluid area of practice that eventually came to be known under the common name of human rights was indeed produced at the crossroads of national and international law and politics.

The chapter seeks to link these interdependent and reciprocal processes to the emergence and transformation of the *field* of human rights. Theoretically, this field is defined as an open, symbolic space held together by the objective relations between institutions and individuals, all seeking to influence the developing issue-area of human rights.[2] This conceptualisation and approach establishes a bottom-up view of the process of building

[1] On the history of the international field, see MR Madsen and Y Dezalay, 'The Power of the Legal Field: Pierre Bourdieu and the Law' in R Banakar and M Travers, *An Introduction to Law and Social Theory* (Oxford, Hart Publishing, 2002) 199. See also C Charle, *La crise des sociétés impériales: Allemagne, France, Grande-Bretagne 1900–1940* (Paris, Éditions du Seuil, 2001).

[2] These conceptualisations draw on the work of Pierre Bourdieu. See for definitions of the original notions, P Bourdieu and L Wacquant, *An Invitation to Reflexive Sociology* (Chicago, University of Chicago Press, 1992) 97 and 101. See also, MR Madsen and Y Dezalay, above, n 1.

this area which seeks to avoid the potential bias produced by analytically staying too close to the legal categorisation of the subject. As with any field, then, human rights was marked initially by the logics of closely related domains whose agents sought to convert their capitals into the fluid domain being constructed before the area developed a greater autonomy and its own particular logics. One consistent feature of the human rights field can, however, be observed throughout its history: as human rights by very definition concern the conduct of the state as well as some of the most essential visions and divisions of state and society, the institutions and agents involved are for the most part to be found inside or in the shadow of the field of state power. This is largely reflected in the following analysis.

THE EXTERIORISATION OF IMPERIAL HUMAN RIGHTS SAVOIR-FAIRE (1945–70)

Internationalisation and Europeanisation of Human Rights

The internationalisation and Europeanisation of human rights as a norm and institution building process after the Second World War was first and foremost the product of competitive international projections of national traditions in areas ranging from established civil and political rights to novel rights deriving from the welfare state projects common to much of Europe in the postwar period.[3] Hence, we should first briefly consider the national starting point of France and Britain since they had considerably different human rights traditions, despite both belonging to the exclusive club of human rights pioneers. Burdened by the Vichy collaboration and general humiliation of the German occupation, postwar France sought to resurrect its place in the world and its political system. Human Rights were, however, only left a declaratory role in the preamble of the Fourth Republic's Constitution (1946) in the form of a list of the great achievements in the area and a proclamation of the new social and economic rights.[4] This document thereby sustained a French tradition of seeing human rights as a mixture of a socio-political struggle and a gradual legalisation of these accomplishments. The period did indeed maintain that human rights in France were the product of a revolutionary transformation, and particularly in the area of social and economic rights, the revolutionary appeal of *les droits de l'Homme* remained integral to the socio-political economy. In Britain, in contrast, human rights or indeed civil rights were

[3] This distinction was replicated in the battles over the status of the right to certain economic, social and cultural benefits to be protected by the UN, as well as the ECHR. In both cases, social, economic and cultural rights acquired lesser legal status than civil and political rights.
[4] D Lochak, *Les droits de l'homme* (Paris, La Découverte, 2002) 28.

the product of a general societal development which by and large had been delegated to the 'closed circuit' of the legal system dominated by an Oxbridge network occupying the majority of seats on the bench. This had produced an archaic jungle of documents, principles and unwritten 'conventions', including the Magna Carta (1215), the Bill of Rights (1689) and the Habeas Corpus Acts (1640 and 1679), all together comprising the UK protection of civil rights and liberties. By all means, human rights in Britain were to a much lesser degree at the centre of the public discourse on the transformation of the postwar state.

Despite these significant differences in the social position of rights in France and the UK — or exactly because of them — both countries held themselves up as the true authors of the concept. This is evidenced in their confident participation in the conferences leading to the drafting of the Universal Declaration of Human Rights and the European Convention on Human Rights, as well as through their eagerness to impose democratic structures modelled in their own ideal images on the former colonies gradually leaving the shrinking empires. This did not imply that these two core imperial societies sought the same ends. On the contrary, their respective traditions were instrumental in forming their views; the clash between grand declarations in the French style and dry 'effective' legal prose as preferred by the British was visible on numerous occasions.[5] Also, their respective positioning in the increasingly bipolar international field conditioned their engagement in the area of human rights. But above all, the inherently contradictory nature of the colonial logic compromised their activism in this new area of international law and politics. First, largely due to their international power and prestige, they managed to keep the subject of decolonisation out of both the UDHR and the UN Charter.[6] Yet, it was the French law professor, diplomat and representative in the UN Human Rights Commission, René Cassin, who engineered that the international human rights declaration was christened the *Universal* Declaration of Human Rights. This discrete change implied a groundbreaking redefinition of the subjects of international law which anticipated the transnational character of the practices of the human rights in the decades to come. This

[5] See for instance É Pateyron, *La contribution française à la rédaction de la Déclaration universelle des droits de l'homme* (Paris, La Documentation française, 1998).

[6] As regards decolonisation, Chapter XI of the UN Charter only called on the so-called 'administering powers' to recognise that the interests of the inhabitants of the dependent territories were paramount and to promote their wellbeing. The administering powers agreed to assist these territories 'in the progressive development of their free political institutions, according to the particular circumstances of each territory'. See further, J Sankey, 'Decolonisation: Cooperation and Confrontation at the United Nations' in E Jensen and T Fisher (eds), *The United Kingdom — The United Nations* (London, Macmillan, 1990) 96ff. On France, see M Bettati, *Le droit d'ingérence. La mutation de l'ordre mondial* (Paris, Odile Jacob, 1996) 25–26.

universalisation of human rights was, however, not designed to undermine colonial politics. Simultaneously, Cassin — like his *confrères* at the Quai d'Orsay and the Foreign Office — was a strong opponent of the concept of peoples' rights that was favoured by national liberation movements at the time. In practice, the imperial powers' common solution was to emphasise national sovereignty over international law and rely on a measured cooperation with the UN over decolonisation issues, thus, limiting the sphere of the new human rights regime.

It is beyond the scope of this work to address in detail the initial negotiations and the subsequent institution-building of the leading French and British actors in charge of pursuing these ends. Also beyond its reach is an analysis of the latter-day imperialist balancing act that kept the colonial matter a question of national sovereignty while continuing a tradition of supplying universals. Generally, we can observe the relative legal-institutional dominance in this process. In Britain, the concept of human rights was translated into the international field by the legal advisors of the Foreign Office, while agents who had participated in the liberation and resistance movements marked the French delegations and nominees to these institutions. This can be exemplified by looking at two key pioneers of international human rights.

Box 1: Pioneers of International Human Rights

Of Jewish origin, in-house counsel to Charles de Gaulle's Free Government in London, the public law expert and diplomat René Cassin was to become the key French player in the preparation of the UN Declaration and probably the most influential member of the UN Human Rights Commission, both during the drafting of the UDHR but also subsequently as a permanent member. His involvement in international issues was long: he had, among others, been an activist in the French Human Rights League in the interwar period as well as being a member of the French delegation to the League of Nations.[7] With his multiple qualifications in and around the field of power, Cassin represented French interest in the UN Human Rights Commission with a personal dedication that was hardly found among the other representatives. His politics of universalism took a starting point in his own ambitious projection of *la France* as representing the possibility of universalisation not replicated elsewhere. Cassin's involvement in international human rights, including the position as president of the European Court of Human Rights for nine years, led him to receive the Nobel Peace Prize in 1968. Internationally and in the French field, he operated very close to the circuits of state power, as well as providing a link between

[7] See below on the role of the French Human Rights League. On the background of René Cassin, see M Agi, *René Cassin: Père de la Déclaration universelle des droits de l'homme* (Paris, LAP, 1998).

official policies and those of the civil society organisations where he was a popular pick for 'president' — or 'porte-drapeau' — supplying a symbolic and juridical power to organisations otherwise defined in opposition to the state.[8]

In the British camp, one pioneer of human rights was Sir Hersch Lauterpacht of Cambridge University. The involvement of Lauterpacht in human rights was immediate and deeply personal. A Polish born Jew, but naturalised as a British subject (1931) and thereby saved from the Holocaust, Lauterpacht personifies the change in perception and outlook that marked the postwar period and with which the investment in international human rights is closely linked.[9] But while Cassin had important connections into the political game, Lauterpacht remained in the dual-role as 'grand professeur' and 'learned international lawyer' operating only in the shadow of the field of international politics dominated by the Foreign Office. He launched a fierce critique of the legal insufficiencies of the high prose of the UDHR in a number of publications, as well as seeking to become involved in the more practical international legal work of human rights: He was a member of the British War Crimes Executive in Nuremberg, as well as an advisor to the UN Secretariat. Eventually, he was appointed judge at the International Court of Justice in The Hague where he sat as British judge between 1955–62 following Lord Arnold McNair (1946–55). Both of them were attached to the same set of chambers as 'door tenants', 20 Essex Street, a leading set of chambers in the area of public international law at the time. They also taught together at the LSE before Lauterpacht joined Cambridge University.

The actual drafting of the human rights conventions and covenants went ahead at different speeds. While it took some twenty long years to complete the international covenants due to the imposition of the Cold War orthodoxy into the area by the superpowers, the ECHR was prepared in an area freed from these constraints and was ready by 1950. Britain was the first state to sign, but only after having secured the so-called 'colonial clause', as well as effectively having obstructed the Council of Europe from becoming a pretext for a federal European master plan. The question of allowing British citizens a direct recourse to the Court by granting a right to individual petition was initially disregarded: it was perceived as irrelevant as the

[8] In the postwar period, Cassin became an important point of reference in international law. He served as president of numerous organisations, including the Society of Comparative Legislation (1952–56), the International Institute of Administrative Sciences (1953–56), the International Institute of Diplomatic Studies and Research (1956), and the French Association for the Development of International Law (1962–67). In France, he was Vice-President of the *Conseil de'État* (1944–60) and then for ten years he sat on the *Conseil Constitutionnel.* Internationally, in addition to his engagement in the Human Rights Commission he was President of the Court of Arbitration at The Hague (1950–60).

[9] Before emigrating to the UK, he had achieved doctoral degrees in both law and political science from the University of Vienna where he was taught by Hans Kelsen. See further, 'The European Tradition in International Law: Hersch Lauterpact' (1997) 8(2), *European Journal of International Law*.

national protection was already extensive, and as it was generally considered unacceptable to have international control of this particular issue-area because of the proud traditions of civil rights under the common law.[10] But as early as 1966, Britain accepted the right of individual petition for British individuals under the ECHR and then in 1967 for individuals in its Crown dependencies and dependent territories. In 1968 Britain signed both international covenants. This accelerated involvement was clearly marked by a strategy of securing the UK maximum influence on the system being built. Moreover, as later noted by one English judge of the ECHR: 'the UK felt pretty confident that [it] was in line with all the requirements of the Convention' (Int 109, no 1, April 25, 2001). Not appearing particularly revolutionary, the ECHR was marked by an old-fashioned public international law attitude and saw as one of its key objectives 'to build up confidence of governments in the system' (Int 109, no 1, April 25, 2001).

Despite this rather inoffensive, slightly introverted appearance of the European system, let alone the central role played by French actors in its genesis and its initial development, it was not until 1974, in the political vacuum during the aftermath of the death of Pompidou, that France ratified the Convention.[11] Individual petition was not granted until 1981. This political course was justified by a few explicit arguments which were influenced by a general disbelief in the prospects of international control in the area of *libertés publiques* — a position that had gained particular momentum during the colonial battles.[12] Generally, France had developed a certain resistance to the ECHR during the 1950s and 1960s. First, there was the general opposition coming from the internalisation of the myth of 'le pays des droits de l'homme' among the actors of the political and legal fields, which in practice led them to conclude that very little, if anything, was to be gained from ratifying the ECHR.[13] Secondly, British law

[10] See H Street, *Freedom, the Individual and the Law* (Harmondsworth, Pelican, 3rd edn, 1975) 291; Sir V Evans, 'The European Court of Human Rights: A Time for Appraisal', in R Blackburn and JJ Busuttil (eds), *Human Right for the 21st Century* (London, Pinter, 1997) 88ff.

[11] One of the chief architects of the ECHR was the French lawyer and former Minister of Justice, Pierre-Henri Teitgen. He helped produce the so-called Teitgen Report of September 1949, laying out the basics of the system and the rights to be protected. Pierre-Henri Teitgen and Sir David Maxwell Fyfe, with Belgian professor Fernand Dehousse, had already in 1949 founded the International Juridical Section of the European Movement. Together they drafted a European Bill of Rights and put forward the argument for a system that included a central court to uphold these fundamental liberties. See JG Merrils and AH Robertson, *Human Rights in Europe: A Study of the European Convention on Human Rights* (Manchester, Manchester University Press, 2001) 6.

[12] See A Pecheul, *Les dates-clefs de la protection des droits de l'homme en France* (Paris, Ellipses, 2001) 118–19. As concerns the colonial aspect, the ECHR system, after French and British pressure, included a so-called colonial clause which secured the member-states the option of limiting territorially the jurisdiction. Also, the right to individual petition and the jurisdiction of the Court were made optional under Art 25 and 46 respectively.

[13] *Ibid.*

unquestionably inspired the ECHR chapter on guarantees in the area of criminal procedure and this seemed *per se* a reason for keeping a certain distance.[14] But France like Britain, needless to say, assumed full compliance with the ECHR as the Convention supposedly was modelled in the images of their own eminent legal traditions.

International Human Rights Strategies under the Welfare State

This brief outline of the French and British positions with regard to the development of international and European human rights necessarily has to be understood in the context of the general transformation of these societies, and how this influenced the civil society activism directed towards the human rights field. To understand these practices, it is beneficial to consider the reconfiguration of the state in France and Britain in the period. The two countries committed themselves to major changes in the set up of the state in the first two decades following the War, in both cases implying a decline in the role and position of law and the legal profession. In France, law and lawyers faced particular challenges. The occupation and the subsequent collaboration had not only disqualified certain right wing political classes, but had questioned the position of law and the legal profession, especially the role played by the judiciary in the Vichy administration.[15] The subsequent legal processes against the collaborators did very little to restore the authority of law.[16] More generally, the decline of the legal profession was cemented by the initiation of the welfare state project of the Fourth Republic, diminishing what was left of the 'Republic of Jurists' — a name attributed to the Third Republic and its domination of lawyers and their legal-liberal ideals of the rule of law and *libertés publiques*.[17] Indeed the period in focus witnessed a considerable drop in the role and power of the legal profession in France, only emphasised by the quasi-exclusion of lawyers in the state bureaucracy by the establishment in 1946 of l'ÉNA (the National School of Public Administration), a new elite educational establishment for civil servants.[18] The welfare state's focus on social and

[14] Another issue was the question of 'laïcité' and how the Republic's clear favouring of public non-religious education was to be considered by the Court. Also, under the Fifth Republic the particular exceptional powers vested with the President in situations of crisis under Art 16 of the Constitution were feared to potentially constitute a violation of the ECHR.

[15] See on the judges under Vichy, A Bancaud, *Une exception ordinaire: La magistrature en France (1930–1950)* (Paris, Gallimard, 2002).

[16] See A Cobban, *A History of Modern France, Volume 3: 1871–1962* (Middlesex, Penguin, 1965) 200–1.

[17] See YH Gaudement, *Les Juristes et la vie politique de la IIIè République* (Paris, PUF, 1970).

[18] L Karpik, *Les avocats: Entre l'état, le public et le marché XIIIè-XXè siècle* (Paris, Gallimard, 1995) 458.

economic rights also contributed to a decline of the relative importance of the classic civil and political rights and, thereby, also the traditional position and influence of the legal profession. Unsurprisingly, among the pioneers of human rights lawyers in the postwar period, we find several who used the welfare state paradigm of rights as a source — politically as well as financially — for their gradual involvement in the human rights field.

In postwar Britain the Labour Government, with a landslide majority behind it, initiated what has been labelled 'the most radical administration of the century' seeking a welfare programme with comparable consequences for the legal profession in the UK as for their French counterparts.[19] However, in the British case, the new welfare state did not only challenge the legal profession and its traditional power as in France it also constituted a challenge to the judiciary and its control and development of the common law. To secure their position in the evolving state structure, the English judiciary responded by emphasising their civil rights practices as a means to challenge the new found belief in welfare state law and associated legal institutions.[20] The choice of terrain, however, was based more upon assumptions and ceremonial traditions than actual practices.[21] Generally, the state's expansionist strategies in the areas of economic and social rights tended to rely more on law than on lawyers, all together helping to transform the power of law and the legal profession in the UK. In other words, the internationalisation of human rights began at a time when law and the legal profession in France and the UK were severely challenged on multiple fronts. International human rights strategies in this context offered a rare opportunity for restoring the role of the lawyer as a political entrepreneur.

France: Defending Human Rights at the Doorstep of the Empire

In France, the production of a vivid, socio-political human rights culture has been considerably influenced by the practices of the French Human Rights League — *la Ligue des Droits de l'Homme et du Citoyen* (LDH) — which was set up at the height of the Dreyfus Affair (1898). In the interwar period, LDH managed to Europeanise its efforts as the Federation of Human Rights Leagues (FIDH), propose a Global Human Rights Declaration

[19] B Abel-Smith and R Stevens, *Lawyers and the Courts: A Sociological Study of the English Legal System 1750–1965* (London, Heinemann, 1967) 285.

[20] Abel-Smith and Stevens note: 'Some judges have gone so far as to claim that the English judges have been more successful in protecting civil liberties than those in countries where civil liberties were written into the constitution'. *Ibid*, at 305.

[21] As one law professor wrote some 40 years ago in the introduction to his book 'Freedom, the Individual and the Law': 'In the United States there are hundreds of books dealing with civil liberties. So far as is known, this is the first book which attempts to survey comprehensively the state of civil liberties in Britain'. H Street, above n 10 at 12–13.

and serve as a platform for denouncing human rights violations on a global scale.[22] The French section of FIDH, the LDH, was indeed the movement's headquarters. The core group of activists were the so called 'Dreyfusards', a name given to the emergence of the new French intellectual, typically to the left of the political spectrum and seeking new ways of doing politics, often with universalistic aspirations, including those for human rights.[23] In the immediate postwar period, however, the French LDH suffered a stern decline in its membership and many of the local sections closed down.[24] Explaining the decline of membership goes beyond this chapter, but it is worth noting that the top leadership of the League was heavily associated with the political elite of the Third Republic. This high profile leadership was only marginally substituted in the postwar period, making the organisation come across as somewhat outdated.[25] A closely related problem was the fact that the organisation could only in a limited way capitalise on the key dynamics of postwar France: the occupation and *la Résistance*.[26] Indeed, it was not until the Algerian War of Independence that the League and 'l'intellectuel Dreyfusard', *mutatis mutandis*, experienced a renaissance during this struggle for justice and basic human rights.[27]

The decline of the LDH in the immediate postwar period should not be equated with a general disinterest in the subject. But it was through the war experience, however, in particular *la Résistance*, that new agents were mobilised. Joë Nordmann — initiator of the 'legal section' of the resistance movement, the National Front of Jurists, as well as lawyer and devout communist — launched the International Association of Democratic Lawyers (IADL) in 1946.[28] Counting among its founding members jurists from most of the allied countries, the organisation was the child of the postwar period and ideally sought to continue the practices initiated by the Nuremberg Process.[29] The early history of the IADL bears evidence of an important dimension of the first decades of the *international* human rights field, namely the paramount importance of the

[22] See C Charle, *Les intellectuels en Europe au XIXe siècle: Essay d'historie comparée* 312.
[23] See C Charle (1996), *ibid* at 308ff. See also P Birnbaum, *l'Afaire Dreyfus: La République en péril* (Paris, Gallimard, 1994).
[24] See É Agrikoliansky, *La ligue française des droits de l'Homme et du citoyen depuis 1945: Sociologie d'un engagement civique* (Paris, l'Harmattan, 2002) 80.
[25] *Ibid*, at 81f.
[26] *Ibid*, at 90.
[27] *Ibid*, at 91.
[28] Of Jewish origin from Mulhouse in the the Alsace region, Nordmann connected himself with the French Communist Party in the interwar years. His postwar legal practice was a general one like most French lawyers at the time. However, his case load also included a significant number of *cause célèbre*, for example the Kravtchenko process. See his memoirs, J Nordmann and A Brunel, *Aux vents de l'histoire* (Arles, Actes Sud, 1996).
[29] Its first president was René Cassin who, however, left the organisation when the political dimension became too apparent.

Cold War. The IADL was soon to be associated with its leading French lawyers — typically communist or otherwise on the political left. Their activism against McCarthyism and their defence of the Rosenbergs led more or less directly to the launch of the International Commission of Jurists (ICJ) as a way to regain, in a Western favour, the terrain of the great principles: human rights, rule of law, etc.[30] Local branches of both organisations were set up. In France the ICJ was to be associated with the moderate lawyer's organisation *Libre-Justice* ('Free-Justice'), an organisation promoting rule of law. And while the CIA discretely sponsored the ICJ, the IADL received money from the Soviet Union. As we shall see in the following, this polarisation was also found in the British field.

On the French terrain many of the lawyers associated with the IADL and its local branch, the Association of Democratic Lawyers, were heavily involved during the Algerian War of Independence as a part of the general anti-colonial stance already advocated by the organisation. The Algerian War of Independence was par excellence the moment of renewed human rights activism in France, and the group of actors mobilised was far broader than the IADL network. For instance, the LDH made a strong comeback in the human rights field. More generally a significant number of French 'avocats engagés' — engaged lawyers — alongside numerous intellectuals, participated in what soon became a vast social movement advocating an anti-colonial stance. While the movement generally focused on the denunciation of the use of torture by the French forces, the 'legal chapter' of the movement developed its own specific activism by establishing an aerial bridge between France and Algeria in order to provide legal counsel to arrested Algerian fighters.[31] Out of the Algerian experience also grew a renewed attention to the FIDH. Beginning in 1964, a group of younger lawyers — Henri Leclerc, Daniel Jacoby and Michel Blum among others — started organising missions as legal observers to a number of countries.[32] This internationalisation of French legal savoir-faire was not limited to the

[30] H Tolley Jr, *The International Commission of Jurists: Global Advocates of Human Rights*, (Philadelphia, University of Pennsylvania Press, 1994), 29, 34. See also Y Dezalay and BG Garth, *The Internationalization of Palace Wars: Lawyers, Economists, and the Contest to Transform Latin American States* (Chicago, University of Chicago Press, 2002) 62f.

[31] See S Elbaz, 'French Lawyers in the Algerian War of Independence (1954–1962): Collective Organization, Legal Strategies and Political Activism', paper presented at LSA, Vancouver, 2002.

[32] H Leclerc, *Un combat pour la justice. Entretiens avec Marc Heurgon* (Paris, Éditions la Découverte, 1994) 137f. The idea of sending observers to witness trials with political stakes was hardly new. In the interwar period, in both Britain and France such missions had been commissioned by trade unions or by political parties with objectives ranging from pure idealism to clearly politically motivated engagements. Looking into the trajectory of, for example, Joë Nordmann reveals a practice of attending legal proceedings in foreign countries and on behalf of a series of groups, including *Secours Rouge Internationale*, the Communist Party and others.

activism of the FIDH and IADL. The International Movement of Catholic Jurists — *le Mouvement International des Juristes Catholiques* — led by future judge of the European Court of Human Rights, Louis Pettiti, together with the IADL and the FIDH formed a loose network of jurists and 'avocats engagés' who from time to time collaborated across the political boundaries on these missions. Altogether, human rights experienced a relative resurrection in France through the struggle to dismantle the empire.

Britain: Promoting Human Rights through the Legitimacy of Law and Lawyers

The history of human rights activism in the UK is in many ways comparable to the French case, however with the important exception that in the UK such activism never achieved a similar central position in the political discourse. First and foremost, the UK did not have the kind of intellectual movement born out of the Dreyfus affair securing human rights a position on the social agenda.[33] In Britain, the pioneer organisation in the area was the National Council for Civil Liberties (NCCL) set up in London in the 1930s by the journalist Ronald Kidd.[34] Somewhat similar to the LDH formula for its central leadership, the NCCL sought to bring together prominent journalists, writers and lawyers and through their collective and complementary capitals serve as a watchdog for civil rights. This all star representation of both the liberal establishment and the leading socialist thinkers of the time provided access to key universities, Parliament, the literary world and the press. The NCCL rapidly came to play a significant role as a voice of civil rights in Britain and a focal point on the political left, encompassing both civil libertarian and socialist agendas. Resembling the situation of the LDH in France, the NCCL suffered a decline after the War, but for different reasons. The NCCL was primarily attacked for being under communist influence and not living up to its own non-partisan role. The emergence of Cold War politics only added political weight to this suspicion.[35] And, the critique was grounded. In practice, the NCCL became the English chapter of the IADL, even if its local activism seemed closer to that of the LDH than the IADL. The international distinction drawn in the image of Cold War bipolarity marked the local terrain and compromised, for instance, the internationally oriented campaigns of the 1950s concerning political imprisonment. However, it should be noted that most of the

[33] Arguable because this kind of autonomous intellectual position on social questions was not yet developed in the UK at the time. See further C Charle, above n 22 at 326.
[34] See M Phillips, 'History of Liberty' on http://www.liberty-human-rights.org.uk/
[35] The internal debate in the NCCL following this critique led to the resignation of the novelist EM Forster from the presidency of the council. See *ibid*.

lawyers engaged in these activities saw themselves as belonging to the same small group of politically engaged lawyers, only making up a marginal minority of the Bar.[36] Needless to say, the issue of colonisation and decolonisation exacerbated the relative opposition of the different political camps in the field of human rights.

The launch in 1957 of JUSTICE, another key lawyers' organisation in the UK, sprang out of this environment, in many ways as a consequence of the political rivalry marking the landscape. One of the founders of JUSTICE, the barrister and later creator of Amnesty International (AI), Peter Benenson, saw this organisation as a means to overcome these competing interests and send observers to political trials no matter what political colour was at stake.[37] It was a short lived utopia as in 1958 JUSTICE became the English chapter of the International Commission of Jurists (ICJ), and thereby came to represent this particular vision. The details of this strategic relationship are explained in Box 2.

Box 2: 'The Strategy of Legitimation'

The local practices of JUSTICE overlap with those of the NCCL but have essentially been focused on miscarriages of justice cases. Its more clear legal project — and apparently less politicised agenda compared with that of the NCCL — made it attract a fair share of prominent barristers, solicitors, judges and legal academics, as well as individuals involved in law reform work. Moreover, the international dimension of JUSTICE, its membership in the ICJ, gave it prominence; it was clearly an institution well-situated for 'national champs' to gain access to international grandeur in the area of law, despite the fact that the organisation's local practices were much more caught up in the day-to-day politics of reforming the legal system. But, this organisational strategy appealed to top members of the profession and academics, contributing to what Yves Dezalay and Bryant Garth have named the 'strategy of legitimation': the pursuit of a transatlantic network of senior noble jurists, constructed in their own eminent images and providing the ICJ with an aura of an international high court on the matters of human rights.[38] JUSTICE was one brick in this ambitious international construction, as well as an important local player.

[36] See T Buchanan, '"The Truth Will Set You Free": The Making of Amnesty International' (2002) 37(4) *Journal of Contemporary History* 575–97, 579.

[37] *Ibid*, at 578. The co-founder of JUSTICE, Tom Sargent, was primarily a businessman and politician. Together with Peter Benenson, he was involved by the mid-1950s to help find legal support for people accused in treason trials in South Africa and to send observers to Hungary after the 1956 uprising. Tom Sargent remained the first secretary and driving force until his retirement in 1982. http://www.justice.org.uk/aboutus/index.html.

[38] Y Dezalay and BG Garth, above n 30, at 62f.

Another crucial legal-oriented organisation set up in London in the early 1960s is Amnesty International (AI). In many ways, the institutional framework and mandate of Amnesty is the further result of the experiences of the NCCL and JUSTICE. While the latter, as a consequence of its 'pure law and lawyers' strategy, lacked a broader appeal, the NCCL seemed disqualified because of its communist dominance. At least Peter Benenson seemed to have reasoned in this way in the 1960s.[39] Timing and publication, as well as depolarisation and internationalisation, characterise the first efforts of AI. By these means AI sought to construct itself with a unique position on relative distance to both the NCCL/IADJ and JUSTICE/ICJ. The mission as such started with the legendary publication of 'The Forgotten Prisoners' on Sunday, 28 May 1961. Numerous newspapers around the world reproduced this 'Appeal for Amnesty' and within months the base for 'a permanent international movement in defence of freedom of opinion and religion' was established through a network of local Amnesty groups.[40] This movement was heavily supported by the media, and the exploitation of this opportunity should have lead to the development of a sophisticated strategy. If the ICJ saw itself as the virtual 'international high court of human rights', Amnesty sought its jurisdiction in the 'tribunal of public opinion'.[41] The power of human rights as a means to mobilise shame, the mere process of scandalisation, was gradually rising in the horizon.[42]

To benefit maximally from the media, a quite subtle strategy was developed by Amnesty. The core principle keeping the movement both focused and impartial was the notion of the 'Three Network': a consciously developed strategy that secured the impartiality of every Amnesty group by forcing them to adopt prisoners of conscience of each of the key geopolitical areas (the East, the West and the 'non-aligned' countries). Further, taking its starting point in the Universal Declaration of Human Rights and a rigorously defined mandate, the tripartition was converted into universalism. This usage of the Universal Declaration provided an important non-partisan common basis for the organisation as such, while the soft law character of the Declaration offered top level management manoeuvrability in the political game of human rights. But alongside the large grassroots membership, the elite group of people attracted added extra fuel to the movement. This

[39] T Buchanan, above n 36, at 583.

[40] See the publication *Voices for Freedom: An Amnesty International Anthology* (London, Amnesty International Publication, 1986) 8. The first AI groups were founded in the UK, West Germany, Holland, France, Italy and Switzerland.

[41] Y Dezalay and BG Garth, above n 30, at 71.

[42] On this phenomenon, see MR Madsen, 'Virtuel legalitet og/eller 'pidgin law'? En præliminær analyse af menneskerettigheder som transnational ret', in H Petersen (ed), *Globaliseringer, ret og retsfilosofi* (Copenhagen, DJØF, 2002).

made AI capable of both acting in the international manners of the ICJ in the area of standard setting and, simultaneously, having clear and broadly appealing objectives.[43]

Peter Benenson's elite background from Eton and Oxford, as well as his involvement in the Labour Party and the politics of the legal profession, served him well when recruiting the very top lawyers to AI. In 1963, the Irish human rights advocate Sean MacBride was elected chairman of the international executive committee of AI. MacBride, signatory of the European Convention on Human Rights, had already played a central role at the ICJ. Like his role at the ICJ, he provided AI not only with a creative spark but also legitimacy: the United Nations gave AI consultative status in 1964 and the Council of Europe did so in 1965. In 1968, another key figure of the early human rights environment was appointed. Martin Ennals (1927–91), leaving a post as head of the NCCL, became the first secretary-general of AI. These recruitment patterns underline how AI managed to position itself between the positions of the previous, competing organisations involved in the genesis of the modern British human rights field.

The relevance of AI's strategy of forced internationalism was to be confirmed in their subsequent campaigning involving the practices of British forces in Northern Ireland, as well as in Rhodesia and Aden in Africa. Questioning the independence of AI, Peter Benenson was in fact forced to retire because of allegations that he had accepted funds from the British secret service for helping political detainees in Rhodesia.[44] He did not resume an active role in Amnesty until the mid-1980s. Also, the Amnesty report alleging the use of torture by the British forces in Northern Ireland caused organisational instability. Even if the report was perceived as a scandalous accusation, the conflict in Northern Ireland reflected a nationalisation of the battle of human rights like that experienced by France through the decolonisation process in Algeria. Generally, the human rights and legal problems associated with the crisis in Northern Ireland indeed helped revitalise human rights in the UK. Additionally, a series of post-colonial problems, in particular racism, increasingly set the British human rights agenda from the 1960s and onwards. In the larger picture, AI represents an important stake in the conversion of the field out of the deadlock of Cold War politics by its ability to generate a national interest that was to go beyond the specific international missions and projects: (international) human rights as a popular, mass political project.

[43] Y Dezalay and BG Garth, above n 30, at 71.

[44] See T Buchanan, 'Amnesty International in Crisis, 1966–7', forthcoming in *Twentieth Century British History* (2004).

THE GROWING NATIONAL IMPORTANCE OF HUMAN RIGHTS (1970–2000)

The socio-legal history outlined in the first part of this chapter argues that modern human rights practices developed interdependently with the transformation of the international order, in particular the politics of postwar, Cold War and decolonisation. Even if the following section focuses predominantly on the national level — the gradual 'homecoming' of the international accomplishments, as well as the revitalisation of the subject in the national context — it equally should be read in light of a series of international events which had great implications for the general development of the field of human rights: from the emergence of the Latin American human rights network of the 1970s, effectively putting Amnesty International on the map, to the process towards the eventual democratisation of Eastern Europe, initiated by the Helsinki Process.[45] The national developments should not be seen, however, as dictated solely by either international practices or national ones. It is important to underline that the emergence of a human rights field was significantly more than simply a 'by-product' of a general macro societal development. Increasingly, the human rights field developed its unique character, implying a set of logics, nomenclatures, mechanisms of evaluation, etc, which in national contexts were translated differently because of the considerably different social position and history of the key actors and concepts: law, including civil rights or *libertés publiques*, and international human rights law, and the legal profession in regard to the field of state power. This implied that the activism and political turf battles involving human rights, either as law or simply political weaponry, were influenced by how the force of human rights was determined nationally through a particular national history. But as the international field of human rights concurrently experienced a significant growth, institutionally and in terms of power, the actors of the national battles sought to utilise this force nationally in various ways: the early investments in international human rights were eventually to pay off in the national struggles over the divisions and visions of the state.

A particular and increasingly powerful point of reference was the European Convention on Human Rights (ECHR) and its associated legal institutions. The ECHR practices, in ways comparable to those of Amnesty but through a different repertoire and set of agents, constituted the conversion of the highly politicised field of human rights, originally influenced by

[45] On Latin America see K Sikkink 'The Emergence, Evolution and Effectiveness of the Latin American Human Rights Network', in E Jelin and E Hershverg (eds), *Constructing Democracy, Human Rights, Citizenship and Society in Latin America* (Colorado, Westview Press, 1996) 59–83. On Eastern Europe see DC Thomas, *The Helsinki Effect: International Norms, Human Rights, and the Demise of Communism* (Princeton, Princeton University Press, 2001).

the legal-politico entrepreneurs of the great social visions of the postwar period, into the lines of the mainstream legal field. This conversion, incomplete however, was facilitated by the Court's delicate balancing between an initial international law attitude marked by hesitance in its activism and its progressive takeover of the contested position as the supreme author of human rights law: for the first 15–20 years the Court essentially focused on the internal build-up of a reliable, respectable legal machinery, before taking a more aggressive route. The project was successful in the sense that the Court was increasingly taken seriously as more than a last resort for desperate individuals and their lawyers, and it represented a forum for contesting the claims of more resourceful agents, including the media, trade unions and more recently even capitalists and kings.[46] This helped situate the Court in a position of the larger, fluid European legal field that allowed it to gain access to the elite of the national legal fields and bridge the gap between national legal elites and international ones.

The Politics of Human Rights at the Core of the State: The Case of France

In the 1970s, France experienced a renewed interest in the subject of human rights. These mêlées over human rights and *libertés publiques* were partly initiated around the campaign leading to the long-awaited ratification of the ECHR, just before the presidential election of 1974.[47] This campaign, strongly supported by the grand old man of human rights in France, René Cassin, helped contribute to a general renewed awareness of the subject. Cassin's strong and at times cynical interventions in favour of ratification helped put the question of liberty back at centre stage and re-constituted a critique of state power through the language of human rights.[48] Generally, the 1970s saw an attempt to resurrect the political engagement of legal agents in France which had generally been lost under the postwar welfare state.[49] Among others, organisations such as Mouvement d'Action Judiciaire

[46] For a critical interpretation of this development, see C Douzinas, *The End of Human Rights: Critical Legal Thought at the Turn of the Century* (Oxford, Hart Publishing, 2000).

[47] Already in 1971 one important step for this general development was taken by the expansion of judicial control.

[48] See É Agrikoliansky, '"Liberté, liberté chérie": La gauche et les libertés publiques dans les années 1970. Usages politiques d'une catégorie juridique', Presentation at l'Université de Picardie, Curapp, 14–15 November 2002.

[49] The mobilisation of legal agents in the national area of human rights in France was closely linked to the activism during the Algerian War of independence. Also, the so-called 'events of 1968' had an impact; many activists quite directly had felt the repressive power of the police and the judiciary. Among the key lawyers of the movement were Leclerc and Jouffa (both associated with the LDH) who developed a significant practice defending demonstrators and activists in the late 1960s and early 1970s. These experiences of the 'extreme Left' led to a renewed interest in law as a measure of challenging State power without precedent in French history.

(MAJ), Syndicat des Avocats de France (SAF) and Syndicat de la Magistrature (SM) were launched and claimed a new, politicised, role for the legal profession.[50] Also, among academics, there was a growing interest in the subject both through publications and participation in these organisations. For the most part close to left wing and extreme left wing political organisations, these practices took part in the general critique of law and politics that marked France in the 1970s.[51] For a legal profession only increasingly excluded from the traditional political career patterns, this form of organisation offered a rare opportunity to perform politics from the platform of law. Providing a unique position in regard to this new activism, the French Human Rights League profited from this interest, and a growing number of lawyers became involved throughout the decade.[52] At the same time, other organisations were set up in France. Most notably the 'French Doctors' — *les Médecins sans Frontières* — who to some extent brought the vision of the FIDH to the terrain of medicine and health by seeking to blend professionalism and political activism into an effective social cure. In the same year, 1971, AI opened its French section, initially providing a basis for a group of activists, many of whom were associated with Christian organisations.[53]

This interest in the subject of *libertés publiques* was also present on the agenda of the political parties. Throughout the 1970s, the left particularly sought to challenge the increasing power of Giscard d'Estaing and an evolving hegemony of the political right. Becoming president in 1974, Giscard d'Estaing responded to this challenge and presented himself as the saviour of human rights/*libertés publiques* from the hands of the left. Already during the election of 1974, Mitterrand had promised to make the drafting of a 'Charte des Libertés' — a Freedom Charter — a top political priority if he was elected. These electoral words were turned into reality by Giscard d'Estaing, when his newly elected government in July 1974 set up a commission of high court judges to draft a 'Code des Libertés Fondamentales de l'Invidu' — A Code of Individual's Fundamental Freedoms. In May 1975, assisted by the eminent lawyer Robert Badinter, Mitterrand responded by proclaiming the birth of a commission to draft a 'Charter of Liberties and Fundamental Rights'.[54] This was only two days

[50] Roughly translated into English: The Movement for Judiciary Action (MAJ), The Syndicate of French Lawyers (SAF) and the Magistrates' Syndicate (SM).

[51] See generally J Commaille, 'La juridicisation du politique. Entre réalité et connaissance de la réalité' in J Commaille, L Dumoulin and C Robert (eds), *La juridicisation du politique. Leçons scientifiques* (Paris, LGDJ, 2000) 241–51.

[52] É Agrikoliansky, above n 24, at 125.

[53] At one point, Amnesty International's French section shared the letterhead with l'ACAT—the Christian Action Against Torture, an organisation with which AI founder Peter Benenson was to be involved.

[54] See in detail on this whole political battle, É Agrikoliansky, above n 48, at 14f.

before the Communist Party was to publish its contribution to this battle, the 'Déclaration des Libertés' (Declaration of Freedoms). As emphasised by Éric Agrikoliansky, this turf war of civil liberties between Giscard d'Estaing, the Socialist Party and the Communist Party took place in a climate of extreme polarisation and with many stakes, including the socialists' attempt to develop an anti-totalitarian, non-communist position as a response to, on the one hand, the Communists and, on the other, the successful liberalism of Giscard d'Estaing.[55] While most of this remained political propaganda, Mitterrand's arrival to power in 1981 brought to the Élysée Palace many of the reformist ideas developed throughout the 1970s. In addition, it brought aboard the presidential ship the aforementioned lawyer, Robert Badinter, as new minister of justice. In his briefcase an ambitious programme of change concerning the legal system was to be found.

Despite being a non-comrade and business lawyer of the Parisian grand bourgeoisie, Badinter soon became a champion among socialists because of his swift abolishment of the capital punishment in France in 1981.[56] Generally, his judicial reform programme, which included the abolishment of the exceptional, emergency court — *la Cour de Sûreté de l'État* — and the 'Security and Liberty' legislation, constituted a reorientation in the relationship between the citizen and coercive state practices.[57] An area where Badinter fared less well was his measures against rising crime in France.[58] Despite interventions by criminologists and sociologists in his favour, some political opponents were quick to present the classic argument of a clear link between the abolition of capital punishment and the rise in crime. At the very least, the Liberal and Conservative opponents perceived the liberal reform programme of the criminal justice system as an example of the Socialists' laissez-faire politics on crime and lack of respect for the victims of crime.[59] The attack on the Socialists in general and Badinter in particular, to some extent, played the card into the hands of Le Pen and the *Front National*, who were quick to explain the problem of crime as related to a series of problems attributed to the massive immigration France had experienced since the 1960s. The question of racism had been a long-term subject for various French human rights NGOs — ex MRAP (the Movement against Racism and for the Friendship between Peoples) and LICRA (the International League Against Racism and Anti-Semitism). But, the battle against Le Pen marked the beginning of the development of a large network

[55] *Ibid.*
[56] Badinter was also a former high-profile member of the French Human Rights League.
[57] *Cour de sûreté de l'État* roughly translates as 'State Security Court'.
[58] Badinter's career as Minister of Justice came to an end when he, in 1986, was promoted to become president of the *Conseil Constitutionnel* by Mitterrand.
[59] JW Friend, *The Long Presidency: France in the Mitterrand Years 1981–1995* (Colorado, Westview Press, 1998) 84–85.

of organisations, including SOS Racisme and GISTI (The Group for Information and Support to Immigrants), mobilising some of the critical lawyers of the 1970s and many others.[60] Further, by the mid-1980s, the glorious years of French economic growth had come to a halt and a focus on the social side of human rights became important — even the 'French doctors' started looking inwards and offered free medical programmes in large French cities. The issues of poverty, racism and illegal immigration were to become the core of the human rights debate in the 1990s, once again mobilising a huge network of organisations, including the traditional human rights organisations such as the LDH which gained support among younger people and younger lawyers in particular.

Another important but considerably less politicised element of the Mitterrand/Badinter reform package was the French acceptance of the right to individual petition before the Strasbourg Court, laying the ground for a full French participation in the ECHR system. Being a monistic legal system, French law did not need a further Act to implement the rights contained in the ECHR into domestic law. In addition, a number of decisions from the *Conseil Constitutionnel* — the Constitutional Council — and the *Conseil d'État* — the State Council — recognised the duty of French courts to enforce international treaties over ordinary statutory law.[61] The ECHR was gradually to get attention up through the legal hierarchies, but compared with the British experience, it was a considerably more silent transformation. Many of the pioneers of the ECHR in France were university professors — typically coming from public international law — or belonged to a small group of lawyers, many associated with the Human Rights Institute of the Parisian Bar and a few specific chambers. Box 3 provides an example of the most high profile of these chambers.

Box 3: 'Le Cabinet Ornano'

The development of a network of progressive lawyers in France is linked to the mobilisation during the Algerian War of Independence and the subsequent engagement in international human rights and rule-of-law missions. One of the key breeding grounds for progressive lawyers in France was co-established in 1973 by the lawyer Henri Leclerc and Georges Pinet, an old friend of Leclerc.[62]

[60] GISTI was driven by the law professor Danièle Lochak who had participated in the *libertés publiques* struggles of the 1970s. She was to pioneer a Master's programme on human rights law at Nanterre University, a university with a long tradition for involvement in political causes.

[61] See C Ban and LF Goldstein, 'Comparing Rule-of-Law Regimes: The Transnational Regime of the European Court of Human Rights', paper presented at LSA, Vancouver, 2002, 11–12.

[62] From 1969–73 Leclerc shared office-space with his FIDH brothers, Jacoby and Blum, but they did not follow him into the Ornano Office. H Leclerc, above n 32, at 171.

Leclerc was until 1972 a keen political activist on the left as well as a prominent member of the French Human Rights League in the 1960s. The so-called Ornano Office was to become the first radical law office in France and was composed of a team of like-minded lawyers aiming at working as a legal collective. The office was set up in a working class neighbourhood in the north of Paris in order to give access to less privileged clients; for a while it even had a 'boutique de droit' — the French equivalent to the British law centres — as an annex to the law office. After some initial problems the office became a success and an attractive starting point for young lawyers interested in the social and political side of law. Some sixty young French lawyers passed through this virtual training camp, many of them — such as Francis Teitgen — were to become leading human rights lawyers in the 1980s and 1990s.

There was little expectation among these progressive lawyers that the ECHR was to have any substantial impact on the ways justice was carried out in France. It was a new legal tool, which at best could serve as a measure for legal fine tuning. As with Britain, France had tested its compliance with the ECHR before ratification and concluded that only insignificant problems could arise.[63] Further, when accepting the right to individual petition, the Quai d'Orsay set up a special office staffed with former magistrates alongside a few career diplomats to take care of French proceedings before the Strasbourg Court. France felt well-prepared when, if slightly late by the standards of comparable European democracies, it fully joined the European regime of human rights protection. But, the gradual development of international organisations tends to be a process towards greater autonomy, and the ECHR — indeed, one of the most successful international institutions ever — was certainly no exception. The growing self-confidence of the Court was manifested in an increasingly progressive interpretive style, only boosted by the general coming of age of international human rights in the 1980s. In other words, the French preparations for compliance were long outdated when the Court started receiving the first cases against France throughout the 1980s. One of the key agents, *la Cour de Cassation* — the French 'Supreme Court' on civil and criminal legal cases — did initially work hard to incorporate the ECHR into its general practices. It issued hundreds of decisions which included reference to or the application of ECHR norms and was swift to incorporate lost cases into its practices.[64] There is no doubt that the perception at the *Cour de Cassation*, as well as its counterpart on administrative law, *le Conseil d'État*, was that the ECHR was a positive endeavour and deeply rooted in the grand tradition of French justice.[65]

[63] M Agi, above n 7, at 318.
[64] Between 1987 and 1997, 'la Cour de Cassation' issued more than 700 such decisions. See C Ban and LFGoldstein, above n 61, at 20.
[65] Among judges it was a shared view that the fact that René Cassin was a former judge at the Conseil d'État seemed to guarantee a deep-rooted French influence on the ECHR regime.

From this background, we can comprehend why it came as a colossal surprise to the highest towers of the French legal system when the European Court of Human Rights, allegedly an insignificant court far from the corridors of Paris, embarked on criticising not only certain police and administrative practices in France, but even the very functionality of the highest courts. The European Convention was suddenly referred to as 'that text of Anglo-Saxon inspiration', according to one French lawyer appearing before the *Cour de Cassation*.[66] In the words of one scholar, Jean-Pierre Marguenaud, the *Cour de Cassation* launched a 'rebellion' against the Strasbourg Court in response. This rebellion was not spurred by the otherwise shameful verdict that France was guilty of applying torture, but by the decision of the Strasbourg Court to question the roles of the general advocates of the *Cour de Cassation* and the equivalent *Commissaires du gouvernement* of the *Conseil d'État*.[67] Subsequently, the relationship between the Strasbourg Court and the *Cour de Cassion* and *Conseil d'État* went through some serious ups and downs but generally established itself on a reasonable level. However, among judges and general advocates it was generally agreed that the ECHR did simply not grasp the complexity of the French legal system, and they attacked what they saw as the Court's superficial, formal programme of standard-setting and uniform compliance with European legal orders. On the national level, these extreme high-level legal battles did not as such contribute to a popular movement. Among lawyers, however, the battles opened the doors for challenging traditions that formerly were untouchable, and the lawyers increased their efforts to bring the ECHR in play before French courts. Moreover, for lawyers, the Strasbourg Court became virtually an appeals court to the supreme French courts. Facilitated by the relative short physical distance to Strasbourg, the number of cases exploded in the 1990s, making France one of the top three violators of the ECHR.[68]

A British-Style Revolution: Towards the Politics of Human Rights Culture

As in France, the recent history of human rights in the UK is made up by a series of social and political events which developed in the shadow of an international human rights movement. The highly politicised discourse

[66] Interview 141, no 1, 14 October, 2002.

[67] JP Marguenaud, 'l'Effectivité des arrêts de la Cour européenne des droits de l'Homme en France' (2001) 24, *Journal des droits de l'Homme* 1–12. See also R de Gouttes, 'Logiques de la Cour de Cassation et de la Cour Européenne des droits de l'Homme', paper presented at Université Panthéon-Assas (Paris II), 10 June, 2002.

[68] In 2001 alone, there were 45 cases concerning France, whereof 32 found France in violation of the ECHR, making France the third biggest violator of European human rights — numerically speaking — only surpassed by Italy and Turkey.

on civil liberties which developed in France in the 1970s and marked Mitterrand's first years in office was however not exported over the Channel. Local issues and events largely determined the progress in Britain. The legal problems emerging from the handling of the crisis in Northern Ireland and the subsequent series of miscarriage of justice cases — most notoriously the 'Birmingham Six', 'Guildford Four' and the 'Maguire Seven' — helped bring 'rights-talk' back to the socio-political agenda. By itself, the crisis in Northern Ireland had already kicked off a civil rights movement in the 1970s, but beyond these particularly contextualised practices, the general British left had little interest in the concept on the home front. Civil rights did, however, come up occasionally as a means to further political goals and challenge the state's sometimes '... cack-handed attempts to punish some [of the] excesses of the Sixties.'[69] This challenge — a mixture of political and social practices with a somewhat common foothold in the events of the late 1960s and early 1970s — was never to be the locus of the transformation of civil rights and human rights in the UK, even though many of its key players would later become central activists. It was not until the 1980s that a considerable *civil rights* counter-strategy was set in motion. This movement took its starting point in a variety of causes marking the time: to begin with the miscarriages of justice, Thatcher's crusade against trade unions in the early 1980s, the miner's strike in 1984, the government's attempts to limit public protests and finally the Poll Tax legislation (1989–90). The attacks on the trade unions were at the same time a declaration of war against very central legal establishments in and around the Labour Party. Also fuelling this counter-strategy, the racial riots in places like Brixton in south London and the Toxteth suburb of Liverpool in the early 1980s brought about more examples of a criminal justice system increasingly having problems handling new social problems. All in all, this fragmented, cause- and case-oriented movement sought to use classic civil liberties and European human rights law as a means to expose the alleged arbitrariness of the Tory government's actions concerning basic liberties, including the fundamental rights to protest, assemble in public places and democratically participate.

In the legal field, developments in the area had already begun in the 1970s, pioneered by a series of lawyers, unsurprisingly many of whom were closely linked to the central organisations of the prior period — the NCCL, JUSTICE and AI — and who had used the welfare state provision of legal aid to help establish 'progressive high street' practices (see Box 4). Further, the British acceptance of individual petition to the ECHR in the late 1960s had an impact on the legal system, helping to push a general advancement of human rights within the British legal field.

[69] G Robertson, *The Justice Game* (London, Vintage, 1999), xi.

Box 4: The Avant-Garde of Human Rights Lawyers

Among the progressive lawyers, it is worth emphasising the practices of Ben Birnberg and Anthony Lester. They represent two different types of legal engagement in the evolving British field of human rights. Both of them managed in an entrepreneurial manner to come to the forefront of the critical environment of the legal profession in the UK. Birnberg, a former head of the NCCL and founder of one of the first radical law offices in the UK, helped to 'educate' a whole generation of progressive lawyers at his premises, including Imran Khan (*Lawrence*-case), Garretth Pierce (*The Guildford Four*, *Birmingham Six* and *Derek Bentley*), John Wadham (head of Liberty), Raju Bhatt and the eminent Professor of International Law at Oxford, Ian Brownlie, whom Ben Birnberg guided into private practice. These disciples, or 'colonies' in the words of Birnberg, were to pioneer a series of new progressive areas of law in the UK, including race, prisoners' rights, immigration, public law and international criminal law, as well as entering straightforward politics. (Int 115, no 1, 12 June 2001).

In comparison, Anthony Lester exemplifies a very different position in the field. Carrying significant cultural capital with law degrees from Cambridge and Harvard, Lester was exposed to the civil rights movement in the US in the 1960s and developed an 'alien' interest in bills of rights and constitutionalism. In 1964 he wrote a book for AI on the Deep South and racial discrimination. Lester argued the first English case before the ECHR and soon pursued the application of the ECHR in the UK.[70] In parallel, he was increasingly involved in Labour Party politics and was working under Labour Home Secretary, Roy Jenkins, on gender equality and race in 1974. In 1975 he became the special advisor for the standing Committee on Northern Ireland. In 1976, he wrote the 'November 1976 call for the implementation of the ECHR', repeating his call from his 1968 tract titled 'Democracy and Individual Rights' (Fabian Society, 1968). In 1976, when returning to the Bar, he left behind a large commercial practice and started focusing entirely on human rights law and comparative constitutional law in British courts as a way of reforming the system. At the same time, he was involved in setting up a series of organisations in the field, most notably Article19 and Charter88.

The increased and surprising importance of the ECHR in UK legal practices received political attention at the highest level. But during the 1970s and 1980s, as a rather unpleasant surprise, the UK became one of the most

[70] This kind of involvement in human rights did not receive a good conversion rate at the time. 'Only one perceived it as good [and] it was a NY Times correspondent in Britain[!]' (int 85, no 1, 26 February 2001). The hostility was great in the courts even in the 1970s with the exception of few liberal judges: 'It was distinctively seen as unfashionable to use the ECHR ... even treacherous ... one was seen being in the last ditch or in a hopeless case if you referred to it ... I was perceived as a maverick that had an obsession that was un-British ... I was regarded at best as an eccentric ... ' (int 85, no 1, 26 February, 2001).

regular customers before the Court in Strasbourg. And politically, as one legal advisor of the Foreign Office under the Thatcher reign recalls, the continuous acceptance of 'the right to individual petition came up as a real question.'[71] But typical of the conservative accommodationist internationalism of the 1980s, the formal response became that 'the UK was not to pull out, but the Court to pull back' (Int 111, no 1, 8 May 2001).[72] The development of human rights law in the Court did accelerate in the 1970s, as did the frequency of dissent from the English judge Sir Gerald Fitzmaurice, a former ICJ judge and legal advisor of the Foreign Office and at the ECHR from 1974–80. The mental *doxa* deriving from schooling in public international law, both academically and professionally, was also reflected in the legal and social outlook of Fitzmaurice's successor in Strasbourg, Sir Vincent Evans. Sir Vincent Evans, however, entered the Court when the jurisprudence of the Court had taken a more aggressive course and saw as its main goal to provide up-to-date human rights protection through a progressive interpretive style, calling for reluctance among the judges who represented the more sceptical countries (Int 109, no 1, 25 April 2001). Generally, the symbolic imperialism of the Foreign Office into the field of human rights described in the first part of this chapter declined and the strongest local agents — in particular the Home Office — became increasingly involved in finding a solution to the ECHR problem. Indeed the progressive transformation of the ECHR implied a change in the national perception of the regime from being purely *international* to becoming a matter between domestically-oriented institutions and the gradually more autonomous Strasbourg Court. In practice, the human rights problem was the UK's administrative tradition, a tendency to rely on administrative procedures rather than more clear cut statutory law. In parallel to the expression of disagreement on the political level, the British response was simply to put in place administrative procedures, screening all new legislation with regard to ECHR standards. Ironically, this allowed the Europeanisation of human rights law to gain a clear priority over national laws and legal projects.

In light of the relative institutional dominance of the gradual transformation caused by the ECHR, it might seem surprising that the idea of advocating for a full British implementation of the ECHR into national law took hold so firmly in the UK. It is only when taking into consideration the series of events in the area of civil rights outlined above that this development can

[71] The 1966 decision to accept the jurisdiction of the European Court and Commission only ran for a renewable period of three years until the incorporation into British law of the ECHR by the 1998 Human Rights Act.

[72] Continued participation was secured by renewing the right to individual petition every three years. Moreover, full effect was given to the rulings of the ECHR causing a discreet but important change in attitude and style of the central ministries.

be explained as a strategy of challenging government and state practices by trying to transplant a series of norms that already had shown their potential as points of reference beyond governmental control. Towards the late 1980s, some of the civil society organisations, which were influenced or founded by the avant-garde of human rights lawyers, became key advocates of the implementation of the ECHR into English law. There was to some extent a clash between the older generations who emphasised the idea of a bill of rights for legal reasons, and a younger generation of socially-aware lawyers and social scientists — including many of the key spokespersons of the movement — who sought to make human rights a question of culture, even of popular culture, as well as a new ethos. The new generation had matured politically in the 1980s during what was perceived as the very long and gloomy 'presidency' of Margaret Thatcher. The profound social battles with Thatcherism, alongside the continuous defeat of the Labour Party, had given them a collective memory of, on the one hand, the questionable protection of civil rights in the UK, and on the other, the limits of representative democracy. As one key player recalls: 'There was no other way to challenge the government than through constitutional changes' (Int 95, no 1, 5 March 2001). Human rights were back at the core debate of society and political weaponry for challenging the government — just as the Tories for a brief moment in the 1970s had sought a new bill of rights as a way of challenging the then Labour Government (Int 95, no 1, 5 March 2001). Yet throughout the 1980s, the response to the idea of a bill of rights from across the political spectrum remained that such an instrument would delegate an unreasonable power to judges beyond Parliamentary control.[73] Basically, both the Tory and Labour parties regarded it as an undemocratic measure.

After Labour's 1987 election defeat, this movement knew that new measures were needed more than ever before. In this climate, Charter88 was founded as a pressure group for constitutional reform with a bill of rights on the agenda as one of ten suggestions for constitutional changes. Rapidly the group collected thousands of signatures and a row of high-profile agents, including Law Lords, lawyers, academics and a few celebrities, joined the effort.[74] The time was literally *right*, and as the name of the organisation suggested with its noticeable reference to the noble Charter77, it was part of the global human rights movement which at the same time was celebrating some of its greatest triumphs. In 1989, the NCCL relaunched itself as Liberty, a 'human rights organisation', and JUSTICE also jumped on the human rights bandwagon. One milestone in the campaign

[73] This argument — the fear of 'government by judges' — was also put forward in the French *libertés publiques* struggles of the 1970s. See JW Friend, above n 59, at 158–59.
[74] See F Klug, *Values for a Goodless Age: The Story of the United Kingdom's New Bill of Rights* 158.

was Liberty's publication of 'A People's Charter' in 1991.[75] This publication contained an indiscrete appeal to the Labour Party, 'a solution that fitted Labour's concerns' in the words of one of the activists (Int 95, no 1, 5 March 2001). In the same year, the Institute of Public Policy Research (IPPR), a think-tank close to the Labour Party, published an outline of a bill of rights. The Labour Party, too, debated internally about a human rights agenda and the heads of the leading NGOs were invited to join some of these discussions behind the scenes. This led to the eventual inclusion into Labour politics of the implementation of ECHR into British law.[76]

The New Labour approval of a human rights policy that included the implementation of the ECHR into English law became a political turning point for the movement. In parallel to the political bargaining, the key NGOs — Liberty, Charter88 and JUSTICE — had pursued a popular outreach campaign in order to maintain the momentum, as well as more practically to seek a realisation of their notion of 'human rights culture'. Once again Tory practices provided a good opportunity for popular rebellion. This time, the most hip of the protests concerned the (human) right to hold techno raves. By mobilising this young environment, Liberty produced significant surplus value for themselves and their projects. Also, Charter88 followed this paradigm of human rights as culture and initiated teaching campaigns aimed at virtually everyone in British society (Int 87, no 1, 27 February 2001). Spending £4.5 million on the training of judges alone and launching a noticeable £1 million publicity campaign concerning the Human Rights Act, the New Labour Government sought to present themselves as protagonists of the fluid idea of human rights culture. And, at the heart of the legal system, due to an unparallelled interest and investment in this new area of practice, solicitors, barristers and academics added to the 'symbolic boom' that followed the Human Rights Act when it came into full force on 2 November 2000. Situated primarily in 5–10 sets of chambers and solicitor's firms, the disciples and 'colonies' of the great British pioneers of human rights generally took the lead in this growing business. Enhanced by their access to and familiarity with the media, this new area of legal practice was communicated widely to the public, only adding to the booming interest. As one leading lawyer states, 'Every single letter I get includes the words human rights' (Int 113, no 1, 9 May 2001).

[75] *Ibid.*

[76] Even if Tony Blair and Jack Straw were to become the political architects of the Human Rights Act, a great deal of the work was prepared by the Scottish lawyer and Labour leader, John Smith. He made a keynote lecture to Charter88 where he embraced most of the constitutional reform programme for which the group was lobbying, including a Human Rights Act incorporating the ECHR into British law. Stuart Weir, former editor of the *New Statesman*, helped Liberty and Charter88 to maintain the momentum by forming a campaign called the 'Labour Rights Campaign', very much directed at the more doubting Labour MPs and grassroots. *Ibid*, at 161.

Alongside this new business of human rights lawyering, the higher courts also invested in the terrain. Most noticeable, the internationalism of the British Law Lords became front page news during the Pinochet extradition trials, a case fuelled by the change in political alliances and perceptions as a consequence of the demise of Cold War bipolarity. This case gave high exposure to a series of human rights NGOs and their allies among lawyers and academics, but in particular the British judiciary came into the spotlight. Indeed the high degree of internalisation of human rights among judges became evident when one of the law lords, Lord Hoffman, was forced to leave the bench during the case because of his long involvement with Amnesty International.[77] At the height of the Pinochet case, a former student leader, Daniel Cohn Bendit, even rephrased his famous statement 'We are all German Jews now' to 'We are all English Lords now.'[78] In sum, human rights had transcended the legal community through the collective force of a general global human rights movement and a specific national campaign, to such an extent that some of the pioneers started publicly questioning this new human rights culture and business. Their objective had only been a better legal protection of human rights in the UK, not a fancy, New Labour-style celebration of a new ethos of society.

CONCLUSION

The United Kingdom and France occupy comparable yet unique positions in the immense social restructuring characterising European history during the last half of the twentieth century, from the common fate of the stern decline of their imperial leadership following the global upheaval of the Second World War, through the emergence of the postwar welfare states, to the reconstruction of the very same. This analysis outlines a little but nevertheless important chapter of this large transformation by focusing on the complex processes of exportation and importation of human rights expertise as part of the international and national developments that helped contribute to the emergence and eventual transformation of an international field of human rights. Adding a particular dimension to the subject of this analysis, there is a close and observable link between the transformation of imperial societies and the emergence of a new international legal order, granting human rights a considerable role. A paradoxical connection can be observed between the decline of the imperial order, which ironically claimed to export civilisation and human rights, and the subsequent

[77] 'Pinochet law lord linked to Amnesty', by J Wilson and N Hopkins, Guardian Unlimited (web), Tuesday 8 December, 1998.
[78] See H Kennedy 'Foreword' in F Klug, above n 74, at xi.

post-colonial social movements using human rights as the backbone of their critique of the treatment of immigrants, whereof the majority came from former colonies. The UK and France did not have to look far to find the question of human rights: the Algerian War of Independence brought the international movement to the doorstep of metropolitan France; the handling of the crisis in Northern Ireland by the UK equally provided the occasion for international human rights organisations to portray the UK as a questionable protector of civil rights. The subsequent national struggles to make human rights a national political priority once again were influenced by international and European developments. This meant that the investments in international human rights were eventually to pay off in the national struggles over the divisions and visions of the state, making the former international players the new national champs through a conversion of their international expertise and capitals

Even though the development of human rights practices were influenced by the general transformation of the international order, the emergence of modern international and subsequent national human rights practices were more than just a by-product of this macro transformation. This is the background for the chapter's emphasis on approaching human rights from the starting point of a human rights *field*. Applying this notion allows the analysis to focus on the particular modes of production that were core to the field of human rights and draw the lines between these particularities and larger social and political transformations. The complexity of analysing human rights in regard to this larger scheme is the fact that the field of human rights is both constructed in opposition to and as an extension of state practices. Further, due to the historically determined close relationship between the legal field and the state, which has found its expression in the state granted monopolies and a legal professional culture of being the guardian of the legality of the state's practices, many of the key legal players encountered in this story indeed exploited the ambiguities of this relationship. The battles to define the subject throughout the story is marked by the stakes of a series of experts operating inside or in the shadow of the state: from the postwar pioneers of public international law and diplomacy, over the investment coming from politically industrious private practitioners seeking international objectives, to the eventual broadening of the field allowing a series of new agents to enter and influence the agenda. The central argument of the chapter is that the reciprocal process between France, the UK and the internationalisation of human rights can only fully be understood by considering how the international field of human rights gradually was being built through the investments by nationally-embedded but internationally-oriented players. The connections are clear between the national positions of these emblematic agents, their international endeavours and the eventual return home of human rights as an effective legal and political weaponry. Indeed, this brief social history of human rights and the transformation of these former imperial societies demonstrates that there is a 'boomerang' effect between the initial eager participation in the internationalisation of human rights and the subsequent process of internalising these accomplishments in the national legal and political fields.

4

'We've had to Raise our Game': Liberty's Litigation Strategy under the Human Rights Act 1998

RICHARD J MAIMAN

INTRODUCTION: INTEREST GROUPS AND BILLS OF RIGHTS

PASSAGE OF THE Human Rights Act 1998 (HRA) marked the successful end of a campaign by human rights NGOs to persuade the government of the United Kingdom to codify the rights recognised by the European Convention on the Protection of Human Rights (ECHR). It was also the beginning of another stage in the process of rights development, one that typically involves efforts by pressure groups to help determine the precise meanings of those rights by bringing test cases in the courts. This chapter examines the post-HRA litigation strategies and tactics of one of the UK's most prominent rights advocacy groups, the organisation known since 1989 as Liberty and before that as the National Council for Civil Liberties (NCCL). The chapter first summarises some of what is known about the litigation strategies of rights organisations in the United States, where interest groups have long played an important role in rights development through judicial interpretation. Drawing largely on interviews with two of Liberty's current leaders, the chapter then describes Liberty's efforts to adjust its litigation programme to the post-HRA world. The research reported here is part of an ongoing project analysing the activities of a number of British human rights NGOs involved in the development and implementation of the Human Rights Act. The overall purpose of this research is to explore the impact of bills of rights on the work of rights advocacy organisations in mobilising support for their political goals.

British pressure groups, like their American cousins, have been resorting to the courts to advance or protect their interests since the mid-nineteenth century.[1] However, academic studies of such activities in Britain have been thin on the ground, making it difficult to draw detailed comparisons between the litigation strategies of UK interest groups.[2] Harlow and Rawlings have attributed this 'black hole' in scholarship in part to the strict bifurcation of the British academic disciplines of law and political science, a division which both reflects and reinforces strong cultural commitments to the interrelated national myths of the apolitical legal system and absolute parliamentary sovereignty.[3] The widespread belief in the UK that law and politics do and should exist in separate universes has discouraged research exploring their conjunctions; according to Harlow and Rawlings, it 'may have disguised the extent to which pressure through law has always been part of the British tradition.' While British interest group litigation has indeed been understudied, it is also true that test cases have played a less important role in the British system than in jurisdictions where judicial activism is a more established (though still often controversial) feature of the political process. Harlow herself has acknowledged that because of the differences in the roles of judges in the UK and the US, 'the achievement of social reform through legal action was a less attainable goal in Britain than in the United States.'[4]

In his comparative analysis of the conditions that produce 'rights revolutions', Epp asserted that Britain has managed a 'modest' revolution despite its notable deficiencies in the three ingredients traditionally thought to be essential, either singly or in combination, to a rights regime: constitutional guarantees, a judiciary receptive to rights claims, and a rights-oriented culture.[5] The British case helped to support Epp's thesis that the expansion of rights through judicial activity depends chiefly on a 'support structure for legal mobilisation' consisting of advocacy organisations,

[1] C Harlow and R Rawlings, *Pressure Through Law* (London, Routledge, 1992).

[2] Notable exceptions have been the case studies of litigation by various pressure groups in J Cooper and R Dhavan (eds), *Public Interest Law* (London, Blackwell Publishers,1986); and separate studies of the work of the Child Poverty Action Group (CPAG) by H Hodge, 'A Test Case Strategy' in M Partington and J Jowell (eds), *Welfare Law and Policy* (London, Frances Pinter Ltd, 1979), and T Prosser, *Test Cases for the Poor* (London, Child Poverty Action Group, 1983).

[3] Prosser similarly has referred to the 'general tradition in English law and law teaching of assuming that what is of legal interest ends with the court giving its decision and not examining the implementation of the decision in practice.' *Ibid*, at 21–22.

[4] Above n 1, at 132.

[5] CR Epp, *The Rights Revolution: Lawyers, Activists, and Supreme Courts in Comparative Perspective* (Chicago, University of Chicago Press, 1998). For Epp, a rights revolution is 'a sustained, developmental process that produced or expanded the new civil rights and liberties' (*ibid*, at 7). His book examines such processes in the United States, India, Canada, and Great Britain.

adequate sources of funding for litigation, and a rights-oriented legal profession. Epp argued that after its emergence in the 1960s and 1970s this structure produced some impressive court victories on behalf of prisoners' and women's rights despite having to operate in a polity that 'appears to be an especially inhospitable site for the development of a judicial rights revolution.'[6]

Since Epp's book was written before the Human Rights Act 1998 was passed, it left out some important developments in Britain's rights revolution, which of course is still a work in progress. While this made it easier for Epp to demonstrate that a support structure for rights 'is not in any simple way a direct response to opportunities provided by constitutional promises or judicial decisions, or to expectations arising from popular culture,'[7] it also meant that he had nothing to say about how the introduction of a bill of rights might affect the behaviour of rights advocacy groups in the UK. In that sense, this chapter picks up where Epp left off by looking at how Britain's equivalent of a Bill of Rights, the Human Rights Act, is influencing the work of one such organisation.

In the United States, litigation has long been seen as 'an integral part of the dialogue by which constitutional standards are shaped and reshaped under changing conditions.'[8] For this reason, the litigation activities of interest groups on behalf of civil rights and liberties in the United States, unlike those of their British counterparts, have been extremely well documented. Such studies are part of a voluminous literature on US interest groups, exemplified by the classic works of Bentley,[9] Truman,[10] Schattschneider,[11] Key,[12] and Olson[13]; and more recent studies by such scholars as Berry,[14] Ornstein and Elder,[15] and Schlozman and Tierney.[16] They belong more specifically to a branch of the interest group literature which examines the strategic use of courts by pressure groups seeking to advance their policy goals. Until recently, most of this research focused on organisations working for liberal and libertarian causes including, among

[6] *Ibid*, at 131.
[7] *Ibid*, at 67.
[8] D Feldman, 'Public Interest Litigation and Constitutional Theory in Comparative Perspective' (1992) 52 *The Modern Law Review* 44ff, 56.
[9] A Bentley, *The Process of Government* (Chicago, University of Chicago Press, 1908).
[10] D Truman, *The Governmental Process* (New York, Alfred E Knopf, Inc, 1951).
[11] EE Schattschneider, *The Semi-Sovereign People* (New York, Holt, Rinehart and Winston, 1960).
[12] VO Key, *Politics, Parties and Pressure Groups* (New York, Crowell, 1964).
[13] M Olson, *The Logic of Collective Action* (Cambridge, Harvard University Press, 1965).
[14] J Berry, *Lobbying for the People: The Political Behavior of Public Interest Groups* (Princeton, NJ, Princeton University Press, 1977).
[15] NJ Ornstein and S Elder, *Interest Group Lobbying and Policy Making* (Washington, DC, Congressional Quarterly Press, 1978).
[16] KL Schlozman and JT Tierney, *Organized Interests and American Democracy* (New York, Harper and Row, 1986).

many others, the rights of women[17] and the poor.[18] Prototypical litigation groups such as the National Association for the Advancement of Colored People (NAACP) and the American Civil Liberties Union (ACLU) have been especially well studied.[19] In recent years the growing use of litigation by conservative organisations has attracted scholarly attention as well, thus providing a fuller understanding of litigation strategies across the political spectrum.[20] A few studies have also been made of efforts to employ international human rights standards through litigation in United States courts.[21]

Litigating and Campaigning by Rights Groups

This literature highlights a number of important strategic and tactical issues typically faced by rights advocacy groups. For any such organisation there

[17] RB Cowan, 'Women's Rights Through Litigation: An Examination of the American Civil Liberties Union Women's Rights Project, 1971–1976' (1976) 8 *Columbia Human Rights Law Review* 373ff; K O'Connor, *Women's Organizations' Use of the Courts* (Lexington, Mass, Lexington Books, 1980); E Rubin, *Abortion, Politics and the Court* (Westport, Conn, Greenwood Press, 1982).

[18] See, eg J Handler, E Hollingsworth, and H Ehrlanger, *Social Movements and the Legal System* (New York, Academic Press, 1978); J Katz, *Poor People's Lawyers in Transition* (New Brunswick, NJ, Rutgers University Press, 1982); B Sard, 'The Role of the Courts in Welfare Reform' (1988) 227 *Clearinghouse Review* 367ff; SE Lawrence, *The Poor in Court: The Legal Services Program and Supreme Court Decision Making* (Princeton, NJ, Princeton University Press, 1990); A Southworth, 'Lawyer-Client Decision-Making in Civil Rights and Poverty Practice: An Empirical Study of Lawyers' Norms' (1996) 9 *Georgetown Journal of Legal Ethics* 1ff.

[19] See, eg CE Vose, *Caucasians Only* (Berkeley, University of California Press, 1959); C Markmann, *The Noblest Cry* (New York, St Martin's Press, 1965); M Meltsner, *Cruel and Unusual: The Supreme Court and Capital Punishment* (New York, Random House, 1973); SC Halpern, 'Assessing the Litigative Role of ACLU Chapters' in SL Wasby (ed), *Civil Liberties: Policy and Policy Making* (Lexington, Mass, Lexington Press, 1976); R Kluger, *Simple Justice,* (New York, Alfred E Knopf, Inc, 1975); RL Rabin, 'Lawyers for Social Change: Perspectives on Public Interest Law' (1976) 28 *Stanford Law Review* 207ff; M Tushnet, *The NAACP's Legal Strategy Against Segregated Education, 1925–1950* (Chapel Hill, NC, University of North Carolina Press, 1987); S Walker, *In Defense of American Liberties: A History of the ACLU* (New York, Oxford University Press, 1990); WB Rubenstein, 'Divided We Litigate: Addressing Disputes Among Group Members and Lawyers in Civil Rights Campaigns' (1997) 106 *The Yale Law Journal* 1623ff.

[20] See, eg K O'Connor and L Epstein, 'The Rise of Conservative Interest Group Litigation' (1983) 45 *Journal of Politics* 479ff; L Epstein, *Conservatives in Court* (Knoxville, Tenn, University of Tennessee Press, 1985); JP Heinz, A Paik, and A Southworth, 'Lawyers for Conservative Causes: Clients, Ideology, and Social Distance' (2003) 37 *Law & Society Review* 5ff. Whether such groups are considered part of the rights movement or a reaction against it probably depends upon one's political perspective. While some see conservative litigation activity as an effort to dismantle the rights revolution, others argue that in making constitutional arguments on behalf of gun ownership, private property, unborn children, and 'victims' of reverse discrimination, conservative interest groups are attempting to establish new rights previously ignored or opposed by traditional civil liberties organisations. See Heinz, Paik, and Southworth at 8, n 5.

[21] B Lockwood, 'The United Nations Charter and United States Civil Rights Litigation 1946–1955' (1984) 69 *Iowa State Law Review* 901ff; S Rosenbaum, 'Lawyers *Pro Bono Publico*: Using International Human Rights Law on Behalf of the Poor' in EL Lutz, H Hannum, and K Burke (eds), *New Directions in Human Rights* (Philadelphia, University of Pennsylvania Press, 1989); H Tolley Jr, 'Interest Group Litigation to Enforce Human Rights' (1990) 105 *Political Science Quarterly* 617–28.

is the crucial threshold question of whether to pursue its policy goals through litigation, legislation, or some combination of the two. Intensive research on liberal rights organisations led many scholars to conclude that litigation is generally the strategy of choice for politically disadvantaged interest groups — those whose small numbers, disenfranchised constituencies, or unpopular causes militate against their exercising much influence in the legislative or executive arenas.[22] However, as studies of interest group litigators have proliferated, the idea that the judiciary is especially accommodating to the interests of the politically disadvantaged has been called into question. Epstein's pathbreaking analysis of conservative organisations showed that the courts have also become targets of opportunity for relatively powerful groups, if only because conservatives can no longer afford to let their opponents monopolise the judicial arena.[23] After finding heavier use of the courts by 'the wealthy and established groups' than by traditional liberal organisations, Scheppele and Walker observed that '[t]he political disadvantage theory does not seem to be wrong, but it captures only a fraction of the interest-group litigation activity.'[24] Similarly, Olson concluded from a study of interest group litigation in a federal district court that while weaker groups may find courts more receptive than other political decision-makers to their demands, more powerful groups frequently use the courts to protect what they have achieved elsewhere in the political process.[25]

The fact that civil rights litigants, like others, often rely in court on statutory rights they have won through legislative campaigning is a reminder that litigation is generally part of a larger strategy employed by civil rights groups to achieve their goals.[26] Assuming that they have sufficient resources to fight on more than one front, most rights groups — like other organisations — seem to prefer a mixed strategy, combining litigation with campaigning in the legislative and executive arenas. The chief virtue of such an approach is that an organisation can build on victories or compensate for defeats in one forum with complementary efforts in the others.[27]

[22] RC Cortner, 'Strategies and Tactics of Litigants in Constitutional Cases' (1968) 17 *Journal of Public Law* 287ff.
[23] Above n 20, at 147–48.
[24] KL Schepelle and JL Walker Jr, 'The Litigation Stratgies of Interest Groups' in JL Walker Jr (ed), *Mobilizing Interest Groups in America: Patrons, Professions, and Social Movements* (Ann Arbor, University of Michigan Press, 1991) 183ff.
[25] SM Olson, 'Interest Group Litigation in Federal District Court: Beyond the Political Disadvantage Theory' (1990) 52 *Journal of Politics* 854ff, 877.
[26] Schepelle and Walker, above n 24, at 169–70.
[27] Morag-Levine has concluded that the rise in litigation activity by two leading environmental groups (one in the US, one in Israel) was not a function of the increased availability of judicial remedies or improvement in the organisations' legal capacities and resources. Rather, it reflected the preference of the organisations' new generations of leaders for an adversarial relationship with the state over the 'partnership' model favored by their predecessors. N Morag-Levine, 'Partners No More: Relational Transformation and the Turn to Litigation in Two Conservationist Organizations' (2003) 37 *Law & Society Review* 457ff.

If a rights organisation has made the basic decision to employ a litigation strategy, other choices will determine more precisely what that strategy looks like. Two of these important choices involve the criteria by which the organisation selects its test cases; and whether the group will sponsor its own cases, provide third-party interventions, or both.

Test Case Selection Criteria

Test case selection is influenced to a considerable degree by the relationship the organisation wishes to maintain between its casework and its overall campaign. If the group is content to use litigation exclusively to influence the development of legal precedents, then it is free to choose cases strictly on their legal merits, without taking account of the quantity or quality of the publicity they may generate. But if the organisation also hopes that its litigation will help shape public opinion, putting a human face on abstract principles, it may be necessary to consider the capacity of a potential client to make a positive impression through the media. Since finding a perfect case or client is not always possible, rights organisations may sometimes have to get on with their work regardless of the public relations consequences. However, it appears that most rights organisations today develop their litigation programmes with at least one eye on how individual test cases will contribute to informing the public about their work. Prosser has even suggested that publicity should be the *ultimate* goal of litigation, since 'the indirect effects of test cases [are] more important than the direct effect.'[28] Smith, on the other hand, has cautioned against ignoring the distinction between media coverage of a pressure group's activities and actual changes in public or elite opinion resulting from such attention.[29]

Direct Sponsorship or Amicus Curiae?

Although most of the classic studies of civil rights and liberties litigation dealt with directly sponsored cases, the use of amicus curiae filings as a litigation tool by pressure groups in the US has also attracted considerable scholarly attention.[30] Most of this research has addressed amicus activity

[28] Above n 2, at 86.
[29] R Smith, 'How Good Are Test Cases?' in J Cooper and R Dhavan (eds), *Public Interest Law* (London, Blackwell Publishers,1986), pp 283–284.
[30] See, eg S Krislov, 'The Amicus Curiae Brief: From Friendship to Advocacy' (1963) 72 *Yale Law Journal* 694ff; L Barker, 'Third Parties in Litigation: A Systematic View of the Judicial Function' (1967) 29 *Journal of Politics* 41ff; S Pruro, 'The Role of Amicus Curiae in the United States Supreme Court: 1920–1966' (PhD Dissertation, State University of New York at Buffalo, 1971); H Jacob, *Justice in America* (Boston, Little Brown, 1978); G Ivers and K O'Connor, 'Friends as Foes: The Amicus Curiae Participation and Effectiveness of the

before the United States Supreme Court, where a virtual 'open door' policy on third party submissions in effect since the early 1960s has allowed many organisations, including some without the resources to sponsor their own cases, to put their views before the Court. There is clear evidence that increasing numbers of interest groups have exploited this opportunity. For example, the proportion of Supreme Court cases accompanied by at least one amicus curiae brief rose steadily from less than 15 per cent in 1950 to more than 92 per cent in 1994.[31] Between 1986 and 1995, the mean number of amicus briefs per Supreme Court case ranged from 3.30 to 5.46[32]; and whereas in the decade between 1946 and 1955 only three Supreme Court cases attracted as many as ten amicus filings each, there were 144 such cases between 1986 and 1995, despite an overall decline in the number of cases heard by the Supreme Court.[33]

Analysing the litigation strategies of a variety of interest groups in the 1980s, O'Connor and Epstein found that conservatives were much less likely than liberals to use direct sponsorship of cases and proportionally more likely to rely on amicus filings.[34] However, this gap has narrowed in the intervening years as conservative legal groups have proliferated and acquired more experience as litigators. O'Connor and Epstein also noted a growing preference by the ACLU for sponsoring its own cases rather than filing amicus briefs.[35] In a survey of litigation groups, Scheppele and Walker found that while 90 per cent of the respondents reported using amicus briefs, less than 10 per cent did so exclusively.[36] This led the authors to conclude that the attention given by researchers to amicus activity has exaggerated its importance and perhaps distorted the overall picture of US interest group litigation. It is apparent that despite the increasing popularity of amicus briefs

American Civil Liberties Union and Americans for Effective Law Enforcement in Criminal Cases, 1969–1982' (1987) 9 *Law and Policy* 161ff; GA Caldeira and JR Wright, ' Amicus Curiae Briefs before the Court: Who Participates, When, and How Much?' (1990) 52 *Journal of Politics* 782ff; AJ Koshner, *Solving the Puzzle of Interest Group Litigation* (Westport, Conn, Greenwood Press, 1998); JD Kearney and TW Merrill, 'The Influence of Amicus Curiae Briefs on the Supreme Court' (2000) 148 *University of Pennsylvania Law Review* 743ff.

[31] Koshner, *ibid*, at 7–11.
[32] Kearney and Merrill, *ibid*, at 765, n 71.
[33] *Ibid*, at 755, n 29. To date, the record for the largest number of amicus curiae briefs filed in a Supreme Court case — 78 — was achieved in the 1989 abortion case of *Webster v Reproductive Health Services* (109 S.Ct. 3040). Forty-six of these briefs (representing 85 separate organisations) were filed in defence of Missouri's restrictions on access to abortion services. The 32 amicus briefs supporting the RHS challenge to these regulations were signed by 335 interest groups. See L Epstein and JF Kobylka, *The Supreme Court and Legal Change* (Chapel Hill, NC, University of North Carolina Press, 1992) 272–73.
[34] Above n 20, at 482. See also Epstein, above n 20, at 149.
[35] *Ibid*. The ACLU's presence before the Supreme Court as an amicus party nevertheles has continued to grow, increasing from 12% of all cases heard by the Court in 1976–85 to 16% of its docket in 1986–95. See Kearney and Merrill, above n 30, at 753, n 25.
[36] Above n 24, at 178.

as a litigation technique, most of the leading rights-oriented groups today invest more of their resources in direct sponsorship than in amicus filings, and whenever possible they prefer to bring their own cases rather than piggy-back on the litigation of other organisations.

LIBERTY AND THE HUMAN RIGHTS ACT

Epp described the rights organisation Liberty as one of the 'main components'[37] of Britain's rights infrastructure; according to Harlow and Rawlings, Liberty 'has more claim than most to be the founder of modern English pressure through law.'[38] Formed as the National Council for Civil Liberties in 1934 to defend left wing activists against police infiltration and repression, the organisation gradually expanded its mission to include the protection and promotion of a range of civil and political liberties. In the early 1990s Liberty began to define its agenda even more broadly by rebranding itself as a 'human rights organisation' and taking up the application of international human rights standards to the UK as a new focus for much of its work. Like its closest (though proportionally much larger and better funded) US counterpart, the ACLU, Liberty has pursued its goals through a mixed strategy of parliamentary campaigning, litigation, and public information, although the exact mix of these elements has varied over time. Litigation began to be an increasingly prominent feature of Liberty's work in the 1970s, as changes in the government's legal aid regime provided a new means of financing casework. For a few years the organisation maintained an extensive but rather haphazard litigation programme driven partly by internal legal aid income targets. Eventually this broad brush approach was replaced by a more purposeful test case strategy involving a smaller number of cases selected for their potential impact on civil liberties law.[39]

Most of Liberty's litigation work has taken place in the UK courts, but the organisation's greatest impact on UK law has been through its litigation based on the European Convention in the European Court of Human Rights in Strasbourg. Liberty has taken more cases to Strasbourg than any other British pressure group, and over the years it has compiled an impressive record of success in high profile cases against the British government.[40]

[37] Above n 5, at 140.
[38] Above n 1, at 292.
[39] B Cohen and M Staunton, 'In Pursuit of a Legal Strategy: The National Council for Civil Liberties' in J Cooper and R Dhavan (eds), *Public Interest Law* (London, Blackwell Publishers, 1986).
[40] See S Grosz and S Hulton, 'Using the European Convention on Human Rights' in J Cooper and R Dhavan (eds), *Public Interest Law* (London, Blackwell Publishers, 1986); C Harlow and R Rawlings, above n 1, at 257.

To understand fully the significance of Liberty's activities in the wake of the Human Rights Act, it is also useful to know something about the role that the organisation played in the development and passage of the Act. Although a detailed account of that story is not possible here, it can be said that while Liberty was by no means the only NGO involved in lobbying for the HRA, it may well have been the most important. Liberty's single most significant contribution to that campaign was to first introduce the principle of 'democratic entrenchment' in its 1991 Bill of Rights proposal, *A People's Charter*. By rejecting the conventional wisdom that a written Bill of Rights must go hand-in-hand with the politically unpalatable notion of judicial supremacy over Parliament, Liberty's proposal was able to attract first the attention and finally the support of the Labour Party in opposition.[41] Although the Human Rights Bill introduced by New Labour after its victory in 1997 differed in some respects from Liberty's preferred model, crucially it did incorporate the principle of democratic entrenchment by preserving Parliament's supremacy over the courts.[42]

Liberty After the Human Rights Act: 'We Had Leverage That We'd Never Had Before'

While the HRA deliberately does not give British judges the power to strike down primary legislation, it does require them, 'as far as it is possible to do so,' to interpret legislation 'in a way which is compatible with the Convention rights.' Thus the law offers rights-oriented NGOs a new tool for advancing their interests through strategic litigation. The codification of rights in a constitutional framework, in Epp's words, 'provides popular movements with a potential tool for tying judicial power to their purposes.'[43] When the Human Rights Act came into force in October 2000, Liberty arguably was the group best positioned to incorporate the new law into its litigation programme because of its unrivalled experience and expertise in human rights litigation, especially with regard to European Convention issues. Liberty capitalised on that experience even before the HRA came into force by contracting with the Legal Services Commission to set up a human rights telephone advice line for lawyers

[41] Liberty proposed that statutes found by the courts to be in breach of the Bill of Rights be scrutinized by a special parliamentary committee and voted on by Parliament itself to determine whether they should remain in effect. See *A People's Charter* (London, Liberty, 1991) 86–87.
[42] 1998 ch 42, ss 3, 4.
[43] Above n 5, at 201.

seeking assistance in using the new law, and conducting HRA training for law firms, barristers' chambers, and government bodies. According to Liberty's former director John Wadham, some of his audiences responded to his message quite differently than they had in the past:

> When I was going to teach the intelligence services or the police or anyone else about the Human Rights Act, what was different was that ... we had leverage that we'd never had before. In 1990 I would go and talk to police officers about human rights, but it would be very, very tense and they would have real difficulties and they would attack us — not physically, but there'd be a real issue. But now, I'd be able to say, 'This is what the law is and if you get it wrong you'll be sued.' And of course that makes a very significant difference in how your audience responds.[44]

Liberty also utilised its expertise at this early stage to try to influence implementation of the HRA in other ways as well. Along with the leaders of other rights organisations, Wadham was appointed to the Home Office Human Rights Task Force charged with overseeing the government's preparations for the Act, as well as promoting greater public awareness and understanding of human rights.[45] A legal practice manual on the Human Rights Act co-authored by Wadham was one of the first of a flurry of such volumes to appear around the time of the Act.[46] It sold an impressive 17,000 copies in its first edition, with the royalties going to support Liberty's activities. Wadham and other Liberty staff members produced a steady stream of newspaper and journal articles discussing various aspects of the Human Rights Act.[47] Even with much of its work now centring on the HRA, Liberty continued its extensive campaigning activities on a wide variety of issues.[48]

[44] All direct quotations are from a personal interview with John Wadham, conducted on 23 April 2003. Wadham resigned from this position in June 2003.

[45] J Croft, *Whitehall and the Human Rights Act 1998* (London, The Constitution Unit, University College London, 2000) 22–27.

[46] J Wadham and H Mountfield, *The Human Rights Act 1998* (London, Blackstone Press Ltd, 1999).

[47] See, eg J Wadham, 'Taking Liberties', *The Sunday Times* (25 January 2000); 'Human Rights Act Update', *Legal Action* [May 2000]; and 'Update: The Human Rights Act', *The Times* (10 April 2001).

[48] For example, in the month of December 2000 alone, Liberty issued press releases or published letters in newpapers on the following topics: reform of the Official Secrets Act; the rights of children of sperm donors; sex discrimination in the provision of bus passes; the privacy rights trial of Catherine Zeta-Jones and Michael Douglas; the government's White Paper on mental health; discrimination against disabled persons in the armed forces; deaths in police custody; due process and the public interest immunity system; e-mail interception by employers; the government's bills on confiscation of financial assets and social security fraud; the government's new Police Complaints Commission; and the Conservative party's stop and search proposals (www.liberty-human-rights.org.uk/press/press-releases-2000).

The New Human Rights Marketplace: 'Losing by Winning'

The first requirement for a successful litigation programme is a continuing intake of potential cases, and before October 2000 Liberty always was assured of a more than adequate supply. Once the HRA was passed, however, Liberty found itself occupying an increasingly crowded piece of turf. Human rights work, once a 'Cinderella specialty', was becoming more widely distributed across the legal profession as lawyers, even those in fields like commercial law, repackaged their expertise to incorporate human rights.[49] Ironically, after playing a leading role in achieving the Human Rights Act, Liberty now found its own prospects somewhat compromised by its success. Describing Liberty's litigation programme in the mid-1980s, Cohen and Staunton had presciently foreseen such a prospect:

> If Britain enacted a Bill of Rights enforceable in its domestic courts, there would probably be a boom in civil liberties cases fully funded by legal aid and not restricted to the present handful of civil liberties lawyers. ... It may be that there is a major dilemma for NCCL that it may lose by winning; by creating more committed civil libertarian lawyers looking for test cases NCCL may lose for itself the central role in such work.[50]

When asked about that prediction in 2003, John Wadham agreed that it had been accurate. Before the HRA, he observed, 'we were on our own, and we became top of the wave, so to speak. And we're still on the top of the wave, but we could be engulfed.' The ranks of what Wadham calls 'newly committed civil liberties lawyers' now included some who 'know more about that particular issue than we know, because they've been working on it.' But many other practitioners with only superficial understandings of the field were now effectively practising human rights law. According to Liberty's director Shami Chakrabarti:

> Because human rights points are now open to all domestic lawyers, it's not a Strasbourg specialism, and so those points are going to be raised, sometimes well and sometimes badly, by just lawyers in general practice.[51]

In this newly competitive market for human rights work, observed Chakrabarti, 'the best Article 6 criminal cases are not automatically going to land on our laps because we are Liberty and no one else is interested in

[49] S Goodchild, 'The Lawyers Won't Be Suffering', *The Independent on Sunday* (20 February 2000).
[50] Above n 39, at 307.
[51] All direct quotations are from personal interviews with Shami Chakrabarti, who was then Liberty's in-house counsel, conducted on 13 March and 22 May 2003. Chakrabarti succeeded John Wadham as Liberty's director in July 2003.

human rights.' Thus, she said, Liberty was having to work harder than ever before to maintain its lead position among human rights litigators:

> The Human Rights Act is out there, and it can be argued in every court in the land, and you can get legal aid for it, and people have to get to grips with it, which means we've had to raise our game.

Building a Strategy: 'I Want the Litigation to Serve the Campaign'

Liberty has begun the process of 'raising our game' by trying to be more self-conscious about what it wants to accomplish through its litigation. According to Chakrabarti,

> That means in operational terms that we're trying to be more strategic about litigation. We can't just sit and wait. People do phone up constantly and want us to take their cases, and solicitors want us to advise them on how to do their cases, and they want us to intervene in their cases. And that's always been the case. But if we want to really make the best litigation and ultimately campaigning impact that we can, we need to be, and are now trying to be, more deliberate, proactive, and strategic.

Balancing the competing demands of campaigning and litigation casework is not an easy task, and since litigation may serve more than one purpose — generating publicity as well as establishing legal precedent — it may not always be clear even to the organisation itself where its priorities lie. But the demands of campaigning and litigating can pull an NGO in opposing directions as well. Since an organisation's influence in the executive and legislative arenas depends partly on its capacity to generate public support for its cause, campaigning groups usually do their best to be seen in a positive light. But litigation, by definition, requires the organisation to take an adversarial stance. In a political culture like Britain's, which remains deeply sceptical about resolving public issues in court, an organisation which appears frequently in court on behalf of unpopular clients risks alienating substantial portions of the populace. While it may be possible for a litigating NGO to seek out more sympathetic causes or clients, such cases may not raise the legal issues that the organisation considers most urgently need its support.

Liberty's former director John Wadham readily acknowledged that balancing the competing demands of litigating and campaigning has been a challenge for his organisation:

> I think there was a tension between the lawyers here and the campaigners here. There still remains that tension. The lawyers, I think, have always been more interested in test cases. The campaigners have wanted us to do high profile cases.

Such 'high profile' cases in the past, he said, included one involving several people arrested under the Public Order Act for wearing t-shirts printed with rude comments about Prime Minister Margaret Thatcher. Liberty took that case because it was seen as a 'winner' in terms of generating favourable publicity for the organisation, even though it was unlikely ever to go to court. However, not all high profile cases have been welcomed by Liberty's campaigners. For example, Wadham recalled that his defence of Sinn Fein leader Gerry Adams in the early 1990s against an exclusion order limiting his right to travel throughout the UK had some Liberty staff members 'very, very concerned,' despite the acknowledged importance of the legal issue. On another occasion, Liberty took up the case of a woman named by a Conservative MP during a parliamentary debate on anti-social behaviour as 'the neighbour from hell.' After rulings in the British courts held that parliamentary privilege protected the MP from being sued by the woman for defamation, Liberty petitioned the European Court of Human Rights on the ground that its client had been denied a fair trial under Article 6 of the Convention. According to Wadham, this stand was not popular with the public nor with some of Liberty's staff:

> We got criticised for daring to suggest that Parliament should be limited in some way or another. So that got us bad publicity. So our campaigners here were concerned about that case because they were saying, 'Everybody's saying we're attacking democracy.'

In Chakrabarti's view, the tension within Liberty between good test cases and good public relations has gradually diminished — a positive development, in her view, since she regards litigation and campaigning as mutually reinforcing enterprises:

> Though I am a lawyer working at Liberty, it's a constant thing in my mind that I want the litigation to serve the campaign. I don't want to be running just a nice little law firm, thank you very much, where we get to do sexy human rights cases. I want everything we do to serve the human rights campaign.

Thus, Chakrabarti said she preferred that decisions about case selection not be confined to the three 'official key-holders' — the director, the legal director, and herself:

> It's a small bunch of people and we have lots of discussion in the legal department, and I'm glad to say increasingly we're spreading some of those discussions through our campaigners' department as well so we can get their input. Because they were concerned — rightly — in previous years that sometimes we were doing silly things like taking cases where a victim would never want to speak to a journalist and wanted complete secrecy for the case, and that's

> no good for Liberty. And it's too easy for lawyers to say, 'Interesting, important human rights case, let's do it.'

Maintaining a litigation programme that is, above all, 'good for Liberty' may mean sometimes passing up legally promising cases that offer little in the way of good publicity. Conversely, it may also mean taking cases with strong public relations potential even when they have little chance of success in court. Even a 'hopeless' case may be worth litigating, said Chakrabarti, because of the positive messages it can send — not only about Liberty as an organisation, but about the larger human rights project as well:

> We're always going to have to do cases of asylum seekers and terrorist suspects and criminal defendants, but it's equally important that we try and show the great British public that human rights might mean something to them too, all the people who aren't ethnic minorities or immigrants or likely to be accused of a terrorist offence or whatever, or likely statistically to ever be in a police station.

'Sending a message' rather than 'winning the case' has long been part of Liberty's approach. Nearly two decades ago Liberty's then general secretary Patricia Hewitt noted that 'a test case, even if lost, may be of considerable value to the broader campaign.'[52] A recent example of such a case — high in potential for positive media coverage but having little chance of succeeding in court — was Liberty's representation of Diane Pretty, a woman terminally ill with motor neuron disease. Liberty argued unsuccessfully on Ms Pretty's behalf in the British courts and in Strasbourg, that the European Convention Article 2 'right to life' includes a right to assisted suicide.[53] John Wadham noted that even though Liberty knew that its argument was unlikely to succeed, 'our campaigners loved Diane Pretty because ... she demonstrated that we were a nice organisation. It was such a sad case, and we were supporting her, so we got so much good publicity.' Chakrabarti is convinced that the media coverage of the Pretty case was valuable because it benefited the Human Rights Act as much or more than it did Liberty itself:

> We had positive headlines in papers like the *Daily Mail* and the *Evening Standard* about Diane Pretty and her human rights challenge. Yes, it is about asylum seekers and so forth, but even your nice *Daily Mail* reader may get a debilitating illness one day, as a mother or a wife or whatever, so it's much easier for them to see.

[52] P Hewitt, 'The NCCL Fifty Years On' in P Wallington (ed), *Civil Liberties 1984* (Oxford, Martin Robertson & Co, 1984) 20ff. Hewitt specifically cited Liberty's representation in 1981 of the Campaign for Nuclear Disarmament (CND) in its challenge to the Metropolitan Police Commissioner's ban on marches in London. Although the case was lost in court, according to Hewitt, 'a number of banning orders were lifted, or re-imposed in narrower form.' *Ibid*, at 21.
[53] *R (Pretty) v DPP* [2001] 3 WLR 1598.

Presenting the HRA to the public in a positive light is especially important, in Chakrabarti's view, because the government itself is doing little to generate such publicity:

> Most of the time, the problem that we have is a government that sponsored the Human Rights Act and then immediately lost heart in it, and so they never say anything positive. So the government, the legislative owners of the Human Rights Act, the sponsors of it, hate it now, or appear to, and never say anything good about it. And we don't have at our disposal the massive communication tools that they have, so we've got to try and find a way of making human rights not a dirty term.[54]

But Wadham suggested that *Pretty* was not a typical Liberty case, most of which are chosen for their potential contributions to the development of human rights jurisprudence:

> We do less of those kinds of ... political cases ... where we can make a noise ... and we do more cases where ... law might be changed. And we've invested more money in our lawyers, so I think now actually we're doing something much more significant than we used to do. ... [W]e've decided that [in addition to] our press strategy, our campaign strategy, our lobbying, etcetera, that we should also have a litigation strategy.

That strategy, Wadham said, gives priority to cases involving criminal justice, policing, equality, and privacy. He was quick to add, however, that 'maybe strategy's too grand a word for it,' since Liberty's litigation agenda inevitably reflects the interests and expertise of its staff:

> In practice, how the litigation strategy works is that people work here for awhile and they work on subjects and they begin to pick up stuff from other lawyers or from the calls that we get, and they have a kind of strategy in their head. ... So it's not as much a strategy as perhaps it should be, but that's because we're a small organisation and we do the best we can.

Furthermore, for Liberty as for any rights organisation, a certain amount of reaction is built into its programme since its primary mission is to respond to government actions. As Chakrabarti pointed out, 'Something like September 11 happens, and the agenda is written for us,' to lobby against the government's anti-terrorism legislation and challenge it in court. For all of its

[54] Chakrabarti thus gives an interesting twist to an argument often made by both friends and opponents of the Act, that respect for human rights principles will not be embedded in the larger culture as long as the HRA is seen by the general public as the exclusive property of lawyers and judges, a view that often is reinforced by litigation. If Chakrabarti is correct, litigation on the contrary may sometimes be a vehicle for building broader understanding and support for human rights.

determination to maintain a litigation programme that reflects strategic priorities, Liberty seldom has the luxury of setting its own agenda.

LIBERTY IN STRASBOURG: 'IT'S THE PERFECT SYSTEM'

There is general consensus among scholars that the longer a group is involved in litigation, the more successful it becomes.[55] Galanter famously identified the many advantages of the 'repeat player' over the 'one shotter' in the legal system, including advance intelligence, expertise, economies of scale, informal relations with institutional actors, and influence over decision rules.[56] An organisation with such resources can engage in 'sequential' litigation, selecting its test cases with an eye towards gradually accumulating favourable legal precedents, as the NAACP did in the decades preceding its landmark victory in *Brown v Board of Education*.[57] The increasing success of conservative litigation groups since their origins in the 1980s further demonstrates the value of maintaining a litigation programme over time.

Liberty has long been acknowledged as the British litigation group with the most experience and expertise in the European Court of Human Rights. Two and a half years after the Human Rights Act came into force, about half of Liberty's litigation docket consisted of Strasbourg filings. Liberty's Strasbourg cases provide the organisation with an opportunity to capitalise on its hard won status as a repeat player, thus continuing to occupy its unique niche in the post-HRA legal marketplace. It is precisely because more human rights cases are now being litigated domestically that it is so important for Liberty to maintain its active Strasbourg practice. According to John Wadham:

> One of the reasons we've got so many cases in Strasbourg is that we know we aren't going to be doing all the key cases. We knew three years ago that we're not going to do all the key cases in the courts.... [T]he Human Rights Act cases arise from the criminal case. They're not constructed beforehand, and the idea that we could be involved in all of them, it's ridiculous. So that's why we thought, well actually we do have continuing expertise in the Convention and we have expertise in the procedure in Strasbourg ... and we would be better going back to that kind of thing. Which is what we've done.

[55] Above n 20, at 152.

[56] M Galanter, 'Why the 'Haves' Come Out Ahead: Speculation on the Limits of Legal Change' (1974) 9 *Law & Society Review* 95ff, 98–100.

[57] During that period the NAACP won 34 of its 38 desegregation cases in the Supreme Court (See J Handler, E Hollingsworth, and H Ehrlanger above n 18, at 26). But see EV Sparer, 'The Right to Welfare' in N Dorsen (ed), *The Rights of Americans* (New York, Random House, 1970) for an account of a less successful sequential litigation strategy in the area of poverty law.

Liberty has discovered, however, that the road to Strasbourg, which once was nearly traffic-free, is growing increasingly congested. The approach that worked well for Liberty in the past — spotting promising 'Strasbourg cases' and offering to take them on when the domestic remedies run out — is no longer as effective since fewer lawyers now are willing to hand their cases over to Liberty. According to Shami Chakrabarti:

> Previously, when domestic criminal cases or other cases had raised human rights issues, another firm of solicitors might take the case and argue such domestic points as they could, and they might hand it to us on a plate, for the purposes of Strasbourg litigation. Because, frankly, they're not going to make any money out of it. There's no legal aid as such for Strasbourg, so why should they bother? Now, they can argue the human rights points domestically, and even though they might not make any money by going to Strasbourg, they might think it's a useful loss leader for them to carry on with the case. It will be good for their reputation.

In Wadham's opinion, by taking their own appeals to Strasbourg some lawyers may be doing themselves more harm than good professionally. Among British lawyers, he suggested, there is still a great deal of ignorance about the European Court, which sometimes is reflected in their Strasbourg submissions:

> I've seen some absolutely appalling applications in Strasbourg from good lawyers, lawyers who'd never do that in domestic courts. But they're not being paid, or they think it's a political process rather than a legal one, so they just kind of send off letters.

This problem is exacerbated by the fact that these inexperienced lawyers are not appearing against each other in Strasbourg, but rather against well-prepared advocates for the government. Some years ago, in a brief description of Liberty's litigation programme, Wadham described the disadvantages inherent in such a contest, in language that echoed Galanter's (1974) observations about 'repeat' and 'one-shot' players:

> [T]he danger with constructing test cases as an 'applicants' lawyer' is that the respondent will have played the game before.... The lawyers that act for the government in the Foreign and Commonwealth Office do virtually no other litigation and have all the reported and unreported cases at their fingertips. They can learn from their mistakes and change their tactics. A 'one-off' player may never get a second chance (or not until he or she has forgotten the lesson).[58]

Still, Wadham now believes that with more lawyers taking cases to the European Court, the quality of Strasbourg appeals will improve over time,

[58] J Wadham, 'Human Rights on Test' *Solicitors' Journal* (15 April 1997) 352ff.

and he expects this eventually to have a salutary impact on European Convention case law:

> I think more individuals will know about the Strasbourg court than before. More lawyers will know about it. The arguments will have had to be rehearsed in the domestic courts so they will have been honed and refined. So I think there'll be more cases going to the Strasbourg court and a substantial number of those will be better cases. ... But we haven't seen the results of that yet.

In addition to Liberty's practical reasons for wanting to maintain a healthy practice in Strasbourg, there is an important strategic incentive as well in the potentially positive impact of European Court decisions on British judicial decision-making. Under the terms of the HRA, British judges are not bound by Strasbourg precedents, but they must take them into account in interpreting Convention rights. Having relied heavily on European Court decisions in the past to force changes in British law, Liberty is keen to see the Court's influence continue in the UK despite the changes in its human rights landscape. According to Wadham, Liberty's litigation strategy has been based on

> the view ... that actually the Strasbourg court was more liberal than the domestic courts, and we wanted to get as many cases to Strasbourg as quickly as possible so the domestic courts know, are told off, so to speak, that they've got it wrong. That process hasn't happened yet because it takes five years for these cases to be heard in Strasbourg.

When the Human Rights Act was under discussion, Wadham said, the government mistakenly assumed that 'nobody would bother to go to Strasbourg any more because everybody will get their results domestically.' When campaigning for the HRA, Liberty was happy to endorse the argument that under the Act British judges would at long last be able to take part in shaping European Convention jurisprudence. But since the organisation anticipated that it would not always welcome the ways in which judges used that opportunity, Liberty's lawyers always expected that Strasbourg would remain an important part of their litigation strategy. Wadham chose not to disclose this line of thinking during the HRA campaign, however:

> There is a bit of deviousness on my part because I always thought this was the case, but I'm afraid to say I never told the government. They would always put out things saying, 'The long road to Strasbourg, we don't want to waste people's time.' Hidden underneath that from their perspective was, 'Well, we'll lose less often.' That's not necessarily the case, and part of the reason of course is that governments can't appeal to Strasbourg. So the only people who appeal are the people who lose here, and inevitably some of them will win there. So it's the perfect system from our point of view.

Wadham acknowledged that with the HRA now in force, judges at the European Court may be more inclined to defer to British court rulings — 'well, the domestic courts have resolved this, so let's not bother' — but since he also expects more and better UK cases to be taken to Strasbourg, in the long run 'there will be more judgments against the UK.' Liberty clearly is determined to contribute to that process by continuing to maintain its long-standing presence in Strasbourg.

Third-Party Interventions: 'The Courts are Quite Keen on Hearing from Us'

As we have seen, Liberty today is working to preserve its leadership role in defining human rights by remaining active as a litigator both in the UK courts and in Strasbourg, and intends for its litigation programme to complement its ongoing parliamentary campaigning and public education. Recognising, however, that it may no longer be able to sponsor directly all or even most of the important human rights cases, Liberty has also taken steps to intervene more frequently in cases where it does not have its own client.[59] Chakrabarti considers third-party intervention to be 'another part of raising our game, because we're not always going to be the solicitor who captures the client in the lead case.' In 1996, Liberty was responsible for the first third-party intervention before the House of Lords, in the case of *R v Khan*,[60] and since then the organisation has averaged several UK interventions per year. Perhaps the chief virtue of intervention, according to Wadham, is that 'it's cheap. We can get lawyers to do the work for nothing.' And while third-party intervention requires the court's approval, Wadham said, 'the courts have virtually never said no to us.' According to Chakrabarti, Liberty is virtually always given permission to intervene because, with few exceptions,

> the claimant always wants us in, and normally the public authority concerned — which in Liberty's case is usually, but not always, the Home Office — is too gentlemanly to actually say, 'No, they shouldn't.' Usually they say, 'We've got

[59] Liberty began making frequent interventions in the European Court of Human Rights in the 1980s. The Court began to allow easier access to third party interveners in 1983, and is now considered quite receptive to receiving written submissions by interested third parties. See, eg *A Matter of Public Interest: Reforming the Law and Practice on Interventions in Public Interest Cases* (London, JUSTICE/Public Law Project, 1996). Previously the Court had followed a much more restrictive practice with regard to interventions. According to Anthony Lester, in the 1978 case *Tyrer v UK* the Strasbourg court made the 'harsh decision' to deny Liberty permission to make oral or written representations even though it had represented the litigant before he withdrew from the case. A Lester, 'Amici Curiae: Third Party Interventions Before the European Court of Human Rights' in F Matscher and H Petzold (eds), *Protecting Human Rights: The European Dimension* (Koln, Carl Heymanns Verlag KG, 1988) 342ff.
[60] 3 All ER 289.

nothing to say about this,' or they say nothing at all. And that seems to be good enough.

Sometimes Liberty might intervene in a human rights case to minimise the damage that might be done by inadequate representation by the case sponsors. Referring obliquely to this point in an article about Liberty's litigation strategy, Wadham wrote, 'In a perfect strategy lawyers would be able to choose their test case or cases from a pool of cases. Unfortunately, often the case that becomes the test case is the one that happens to arrive at the door of the court first.'[61] Liberty's view is that by intervening in a poorly argued case, it may be able to save it, either by making a different set of arguments or perhaps by simply making the same points more effectively. 'To be honest,' said Chakrabarti, 'sometimes we don't have anything new to add, but we just do it better, because we know what we're doing, and sometimes the solicitor and counsels don't.' There also may be advantages in being able to represent a cause instead of a client:

> Sometimes, even though we're on the same team, we are just going to lend something to the intervention because there's something quite pure and convenient about not having to be trammeled by facts, facts that may be unattractive, clients that may be unattractive, to be able to come in as fairy godmother and say, 'These are points of principle, and this is what we say about them.'

Chakrabarti acknowledged that there was some arrogance in this stance but contended that it was justified by Liberty's record as a third-party intervener:

> Some academics have ... written that [intervention] is basically wrong because who are these people? Who's deciding who should intervene and who shouldn't? We're neither the democratically elected government, nor are we the parties. Who are we to suggest we've got anything to say? But I think the crude reality is that the courts are quite keen on hearing from us ... because we've been doing this stuff for so long ... and we always use very top-notch counsel when there's an oral intervention.[62]

Liberty's use of interventions to extend its influence over the development of the law is similar to the amicus strategy adopted by many of the

[61] Above n 58, at 352.

[62] One of the 'academics' to whom Chakrabarti apparently is referring is Carol Harlow, who recently published a stinging critique of the rise of 'group litigation' resulting from the relaxation of traditional rules governing standing and third party interventions. C. Harlow, 'Public Law and Popular Justice' (2002) 65 *The Modern Law Review* 1ff. Harlow suggests that this trend reflects the desire of British courts to be 'seen to be participatory and responsive,' so that 'they too can claim a sort of democratic legitimacy, based not on the representativeness of election but on popular participation' (*ibid*, at 14). She deplores the development of a 'symbiotic relationship between courts and campaigning groups' by which 'courts can legitimate the political lobbying of campaigning groups at the same time as campaigners legitimate ever deeper forays into the realm of policy and politics' (*ibid*, at 17–18).

leading US rights advocacy groups. Liberty, like most rights NGOs, has no interest in performing the traditional British amicus curiae function of providing the court with neutral information relevant to the case. In litigation under the Human Rights Act, Liberty's interventions would virtually always support interpretations of the law which would benefit individual appellants against the government. The only exceptions would be cases where Liberty chose to argue tactically for a narrower interpretation of the Convention than one which would be most helpful to the appellant in that particular case. For example, in *R v Khan*, the first House of Lords intervention in 1996, Liberty's strong interest in having Article 8 of the European Convention recognised in British law, led it to present a relatively narrow argument that not only did not support the appellant's case but may actually have weakened it. However, when the case was subsequently taken to the European Court of Human Rights, Liberty fully supported the appellant's position.[63]

Although third-party intervention is not a new litigation strategy for Liberty, the organisation appears to be going about it even more deliberately than in the past, frequently as part of its coalition building activities with other organisations in the human rights advocacy community.[64] Early in 2003, for example, Liberty intervened in a set of test cases challenging enforcement of provisions of the Nationality, Immigration, and Asylum Act 2002, which denied subsistence grants to 'late' asylum seekers — those who did not make asylum claims 'as soon as reasonably practicable' after arriving in the UK. Chakrabarti described the careful preparation by Liberty that preceded this intervention:

> [The amendments] came into force on the 8th of January, and we geared up for that even before the 8th of January, because we campaigned against the policy when it was first introduced as an amendment to the Act. We campaigned against it, we did media work, we said this is appalling. ... And that built up a head of steam when the Act was passed. And we coordinated

[63] A Loux, 'Losing the Battle, Winning the War: Litigation Strategy and Pressure Group Organisation in the Era of Incorporation' (2000) 11 *Kings College Law Journal* 90ff.

[64] There is little systematic research to date on whether, and how, the litigation strategies of rights NGOs are affected by their relationships with like-minded groups. See, eg M Hojnacki, 'Interest Groups' Decisions to Join Alliances or Work Alone' (1997) 41 *American Journal of Political Science* 61ff. However, the case studies of civil rights litigation are replete with examples of both formal and informal cooperation among liberal organisations. See, eg Epp, above n 5, at 53. There is reason to suspect that this pattern may not be consistent across the political spectrum. In the mid-1980s, Epstein contrasted liberal litigators, who 'often file amicus curiae briefs in support of each others' efforts,' with conservatives, who 'have avoided what they call 'me-too' participation, with the intention of eliminating needless duplication of effort.' Above n 20, at 155. Likewise, Heinz, Paik, and Southworth found relatively little cohesion among lawyers representing different conservative causes, and in fact observed that 'considerable antipathy' seems to exist between libertarian and 'family values' conservatives. Above n 20, at 26.

> meetings with all the major refugee and asylum organisations so that essentially people were out looking for just case victims from the second that policy came into force.

As it happened, Liberty had arranged to represent a group of asylum-seekers affected by the regulations. However, according to Wadham,

> Everybody rushed to court, and we got to court in the evening, and somebody else got to court in the morning, and they got the case. So we then intervened with all these other organisations. We were part of another five [cases] that were pending. [We were] irritatingly close!

Unsuccessful in its effort to bring one of the leading cases against the new regulations, Liberty instead intervened with the Joint Council for the Welfare of Immigrants (JCWI) and eight other organisations — the largest joint intervention in the UK to date — in support of the challenge, which was successful.[65] According to Chakrabarti, this case was one that 'needed to be brought, in a certain way, by the right advocates. And [for Liberty] all that kind of pre-negotiating and strategising and pulling organisations together is a new way of working.' The success of that experience and other similar ones has led Wadham and his colleagues to consider how Liberty might expand and institutionalise its intervention work:

> What we've thought about doing in the future is to provide a kind of service to smaller NGOs and campaigners and say, 'Look, there's these cases coming up, and you know more about them than we do, but we know more about the law and how to intervene. Let's work together.' We hope we can get some funding to do that kind of intervention work because at the moment we're just doing it from our [budget].

Thus, by making its expertise available to like-minded but more narrowly focused pressure groups, Liberty is trying to magnify the impact of its voice in the increasingly crowded field of UK human rights jurisprudence.

CONCLUSION

Formidable cultural, political, and legal barriers stand in the way of a full embrace of US-style litigation in the UK in the foreseeable future. There is no doubting, however, that the Human Rights Act takes a major step in that direction. By codifying a set of political and civil rights in British domestic law, the HRA has created new opportunities for claiming protection

[65] *R (Q and Others) v Home Secretary* [2003] EWCA Civ 364.

for rights through test case litigation. Just how significant a source of rights the HRA proves to be will depend largely on how effectively British interest groups can mobilise their resources to exploit its potential.

This case study of Liberty's early post-HRA mobilisation efforts suggests that the relationship between interest groups and Bills of Rights is mutually constitutive. Because of its previous experience both domestically and in Strasbourg, Liberty was able to incorporate the HRA quite seamlessly into its programme, with only marginal adjustments consisting mainly of more purposeful selection of test cases and increased use of third party interventions to supplement direct case sponsorship. But the impact of the HRA on Liberty cannot be isolated from its effects on other legal-political actors as well, since whatever opportunities the HRA has provided for Liberty are now generally available. Liberty's post-HRA work has been shaped in part by its leaders' perception that the Act carries a threat to Liberty's long-standing hegemony in UK rights litigation. The danger is not that any single organisation might assume Liberty's traditional leadership role, but rather that Liberty's influence could diminish as litigation is pursued by a larger number of groups and individual practitioners working in an increasingly crowded field. Liberty has responded thus far not by engaging in aggressive competition for cases, but rather by attempting to join forces and pool its resources with like-minded organisations. The outcomes of these efforts will help shape HRA jurisprudence in the United Kingdom.

Liberty's prominence as a human rights litigator makes its post-HRA experiences especially important, but it may also make them unique. If socio-legal scholars are to achieve a more comprehensive understanding of how the work of rights advocacy groups affects and is affected by the codification of rights, further research needs to be done on how other organisations are faring under the Human Rights Act. We might begin by examining the legal landscape to discover whether new rights litigation groups have appeared since the HRA; whether rights advocacy organisations that once avoided the courts are now developing litigation programs of their own; whether NGOs without previous interests in human rights have broadened their litigation activities to incorporate such concerns; whether litigation groups are making greater use of third party interventions in addition to or instead of conventional test cases; and whether, in general, the HRA has affected the balance between litigation and non-litigation activities undertaken by British rights advocacy groups. The literature on US rights interest groups cited in this chapter could be productively mined for hypotheses and methodologies to help explore such questions, the answers to which will assist us in understanding the dynamics of the relationship between written bills of rights and interest group behaviours.

5

Implementing the Human Rights Act into the Courts in England and Wales: Culture Shift or Damp Squib?

JOHN W RAINE AND CLIVE WALKER

THE HUMAN RIGHTS CONVENTION AND THE COURTS

THE DECISION TO incorporate the Human Rights Convention into English law was always likely to be of special significance for the courts — perhaps more so than for any other public organisation, given that it would be within the courtrooms of the land where so many of the new human rights questions would be raised and resolved. Within that environment, and particularly in the run up to enactment, it was expected that Articles 5, 6 and 8 would figure most prominently in litigation.[1] But more than that, it was widely anticipated that the Act could have a major impact on, not just the courts, but on legal thinking in general, as reflected in a profusion of commentaries on the legislation.[2] With hindsight perhaps, this expectation might have been somewhat overblown. The Convention rights were drafted with English law models in mind, models in which pragmatism and social compromise are more recurrent features than libertarianism. Furthermore, what began as a rather reticent and conservative statement of rights has since been applied by the European Court of Human Rights with a great deal of respect for national foibles, including the development of the concept of 'margin of appreciation' which allows

[1] N Rose, 'Crime cases dominate ECHR bids' (1998) 95 (07) *Law Society's Gazette* 10ff; G Chambers, *Practising Human Rights* (London, Report 28, RPPU, Law Society, 1998).
[2] See, eg HWR Wade, 'Human rights and the judiciary' (1998) 520 *European Human Rights Law Review* 532, describing the Human Rights Act as '... a quantum leap into a new culture of fundamental rights and freedoms.'

for national difference.[3] In addition, the Home Office's White Paper, *Rights Brought Home: The Human Rights Act*, itself adopted a line which is pragmatic and expressly respectful of English constitutional traditions such as sovereignty.[4] The English judiciary have also been said to be conservative-minded when it comes to major legal innovation, such as the development of rights to privacy or against discrimination.[5] Moreover, the higher courts had already encountered the European Convention which was being increasingly cited as persuasive[6] and so were not encountering an entirely unknown influence. Even the executive in Whitehall did not exactly face a revolution, for it had long worked with the Convention and had already engaged in 'Strasbourg proofing',[7] as a consequence of which it did not expect many challenges to succeed or many major legal reforms to be undertaken to ensure compatibility.

Despite all these restraints, the courts, like the legal profession more generally, tended to expect a significant level of interest and challenges based on the Act. Indeed, in the minds of some, it was feared that '... the lawyers [will] ... dominate all the debates.'[8] While this viewpoint now seems to have been exaggerated, even the Lord Chancellor, Lord Irvine, asserted in December 1997[9]:

> This Bill will therefore create a more explicitly moral approach to decisions and decision making; will promote both a culture where positive rights and

[3] See *Handyside v UK*, App no 5493/72, Ser A vol 24, (1976) 1 EHRR 737 and see also *Müller v Switzerland*, App no 10737/84, Ser A vol 133, (1991) 13 EHRR 212; *Scherer v Switzerland*, App no 17116/90, Ser A vol 287 (1994).

[4] N Bamforth, 'Parliamentary sovereignty and the Human Rights Act 1998 [1998], *Public Law* 512ff; Lord Irvine, 'Activism and restraint' [1999] *European Human Rights Law Review* 350ff, 371.

[5] See *Malone v UK*, App no 8691/79, Ser A vol 82, (1985) 7 EHRR 14; *Nagle v Feilden* [1966] 2 QB 633; *Edwards v Society of Graphical and Allied Trades* [1971] Ch 354; *Constantine v Imperial Hotels Ltd* [1944] KB 693; *Rothfield v North British Railway Co* 1920 SC 805.

[6] See MJ Beloff and H Mountfield, 'Unconventional Behaviour? Judicial uses of the European Convention in England and Wales' [1996] *European Human Rights Law Review* 467ff; R Singh, *The Future of Human Rights in the United Kingdom* (Oxford, Hart Publishing, 1997); M Hunt, *Using Human Rights Law in English Courts* (London, Hart Publishing, 1997). For its relationship at that time with English law, see *R v Secretary of State for the Home Department, ex parte Brind* [1990] 1 All ER 469.

[7] See N Lyell, 'Whither Strasbourg?' [1997] *European Human Rights Law Review* 132ff; I Bynoe and S Spencer, *Mainstreaming Human Rights in Whitehall and Westminster* (London, IPPR, 1999). Some studies were undertaken ahead of the implementation of the Human Rights Act (see for example, Law Commission, Bail and Human Rights, Consultation Paper no 157, Stationery Office, London, 1999) and some legislative changes were undertaken (most notably the Terrorism Act 2000 and the Regulation of Investigatory Powers Act 2000).

[8] KD Ewing, 'The Human Rights Act and Parliamentary Democracy' (1999) 62 *Modern Law Review* 75ff, 79. Compare Lord Irvine, 'Activism and Restraint: Human Rights and the Interpretative Process' [1999] *European Human Rights Law Review* 350ff, 371.

[9] Tom Sargant memorial lecture, December 1997, http://www.lcd.gov.uk/speeches/1997/tomsarg.htm.

> liberties become the focus and concern of legislators, administrators and judges alike; and a culture in judicial decision making where there will be a greater concentration on substance rather than form.

Thus, a new era of 'rights review' rather than 'judicial review' was anticipated,[10] albeit that it would be achieved through an evolutionary rather than revolutionary transformation, reflecting the reality that English law already resonates with the values of individual liberty and would not require radical surgery. But an acute worry at the time was that the process by which that transformation would be achieved might engulf court business and resources.

This chapter draws on findings from a research project undertaken for the Lord Chancellor's Department in 2000–02 designed to assess the early impacts of the Act on courts through a longitudinal study covering the pre-enactment planning stage and post-enactment implementation in nine courts through the first year after commencement on 2 October 2000.[11] The study had a particular focus on impacts in terms of court workloads and productivity in the throughput of cases — this being an aspect of some concern to policy-makers and practitioners in the courts ahead of enactment. But, more than that, the study also set out to explore more widely the effects of the new Act for the ways the courts worked and to assess the extent to which behaviour and culture within the judicial and administrative organisation was affected by the new expectations and legal provisions of the legislation.

The study was primarily based on analysis of impacts at a sample of nine courts in England and Wales — three Crown Court centres (Guildford, Liverpool and Chester), three county court centres (in the same three locations) and three magistrates' courts (Stafford, Camberwell Green and Leeds) — purposefully chosen for their differences in scale of organisation and geographical spread. Particular emphasis was placed in the study on the lower tier, first-instance courts because it was anticipated that it would be there, more than elsewhere, that the impacts would be most significant. Not least, of course, this was because these are the courts which handle the great bulk of judicial business, even though they are generally less visible to the public as compared with the High Court or Court of Appeal, wherein cases, impacts and outputs are more widely reported.[12]

[10] Compare D Feldman, 'The Human Rights Act 1998 and Constitutional Principles' (1999) 19, *Legal Studies* 165ff; Lord Irvine, 'Activism and Restraint 350ff, 369.

[11] *The Impact on Courts and the Administration of Justice of the Human Rights Act 1998* (London, LCD Research Series 9/02, 2002).

[12] A full list of Human Rights Act cases in the higher courts is indeed being compiled: EM Salgado and C O'Brien, 'Table of cases under the Human Rights Act' [2001], *European Human Rights Law Review* 181, 376, 677; J Arkinstall and C O'Brien, 'Table of Cases under the Human Rights Act' [2002] *European Human Rights Law Review* 80, 239.

The research involved a series of interview rounds with court managers, members of the judiciary and other personnel involved in court-based work at the courts (a first round, shortly ahead of implementation of the Act to focus on preparations; a second round, shortly after implementation to focus on immediate effects; and a third round, some nine months later to assess longer-term implications).[13] In addition, data gathering arrangements were made to provide a 'log' of all cases arising in the selected courts with a Human Rights Act implication over the period of the project. Observational work was also undertaken in the courtrooms at two of the magistrates' courts specifically to examine the issue of 'giving reasons' for decisions — a key change in practice for the lower courts implied by the Act. Finally, various national agencies[14] were contacted ahead of the Act being implemented with questionnaires to ascertain information on their preparations for the Act and to gather views on anticipated impacts. Further contact was made with some of these agencies one year later to provide further perspective on their experiences and reflections about impacts.

PREPARING FOR THE ACT

The fact that the European Convention on Human Rights was enshrined in legislation in 1998 but was not actually implemented in England and Wales[15] for another two years meant that there was a significant period of time for the courts and associated agencies to prepare for the new legislation.[16] Perceptions and expectations about possible impacts varied, but with the formal policy/practice guidance and various promotional materials being compiled and provided by the Lord Chancellor's Department, the courts collectively committed themselves to an ambitious programme of preparation and training in readiness for the new Act.

The details of that preparation work were explored and highlighted in the research study which revealed the considerable intensity to the preparation

[13] At each site we conducted separate interviews with the court manager/justices clerk, with senior representatives of the judiciary (the chair or deputy chair of the local magistracy and/or presiding judge) and also administrators from the courts and officials from court user organisations—the Police, the local Bar, and Law Society, the Crown Prosecution Service, Probation and Prison Services.

[14] The Association of Chief Police Officers, The Court Service, The Crown Prosecution Service, The General Council of the Bar, The Judicial Studies Board, the Justices' Clerks' Society, the Law Society of England and Wales, the Legal Services Commission, the Magistrates' Association, the Magistrates' Courts Service Inspectorate, and the Lord Chancellor's Department.

[15] It was implemented more than a year earlier in Scotland in regard to 'devolution matters' through the operation of the Scotland Act 1998 ss 29, 57.

[16] See further N Pleming, 'Assessing the Act: A Firm Foundation or a False Start?' [2000] *European Human Rights Law Review* 560ff; J Croft, 'Whitehall and the Human Rights Act 1998' [2000] *European Human Rights Law Review* 392ff.

efforts undertaken within the courts.[17] All district judges and Crown Court judges submitted themselves to a training programme organised by the Judicial Studies Board, with many individuals subsequently 'topping up' by attending other conferences and seminars, typically organised within the legal profession. Views on the adequacy of the training provided to the judges, as revealed through the research study, varied from 'quite sufficient' to 'hardly adequate'. But on a wider national scale, the evidence collected centrally suggested generally positive views on the Judicial Studies Board (JSB) training (with 89 per cent of participants who completed JSB evaluation questionnaires considering that the seminars had 'substantially met their needs').

In the Crown and county courts, managers were also all invited to attend a one-day training event organised by the Court Service during Summer 2000. This, too, was generally felt to have provided a satisfactory grounding, although some respondents felt it had not been as specific and detailed as they would have wished and had left unanswered some of the questions which they had felt to be important. A further important component of the preparation/training of such court managers took the form of additional written information provided through editions of the Court Service's *Court Business* (September 2000 edition in particular) and through other guidance issued, for example, for court users and on the use of language interpreters in civil hearings. As part of the preparations for implementation, at each county and Crown Court, a named person was also made responsible for acting as the principal 'point of contact' for Human Rights Act issues and as a conduit through which to disseminate any information to colleagues.

So far as the magistrates' courts were concerned, the district judges (magistrates' courts) similarly attended a standard training session for the professional judiciary organised by the Judicial Studies Board, plus one or two additional special training events, notably on 'giving reasons' in youth court and family court proceedings. In addition, many again chose to attend other relevant conferences for their own professional development and interest. For lay magistrates, on the other hand, the basic pattern of training comprised a one-day training event for every justice, mostly arranged in spring/summer 2000 as part of the locally-organised training. This was prefaced by an initial training day for justices' clerks/training officers (who would be delivering the training to lay justices (organised by the Magistrates' Courts Division of the Lord Chancellor's Department).

[17] At each of the three Crown and county court centres interviews on this subject were conducted with the court managers and in some instances with judges as well. At the magistrates' courts, interviews were arranged at this first stage mainly with justices' clerks but at some centres also with magistrates, district judges, prosecution and defence lawyers, and administrative staff.

The training for lay justices was based mainly on materials prepared for this purpose by the Judicial Studies Board, which also provided training on use of the materials. Additional events (typically a further half-day session) were organised for family panel members. Beyond this basic provision, different local magistrates' courts arranged their own additional training to differing degrees. At one of the three courts visited within the research, for example, an additional training event was arranged with other agencies (on a Saturday morning), as well as an evening session on 'giving reasons' and a day event specifically for youth court panels.

Reactions by magistrates to the training were generally positive, though at the time, there were some anxieties (and not a little complaint) about the potential impact of the new legislation and concerns about the apparent complexity of the requirements. Inevitably, with some 30,000 lay magistrates to undergo the training for the new Act, the organisational arrangements were quite demanding for magistrates' courts committees and their training teams — with the events having to be run many times in each area (and at several different courts) to accommodate everyone on the local benches in each commission area. However, much of the direct resourcing of this effort was met by the provision by the Lord Chancellor's Department of funding to the extent of £50 per magistrate.

Legal advisers to magistrates (justices clerks and their assistants) undertook their training on the Act over a more extended period — from September 1999 onwards (save for those who were themselves acting as trainers). This was initiated with a two-day residential programme for justices' clerks followed by systematic programmes of training for court clerks organised mainly on a regional/commission area basis). Mostly, the programmes had followed the format of the training packages issued by the Judicial Studies Board for the professional judiciary and were drawn up in consultation with the Magistrates' Association and the Justices' Clerks' Society. A refresher day was held in early autumn 2000, immediately ahead of implementation. Senior administrative staff at each of the magistrates' courts were also provided with briefing sheets and/or other relevant information and most such personnel were given the opportunity to attend short training sessions (mainly in the form of half-day sessions for small groups of administrative staff from across each magistrates' courts committee area).

The research revealed that this amount of training and preparation within the magistrates' courts, compared favourably with most of the other public sector organisations with which those courts have to work — notably police, probation, youth offending teams. Only the Crown Prosecution Service (CPS) appeared to commit anywhere near equivalent time to its preparations. Here prosecutors, from an early stage, were required to apply an additional test for each case — of compliance with the Human Rights Act and were given very comprehensive training on the Act (as were administrative staff within the CPS).

Yet, despite the fact that implementation coincided with the early stages of the policy development to 'join up' criminal justice, there was comparatively little commitment towards joint organisational training and preparation for the Act — each agency tending to develop its own response separately. That said, one of the magistrates' courts visited in the research did provide a notable exception to this general state of affairs in that the court had invited other local criminal justice agencies to join the magistrates' training sessions, and the justices' clerk had made contact with all the local agencies individually to brief them on expectations of the court and to offer advice and assistance. For example, the court actively helped the Young Offenders Team (YOT) with their training.

PRE-IMPLEMENTATION EXPECTATIONS

Interviews with practitioners in, and associated with, the courts revealed a number of key issues as dominating expectations about the impact of the new legislation — mostly, it should be said, relating to magistrates' courts. These included bail decisions, conduct of trials, giving reasons for decisions, court clerks' giving of advice in open court, providing support for unrepresented defendants, use of bailiffs for recovery of unpaid fines and conduct of fine enforcement courts, and treatment of the public and prisoners at court.

On bail decisions, concerns were particularly aired about the possible effects of the Bail Act 1976 in relation to the inevitably difficult issue of achieving consistency in its interpretation in different courtrooms, with different defence and prosecution lawyers, and on different days (with different members of the lay bench). And that problem, it was suggested, would always be compounded by the general pressures of time and limited information that were so characteristic of remand courts, with many cases being added to the list at very short notice following overnight arrests. Concerns were also articulated about achieving full compliance in relation to the giving of reasons in bail decisions. On the other hand, it was acknowledged that the Bail Act already required a structured approach to decision-making, so that here perhaps the formulation of reasons would be more straightforward than in many other instances, such as, trials.

Some anxieties also existed at the outset in magistrates' courts about the prospect of legal challenges to the assumption that magistrates would continue to adjudicate in hearings where evidence presented earlier had been deemed inadmissible by the same bench. Here, several justices' clerks/court clerks pointed to the potential acute difficulties for courts in meeting completely the conditions of impartiality implied by Article 6, at least for a purist interpretation of the requirements.

But undoubtedly of most concern in the magistrates' courts ahead of implementation of the Human Rights Act was the matter of giving reasons in open court for the decisions. It was being widely assumed to be a requirement of fairness under Article 6 that the court process in each case must conclude with a reasoned judgment, such as would allow a defendant to understand not just what had been decided but also why.[18] Generally this was perceived as potentially problematic for many lay magistrates, unused as they were to such reason-giving.[19] There was concern within many local benches at the prospect of being found wanting in this respect and also about the amount of time clerks might need to spend with the justices in helping them to formulate their reasons and in articulating them in court and in full thereafter.

At one of the three case-study magistrates' courts visited, a 5–10 per cent increase was proposed in the time provision to be made for each contested hearing on account of this new reason-giving requirement (allowing time both for formulation in the retiring rooms and delivery in court). And at all three courts where the research was based, efforts were made to develop special templates for the bench to help simplify and shorten the task of compliance in this respect (through a form of structured decision sheet, setting out all the questions/issues that needed to be considered/decided etc in each case, much along the lines that were already in use in family courts).

Further anxieties ahead of implementation surrounded the question of the role of the clerk in open court. The general advice here from justices' clerks at the time was that clerks should concentrate on giving their advice in a confident and open manner (rather than, as often the case previously, through whispered communication with the bench or through additional retirements). But at the same time there was disquiet about the impressions likely to be given to the observing public in this context if clerks felt the need to intervene with legal points (or corrections) during pronouncements by magistrates.

On the particular question of clerks being invited by the justices to the retiring room to give advice, the consensus view from the outset was that this would still be an acceptable practice. However, some justices' clerks were noted to be considering recommending that their clerks should, on their return to the courtroom, formally explain to the court precisely what their role in the retiring room had been.[20]

Likewise there was concern about the role of the court clerk in the traditional task of assisting any unrepresented defendants and, in the view of one justices' clerk at the time, a greater propensity to grant

[18] See *(John) Murray v UK*, App no 18731/91, Ser A vol 300-A, (1996) 22 EHRR 29; *Condron and Condron v UK*, App no 35718/97, (2001) 31 EHRR 1. In *Degnan v HM Advocate* 2001 SLT 1233, it was decided that matters relating effectively to court administration did not have to take place in open court.

[19] Compare the position in regard to professional magistrates: *R v Harrow Crown Court, ex parte Dawe* (1994) 158 JP 250.

[20] See *R v Chichester Justices, ex parte DPP* (1993) 157 JP 1049.

legal aid was felt likely as an alternative simply to ensure 'equality of arms'.[21] A number of clerks also foresaw the need for improved provision of interpreter services, again particularly in relation to unrepresented defendants.

A further area of widespread concern at the magistrates' courts in the pre-implementation phase related to the implications for fine enforcement policy and practices, again a setting in which the preponderance of those listed to appear (as defaulters) were unrepresented. The main concern here was that the procedures and methods traditionally applied might not be viewed as compliant with Article 6 of the Act. Some courts even talked of wholesale abandonment of defaulters' courts (presided over by magistrates) and their replacement with 'fines clinics' run by court clerks and at which the reasons for default and ways of responding to default problems might be investigated and approached through a less intimidating environment and style of interaction. Also under discussion at the time was the question of the role of court clerk in relation to the conduct of means enquiries within enforcement proceedings. Here several courts were contemplating training some of their administrative staff to undertake the courtroom role traditionally performed by court clerks of conducting the enquiries. The aim here was to create the impression of a cross-examination that would be 'independent' of the bench and their clerk (whose role would be seen to be confined to that of advising magistrates). However other justices' clerks interviewed during the research questioned whether such a change would necessarily achieve the desired compliance, given that administrative staff, like clerks, were employees of the court.

Related to this area of concern was that of the use by the courts of bailiffs to execute warrants for non-payment of financial penalties. The issue here was particularly related to the long track-record of complaints made to the courts about alleged malpractices by bailiffs, with the focus, being above all on rights to privacy and property in the context of any attempts by bailiffs to exercise distraint (seizure of assets). Some doubts were expressed in this context about the robustness of the codes of conduct that had been agreed with the bailiffs as part of the contracting process, if the court's enforcement policies and practices were to become subject to legal challenge. Likewise, it was suggested at one court that the exercise of arrest powers by civilian enforcement officers would also need to be reviewed and the staff concerned given extra training, particularly in relation to the giving of reasons for their actions.

Interviews in the research also highlighted the existence of concerns about the Act in relation to standards of personal treatment, for example, of

[21] See A Le Sueur, 'Access to justice rights in the United Kingdom' [2000] *European Human Rights Law Review* 457ff.

the possibilities of the court becoming subject to challenge over allegations that wrong advice had been given, or of inappropriate behaviour by security staff or of the procedures that could and could not be followed in checking and searching people on arrival at court. A commonly cited further dilemma concerned the ordering of cases on court days — and whether it would or would not be right to give priority to parents in case-listing if they claimed a need to leave court early enough to collect their children from school. Aspects of the design and condition of accommodation, particularly the cell areas, also gave rise to worries about compliance (such as arising from standards of cleanliness and the removal of graffiti, the separation of different categories of prisoners and the adequacy of facilities for consultations between prisoners and their lawyers). Within the courtroom too, there was vexed debate about dock facilities, with differing views as to what might constitute compliance in design terms. At one court it was felt that the absence of a roof on a 'secure' dock would be deemed satisfactory from the compliance viewpoint (again, in relation to the right to humane treatment). But elsewhere, the view taken was that 'roofed' docks would not be a particular problem (many courts having only comparatively recently increased the security of their docks by 'roofing' them to minimise the problem of 'runners' escaping custody). In contrast, there was general agreement about the need to avoid situations in which prisoners would be accompanied handcuffed in public areas (in the street or in the court precincts).

Finally, there were anxieties about the provision of information about the ways of working of the courts and of its expectations in relation to users. At one county court, plans were being made for a 'question and answer' leaflet on court procedures (a draft had been circulated) — something that many magistrates' courts had been providing for some time. But even at those courts where such leaflets were already available, the view ahead of implementation was that all such documentation would need to be reviewed to ensure that the information was in compliance with the Act. At one court, too, there was discussion about the quality of 'sign-posting' in the public areas of the building — particularly concerning the clarity of communication as to which hearings/sessions would be open to the public to observe.

EXPECTED WORKLOAD IMPLICATIONS

As indicated, a key focus of the research was with the workload implications of the Act, and in this respect perspectives about the amount of extra case-work anticipated varied quite markedly. Some foresaw a significant amount of new human rights challenges. Others simply predicted a general lengthening in the average time per (existing) contested case, particularly because of having to comply with the giving of reasons, as described above. Others again anticipated pressures in relation to bail cases, in particular, with more contested bail applications expected as a result. At one of the Crown Court centres it was suggested that the consequence might show itself in more compensation payments for wrongful imprisonment. There was also a fairly widespread view that many of the Human Rights Act issues would be raised *within* forms of process grounded on other bases (as opposed to being the subject of suits in their own right).

Furthermore, there was also a fairly widespread expectation (though by no means universally shared) of an initial flurry of Human Rights challenges and applications followed by a 'plateauing' of interest, once a new equilibrium of understanding between parties and the courts had been established. The view of the courts in the pre-implementation period was that any initial flurry would be more likely to reflect the use of the Act by defence lawyers as a (delaying/testing) tactic, rather than in the pursuit of substantive human rights claims per se. This anticipated effect had generally prompted the courts to publicise their intention to respond robustly to any 'shooting in the dark' challenges by requesting precise and full clarification of the particular Articles and legal points to which they would be referring in their submissions. Court managers also indicated that the judiciary was expecting to take a firm stand in dealing with repetitive or hopeless human rights pleas.

At one Crown Court the main impacts on workloads were anticipated to be in relation to 'administrative courts' for pre-trial issues (for example, plea and directions hearings and issues regarding disclosure). Here there was also some speculation about a possible perverse effect of more matters being put before judges by the court managers simply as a way of passing over the responsibility for potentially difficult/challengeable decisions. And at both Crown and magistrates' courts, many practitioners indicated their expectation of more 'cracked trials' (ie changes of plea to 'guilty' on the day of cases previously notified as 'not-guilty'). This expectation at the time reflected the general expectation that many defence lawyers would use the Act as an additional opportunity for delay.

THE EFFECTS FOR THE COURTS OF THE ACT IN PRACTICE

The implementation of the Human Rights Act in October 2000 has in fact produced a mixed picture for the courts.[22] In the first year or so at least there were comparatively few challenges by way of declarations of incompatibility, but certain areas of law were repeatedly brought into

[22] See further F Klug and K Starmer, 'Incorporation through the "front door": the first year of the Human Rights Act' [2001] *Public Law* 654ff.

question which in turn added to the work of the courts, even if there was limited change as a result. Such areas included presumptions in criminal law[23] and the relationship between breach of rights and either the exclusion of evidence[24] or appeal grounds.[25] However, other jurisdictions and procedures which some had anticipated to be vulnerable, such as coroners' proceedings and the drug testing of prisoners, did not (immediately) become subject to much challenge. As expected, it was criminal process that proved to be the busiest area for challenge based on the Human Rights Act.[26] As regards civil litigation, fundamental decisions about the 'horizontal' effect of the Human Rights Act are still awaited to determine the broad impact.[27] In *Douglas v Hello! Ltd*,[28] Lord Justice Sedley regarded section 12(4) of the Act as ensuring that Article 10 at least had horizontal effect.[29] There were in the meantime some major cases in the medical field.[30] But there was little sign of the development of radical new perspectives in civil law,[31] and, overall, it could be said that the courts have been 'generally rather cautious'.[32] Table 1 summarises the position nationally for the first year in quantitative terms.

Four features in particular emerge from an analysis of that first year's experience (each borne out at the case study courts on which the research was particularly focused). First was the very small caseload: a total of 297 cases (compared with a typical Crown Court annual caseload of around 30,000 criminal cases and a civil caseload of around 160,000). Second was a weighting in favour of criminal business over civil/private business

[23] See *R v Secretary of State for the Home Department, ex parte Kebilene* [1999] 3 WLR 972; *R v Benjafield* [2002] 2 WLR 235; *R v Lambert* [2002] 2 AC 545.
[24] See *R v P* [2001] 2 All ER 58.
[25] See *R v Francom* [2001] 1 Cr App R 237; *R v Kansal (No 2)* [2001] 3 WLR 751; *R v Lyons (no 3)* [2003] 1 AC 976.
[26] Though there may also be much happening at tribunal level especially within immigration tribunals.
[27] See R Buxton, 'The Human Rights Act and private law' (2000) 116 *Law Quarterly Review,* 48ff; W Wade, 'Horizons of Horizontality' (2000) 116 *Law Quarterly Review* 217ff; A Lester and D Pannick, 'The Impact of the Human Rights Act on Private Law' (2000) 116 *Law Quarterly Review* 380ff; N Bamforth, 'The True "Horizontal Effect" of the Human Rights Act 1998' (2001) 117 *Law Quarterly Review* 334ff; T Raphael, 'The Problem of the Horizontal Effect' [2000] *European Human Rights Law Review* 393ff; T De la Mare and K Gallifant, 'The Horizontal Effect of the Human Rights Act 1998' [2001] *Juridical Review* 29ff; I Hare, 'Vertically Challenged: Private Parties and the Human Rights Act' [2001] *European Human Rights Law Review* 526ff.
[28] [2001] 2 WLR 992.
[29] *Ibid,* at 1027.
[30] *NHS Trust A v M* [2001] 2 WLR 942; *R (Pretty) v Director of Public Prosecutions* [2001] 3 WLR 1598.
[31] See, eg *Ashdown v Telegraph Group* [2001] 2 WLR 967; *R (Mellor) v Secretary of State for the Home Department* [2001] 3 WLR 533; *Venables and Thompson v NGN* [2001] 2 All ER 908; *R v Secretary of State for the Home Department ex parte Wainwright* [2002] QB 1334.
[32] Scottish Executive Central Research Unit, Public Authorities and the Human Rights Act (Scottish Office, Edinburgh, 2001) para 1.17.

(94 criminal cases compared with just 56 civil/private cases). Third was (and continues to be) the predominance of Article 6 (fair trial) issues over other articles in the Act (some 42 Article 6 cases compared with just 14 for Articles 3 and 4). Fourth was that the outcome in most cases was that no ruling or remedy was directly related to a sustained Human Rights Act point (233 cases of 'no remedy' compared with around 25 for injunctions/quashing decisions and fewer than 10 for other outcomes such as retrials or administrative actions).

Further quantitative evidence was gathered from the Lord Chancellor's Department's quarterly returns published in the wake of the Act coming into force (see Table 2). Overall, those returns suggested that most of the cases had impacted on the higher courts but with very little impact on courts of first instance and showed the court system was '... matching up very well to the demands of the Act ...'[33]

Table 1: Case Loads in All Courts from 2 October 2000 to 13 December 2001[34]

Cases analysed:	Civil and private	56	
	Civil and public	147	
	Criminal (including judicial review)	94	
Total			297
HRA claims upheld:	Section 3	11	
	Section 4	3	
	Section 6	42	
Total			56
Outcome of HRA challenge	Made no difference	90	

Continued...

[33] Joint Committee on Human Rights, Implementation of the Human Rights Act 1998 (2000–01 HL 66, HC 332), memorandum from Lord Irvine.

[34] Statistics based on information supplied to the Human Rights Unit by the Human Rights Act Research Unit, Doughty Street Chambers, London, based on cases reported in Lawtel Human Rights interactive and Butterworths Human Rights Direct from case transcripts available. This table is reproduced from http://www.lcd.gov.uk/hract/statistics.htm. Corresponding data is available at http://www.doughtystreet.co.uk/hrarp/summary/index.cfm.

Table 1 Continued…

	Affected outcome, reasoning or procedure	207	
Total			297
Remedies:	No remedy	233	
	Declaration, injunctions or orders	22	
	Quashing of order or decision	23	
	Retrial	4	
	Administrative action	3	
	Declarations of incompatibility	3	
	Damages	1	
	Other	8	
Total			297

Table 2: Impact of the Human Rights Act by Court Type[35]

Court of Appeal (Criminal Division)	**Total caseload**	**Total HRA**	**Impact on court affected cases**
2 Oct–31 Jan 2000	2491	277	Average sitting time per casedown by 5 minutes
1 Jan–31 March 2001	1872	161	Overall no change
1 Apr–30 Jun 2001	1971	123	Overall no change
Court of Appeal (Civil Division)	**Total caseload**	**Total HRA affected cases**	**Impact on court**
2 Oct–31 Dec 2000	1260	93	Average sitting time per caseup from 0.77 to 0.79 days

Continued…

[35] See http://www.lcd.gov.uk/hract/hrimpact1.htm, http://www.lcd.gov.uk/hract/hrimpact2.htm, http://www.lcd.gov.uk/hract/hrimpact3.htm.

Table 2 Continued...

Court of Appeal (Civil Division)	Total caseload	Total HRA affected cases	Impact on court
1 Jan–31 March 2001	1262	87	Not available
1 Apr–30 Jun 2001	1105	38	Not available
High Court	**Total caseload**	**Total HRA affected cases**	**Impact on court**
2 Oct–31 Dec 2000	Not available	383 (303 in the Administrative Court)	Not available
1 Jan–31 March 2001	Not available	343 (261 in the Administrative Court)	Not available
1 Apr–30 Jun 2001	Not available	288 (261 in the Administrative Court)	Not available
County Court	**Total caseload**	**Total HRA affected cases**	**Impact on court**
2 Oct–31 Dec 2000	Not available	Less than 0.05% of total cases	For trials, increase from 3 hours 35 minutes to 3 hours 44 minutes
1 Jan–31 March 2001	Not available	Less than 0.01% of total cases	Not available
1 Apr–30 Jun 2001	Not available	Less than 0.01% of total cases	Not available
County Court	**Total caseload**	**Total HRA affected cases**	**Impact on court**
2 Oct–31 Dec 2000	Not available	168	Average hearing time up from 4.83 to 4.85 hours
1 Jan–31 March 2001	Not available	46	Average hearing time 4.48 hours.

Continued...

Table 2 Continued...

County Court	Total caseload	Total HRA affected cases	Impact on court
1 Apr–30 Jun 2001	Not available	4	Average hearing time 4.45 hours
Magistrates' courts	**Total caseload**	**Total HRA affected hearings**	**Impact on court**
2 Oct–31 Dec 2000	Not available	166	Throughput per sittinghour, down from 10.52 to 9.96
1 Jan – 31 March 2001	Not available	9	Throughput=11.90 (compared with 10.52 in the equivalent period of 2000)
1 Apr–30 Jun 2001	Not available	8	Throughput=10.30 (compared with 10.60 in the equivalent period of 2000)

The data in the third column of Table 2 suggests an initial period of experimentation on the part of advocates in the courts of first instance, followed by a substantial tailing-off of interest (for example, 277 cases in the Criminal Division of the Court of Appeal and 166 in the magistrates' courts in the first quarter after implementation yet only 161 and 9 respectively in the second quarter). In other words, the pattern in practice rather supported that which had been quite widely anticipated ahead of implementation — of an initial flurry of human rights challenges and applications followed by a 'plateauing' of interest once a new equilibrium of understanding between parties and the courts had been established.

Overall, then, any speculation ahead of implementation that the Human Rights Act would cause major disruption in the courts did not materialise: '... there does not seem to be the flood of spurious or vexatious challenges which might have damaged public confidence in the operation of the Act ... '[36] There was not even the '... significant impact ... ' that had been predicted at least as an initial response.[37]

[36] Joint Committee on Human Rights, Implementation of the Human Rights Act 1998 (2000–01 HL 66, HC 332), Memorandum by the Home Office, para 20.
[37] A Finlay, 'The Human Rights Act: The Lord Chancellor's Department's Preparations For Implementation' [1999] *European Human Rights Law Review* 512ff, 514.

That said, it is fair to say that some of the other specific concerns raised in anticipation of implementation of the Act did indeed prove to be realities in the courts. While arguably the difficulties were over-emphasised initially in terms of the likely number of challenges and their possible negative outcomes, the problem areas were in the main correctly predicted in the institutional training programmes and by practitioners at the sampled courts. This assertion was evident in the following litigation:

> In bail procedures, the requirement for evidence to be adduced in cases of breach (Bail Act 1976, section 7) is confirmed by the decision in *R (Director of Public Prosecutions) v Havering Magistrates' Court; R (McKeown) v Wirral Borough Magistrates' Court.*[38]
>
> In *St Brice v Southwark London Borough Council*,[39] a claim under Article 6 for further notice to be given of the issuance of a possession order was rejected.
>
> In *R (M) v Commissioner of Police for the Metropolis*,[40] it was suggested that the police were not bound to provide ideal conditions for consultations with lawyers and that an interview in a cell was acceptable.
>
> In *Moran v DPP*,[41] it was accepted that there is no need to give reasons when dismissing an application for no case to answer. But in *Hyams v Plender (Practice Note)*[42] a litigant who is refused permission to appeal from a decision of a lower court should be given reasons. In *Flannery v Halifax Estate Agencies Ltd*,[43] the Court of Appeal granted an appeal on the basis that the judge had failed to give adequate reasons for his decision to prefer the evidence of one expert to another. Further elucidation was provided by the Court of Appeal in *English v Emery Reimbold & Strick Ltd.*[44] Reasons are necessary to the extent that a litigant must be able to understand how they won or lost — vital or critical issues should be identified and explained but not every factor which weighed with the judge.[45] Another limit on reason giving concerns the impact of the decision: 'Where a judicial decision affects the substantive rights of the parties we consider that the Strasbourg jurisprudence requires that the decision should be reasoned. In contrast, there are some judicial decisions where fairness does not demand that the parties should be informed of the reasoning underlying them. Interlocutory decisions in the course of case management provide an obvious example.'[46]

[38] [2001] 1 WLR 805.
[39] [2002] 1 WLR 1537.
[40] [2001] EWCA (Admin) 553.
[41] [2002] EWHC (Admin) 89.
[42] [2001] 1 WLR 32.
[43] [2000] 1 WLR 377.
[44] [2002] EWCA Civ 605.
[45] *Ibid*, para 19.
[46] *Ibid*, para 13.

The 'judgement summons' procedure used by the Family Division was declared incompatible with Article 6 in *Mubarak v Mubarak*[47] and so a new Practice Direction (Committal Applications) has been issued.[48]

The work of bailiffs and the issue of representation arose in *Newman (t/a Mantella Publishing) v Modern Bookbinders Ltd.*[49] It was emphasised by the Court of Appeal that in proceedings for contempt of court under s 92(1) of the County Courts Act 1984 against a person rescuing goods seized in execution under the process of a county court, adequate notice must be given of what was being alleged, both at the time of arrest by bailiffs under a warrant of committal and at the time of a court hearing. When it appeared that the contemnor could be facing imprisonment, it was important for the court to ask an unrepresented defendant whether he wished to be represented.

BEYOND THE IMMEDIATE EFFECTS

As indicated, the reality of these general patterns at national level was amplified in two further rounds of research interviews at the sample of case study courts around the country — one in autumn 2000, soon after implementation, and another almost a year later in summer/autumn 2001, when the aim was to take stock of the longer term implications.

In fact, the story revealed in the second round was hardly different from the first. The most important finding remained one of the general 'quietness' of the effect for the courts of the Act. In some contrast to the general expectations of a large proportion of those interviewed ahead of October 2000, most court officials expressed surprise after implementation at the very limited impact and regarded the whole state of affairs as something of a '… damp squib …'. At two of the County Courts, there were no cases recorded at all in the first six months, and only five at the largest in the sample. Similarly, at the Crown Court the number of Human Rights Act cases was very small indeed (at one of the court centres there was just one such case recorded), with most such cases involving Article 6 points.[50]

Moreover, at the magistrates' courts, the number of cases recorded was hardly any greater — three at one city court (one of the largest magistrates' courts in England and Wales), four at a county town court and seven at a London-based court. All such cases before magistrates were issues being brought within a criminal prosecution. For example, in one case which arose

[47] [2001] 1 FLR 698.
[48] [2001] 2 All ER 704.
[49] [2000] 2 All ER 814 .
[50] More precisely, there were 30 cases, producing 44 claims between 2 October 2000 and 31 March 2001. Of the 44 claims, 22 were at the sample magistrates' courts, 17 at the sample Crown Court sites and 5 at county courts; 22 related to Art 6. For the Scottish experience, see JW Raine and CP Walker, *The Impact on Courts and the Administration of Justice of the Human Rights Act 1998* (London, LCD Research Series 9/02, 2002) Appendix II.

in a prosecution for robbery, an unsuccessful Human Rights Act challenge was made to the court's refusal to make available a video link facility to a defendant, who it was claimed was 'vulnerable' along the same lines as vulnerable victims or witnesses within the Youth Justice and Criminal Evidence Act 1999. In another case at the same court, an issue of self-incrimination arose in relation to section 172 of the Road Traffic Act 1988, this being quickly dealt with because of the potential precedent that it might set in the same way as the Scottish case of *Brown v Stott*.[51] And in a further case at the same court, the question arose as to whether an application under section 135 of the Mental Health Act 1993 should have been made in the absence of the defendant and without prior notice of the hearing. Complaints under Articles 5, 6 and 8 were all dismissed.

In the cases encountered at the magistrates' courts, the most common categories concerned breaches of bail and whether or not such matters needed to be treated as trials with cross-examination of witnesses (therefore being subject to Article 6). At one court, for example, it was reported that one such case had led the justices' clerk to issue a clarifying memorandum to all legal staff at the court. In this memorandum, he had recommended no cross-examination of witnesses where defendants admitted the breach but in all other situations advised that the prosecution be given the opportunity to do so.

As indicated earlier, compliance with the Act was perceived as a particularly key issue within the magistrates' courts context in a number of respects, especially concerning courtroom behaviour and protocols and the respective roles of Bench and clerks. Many magistrates (and their clerks) were also quite anxious ahead of implementation about the new expectations, notably around giving reasons for decisions, and about their implications for the pace of progress in case handling. Accordingly the research involved courtroom observational work at three of the magistrates' courts and monitoring to ascertain the impact of the Act on the conduct of the cases and of the time spent in reaching decisions (with 'before and after' samples — some 132 cases being observed in the pre-implementation period and a similar number (137) in the post-implementation period).

As perhaps might have been anticipated, the *numbers* of 'retirements' by magistrates[52] to decide cases did not vary significantly between the pre-implementation and post-implementation samples (in about 22 per cent of the cases observed in the pre-implementation sample and in 24 per cent of the cases in the post-implementation sample). However, a slight increase was noted in the average *length of time* spent in 'retirement' (by the lay bench)

[51] [2001] 2 WLR 817, as applied in *HM Advocate v McLean* 2001 SLT 189.

[52] Because lay magistrates usually sit as panels of three, it is common practice for them to leave the court-room and 'retire' to a separate room to discuss the evidence they have heard and to formulate their decisions before returning to make their pronouncements.

between the samples — from 15.4 to 19.5 minutes over the two courts. The extent to which this could be confidently attributed to the effect of the Human Rights Act and particularly to the need to 'formulate reasons' was, of course, a more difficult issue on which to reach a conclusion. The observational work was confined to the courtroom only, and the researchers therefore had no direct knowledge of how time was assigned within the retiring room, for example, between deciding verdict and sentence and formulating reasons.

Considerable variance was noted from the courtroom in the individual case lengths (ranging from 5–35 minutes) that was probably attributable to a number of different factors (of which formulating reasons was but one). Nevertheless, at one of the courts at least, the unequivocal view of the practitioners tended to support the conclusion from the pre- and post-implementation case-time analysis and was that the giving of reasons *had* made a significant difference to the length of sittings — indeed, this, it was said, had been formalised in a policy decision to allow an extra half hour per trial in scheduling cases expressly to allow for the formulation and articulation of reasons. Moreover, while the extension of average case lengths had not reached the point where extra court sittings had became necessary, it was pointed out that partly this was due to the offsetting effect of the court requiring prior notice from the prosecution and defence parties of any anticipated Human Rights Act issues (which could be addressed in pre-trial reviews, thus clawing back some court-time that might otherwise have been absorbed).

One further aspect from the observational research in this context, concerned the practice of court clerks joining magistrates in the retiring room to provide advice. In this respect, in the post-implementation sessions observed, of the occasions when the Bench retired, the clerk was asked to join magistrates on less than half of them (46 per cent). In only one of these cases was the public court informed of the nature of the advice given (despite the advice given ahead of implementation that it would be wise so to do from the point of view of compliance).[53]

Regarding the time taken to pronounce the Bench's decisions and to articulate the associated reasons, the courtroom monitoring yielded an average time of 3.3 minutes for those cases on which the Bench had retired (and with a range from 1.5 minutes to 5 minutes). In cases where the Bench had not retired (including the cases heard by the District Judges

[53] The advice concerned whether the defendant had the right to choose between having the case heard in the Crown or magistrates' court. The doubt emanated from the fact that the offence had been committed when the defendant was a juvenile, but at the time of the case he was, legally, an adult. It is also relevant here to note that in this case (as in several others) the researchers were asked by the clerk about their role in court — so it is possible that awareness of the monitoring process may have affected behaviour on this occasion.

(the professional lawyer magistrates), the average time taken to make the announcements was distinctly shorter — with the overall average being approximately 1.75 minutes. Here, again, however, the individual circumstances and nature of decisions/reasons required in different types of case would clearly have some bearing on the time taken (and indeed, it seemed very likely that most of the cases on which retirements took place would be those involving the more complex or multiple decisions/reasons).

Overall, then, the research suggested that, at least in the early period after implementation, the Human Rights Act had had only small effects on time frames in case processing times in court and these were mostly not of great concern to the courts in terms of pressures of time and associated resources. As one justices' clerk argued, variation in case lengths on any particular day, and sometimes the effects of just one or two individual cases on a typical list, would probably be of more significance in determining the length of sittings than the effects of Human Rights Act compliance in relation to the 'giving of reasons'.

Nor did the prior concerns about reason giving in the magistrates' courts prove in practice to be wholly justified in the light of implementation of the Act. In this respect, the observational research involved assessments of the 'clarity', 'fluency' and 'conciseness' of articulation by the presiding magistrate (on five point scales ranging from 'excellent' to 'poor'), and the results were fairly uniform and generally quite positive at each court. While overall, District Judges scored slightly better than the lay Benches in terms of 'conciseness' and 'fluency', and while the lay bench at one court consistently scored more highly than the others, very few 'weak' presentations were observed. Often the decisions/reasons given seemed somewhat 'rehearsed' (ie, with all the required information presented in an apparently standard manner — as if following a model script) and usually the stated reasons were given in quite general terms (for instance, explaining that the defendant had been found guilty of crime 'X' and so punishment 'Y' was applicable). In very few instances was there much in the way of elaboration as to the thinking behind the decisions or, for example, reference made to specific statutes or case law, this reticence probably reflecting the fact the justices' clerks had advised magistrates against taking the matter of 'giving reasons' further than was absolutely necessary.

Within 6–12 months of implementation, most bench chairs with whom the matter was discussed reported feeling reasonably confident about constructing and articulating reasons. At one court, the point was made by the justices' clerk that the priority in raising standards of communication in the courtroom should now be less with magistrates and more with clerks — some of whom, he felt, needed to be able to demonstrate greater confidence in the courtroom, by projecting themselves and appearing more authoritative in their conduct of the cases. In this respect the justices' clerk perceived the need for court clerk training programmes to be extended from their traditional law and practice focus to include skills of communication and public speaking.

Likewise in relation to other matters of concern ahead of implementation, the Act in practice seemed to have had comparatively little impact on the practices and procedures of the courts. For example, in relation to the treatment of unrepresented defendants, the research study identified little evidence of any substantive shifts in policies and practices. In relation to fine enforcement courts (where so many defaulters tend to be unrepresented), a carefully planned scheme at one court to abandon the traditional default hearings before magistrates in favour of 'fines clinics' to be run by administrative staff, was quietly shelved (although at another of the courts visited a similar scheme of 'lay presenters' was indeed implemented into the fines courts).

Similarly, despite the fact that some of the courts had indicated their intention to be more active in encouraging referrals to duty solicitors of any defaulters at risk of imprisonment, the research study identified little evidence of this happening in practice. Two factors seemed mainly to account for the limited nature of change in this context. First, it was apparent in the first year of the Act that some of the practicalities still had to be worked out (such as training administrative staff in conducting means enquiries and arranging back-up for them in relation to their 'normal' duties). Secondly, there seemed to be rather more confidence six months on that previous practices might after all be acceptable in terms of human rights compliance. Perhaps the main visible change in this respect concerned the role of court clerks in fine default courts, where they were clearly seen to be undertaking a much less dominant role and profile than in the past (leaving the enquiry and scrutiny process to the magistrates and confining their own role to that of information-gathering only).

In much the same way, little evidence was found of the Act actually leading to significant change in arrangements for handling prisoners — another aspect of prior concern in relation to compliance. At none of the courts were any significant problems raised in relation to prisoner handling — indeed, only one such instance was reported, this being a query by a solicitor about the magistrates' retirement over lunch time while a prisoner remained in the cells (though this was given short shrift). And at one of the Crown Court centres, forward plans for refurbishment/graffiti-removal work in the cells had still not taken place one year after implementation of the Act. Once again, it seemed that initial fears of challenges in relation to humane treatment had dissipated to a considerable extent. On the other hand, it was interesting that, at one court, the tables were turned and the Act used by the judges to limit the use of handcuffs in the courtroom (against the requests and wish of the private security firms responsible for prisoner escort services and in the light of a series of 'escapes').

CONCLUSIONS

The assessment of the full implications of the Human Rights Act on the courts must, of course, be an ongoing process. Although the research study reported in this chapter offers many important insights on the impacts, these need to be qualified by recognition that the European Convention on Human Rights is regarded as a 'living instrument', the implications of which can be expected to develop over time. There is also the proviso, already demonstrated from the Scottish experience, that just one case from the higher courts (for example, in relation to the security of tenure of part-time judges)[54] can inflict widespread and lasting dislocation on the courts' processes.

Nevertheless, one year after enactment at least, the clear message from the research was that the Human Rights Act had *not* had the impact that many anticipated in relation to the number or complexity of challenges. The consensus experience to date has been that relevant court business has been fairly tranquil. Furthermore, as time has elapsed, the likelihood seems to have diminished that this could be 'the lull before the storm'. Instead the research study recorded a growing view among court practitioners that, on the whole, the Human Rights Act is now unlikely to create significant additional workload for first instance courts, although that is not to ignore its importance in relation to particular cases. Moreover, some of the other concerns that were very apparent in the period ahead of implementation, notably regarding the giving of reasons and the conduct of means enquiries in the magistrates' courts, have also proved to be less worrying than was envisaged, and indeed, practice has quickly become quite routinised and instinctive for most of those concerned.

With the benefit of hindsight, an obvious question is whether all the careful preparatory work that most courts undertook was indeed necessary or worthwhile. But on this issue the widespread view of the court practitioners at least was that, given all the uncertainties about impacts, it

[54] See *Starrs v Ruxton* 2000 SLT 42. See also: *Gibbs v Ruxton* 2000 SLT 310; *Lafarge Redland Aggregates v Scottish Ministers* 2000 SLT 1361; *McFarlane v Gilchrist* 2002 SLT 521; *Millar v Dickson* [2002] 1 WLR 1615; A O'Neill, 'The European Convention and the Independence of the Judiciary' (2000) 63 *Modern Law Review* 429ff. In *Stott v Minogue* 2000 SLT (Sh Ct) 25 an argument that there should be a positive declaration by a judge that he was not a Freemason was not sustained as the judicial oath and ethical duties provided sufficient safeguard. In Scotland, a resolution came in the form of the Bail, Judicial Appointments etc (Scotland) Act 2000. The matter was dealt with by administrative changes to terms of judicial appointment and conditions of service for part-time judicial office holders south of the border: Joint Committee on Human Rights, Implementation of the Human Rights Act 1998 (2000–01 HL 66, HC 332) evidence of Lord Irvine, q 45; Lord Chancellor's Department, Judicial Appointments Annual Report 2000–2001 Cm 5248, London, 2001) Annex C.

was both justified and appropriate to have undertaken that work. While many respondents were surprised at the comparatively low number of cases within which Human Rights Act issues were being raised, let alone, the very few substantive cases of a human rights nature *per se,* equally, a number suggested that this might in part at least be a reflection of the preparation work, and more importantly, the fact that the message had got about that the courts were well-prepared and were likely to give short shrift to spurious or ill-conceived applications. Equally apparent was the generally tardier pace at which many private practitioners had gained familiarity with the Act, meaning that there would probably be some reluctance on the part of all but the foolhardy and the specialist human rights firms to raise human rights points or bring cases before the courts without being very sure of their grounds.

And confidence was undoubtedly quickly bolstered among the lay magistracy, in particular about their competence and authority under the new Act. While variance in skills with which different bench chairs now articulate and communicate their decisions and associated reasoning is likely to remain significant within a lay magistracy of around 30,000 part-time volunteers, the courts in general have certainly not been found wanting, and, indeed, as the research revealed, have earned themselves some praise and respect from professional practitioner quarters along the way.

Nor, as the research study demonstrated, has the Act added significant pressures to the resource base of the courts — with only slight increases in case lengths (especially in the magistrates' courts as a result of the requirement to formulate and articulate reasons for all decisions). Within a context of general constraint on resources in criminal justice, this has been a considerable relief to court managers, as there seemed little prospect at the time of the study of obtaining additional clerks, prosecutors and other personnel.

But what of the impact of the Human Rights Act upon the *legal culture and ethos* of the courts? In this respect, most people interviewed in the research study were of the view that, despite the very limited workload or resource implications, there was from the outset a discernible effect in terms of greater consciousness of human rights issues, as a result of the requirement of compliance. While, as one practitioner argued, '... it would be an overstatement to talk (yet) of a human rights culture descending on the courts ... ,' the research did highlight a continuing preoccupation within the courts (at least through the first year) with the Act and with the associated compliance issues. This suggested that a new perspective had indeed come to be adopted into the thinking of most professionals, which in turn was having its effect in rethinking and, in some cases, reshaping both the minutiae of many operational practices and some more strategic matters of policy.

Yet, the limited practical impacts in terms of resource effects and case-loadings, and the apparent ease with which the courts immediately coped with the Human Rights Act — without the need for substantive adjustments — could be a hindrance to a more fundamental reformation and development of a more rights-conscious environment within the courts. Indeed, even early on in the life of the Human Rights Act, there were signs that indicated that responses were becoming routinised, such as through local protocols agreed between the courts and local defence solicitors that prior notice would be expected before Convention challenges were raised at court. As a result, there is still some considerable distance still to be travelled before the Human Rights Act can achieve its full and intended potential in the courts.[55]

[55] It follows that the establishment of a more proactive and systematic human rights commission remains a live issue. See Joint Committee on Human Rights, The Case for a Human Rights Commission (2002–03 HL 67). The case for a Commission for Equality and Human Rights has been accepted by the government (HL Debates vol 654, col 54wa, 30 October 2003, Lord Falconer), and the appointment of a 'champian' of this kind is timely in view of the report finding by the Audit Commission (Human Rights: Improving Public Services, London, 2003, para 37) that the impact of the Human Rights Act is in danger of stalling in public services.

6

The Effectiveness of National Human Rights Institutions

STEPHEN LIVINGSTONE AND RACHEL MURRAY*

INTRODUCTION

STARTING WITH THE National Consultative Commission on Human Rights, established in France in 1947 the period since the end of the Second World War has witnessed a significant growth in National Human Rights Institutions (NHRIs). The Vienna Conference on Human Rights provided a significant boost to the development of such institutions by calling for 'the establishment and strengthening of national institutions on human rights'[1] and there are now over sixty of these institutions around the world. Such institutions come in a variety of shapes and sizes with great differences in their authority, composition, remit and powers. At best such institutions mark a recognition that the growing range of international human rights standards are not self-executing and that if rights are to become a reality for many people then there must be a public institution whose task is to promote and protect them, especially where government,

* It is with great sadness that the editors and co-author of this chapter report that Stephen Livingstone disappeared in March 2004 and is now sadly presumed dead. Stephen had displayed a commitment and enthusiasm for the cause of human rights since student days at Cambridge, and made huge contributions, practically and academically, to the greater understanding of human rights. For many years chair of the Committee for the Administration of Justice in Northern Ireland, he became a familiar and much respected figure on the Northern Irish legal scene. He taught briefly at Nottingham University, becoming an expert on the ECHR long before the human rights revolution began in the UK. Moving back to Queen's University Belfast, he became, fittingly, Professor of Human Rights Law. He wrote or co-wrote countless articles and contributed to a number of books, including *Prison Law* (now in its third edition), which he co-wrote with Tim Owen QC and Alison Macdonald. He will be remembered with much love and respect, not only at Queen's, but among human rights scholars throughout the world.

[1] Vienna Declaration, para 36.

courts and the media are unwilling or unable to do so. In many parts of the world NHRIs are promoted as a way of making rights accessible, especially to poor and marginalised people who may lack the resources or knowledge to access lawyers and the courts. At worst though they can become mere apologists for governments with little interest in the protection of human rights, both on the domestic and international stage. Such apologies may be all the more insidious if the NHRI is presented as being 'independent'.

Mindful of these risks the UN has sought to provide a definition of an NHRI[2] and to develop certain standards and criteria against which these institutions should be measured. The main guidelines are the 'Paris Principles', adopted by the UN General Assembly in 1993,[3] which have been applied in their dealings with states and institutions and upheld by other organisations and individuals as the benchmarks against which a National Human Rights Institution should be measured.[4] The Paris Principles set out good practice on the legal basis for an NHRI, how it should be appointed, who should be appointed to it, its funding arrangements, remit and powers. However, they offer relatively little on what such a body should do and how we can assess its success or failure. Until relatively recently most literature on NHRIs was produced by such bodies themselves and focused on what powers they had and what they did with them.[5] Issues of how best an NHRI can promote and protect human rights were not extensively discussed but as more such bodies are established these matters are becoming of increasing importance, notably for people who become members or staff of such organisations but also for all the other parts of society which interact with them.

The establishment of the Northern Ireland Human Rights Commission (NIHRC) in the Northern Ireland Act 1998, following the commitments given to create both this institution and its Irish equivalent in the Belfast/Good Friday Agreement,[6] provided an ideal opportunity to us, as researchers based in Northern Ireland, to conduct such an assessment.

[2] 'A body which is established by a government under the constitution, or by law or decree, the functions of which are specifically defined in terms of the promotion and protection of human rights', United Nations, National Human Rights Institutions. *A Handbook on the Establishment and Strengthening of National Institutions for the Promotion and Protection of Human Rights*, Professional Training Series, 4 (1995), para 39.

[3] Principles Relating to the Status and Functioning of National Institutions for Protection and Promotion of Human Rights.

[4] See *National Human Rights Institutions. Best Practice*, Commonwealth Secretariat (2001) 1.

[5] We would say until recently as two publications in particular have seen a move away from this trend, namely *Protectors or Pretenders?: Government Human Rights Commissions in Africa* (New York, Human Rights Watch, 2001) and *Performance and Legitimacy: National Human Rights Institutions* (International Council on Human Rights Policy, 2000). We have drawn extensively on both of these reports in our study.

[6] This also provided for a number of other institutions including an Equality Commission which unified the previous Fair Employment Commission, Equal Opportunities Commission (NI), Commission for Racial Equality (NI) and the Disability Council.

While focusing on the Northern Irish Commission in its first years we decided also to look at the South African Commission on Human Rights (SAHRC). The South African Commission had been established in 1995 and like the Northern Irish commission was established after a political agreement designed to transform a political conflict in a deeply divided society, a conflict where claims of human rights abuse had played a major role. This is one of the main contexts in which NHRIs are established, though they have also been set up in societies where the government has come in for significant criticism of its human rights record[7] and in societies with generally good human rights records.[8] Despite the significant differences in the two societies, the fact that both were established as part of peace agreements and in similar legal systems led us to believe that we could draw upon the longer experience of South Africa to help us examine Northern Ireland.

THE AIMS OF OUR PROJECT

Our project had three main objectives:

1. To develop criteria for evaluating the effectiveness of NHRIs. These criteria would draw upon but go beyond the Paris Principles to look especially at how an NHRI has used the powers and resources given to it and what impact this had on the promotion and protection of human rights.
2. To use these criteria in assessing the performance to date of one NHRI, namely the Northern Ireland Human Rights Commission. We also aimed to look at the work of the SAHRC, not as a full comparison but to help us to refine our analysis of the NIHRC.
3. To draw upon the critical analysis of the NIHRC and South African Commission in order to make recommendations with regard to the composition, powers, resources and operation of human rights commissions, with particular reference to other potential commissions in the United Kingdom.

SETTING BENCHMARKS: EVALUATING THE EFFECTIVENESS OF A HUMAN RIGHTS COMMISSION

Given the variety in the character of NHRIs and the different contexts within which they operate it is difficult to develop a single set of criteria

[7] For example in Nigeria or Indonesia.
[8] For example Australia or Canada. It is notable in such societies that much of the NHRI's work has focused on the treatment of marginalised groups in society, notably indigenous peoples.

which can be applied to all of them to assess their effectiveness. Even among those organisations that fund the establishment of national institutions, there does not appear to have been clear guidelines or benchmarks against which the funding is assessed. Indeed, it has been noted that the United Nations Development Programme and the United Nations High Commissioner for Human Rights have been too quick to provide funding without evaluating the extent to which it is used effectively or evaluating the effectiveness of the organisation to which it is being given.[9] A very simple measure would be to ask to what extent the human rights record of a country had improved since an NHRI began operating. Leaving aside the difficulties of assessing the extent to which a state's human rights record has 'improved' or 'declined'[10] this may be inappropriate for a number of reasons. The main one is that the work of an NHRI is likely to be only one influence on the condition of human rights in a state, it will often be difficult to decide what is attributable to its work and what is attributable to the work of others. It is perhaps easier to begin by giving examples of what are generally seen as effective and ineffective commissions. Those that are seen as effective display a willingness to engage with the most serious human rights issues in a society, are prepared to challenge powerful groups (especially government) where they feel such groups are failing to fulfil their responsibility to protect human rights, enjoy a prominent place in public discourse on human rights, are well respected both nationally and internationally (especially by human rights NGOs and also by government even if it does not always agree with the NHRI) and are professional in their dealings with others. Those viewed as ineffective at worst become simply apologists for government abuses of human rights.[11] Even if they do not engage in this they may fail to engage with the key human rights issues in a society, put less emphasis on protection activities and instead focus on 'softer' work such as education, demonstrate reluctance to challenge government, fail to develop good relationships with other key actors and lack administrative competence.

Rather than seek an absolute measure of effectiveness we felt it was better to set out a series of benchmarks against which to evaluate an NHRI. Such benchmarks allowed us to take account of the variety of different circumstances in which NHRIs are established (especially as regards their composition, resources and powers) and to assess them in relative rather than absolute terms. We sought to develop our benchmarks

[9] Human Rights Watch, *Protectors or Pretenders? Government Human Rights Commissions in Africa* 77.

[10] M Green, 'What do we talk about when we talk about Indicators: Current Approaches to Human Rights Measurement' (2001) 23, *HRQ*, 1062ff.

[11] For example if they are involved in the drafting of reports to international bodies which deny or justify human rights abuses.

drawing upon reflection on the purposes for which such institutions are established, literature by such organisations themselves and previous literature in the field, including the studies by Human Rights Watch and the International Council on Human Rights Policy referred to earlier. Work on the effectiveness of NGOs in the human rights field was also valuable in this task[12] and organsational literature was particularly useful in examining the internal functioning of the commission as an organisation and the importance of leadership.[13] While not a formal evaluation, the approach we have adopted draws on literature on evaluations[14] and includes elements of both *Accountability Evaluation* — which is primarily concerned with outcomes and *Develop-ment Evaluation* — which looks more to providing ideas on how an institution might be developed and improved.[15]

Using the above material we attempted to identify a number of benchmarks and indicators to evaluate the success of a national human rights commission. We found that there were a considerable number of issues which had an impact on the ability of a commission to be effective and that each impacted on the others. In addition, it was the combination of factors, rather than one alone, which seemed important. We saw in the course of our research that one needed to separate out those factors which were within the control of the institution itself, and those which were not. In addition, it seemed important that an effective national commission was one which had a certain level of resources, used them to their fullest effect, and was perceived as legitimate in the eyes of the public and key stakeholders in society. It was thus useful to separate out our criteria in the light of these considerations. We therefore identified 18 benchmarks against which national commissions could be established and divided these into three categories. These are:

1. *Capacity* — which refers to the NHRIs powers, resources, composition and the context within which it operates.
2. *Performance* — which looks at how an NHRI exercises the powers given to it.
3. *Legitimacy* — which considers its standing and relationships.

[12] A Hudson, 'Organising NGOs International Advocacy: Organisational Structures and Organisational Effectiveness', presented at the NGOs in a Global Future Conference, University of Birmingham, 11–13 January 1999, on file with author, at 13.

[13] See, eg J Kotter and J Heskett, *Corporate Culture and Performance* (Simon and Schuster Free Press, 1992); C Handy, *Understanding Organisations* (Penguin, 1997); Mullins, *Management and Organisational Behaviour* (6th edn, FT Prentice Hall, 2001).

[14] See T Newburn, 'What do we mean by Evaluation? (2001) 15 *Children and Society* 5–13; M Morris and LR Jacobs, 'You Got a Problem with That? Exploring Evaluators' Disagreements about Ethics' (2000) 24(4) *Evaluation Review* 384–406.

[15] See E Chelimsky 'Thoughts for a New Evaluation Society' (1997) 3 *Evaluation* 97–118.

Capacity

There are a number of factors that are key for a commission's effectiveness which are determined at its creation. The conditions under which a commission are created lay the foundations for its future effectiveness. Although there are examples of national human rights institutions being established in ideal situations, limitations in this regard have an impact on the extent to which they can be effective. The Paris Principles, in particular, focus on many of these issues;

- Legal status: a clear legal foundation for the establishment of such a body
- Protection of its independence, from both government and others
- Political support in its creation, the process of establishing a commission is critical to its success[16]
- Political context in which they are established and the need for independent and democratic state institutions
- Adequate powers and resources to fulfill its mandate; broad mandate and defined jurisdiction
- The necessary financial resources
- Clarity of the role of Commissioner, and their role vis-à-vis staff of the commission

Performance

Although the manner in which a commission is established can impact on its effectiveness, it is also clear that even those established in the ideal conditions can fail to deliver. There are numerous factors that are within the commission's control which can determine its effectiveness:

- The Commission must have a clear strategic plan for the most effective use of what may be limited resources
- It must make full use of the powers and resources that it does have
- It must have a coherent management and internal structure and operational efficiency
- It should be influential, a catalyst for change
- It should be able to deal with crises and reflect on its own problems

[16] International Council on Human Rights Policy, *Performance and Legitimacy: National Human Rights Institutions* (Switzerland, IPPR, 2000) 106–7.

Legitimacy

These matters again fall partly beyond the commission's control but are central in determining the extent to which it can be effective. A NHRI which is performing well would enjoy widespread legitimacy, but this cannot be taken for granted. Legitimacy requires consideration of its standing in the eyes of others and the nature of the relationship it has with others.

Factors which are relevant here include:

- The relationship with the government: A human rights commission is in a difficult position. Its legitimacy and credibility and therefore effectiveness, depend on its ability to be perceived as independent of the government, yet the manner of its creation and its special status derives from its closer relationship with the government than that which, for example, an NGO would have
- Accountable and regular relationship with the legislature
- Build upon, yet remain independent from, NGOs and civil society
- Carve out a role for itself amidst other statutory or constitutional bodies
- Must be accessible
- Must develop a clear coherent media and communication strategy

METHODOLOGY

Having set out these benchmarks we then sought to draw on a wide range of evidence to assess the experience of the Northern Ireland Human Rights Commission in relation to them. We looked at the published documentation of the Commission itself, in the form of its press releases, publications, minutes and annual reports. As required by the legislation establishing the Commission it had conducted its own evaluation of its powers and effectiveness after two years, which the government eventually responded to.[17] Before, and in the course of our project, the NIHRC was subjected to a number of other examinations. These included reports it commissioned into its organisation and effectiveness from consultants Peter Hosking[18] and Roger Courtney. We were given access to the

[17] Northern Ireland Human Rights Commission, *Report on Effectiveness: Report to the Secretary of State as Required by Section 69(2) of the Northern Ireland Act 1998*, (NIHRC, 2001). Northern Ireland Office, *The Government's Response to the Northern Ireland Human Rights Commission's Review of Powers Recommendations* (NIO, 2002).

[18] P Hosking, *The Northern Ireland Human Rights Commission. An Evaluation of its Powers, Effectiveness and Structure*, April 2001, on file with the author.

Hosking report but not that of Courtney. The UK Parliamentary Joint Committee on Human Rights also examined the NIHRC, reporting in July 2003, and we drew on both the final conclusions and the evidence presented to it.[19] The Commission has also been the subject of a fair amount of press attention, both that which it has generated and that which has been critical of it. Some, relatively recent data was available on public opinion regarding the Commission. We used this but did not feel it was useful to commission further surveys as it was not far enough away in time to do anything but replicate these surveys. Moreover, it was unlikely to tell us much more than the level of public awareness of the existence of the Commission, as opposed to an assessment of what it was doing.

We were able to draw on some quantitative data to assess the *activity* of the NIHRC (for example the number of complaints received and assisted or the number of submissions made to Parliament) but it was more difficult to use this to assess its *impact*. The Commission would often be only one of a number of actors seeking to change legislative proposals or influence judicial decisions.[20] It is difficult to say when their intervention is decisive as opposed to that of anyone else. Therefore, we decided to rely to a significant part on a series of semi-structured interviews with government, parliamentarians, NGOs, civil society, religious organisations, trade unions, the legal profession, academics and those who had used the Commission's services. Finally, we concluded with interviews of the staff and all commissioners themselves. We also conducted similar interviews in South Africa. The extensive use of interviews was particularly relevant to the study for two reasons. First, as in any case of studying the practices of an institution much of what takes place is not committed to written form, moreover it is important to know *why* things were done as well as *what* was done. Secondly, as already noted above, much of the literature about NHRIs is produced by such bodies themselves and represents their view of the world. Especially given our concerns with legitimacy it is important to speak to others with whom they have had dealings to assess how accurate that is. Working in a small jurisdiction gave us a good opportunity to have access to a number of key players who interacted with the Commission and hence an opportunity to assess its impact in practice.

[19] Joint Committee on Human Rights, *The Work of the Northern Ireland Human Rights Commission*, HL 132 HC 142 (2003).

[20] The Commission itself has alluded to this in its annual reports but has indicated in these that its own view has been that it has had a limited effect, especially on proposed legislation. This has also been echoed by the Chief Commissioner in another context, see B Dickson 'The Contribution of Human Rights Commissions to the Protection of Human Rights' [2003] *Public Law* 272, 280.

Before looking at our assessment of the NIHRC it is worth one final observation on the methodology and context in which we worked. From its creation the NIHRC was a controversial body, which some in Northern Ireland opposed from the beginning and others were unhappy with from the initial appointments. We were acutely aware of the difficulties of evaluating the effectiveness of an institution within a complex political environment[21] and the impact that our research could have on this.[22] However these issues became even more complex as divisions within the Commission widened, leading to a number of resignations discussed below. By the time we finished the research almost as many people had resigned from the Commission as remained on it.[23] Views about the performance of the Commission had become increasingly hardened and personalised. Since we had interviewed most of those with an interest in the Commission there was increasing interest in the outcome of our research and on more than one occasion people, from different perspectives, expressed concerns to us about what we would say. This included concern from people outside Northern Ireland on the impact of our views on the prospects for strengthening human rights commissions elsewhere.[24] This level of interest and concern placed us under more immediate pressure than is normal in academic research, especially as many of those on all sides of the debate were well known to us. We can only say that have had to carefully consider our role in this arena[25] and have striven hard to ensure that, by playing close attention to the original benchmarks we established, our conclusions are as independent and impartial as possible.

[21] See eg E Chelimsky and W Shadish (eds), *Evaluation for the 21st Century* (Thousand Oaks, CA, Sage, 1997); R Pawson and N Tilley, 'What Works in Evaluation Research?' (1994) 34 *British Journal of Criminology* 291–306; I Crow, 'Evaluating Initiatives in the Community' in V Jupp, P Davies and P Francis (eds), *Doing Criminological Research* (London, Sage, 2000).

[22] See RA Berk and PH Rossi, *Thinking about Program Evaluation* (Newbury Park, CA, Sage, 1990).

[23] When we finished our research in December 2003 a total of 7 members of the NIHRC remained active. During the period since the initial appointments 3 had resigned expressing dissatisfaction, 2 had withdrawn from active involvement on the same grounds, 1 had resigned for personal reasons but was also critical of aspects of the NIHRCs performance and 1 had been required to resign by legislation on standing for election for the Northern Ireland Assembly.

[24] As noted below the NIHRC has enjoyed high visibility and a good reputation internationally. It has contributed regularly to international forums on the developing and strengthening of NHRIs.

[25] See M Matassa and T Newburn, 'Problem-Oriented Evaluation? Evaluating Problem-Oriented Policing Initiatives', on file with author; E Chelimsky, 'Thoughts for a New Evaluation Society' 97–118; MQ Patton, *Utilization-Focused Evaluation* (Thousand Oaks, CA, Sage, 1997); JM Owen and PJ Rogers, *Program Evaluation: Forms and Approaches* (St Leonards, New South Wales, Allen and Unwin, 1999); H Newby, *Social Science and Public Policy* (Swindon, Economic and Social Research Council, 1993).

THE EXPERIENCE OF THE NORTHERN IRELAND HUMAN RIGHTS COMMISSION

Overview

The Northern Ireland Human Rights Commission, as established by the Good Friday/Belfast Agreement, was not the first body of its kind in the jurisdiction. The Northern Ireland Constitution Act 1973 provided for a Standing Advisory Commission on Human Rights (SACHR),[26] but, despite some successes,[27] it was not seen as an effective body given its lack of powers and perceived lack of independence.[28] By referring to the Human Rights Commission as a body which should be 'independent of government, with an extended and enhanced role beyond that currently exercised by the Standing Advisory Commission on Human Rights,' the Agreement gave some hope that it would be more successful than its predecessor.

The Good Friday/Belfast Agreement thus provides that Westminster legislation will create the NIHRC, 'with membership from Northern Ireland reflecting the community balance,' and whose tasks would include 'keeping under review the adequacy and effectiveness of laws and practices, making recommendations to Government as necessary; providing information and promoting awareness of human rights; considering draft legislation referred to them by the new Assembly; working in a Joint Committee with the Irish Commission on Human Rights; providing advice to the Secretary of State on the scope for additional protections beyond those contained in the Human Rights Act through a Bill of Rights for Northern Ireland, bringing court proceedings or providing assistance to individuals doing so.'[29] Subsequently, the Northern Ireland Act set out the powers and remit of the Commission, the method of its appointment and funding and to whom it is accountable. The Commission reports annually to the Secretary of State for Northern Ireland.[30]

All commissioners including the Chief Commissioner are appointed by the Secretary of State for Northern Ireland under the Code of Practice for Public Appointments. The Chief Commissioner is appointed separately, rather than from among members of the Commission, as is the practice in some institutions.[31] The Chief Commissioner, Brice Dickson, was

[26] Section 20(1) Northern Ireland Constitution Act 1973.
[27] Eg its 1987 report on employment discrimination influenced the Fair Employment Act 1989 and produced a number of other reports which were also seen as important and led to other legislation, although it was less successful in terms of influencing terrorism legislation, S Livingstone, 'The Northern Ireland Human Rights Commission' (1999) 22 *Fordham International Law Journal*.
[28] S Livingstone, *ibid*. SACHR was dissolved by the Agreement.
[29] Good Friday Agreement, Part IV, para 5.
[30] Para 5(1) Sched 7 of the NIA.
[31] For example, the South African Human Rights Commission.

appointed on 18 January 1999 and an additional nine commissioners appointed in March 1999. One commissioner, Angela Hegarty resigned in January 2001 and in November of that year all other existing Commissioners were confirmed in their positions[32] and four new commissioners were appointed. In September 2002 Christine Bell and Inez McCormack resigned with significant press attention.[33] Patrick Yu then resigned in July 2003 and two commissioners, Paddy Kelly and Frank McGuinness, have recently withdrawn from active service calling for the resignation of the chair.[34] Paddy Sloan, the Chief Executive, started her post on 1 November 1999, eight months after the Commission began. At present, besides the Chief Executive, the Commission employs 14 members of staff.[35] A number of others have been employed, including on the Bill of Rights project specifically, and there have been a number of interns and volunteers who have assisted the Commission. The NIHRC was given an initial annual operating budget of £750,000, which has recently been raised to £1.3 million.

Overall our conclusion is that the NIHRC to date has not proved as effective as many hoped it would and is struggling to make a significant impact on the promotion and, in particular, the protection of human rights in Northern Ireland. It is an organsation which has demonstrated significant industry and can claim some successes as regards the promotion of human rights and the publication of research studies. However, these are overshadowed by its problems. These include the failure to deliver on its major project, the provision of advice on a Bill of Rights, significant internal divisions leading to resignations and an ebbing of public confidence in the wake of its handling of the dispute at Holy Cross Girls School. Many of these problems spring from the context in which it has operated, notably the limited powers and resources it was given plus the very difficult and highly politicised context in which it must operate. Any human rights commission in Northern Ireland would have faced significant problems in these circumstances. They are arguably more difficult than those of the South African Commission, which also faced resource problems but a rather more favourable political context. However the NIHRC has not responded well

[32] With the exception of Christine Bell who was not confirmed in her position until early 2002.
[33] See, eg I McCormack, 'Comment/Analysis: North's Human Rights Body Cannot Deliver', *The Post.IE, Sunday Business Post Online*, Dublin, Ireland, 22 September 2002; I Graham, 'Ulster Human Rights Commissioners Quit', *The Independent*, 10 September 2002, http://news.independent.co.uk/uk/politics/story.jsp?story=331990; 'Human Rights Members Resign', 9 September 2002, http://news.bbc.co.uk/1/hi/northern_ireland/2247268.stm
[34] Chris McGimpsey also resigned in November 2003 upon nomination as an Ulster Unionist Party candidate for the Northern Ireland Assembly elections.
[35] Four administrative officers, a development worker, one assistant caseworker, an education worker, an information worker, three investigations workers, two research workers and a cleaner. Of these, four are occupying job-shared posts and there are twelve full time positions along with the post of chief executive and the vacant post of caseworker. These are appointed by the Commission, Northern Ireland Act 1998, Sch 7, s 4.

to these challenges. After exploring these issues in more detail through examination of the themes of capacity, performance and legitimacy we will outline some recommendations designed to improve the effectiveness of all NHRIs in general and the NIHRC in particular.

Capacity

The Commission was established by a statute rather than administrative fiat[36] and indeed in a statute that has the character of a constitutional provision. However, while human rights and equality provisions were seen as integral to the Agreement, it would not seem to the case that detailed attention to the mandate, composition and functions of the Commission was battled out at this stage of the process. This was not a particularly auspicious start, for what seems from reading the Agreement, to be the principal human rights institution for Northern Ireland. Our interviews with Northern Irish political parties and the two governments suggested that while nationalist parties were more interested than unionists in the creation of a Commission even they gave it much less priority than, for example, policing reform or prisoner release. While the UK government was supportive it was clearly much less convinced of the need for such an institution than, for example, South Africa where government worked with the Commission to establish a National Action Plan for the Protection of Human Rights.

From the start the NIHRC was dogged by criticism of its membership, with unionist politicians in particular claiming that this was not sufficiently 'representative of the community'.[37] While the initial appointments did reflect accurately the Protestant/Catholic community background percentages in Northern Ireland, unionists claimed that while none of those from a Protestant background had been clearly identified with unionist politics[38] two from a Catholic background had been involved in nationalist politics. Unionists opposed to the Agreement were especially scathing about the composition arguing that since it did not contain anyone avowedly anti-Agreement it could not, by definition be representative of the community. Our interviews suggested that this opposition had not been assuaged by the second round of appointments, which included a prominent pro-Agreement Unionist politician,[39] but that instead this appointment had concerned nationalists who now felt that political considerations

[36] Unlike, for example, the Prisons Ombudsman in the United Kingdom.
[37] As required by s 68(3) Northern Ireland Act 1998.
[38] Indeed some were accused of being pro nationalist largely because of their involvement in organisations which had worked on human rights in Northern Ireland.
[39] Chris McGimpsey, who subsequently resigned to run for the Northern Ireland Assembly.

were openly being taken into account in Commission appointments and that these were no longer being made on the basis of knowledge and commitment to human rights. What is also of concern is that government, which was responsible for the appointments and ostensibly made them on merit, seemed slow to defend the commissioners when they came under repeated attack in Parliament for being unrepresentative and too sympathetic to one community.[40]

In addition to concerns about *who* was appointed there were also concerns about *how* they were appointed. The fact that appointments were made by the Secretary of State meant that there would always be some suspicion as to how independent those appointed would be. While the positions were publicly advertised and an appointment panel, including some people from outside the Civil Service, established to make recommendations to the Secretary of State, the process was some way from being entirely transparent. There remains a degree of secrecy regarding, for example, what weight was given to each of the criteria for appointment and whether the panel's recommendations were always accepted. While a more transparent process might have done better to establish the independence of the Commission it must be acknowledged that some critics of the lack of transparency, notably from political parties, would have been a lot less vociferous if more of 'their people' had been appointed.

In respect of its powers the NIHRC did have the broad remit and most of the powers recommended by the Paris Principles. It was not confined to the rights guaranteed by the Human Rights Act but could look at a broader range of international treaties. However there were some significant gaps. Of particular concern has been the fact that while the legislation states that 'for the purpose of exercising its functions under this section the Commission may conduct such investigations as it considers necessary or expedient'[41] it contains no specific powers to compel individuals to talk to the Commission or provide it with documents during its investigations into particular matters. Although government gave undertakings during the passing of the legislation that government departments would cooperate with the Commission, the NIHRC always was of the view that this might prove problematic. This turned out to be the case when it began to conduct its first investigations and it was no surprise that when the Commission produced its review of powers and effectiveness after two years of its

[40] 'Having decided on appointments to the NIHRC, the NIO must stand by these choices and make clear its support for, and confidence in the impartiality of, the Commissioners it has appointed. ... We recommend that the NIO be more robust in support of the Commission, its work, its impartiality and its independence', Joint Committee on Human Rights, Fourteenth Report: Work of the Northern Ireland Human Rights Commission, 15 July 2003, HL 132, HC 142, at para 30.

[41] Section 68(8) Northern Ireland Act 1998.

existence stronger powers on investigations were at the top of its list. Although the Commission was very positive about the power to make recommendations on a Bill of Rights, several of the commissioners we interviewed having placed the opportunity to do this at the top of their reasons for applying to join the Commission, it may be wondered if it was wise to give this potentially massive task to a new body which already had many other difficult tasks. In South Africa, as in many other societies, the task of drafting a Bill of Rights was seen as an essentially *political* one with the Commission having the subsequent role of enforcing a Bill of Rights others had devised and committed themselves to. In Northern Ireland the Commission, whose political legitimacy was already in question following the appointments, would have to resolve a number of controversial issues and then push for its adoption with politicians who may have had little part in its creation.

If the powers were generally adequate this was certainly not true of resources. Initially the Commission was allocated only £750,000 per year, with the Chief Commissioner informing us efforts were made to reduce this to only £400,000 before he persuaded the United Nations High Commissioner on Human Rights to intervene with the government. How this was arrived at no one is very clear, even the responsible minister has suggested it may have been simply by multiplying the existing budget of SACHR by three.[42] This was clearly likely to prove inadequate, especially if the Commission was going to do anything significant in terms of investigations, supporting litigation and conducting a consultation on a Bill of Rights. The NIO made it clear that the Commission could seek supplementary budgets for programme activities but this only resulted in significant energy being diverted into financial negotiations. The Hosking review suggested that a budget of £1.5 million might be more appropriate for the Commission's activities. Interestingly the budget it is given has crept up towards this.

The relationship between commissioners and staff was largely left for the commissioners themselves to define. While it was important for the independence of the Commission that it got to appoint its own staff, unlike those of SACHR who were always seconded from the NIO, the absence of a previous organisation meant that staff as well as commissioners would be coming to the institution with little experience. Whereas in many parts of the world all or most of the commissioners are full time[43] government decided, in keeping with the tradition for regulatory commissions in the

[42] In his evidence to the Joint Committee on Human Rights, Minutes of Evidence, Mr Desmond Browne MP and Ms Kirsten McFarlane, 2 December 2002, para 75, http://www.publications.parliament.uk/pa/jt200203/jtselect/jtrights/132/2120203.htm

[43] South Africa for example has a mixture, with full time commissioners predominating.

United Kingdom, to make most of the appointments part-time. One former human rights commissioner from another jurisdiction, with extensive comparative experience, expressed doubts to us as to whether a predominantly part time commission can deal with the many issues likely to be presented to it. Only the Chief Commissioner was appointed on a full-time basis. This structure, plus the fact that the Chief Commissioner was appointed ahead of the other commissioners, created a potential tension between the role of Chief Commissioner as leader of the Commission, supported by other commissioners and staff, and their role as chair of a group of commissioners of equal status. Against this it must be said that most of those to whom we spoke commented favourably on the human rights expertise and commitment of those selected as commissioners, even if some questioned their political allegiances.

The issue of political allegiances leads us into the issue of context. The NIHRC was established in difficult political circumstances, after a period of conflict and violence. There are sharply differing views in Northern Ireland as to the extent to which human rights were infringed in that period and whose human rights were most under threat. These also lead to differences about what should be promoted in the future. In a context where human rights issues are matters of pressing political concern the NIHRC was always likely to be closely scrutinised as to whether it was giving an advantage to one political side or another, hence the close interest of politicians in its appointments. However, the situation was not entirely bleak. The Agreement also created the policing and criminal justice reviews. In both, the need to mainstream the protection of human rights as one of the key organising principles was quickly accepted. The creation of the Equality Commission and Police Ombudsman further strengthened the culture of rights in Northern Ireland and the means of their enforcement. The introduction of the Human Rights Act 1998, making the ECHR rights part of Northern Irish law, fulfilled a twenty-year-old demand of SACHR and one which had been echoed by many human rights NGOs in Northern Ireland. It gave the NIHRC what had long been denied to SACHR, a set of legally enforceable human rights standards on which to base its recommendations and the new litigation and investigation powers the NIHRC had been given. Finally, unlike the situation faced by SACHR, the Commission began life in circumstances of relative peace in Northern Ireland. Though the republican and loyalist ceasefires of the 1990s had not brought a complete end to political violence in Northern Ireland, this had diminished significantly.[44]

[44] For example statistics provided by the Police Service for Northern Ireland show that the number of deaths related to the security situation had declined from an average of 82 per year 1987–95 to 20 per year 1995–2002.

Performance

With regard to its performance, one key factor in a Commission's effectiveness, which a body with limited resources and powers can still ensure impact, is through defining a clear and coherent strategy for its work. This can be a particularly difficult task for a commission, as the experience in South Africa also illustrated. While the South African Human Rights Commission had a broad mandate and extensive powers, and it is possible to identify a number of themes that run across all aspects of its work, it has failed to project a clear overall strategy for its work. As a result it has been criticised, often on the more high profile issues in which it chooses, or not, to become involved. For example, despite having paid some attention in its work to HIV/AIDS, when it came to a case before the Constitutional Court which received international attention challenging the refusal by the government to provide drugs to pregnant women to prevent transmission of HIV,[45] the Commission was noted for its absence amid allegations of government pressure.

Developing a clear strategic plan has also proved difficult for the NIHRC. It took some considerable time over this, with discussions on the draft strategic plan continuing within the Commission for over a year. However, what emerged remained very broad and did not appear to set the Commission's priorities or provide a basis for deciding which among the many issues brought to it the NIHRC would focus on. The director of one human rights NGO working in Northern Ireland commented to us that it looked simply like a 'wish list', while an academic felt it left the Commission open to having its priorities set by whoever complained most loudly to it. Ultimately several commissioners acknowledged to us that little of what the NIHRC did in its first three years was guided by its strategic plan. The fact that commissioners spent so much time on the initial plan to produce such an unsatisfactory response suggests that while there was a lot of discussion of detail, issues of overall vision remained unclear.

This indeed has been a major problem for the NIHRC, with internal divisions opening shortly after its creation and widening to lead to a number of resignations. Divisions have emerged over a number of issues such as the content of the Bill of Rights, the extent to which the Commission should tackle the activities of non-state actors such as paramilitary groups as well state bodies, how strongly the Commission should push government on collusion allegations and the extent to which it should become involved in mediating high profile disputes. Many of these issues concern the role of human rights and what a human rights commission should do.

[45] *Minister of Health and Others v Treatment Action Campaign and Others*, Constitutional Court, CCT 8/02, 5 July 2002.

What is worrying is that while some within the Commission feel this has been fully explored, those who have resigned do not. One of the former commissioners stated to us that 'In a sense there was never, ever a serious discussion of what we consider the purpose of the NIHRC to be.' Instead there appears to have been allegations of bad faith, an increasing emphasis on proceduralism[46] and extensive leaking of divisions within the commission to those outside, including political parties and governments. Although these divisions existed from early in the Commission's life they were to be magnified in the context of responding to events, notably the crisis around the protests at Holy Cross Girls School, which will be discussed further below.

The Commission produced a second strategic plan for 2003–06 which does appear to be more focused and sets out a series of performance indicators. There is evidence here that it has learned from its early years. Even without a clear plan though the NIHRC did display impressive industry and make use of all its powers in its first three years. It has produced a significant range of reports, including some on very contentious, issues;[47] supported a small number of cases before the courts,[48] intervening as third party in some of these and taking cases in its own name, one of which included bringing a case before the House of Lords to confirm its power intervene as a third party.[49] It has undertaken a review of laws on those with mental health issues in Northern Ireland, and has proofed and submitted evidence on draft legislation before both Westminster and the Northern Ireland Assembly.[50] It has also appeared before various committees.[51]

[46] The minutes of the 9th Commission meeting on 9 September 1999, for example, disclose extensive discussion of minutes of previous meetings and concern by the Chief Commisioner that he has to obtain the agreement of all commissioners before making a statement.

[47] Eg *Baton Rounds: A Review of the Human Rights Implications of the Production and Use of the L21A1 Baton Round in Northern Ireland and Proposed Alternatives to Baton Round*, April 2003; *In our Care: Promoting the Rights of Children in Custody*, March 2002; *Enhancing the Rights of Lesbian, Gay and Bisexual People in Northern Ireland*, August 2001; *The Recording of the Use of Plastic Bullets in Northern Ireland*, May 2001, *Human Rights and the Victims of Violence*, July 2003

[48] See On-Going Report of the Commission's Activities, www.nihrc.org/files/On_Going_Report_1.htm

[49] Re Northern Ireland Human Rights Commission, [2002] UKHL 25; *Northern Ireland Human Rights Commission. In the Matter of an Application for Judicial Review*, NIQB 61, 8 December 2000.

[50] Eg NIHRC Response to the White Paper 'Legislation Against Terrorism', April 1999; Submission on the Family Law Bill (NI), May 2001; Anti-Terrorism, Crime and Security Bill, Brief from the Northern Ireland Human Rights Commission, Committee Stage, House of Lords, 28 November 2001; Suggested Amendments to the Justice (NI) Bill 2002; Comments on Assembly Ombudsman for Northern Ireland (Assembly Standards) Bill, September 2002; Response to the Draft Firearms (NI) Order 2002, October 2002; Response to the Coroners (practice and Procedure) (Amendment No 2) Rules (NI) 2002.

[51] For example, before the Northern Ireland's Assembly Committee re views on role of a Children's Commissioner for Northern Ireland.

The Commission has also submitted reports on reviews and policies of the government.[52] It has visited a number of prisons and places of detention in Northern Ireland, and initiated investigations into, for example, juvenile justice centres in Northern Ireland and the policing of parades.[53] It has worked with others to introduce human rights into the school curriculum in Northern Ireland and also done some broader public education on human rights. Much of this has been pursued through its work on proposals for a Bill of Rights for Northern Ireland. It began a major consultation on this in March 2000 and recently published a summary of the submissions received.[54] It published draft advice on a Bill of Rights in the form of a consultation document in September 2001,[55] but has yet to produce its final advice to the Secretary of State.

At the international level it has made submissions on UK government reports before various treaty monitoring bodies[56] and made statements at international meetings.[57] The Commission has placed most of its publications and minutes of its meetings on its website, produced one edition of a newsletter and training material on the Bill of Rights. The NIHRC has also produced guidance to public authorities in Northern Ireland and a booklet for the public on the Human Rights Act, and reported on a training programme for officers in the police service of Northern Ireland.[58] They have also commented on various documents produced by the police including their Code of Ethics and orders on handling threats and defence lawyers. It has also held and cooperated with others in the holding of a number of conferences.

Most of the NIHRC's output has been well received in terms of its quality although there are occasions when it has fallen short on this criteria, notably its report on victims where an opportunity to frame a debate of major public importance was missed.[59] However, of greater concern is

[52] For example, in relation to post-primary education.

[53] Northern Ireland Human Rights Commission, *In Our Care. Promoting the Rights of Children in Custody*, April 2002.

[54] Northern Ireland Human Rights Commission *Summary of Submissions on a Bill of Rights*, July 2003.

[55] Northern Ireland Human Rights Commission, *Making a Bill of Rights for Northern Ireland*, September 2001.

[56] For example, it submitted reports to the UN Committee on the Elimination of Discrimination Against Women, the Committee on Social Rights of the Council of Europe, the Council of Europe's Monitoring Committee on the Framework Convention for the Protection of National Minorities, the UN Committee on Economic, Social and Cultural Rights and the UN Committee on the Rights of the Child.

[57] For example, before the UN Special General Assembly on children's rights and the UN Commission on Human Rights, as well as the International Coordinating Committee of National Human Rights Institutions.

[58] Northern Ireland Human Rights Commission, *An Evaluation of Human Rights Training for Student Police Officers in the Police Service of Northern Ireland*, November 2002.

[59] Unlike South Africa, Northern Ireland has had no truth commission. However a number of specific official inquiries have already been undertaken, notably the Saville Tribunal into the

the lack of impact of its work. The NIHRC itself acknowledges that it has had relatively little impact on legislation or through the use of litigation. In respect of the former, the Chief Commissioner has stated 'like the purely advisory body which preceded us in Northern Ireland — the Standing Advisory Commission on Human Rights — we cannot honestly claim that the United Kingdom government has taken our concerns or legislative proposals seriously.'[60] In respect of the latter the only litigation 'success' it can point to in its 2000–03 review of activities is its appeal to the House of Lords on the scope of its own powers to intervene in litigation, a decision which restored powers it already thought it had. On the basis of the evidence we have looked at it is difficult to disagree with these conclusions. Limitations on its powers, as noted already, have constrained what it can do by way of investigations. Its human rights promotion activity has generally been well received, but this is overshadowed by the fact that it has failed to deliver on its main promotion task, providing advice on a Bill of Rights. Indeed concerns regarding both the management of the Bill of Rights process and its likely final content have been stressed both by those who have resigned and by many critics outside the Commission.

Perhaps due to divisions over strategic issues the Commission did not devote as much time to structural and management issues as it might have done. Initially it sought to work without a chief executive, throwing even more responsibility onto a heavily burdened Chief Commissioner. This was changed within six months but all those we spoke to agreed that important time was lost as a result. Initially it settled on a series of committees (rising to seven) for its various functions, with a staff member appointed in respect of each topic. This appears to have led to some confusion as to whether the staff were to do the work of the Commission, with commissioners having an oversight role, or whether commissioners were to do most of its work, with staff in a support role. The former would seem more appropriate for a predominantly part-time body and is now coming to be the case, after the reviews of Hosking and Courtney, with the number of committees reduced and more responsibility being given to

shootings by the Paratroop Regiment in Derry in 1972, and others may be announced following reports commissioned by the British and Irish governments by a former Canadian Supreme Court judge. Government also commissioned a report into the circumstances of victims. In addition there have also been a number of unofficial inquiries. While those imprisoned as a result of criminal convictions relating to the conflict have largely been released discussion of the issue of what to do about 'on the runs', those suspected of involvement in terrorist activity but never charged, raised again the question of what to do more generally about issues of truth, justice and the past. For an overview see C Bell 'Dealing with the Past in Northern Ireland' (2003) 26 *Fordham ILJ* 1095ff.

[60] B Dickson, 'The Contribution of Human Rights Commissions to the Protection of Human Rights' 272, 280.

staff. The role of the Chief Commissioner has remained a matter of dispute. Although he has indicated to us that both he and the NIO see the role very much as a chair of the Commission and first among equal of the commissioners others on the Commission, especially those who have resigned, have suggested that at times the leadership role has eclipsed the chairing one. As a result at times the Chief Commissioner appears frustrated that his freedom to respond quickly to events has been constrained while other commissioners have been concerned that he is departing from an agreed position. In South Africa, with a greater number of full time commissioners, the chair is elected by other commissioners rather than being appointed by government.

One issue where the actions of the Chief Commissioner became especially controversial was in respect of the Holy Cross dispute. This arose in the summer of 2001 when Protestant parents sought to block the route normally taken by children to a Catholic girls primary school. The dispute received international media coverage, focusing especially on the actions of the protestors, including at one time throwing urine over those walking to school, and the distress of the children. There were clear tensions within and without the NIHRC over what its role should be. Initially it issued a statement referring to the rights of all sides but stressing the priority of childrens' rights. Subsequently though it decided commissioners could walk with the children through the protest, sometimes it appeared as commission representatives, at other times in their individual capacity. The Commission also investigated the possibility of taking legal action against the police for their handling of the demonstration. A full Commission decided not to do so after taking legal advice[61] but the Commission's casework committee subsequently decided to support an application by a parent raising similar issues. In response to concerns expressed by the Chief Constable of the RUC, the Chief Commissioner subsequently wrote to him indicating that he and a number of other commissioners did not agree that the police action breached the Human Rights Act. This decision was criticised within the Commission as a breach of confidentiality and the Parliamentary Joint Committee subsequently expressed concern that it jeopardised the Commission's independence. While there is insufficient time here to go into this complex and controversial dispute in full it can be observed that nearly everyone within and without the Commission agreed its involvement with Holy Cross proved a disaster and magnified its internal divisions under the pressure of responding to a controversial event.

[61] Which appears to have focused as much on the Commission's standing as on the substance of the issue.

Legitimacy

The need for government support for the Commission's work is particularly important given the manner in which the Commissioners are appointed, as detailed above. More generally, it is important that a human rights commission is able to have some influence over government and in this regard must be respected and taken seriously by it. Yet, there have been considerable criticisms of the relationship between the Commission and the main government department with which it interacts, the NIO. As noted, the Commission has had little impact on legislation and has frequently complained that it has not been adequately consulted on legislative proposals. The issue of funding has continued to be a matter of dispute and when the government finally responded, after 14 months, to the Commission's review of powers document it accepted only three of the 25 recommendations. Most significantly it rejected the recommendations on investigations, advancing arguments that clearly could have been produced in 1998 and were not based on subsequent experience.

The Commission has consistently come under attack from unionist parties. Most of this has been centred around its appointments and composition.[62] However, in recent months there has been increased dissatisfaction from among nationalist parties about the manner in which the Commission is functioning, without a notable decline in unionist concerns. The depth of the lack of confidence from across the political spectrum is clearly indicative of a crisis point in the history of the Commission.

The Commission should be accountable to Parliament and to the public which it serves. Operating within a particular constitutional context, it was essential that the NIHRC be accountable not only to Westminster, but in particular to the Northern Ireland Assembly. The latter was clearly fundamental for its legitimacy. Yet, the Commission has been deprived of the opportunity to develop its relationship further with the Assembly given its suspension and dissolution. This could have been the main way for the Commission to interact with the politicians. There is no sense of normalcy in this regard.

The relationship with NGOs has in general been positive with many organisations having been supportive of the Commission's work. The NIHRC has been praised especially for its accessibility and willingness to meet those not previously involved in human rights work. However, it is significant that those NGOs most active and internationally respected in terms of human rights work in Northern Ireland have been most dissatisfied with the Commission's work to date. Such organisations had especially high hopes for the Bill of Rights and now appear to be confused and deflated as to the way forward on this.

[62] See ch 2.

The Commission was established along with numerous other statutory bodies as part of the Agreement and has had to fit itself in between these, many of whom have potentially overlapping mandates. It has generally worked out its relationship with them through Memoranda of Understanding,[63] the process of discussing which has generally facilitated the relationship in practice. These, it sees, as allowing it to '*complement* the work of others, not repeat it.'[64]

One relationship which appears to be underdeveloped is that with the media. Several journalists to whom we spoke commented that it was a fairly low profile organisation, one suggested lower profile than the Federation of Small Businesses, and that stories about its difficulties were more likely to be covered than stories about its activities. The way it had handled Holy Cross did not appear to have helped with even journalists interested in human rights claiming they were confused as to what the Commission's position was. It was noted that the NIHRC lacked a clear media strategy and that while the Chief Commissioner was very approachable, the Commission had difficulties in responding to inquiries when he was unavailable. Overall it did not appear that the NIHRC had established itself as the first port of call for journalists dealing with human rights issues and this was reflected in its lack of appearance in stories on key issues such as collusion allegations. One former human rights commissioner in another jurisdiction commented to us that, where powers and resources were limited, the media could become a very important ally. This does not appear to have been fully taken on board by the NIHRC. While the SAHRC has also complained about an unfavourable media, it has taken steps to deal with this by having regular meetings with editors and broadcasters.[65]

RECOMMENDATIONS

Interestingly it was clear to us that while a few people we spoke to felt the idea of a human rights commission was a bad one from the start, that

[63] For example, with the Equality Commission, Memorandum of Understanding between the Northern Ireland Human Rights Commission and the Equality Commission for Northern Ireland, 23 October 2000; the Police Ombudsman, Memorandum of Understanding between the Northern Ireland Human Rights Commission and the Police Ombudsman for Northern Ireland, 2 November 2001; the Police Service of Northern Ireland, Memorandum of Understanding between the Northern Ireland Human Rights Commission and the Police Service of Northern Ireland, 16 January 2003; and the Court Service of Northern Ireland, Memorandum of Understanding between the Northern Ireland Court Service and the Northern Ireland Human Rights Commission, 6 December 2002.

[64] The Commission's italics.

[65] B Pityana 'National Institutions at Work: The Case of South Africa' in K Hossain, L Besselink, H Selaisse and E Volker (eds), *Human Rights Commissions and Ombudsman Offices: National Experiences Throughout the World* (Kluwer, 2001) 627, 638. Pityana's main concern appears to be that the media condemned it as financially wasteful.

human rights were either a bad idea or were already sufficiently protected in other ways, there is still widespread support for a human rights commission in Northern Ireland. Even those most critical of the performance of the NIHRC still felt a human rights commission had an important role to play in Northern Ireland. That role included developing a broad societal awareness of human rights, monitoring public authorities to ensure their compliance with human rights, being an authoritative respository of information and advice on human rights and taking a range of actions to protect human rights when abuses came to light. Such ambitions are not greatly dissimilar from those the Commission has had for itself over the past five years. They are also similar to the ambitions for NHRIs in most parts of the world. So what should have happened to increase the chances of this occurring in Northern Ireland and what can be learned that is of advantage to other NHRIs already existing or about to be established in other parts of the world?

First, that there are a number of things for which government, both its legislative and executive branches, bears a responsibility. Attending to these would increase the chances that a human rights commission would be effective. These include:

— Ensuring adequate funding. The NIHRC was clearly underfunded from the start, especially as regards staff, a legal budget and the Bill of Rights process. The lack of funding increased tensions within the Commission over priorities and contributed to public disappointment with its limited activity. There appears to have been little detailed thinking on how the Commission's budget should be set and when it quickly became clear that it was inadequate, the Commission was forced to spend a significant amount of time and energy arguing for an increase in its funding. This distracted it from other important issues at its inception and did little to protect its independence. As has been seen around the world there is little point in government establishing independent human rights commissions if it then deprives them of the resources needed to ensure their independence.

— Ensuring a transparent appointments process. Although the process for the NIHRC appointments did provide for the advertising of positions, a published set of criteria for appointments and the involvement of people other than government officials in the selection, it still fell short of demonstrating sufficient transparency. In particular we have suggested that government might include a more independent element in the selection process. This could draw upon some of the models now being developed for judicial selection, which include a mixture of lawyers and lay people.[66] Similarly a selection panel for NIHRC members might include a range of officials, politicians and lay people. It might make recommendations to the Secretary of State but would be entitled to an explanation if any of its recommendations were rejected. Government could also produce a more detailed set of criteria for appointment and clarify what it understands both as to the definition of the concept 'representative of the community' and what the purpose of having this criteria for appointments is. A certain degree of confusion appears to exist regarding this which was not helpful for the Commission once it was established. However, we would not endorse the view either that there should be direct political representation on the NIHRC or that people should be appointed primarily because of their political background, still less that there is a need to appoint people who are hostile to the whole idea of human rights. Nor did we feel that there was much support for direct political appointments even among those who were critical of the initial appointments to the Commission. Knowledge and experience of human rights plus a willingness to work for their promotion and protection should be the key criteria for appointment but this should not be defined narrowly to focus only on academic or NGO expertise; there are many other walks of life in which people can gain experience in human rights. Also, where government is responsible for selecting the Commissioners, it is important that it defends its choices. Early in its existence the NIHRC came under substantial criticism from some Unionist politicians in particular less for what it had done, which is a matter for the Commission itself to deal with, but for who was on it. The government rather than the NIHRC was responsible for its composition but at times it seemed that it left the Commission to defend the choices government had made.

— Ensuring the Commission has adequate powers. We have noted that the powers given in respect of investigations were inadequate and that this has already caused difficulties for the NIHRC in exercising its investigative function. Moreover, the reasons given for not conferring adequate investigation powers are unconvincing. The failure to confer adequate investigation powers is especially disappointing given that litigation will probably always play a minor role for the NIHRC (especially

[66] See *Constitutional Reform: A New way of Appointing Judges* (Department of Constitutional Affairs, 2003).

given the limited funding and the possibility for individuals to pursue human rights claims through the use of private lawyers funded by legal aid) and investigations have an important potential to deal with issues where litigation is too slow or inappropriate. However, it is also important not to overburden a Commission with tasks it is not effectively equipped to perform. We suggest that the power to advise on a Bill of Rights comes into this category, even though many both within and without the Commission welcomed this and have devoted considerable energy to it.

— Ensuring that there is effective engagement with the Commission. There have been delays in producing memorandums of agreement with a number of government departments, notably the NIO and OFMDFM. Partially because of this the NIHRC has not been consulted as frequently and as early about policy development regarding human rights as it should have been. Ultimately it is for government to make decisions and it can reject the advice of the Commission if it chooses to. There remains the risk that its decisions will be challenged in the courts. Therefore we would not endorse the proposal of the NIHRC that there should be some sort of statutory duty placed on government to accept the recommendations of the Commission.[67] This would come close to giving the Commission a wholly inappropriate judicial power. However, it would not be inappropriate to require United Kingdom government ministers when making a statement under section 19 of the Human Rights Act 1998 as to a Bill's compatibility with that Act or Northern Irish ministers when indicating under section 9 of the Northern Ireland Act 1998, that proposed legislation is within the competence of the Assembly, to acknowledge any contrary views they have had from the Human Rights Commission. This would at least ensure that the Commission's views were brought to the attention of the legislature, and perhaps later to the courts, which might encourage the executive to respond to them more fully before the stage of making such a statement is ever reached.

These are important responsibilities for government. Although directed to government in the United Kingdom we feel they may also have resonance for many parts of the world where NHRIs are established. However, as our and other studies have indicated there are also responsibilities on those appointed to

[67] This was advanced in the review of powers document.

commissions to ensure their effectiveness, even when they operate in a context of limited funding, powers and political support. As Human Rights Watch has observed, 'What is clear is that even under constrained political circumstances, human rights commissioners have scope to make important choices.'[68] Our study suggests that there are a number of things commissioners can do to strengthen the effectiveness of their institution. These include:

— Developing a clear purpose and vision for the Commission. Especially where a Commission has a broad mandate it will face demands to take action on a very broad range of issues. It is important that commissioners reflect on what they feel are the most important human rights issues for their society and that they develop an agreed policy on how to take this forward. In a society with a history of division this especially may not be an easy task but it is vital that the commissioners undertake such work if they are not to face difficulties in the future when criticism comes their way. We have argued that such discussion did not take place initially in the NIHRC. Instead important differences were deferred or glossed over. Partially as a result the Commission fell into reactive mode and spread its resources too thinly. When difficulties did arise it did not display a shared purpose and such disunity undermined its legitimacy. The lack of a shared purpose has had a significant adverse impact on things like the litigation strategy and the proposals for a Bill of Rights.

— Fully understanding the idea of independence in this area and distinguishing it from isolation. Independence from government is often stressed but as noted in the observation above it is also important that a NHRI displays independence from all those who urge it to act in various ways. However, maintaining independence, that ultimately it is for a Commission itself to decide what is best to promote and protect human rights, should not become isolation where it avoids engagement with others for fear that they 'taint' its agenda. A number of key NGOs in the human rights field have expressed concern that the Commission has not worked as closely with them as they expected and indeed has been concerned to keep them at arms length. A number of those we spoke to, both within and without the Commission, have indicated that there has been a reluctance to become too closely involved with politicians, whether in Belfast, London, Dublin or

[68] *Protectors or Pretenders?* p 26.

Washington. However if an NHRI is to prove influential in respect to matters which have a high political profile in most societies, then it is important that it devotes significant energy to its visibility and reputation in the political world. Such visibility should always be orientated towards the advancement of the promotion and protection of human rights rather than being an end in itself. However, especially where an NHRI feels it lacks sufficient powers and resources it is important that it develops alliances and partnerships with those who may help it to achieve its aims.

— Building on what exists in the human rights field. Members of Commissions may feel that there is much that needs changing as regards law and policy if the protection of human rights is to be achieved. Making recommendations as to these tasks is one of their key functions. However, they cannot always guarantee that such changes will take place, especially in a society characterised by significant division. It is important to make full use of whatever legal structures already exist, except where these are largely discredited from the perspective of protecting human rights and there is a danger of legitimating them. One thing the NIHRC could have made more use of initially was the Human Rights Act. This was accepted as a legitimate provision by government, a broad spectrum of political opinion and civil society. It was a major innovation in the legal protection of human rights on which many were looking for advice and information. It could have formed the basis for a critical but constructive relationship with a number of government departments and given the NIHRC a more detailed grounding for its proposals as to where there was a need for a Bill of Rights to go further. However, as the Chief Commissioner acknowledged, 'We've done very little on the Human Rights Act, as it happens, a lot more on the Bill of Rights.' While the HRA has undoubtedly featured in the NIHRC's work it has not been given the prominence that the South African Bill of Rights plays in the SAHRC's work, for example.

— Paying sufficient attention to organisational issues, especially where one is building a new institution. The NIHRC's commissioners, perhaps anxious to move onto the 'real work' of the Commission, did not pay as much attention to matters of staffing and organisation as they might have. The NIHRC has been dogged by such issues ever since, with two internal reviews over the past three years and more changes still to be made. This has caused several problems as regards its effectiveness, most notably with regard to its relations with the media. This has the potential to be one of the most significant relationships for the Commission, especially where it claims to be lacking in adequate powers and resources, but the Commission initially appeared to take media interest for granted rather than develop the organisational structures to ensure it was developed and sustained.

7

When Do Rights Matter? A Case Study of the Right to Equal Treatment in Sweden

REZA BANAKAR

THE PRINCIPLE OF equality and its underlying civil and political rights constitute the cornerstone of all documents on international and domestic human rights. These rights are already incorporated in one form or another in many domestic legal systems. It is, however, one thing to ratify the Universal Declaration of Human Rights or to adopt the European Convention on Human Rights, quite another thing to successfully implement them. An effective implementation of human rights and freedoms requires a multi-layered institutional infrastructure for legal decision-making, such as a hierarchy of courts and public authorities, which facilitates the incorporation of human rights into the domestic law, but also safeguards the due process rights. In addition, it requires a legal culture — comprising both the legal consciousness of the judiciary and ordinary citizens — which is committed to upholding the underlying values of human rights and freedoms. To mimic or to construct the institutional basis for introducing human rights and freedoms might indeed not be a simple operation, but one which is at worst largely dependent on adequate material investment and political will. In contrast, the legal culture needed for the realisation of the spirit of human rights and freedoms can neither be mimicked nor introduced from above by a political elite or the state administration.[1] This does not mean that values

[1] Legal culture consists, partly, of the taken-for-granted values and behavioural patterns of the judiciary and, partly, of ordinary men and women's knowledge of laws, but also of their attitude towards, and perception of, the judicial order in general and laws in particular. In that sense, legal culture is an integral part of the mainstream custom and tradition of a group of people. Cf LM Friedman, *The Legal System: A Social Science Perspective* (New York, Russell Sage Foundation, 1975).

and principles which lack popular support cannot be introduced in, or imposed on, a society by the legislature from above, but that the reception and effectiveness of laws which try to introduce new values and behavioural patterns can be fundamentally different from laws whose values are already entrenched in the custom and mores of some sections of the society.

The discussions in this chapter should be viewed as a limited contribution to the debate on how to introduce the right to equal treatment through legislation. In the coming pages, I shall use a case study to demonstrate the differences between rights, which emerge organically from below and work bottom up, and rights which are introduced through political pressure from above and work top down. This study is limited in its legal and jurisdictional scope in that it addresses only the emergence and enforcement of rights to equal treatment in regard to two Swedish anti-discrimination laws.[2] It begins by comparing the Equality between Women and Men Act (EWMA) with the Act Against Ethnic Discrimination (AED). These two Swedish anti-discrimination laws are comparable in many respects and, in fact, the AED is modelled on the EWMA. Yet, in practice, the EWMA is relatively more effective than the AED. This disparity is explored, partly, by examining how these two Acts are enforced by ombudsmen and, partly, by comparing the socio-cultural sources and political interests which underpin them. It is, then, argued that anti-discrimination laws and their corresponding rights need to be viewed as a part of an ongoing discourse on socio-cultural values pertaining to the organisation of our societies.

COMPARING ANTI-DISCRIMINATION LAWS

Both lawyers and policymakers who are involved in combating racism and ethnic discrimination appear to foster an understanding of the law as an *independent* instrument of social change, or 'a technical device that is capable of doing as much for ethnic relations as the microchip has done for communications.'[3] Seen this way, law is employed in the hope of furthering the ideals of socio-economic equality, ethno-cultural diversity and tolerance. Factors which determine the success or failure of anti-discrimination laws are, then, sought in the internal structure of the rules constituting such laws or the way their rules of evidence are

[2] The main part of this study is based on ch 9 in R Banakar, *Merging Law and Sociology* (Berlin, Galda & Wilch, 2003).

[3] B Hepple, 'Have Twenty Years of Race Relations Act in Britain Been a Failure?' in B Hepple and EM Szyszczak (eds), *Discrimination: The Limits of Law* (London, Mansell, 1992) 18ff.

formulated.[4] This prevailing view, which regards law as a social factor capable of standing apart from and acting upon the social conditions which it intends to regulate, informs attempts to outlaw discrimination on grounds of gender, nationality, religion, race and ethnicity in most European and North American countries and the EU.[5]

In a recent collection of essays on discrimination and human rights, for example, Sandra Fredman, conscious of the reality of racism and discrimination, questions the likelihood that new legal measures make a real impact on racism, which although not necessarily the root or cause of ethnic discrimination, is nevertheless a closely related social evil.[6] She writes:

> The contrast between legislative attempts and the reality of racism prompts a closer scrutiny of the legal instruments themselves. Does the problem lie in the goals and purposes of the legislation, or in the substantive provisions, or in the remedial structures? And can we even be sure that the correct answers are being given to the foundational questions: What is race? And what is racism?[7]

Whenever the law fails to bring about the intended effects, one should, according to the standpoint presented above, start re-evaluating the goals, substantive provisions and remedial structures of the law. In other words, if the law is ineffective and does not deliver the policy goods, it must be *technically* flawed.

Important though the lawyer's perception of the law is for counteracting ethnic discrimination, it hardly exhausts the understanding of the regulatory limits and possibilities of the law with respect to discriminations. That is why this study adopts a somewhat broader approach than that common to legal studies and argues that any assessment of the efficacy of anti-discrimination laws needs to take into consideration the societal context which produced them and in which they operate. An important aspect of this discussion is the ongoing discourse on the social organisation of society, ie how people in their everyday interactions, exchanges and endeavours to cooperate with each other envisage, plan and finally construct their relationships. The other decisive discursive factor is the general perception of race, ethnicity, gender, nationality, religion, sexual orientation, age,

[4] For an examination of the normative structure of the Swedish anti-discrimination laws see A Christensen, 'Strukturella aspekter på diskrimineringslagstiftning och normative förändringsprocesser' in A Numhauser-Henning (ed), *Perspektiv på likabehandling och diskriminering* (Lund, Juristförlaget, 2000).

[5] For an introduction to anti-discrimination laws and theories addressing the legal regulation of discrimination see C McCrudden, *Anti-discrimination Law* (Aldershot, Dartmouth, 1991).

[6] S Fredman, *Discrimination and Human Rights: The Case of Racism* (Oxford, Oxford University Press, 2002).

[7] Fredman, *ibid*, at 1–2.

disability or any other characteristic which might be used for the purposes of inclusion or exclusion of people.

EQUALITY BETWEEN WOMEN AND MEN ACT (1991)[8]

The Equality between Women and Men Act (hereafter the EWMA) of 1 July 1980 was introduced to promote the equal rights of women and men in working life. This Act was revised in 1991[9] and amended in January 2001 to strengthen its provisions on the obligation of the employers to draw up an annual wage plan and to clarify matters related to sanctions for non-compliance and the rules of evidence.[10] This was done as part of the attempt to harmonise Swedish legislation on equal opportunity in employment with European Community law and other Swedish anti-discrimination laws.[11] The new EWMA is concerned with the employment and working conditions of women and men and aims to counteract gender discrimination and harassment in working life. It is formulated in a gender-neutral manner but, as emphatically spelt out in section 1 of the Act, its underlying intention is to improve the terms and conditions of employment and opportunities for development in work for *women*.

According to section 15 of the Act an employer may not treat a job seeker, or an employee, less favourably than the employer treats or would have treated a person of the opposite sex in a comparable position, unless the employer can demonstrate that this less favourable treatment is not based on gender differences. The prohibition does not, however, apply if the treatment is designed as part of an effort to promote equality in working life, provided it does not involve pay discrimination or undermine the principle of equality in working life. The Act then goes on to address indirect discrimination in section 16, by prohibiting the application of provisions or procedures that although they might appear to be neutral and objective, nonetheless (1) disadvantage persons of one gender in practice

[8] The Swedish title of this Act is *Jämställdhetslagen*.

[9] See Swedish Legislation SFS 1991: 433.

[10] See H Göransson and A Karlsson, *Supplement till 'Diskrimineringslagarna'* (Stockholm, Norstedts Juridik, 2001).

[11] Sweden does not have an all-embracing legislation against various forms of discrimination in working life. Instead, the Swedish law contains four anti-discrimination Acts, which have been introduced in a piecemeal fashion. The first and the oldest of these is the Equality between Women and Men Act, 1980. The Act Against Ethnic Discrimination is the second oldest and was introduced in 1994. More recently, in 1999, two other Acts, one prohibiting discrimination on the basis of sexual orientation and, the other, on the basis of disability, have also been introduced to protect homosexuals and people with physical disability against unlawful discrimination in working life. In this study we are concerned with the first two acts. For a presentation of these four acts see H Göransson and A Karlsson, *Diskrimineringslagarna: En praktisk kommentar* (Stockholm, Norstedts Juridik, 2000).

and (2) cannot be justified by any other objective motive which is independent of the gender of the employee or job applicant.[12]

An employer who is found in breach of these prohibitions shall pay damages to the person he/she discriminated against. The employer shall also compensate the employee for other losses that might have been incurred by the employee as a result of this discriminatory treatment. The Act, furthermore, provides that if a contract of employment permits discrimination as prohibited in this Act, any conditions of the contract or decisions made by the employer on the basis of the contract may be declared void. Civil proceedings under the EWMA (this also applies to the Act against Ethnic Discrimination which will be discussed in the next section) are conducted in accordance with the Act on Litigation in Labour Disputes.[13] The ombudsmen can, within their specific jurisdictions and field of competence, bring a case to the Labour Court. This must, however, be done with the consent of the individual complainants, and if the ombudsman considers that litigation would benefit the practice of the anti-discrimination law or counteract discrimination in other ways. However, this privilege of the ombudsman is secondary to the rights of the trade unions to represent their members in such disputes, ie the ombudsman can only initiate an action if the trade union decides not to do so.[14]

Besides prohibiting gender discrimination, the Act requires employers, whether in the public or private sector, to undertake 'active measures' to promote equal opportunities for women and men. The Act also instructs those employers with ten or more employees to prepare an annual equal opportunities plan. Also, all employers are expected to conduct an annual survey of wage differences between women and men in an attempt to discover, rectify and prevent unjustifiable pay differences between women and men and unwarranted terms of employment.[15]

According to sections 30–32, an equal opportunities ombudsman and an equal opportunities commission are appointed by the government to

[12] See Swedish Legislation SFS 2000:773.

[13] See Swedish Legislation SFS 1974:371.

[14] A Numhauser-Henning, 'Labour Law' in M Bogdan, *Swedish Law: In the New Millennium* (Stockholm, Norstedts Juridik, 2000) 365. For more detailed and more recent statistics on the socio-economic status of women in Sweden see ch 3 in A-K Roth, *Nya jämställdhetsboken: från teori till praktik* (Stockholm, Norstedts Juridik, 2002).

[15] About 75% of Swedish women between the ages of 16 and 64, as compared with 79% of Swedish men, were in employment in 1997. Despite the fact that women's participation in the labour market matches that of men, the Swedish labour market remains highly gender-segregated. Women dominate the public sector, which includes medical, child and elderly care, while men dominate the private sector. Moreover 'within all professions there is a disproportionate amount of men in top managerial positions and wage differentials still exist' (*ibid*, Numhauser-Henning 366). Also, according to the Equal Opportunity Ombudsman (see

monitor and ensure compliance with the Act. The ombudsman is instructed, in the first instance, to encourage employers to comply voluntarily with the provisions of the Act. While the ombudsman focuses on promoting better working conditions for women, the Equal Opportunity Commission considers matters arising out of orders for default fines and appeals. In the following we shall primarily focus on the effects of the EWMA and the Equal Opportunity Ombudsman.

The EWMA in Action

This study also hopes to examine the interplay between legislation and law in action. So this section draws attention to how the EWMA operates by considering the number of complaints that are annually lodged with the Equal Opportunity Ombudsman (hereafter the EO) and how the complaints are processed.

The ombudsman receives a large number of complaints from both men (about 10 per cent) and women (about 90 per cent) some of which fall outside the ombudsman's jurisdiction, ie do not concern working life. These can concern a host of gender-related issues ranging from the degrading tone or images of certain advertisements, entrance fees, decisions made by the Inland Revenue, social security authorities or the treatment of prisoners. The ombudsman replies to all these complaints, even though he/she does not necessarily process them all, for many of them fall, as already mentioned, outside the terms of reference of the office. The total number of enquiries and complaints received by the ombudsman is influenced by a host of social, political and economic factors and varies from year to year.[16]

Nonetheless, the number of complaints processed by the ombudsman each year which specifically addressed discrimination in working life, is somewhat more stable. It fluctuated slightly around 100 cases per year during the 1990s with any sudden dramatic increases during this period indicating group actions rather than a change in the overall propensity of the public — which in this case consists mainly of women — to lodge complaints. However, during recent years this figure has been steadily

Förändringar i jämställdhetslagen, JämO, januari 2001) women earn on average about 80% of men's pay. This disparity can only be partially attributed to the differences which exist between women and men's working experience, education and the type of work they are engaged in. The other part of this difference is due to the fact that existing structures in the labour market and employment act to the disadvantage of women. This difference has not diminished, even though the provision requiring that employers discover, rectify and prevent unwarranted pay differentials was enacted in 1994.

[16] According to the EO's Annual Reports the Ombudsman received 571 cases in 1997, 471 cases in 1998, 285 cases in 1999, 461 cases in 2000 and 296 cases in 2001.

rising due to the increased number of complaints related to maternity leave or pertaining to discrimination on the basis of pregnancy.[17] Also see Table 1 below.

Table 1: Cases Regarding Working Life Lodged with the Ombudsmen against Ethnic Discrimination (the DO) and the Equal Opportunity Ombudsman (the EO)

	1998	1999	2000	2001	2002
Cases lodged with the DO	121	184	164	272	306
Cases lodged with the EO	91	110	120	177	129

Sources: The DO's and the EO's Annual Reports

The steady flow of these cases is the result of two factors, each representing a specific standpoint on unlawful discrimination. One factor is internal to the law and reflects, above all, the working capacity and institutionalised practices and routines of the EO. The other factor reflects the frequency of gender discrimination, on the one hand, and women's propensity to register complaints with the ombudsman, on the other, which is in turn related to women's knowledge of, and attitude towards, the EWMA in general.

If the efficacy of this Act is to be judged by the number of cases brought before the labour courts and won by the ombudsman, then the Swedish legislation on equal employment opportunity is a total failure and its ombudsman a 'toothless tiger'. A different picture of the impact and significance of the EWMA emerges if we disregard the ombudsman's poor litigation record and instead focus on the cases it actually resolves. A large number of cases are either settled through the ombudsman's direct involvement as a mediator or in the 'shadow of the law' through the indirect effect of the EWMA, ie through the initiative of the parties to the disputes to resolve their differences out of court.

More importantly, the auditing effects of the ombudsman, ie the fact that he/she instructs employers to draw up equal opportunities plans, the implementation of which can then be monitored by the ombudsman, is not reflected in the figures above. This auditing function of the ombudsman is highly significant with regard to the overall assessment of the efficacy of the Act because it provides a means of conflict avoidance. Without this function, it is highly probable that the number of complaints per year would be many times larger.

In practice, the EWMA appears, at first glance, to only partially address the objectives envisaged by the legislature to combat gender discrimination. The provisions on prohibitions and remedies appear to be obsolete and exist only for cosmetic purposes. The sanctions provided against discrimination belong, in fact, to law on the books which, when put into practice

[17] See the Equal Opportunity Ombudsman's Annual Report 2002, at 20.

by the ombudsman, are mysteriously transformed into alternative dispute resolution (ADR) and a technique for avoiding conflicts. Although the legislature urged the ombudsman to try to achieve equal employment opportunities for women and men, 'in the first instance,' by encouraging the employers to voluntarily comply with the provisions of the Act,[18] nowhere in the Act is it indicated that the office of the ombudsman is to function as an institution for alternative dispute resolution. Moreover, the office of ombudsman as it was originally introduced in Sweden by the Parliamentary Ombudsman, was not meant as a forum for alternative dispute resolution and mediation but a governmental instrument of internal control. Clearly, how the EWMA is in actual fact enforced does not reflect the image of the law as a technical device designed for litigation.

A number of hypotheses can be formulated with reference to Swedish legal culture and the social sources of the EWMA to explain this disparity. First, since it is difficult to bring discrimination cases to court and to successfully present evidence of unlawful discrimination, then it is possible that the ombudsman finds no other alternative than to resort to other methods to combat discrimination. According to this hypothesis, the employment of ADR is not by choice, but a sign of desperation. Secondly, one needs to consider the political and legal culture of Sweden, which on the whole favours decision-making by consensus. This approach has also shaped the attitude towards legal action in the sense that, when possible, negotiations in the shadow of law are preferred to litigation. Anti-discrimination laws have been brought about through a long and elaborate process of negotiation and bargaining between established groups with vested interests in the labour market, such as organisations representing employees and employers and the different political parties. The results of these negotiations and the compromises reached are then reflected in the preparatory legislative documents, *travaux préparatoires*, which are regarded as one of the important sources for statutory interpretation by Swedish lawyers.[19] One can therefore postulate that the enforcement of the EWMA bears the consensual hallmark of its social sources. However, these two hypotheses do not necessarily exclude each other. It is also possible that while the ombudsman finds resorting to ADR more effective than litigating, he also finds tacit political and cultural support for making this choice.

We shall now move on to the Swedish legislation on ethnic discrimination, which aims to promote equal rights and opportunities in working life regardless of the ethnic background of employees or job applicants. This

[18] See s 31 of the EWMA 1999.

[19] Although the Swedish *travaux préparatoires* are considered as a source of law and a guide for interpretation they are, however, not formally binding. See H-H Vogel, 'The Sources of Swedish Law, in M Bogdan (ed), *Swedish Law* (Stockholm, Norstedts Juridik, 2000).

anti-discrimination Act, as we shall see below, is to a large extent modelled on the legislation on equal employment opportunity.

THE ACT AGAINST ETHNIC DISCRIMINATION (AED)[20]

The Act Against Ethnic Discrimination (1999) bears a structural resemblance to the EWMA. It starts by emphasising the importance of 'cooperation' between various actors with an interest in the labour market, such as the employers, the unions representing employees and the ombudsman, to promote ethnic diversity in working life and to work towards eradicating ethnic discrimination. More significantly, it also contains two sets of rules: one prescribing 'active measures' and the other prohibiting discrimination. The provisions on active measures require that employers systematically promote ethnic diversity by (1) creating working conditions suitable for the ethnic background of their employees; (2) preventing ethnic harassment in the workplace; (3) ensuring that members of ethnic groups are given the opportunity to apply for vacant positions through the direct advertising of job openings and (4) applying affirmative action with regard to training and employment opportunities. However, taking measures of affirmative action is not a statutory obligation and employers are only encouraged to take such measures.

The Act Against Ethnic Discrimination (hereafter AED) does not, however, require employers to draw up an annual equal opportunity plan and maintain a documentation of their ethnic equality plans. This means that the AED lacks conflict avoidance mechanisms, a fact that is, needless to say, highly significant for its actual impact on counteracting ethnic discriminatory behaviour. As we shall see later, the absence of a mechanism for conflict avoidance is a function of the social sources of the AED in the sense that the values which it represents are not sufficiently embedded in the Swedish culture to compel employers to draw up equal opportunity plans of the type required by the EWMA. In this sense, the AED is a weaker version of the Equality between Women and Men Act, 1991.

The AED contains sanctions against direct and indirect discrimination which are applicable to the entire recruitment and employment process. According to section 8 of the Act, it is unlawful to unfairly treat a job applicant or an employee by treating him or her less favourably than the employer treats or would have treated persons with another ethnic background in a comparable situation, unless the employer shows that the less favourable treatment has no connection with ethnic background. This ban does not, however, apply if the discriminatory treatment is motivated by

[20] Swedish Legislation SFS 1999:130.

special interests that are clearly of more importance than preventing ethnic discrimination. In section 9 of the Act, the legislature goes on to prohibit indirect discrimination. According to this section, an employer may not treat a job applicant or employee less favourably by using a rule, requirement or procedure that appears impartial, but which in practice particularly disfavours persons of a particular ethnic background. This does not apply if the intention behind the application of such a rule, requirement or procedure is rationally justifiable and the measure suitable and necessary for realising this intention.[21] For example, requiring Swedish high school diplomas for a specific position may be indirectly discriminatory for it automatically excludes the overwhelming majority of immigrant applicants. Such a requirement would be, however, lawful if the employer could demonstrate that to successfully perform the job in question, one necessarily requires a specific form of knowledge or experience, which only a person with a Swedish high school diploma can possess and that there are no other alternatives to this requirement. The employer might also need to demonstrate that the chosen procedures used for evaluating this requirement are suitable for the task at hand.

The AED does not require any evidence of the employer's ethnic discriminatory intent. However, the employer's intent will have a bearing on the size of compensation that is to be awarded in the sense that an intended discrimination will lead to awarding higher damages. A prima facie case of *direct* discrimination exists where the complainant can demonstrate that (1) ethnicity was a factor of consideration; (2) that the applicant was treated less favourably than another person with a different ethnic background was treated or would have been treated and (3) that he or she was in a position similar to the other person. A case of *indirect* discrimination exists if the complainant could prove that there is an ethnic factor influencing the employer's decision making and that the employer uses rules and procedures that although in theory appear neutral, nonetheless, in practice, disadvantage most applicants from the same ethnic background as the complainant.

The enforcement of the AED is procedurally similar to that of the EWMA. A special ombudsman, the Ombudsman against Ethnic iscrimination

[21] The language expressing the second part of the exception to the rule of indirect discrimination (... rationally justifiable and the measure is suitable and necessary for realising the intention) is closely based on the original text of the Act (Detta gäller såvida inte syftet med bestämmelsen, kriteriet eller förfaringssättet kan motiveras av sakliga skäl och åtgärden är lämplig och nödvändigt för att syftet ska uppnås), which is not formulated in a straightforward manner. To clarify this rule we can divide it into three separate conditions. First, the intention behind rules, requirements and procedures used by the employer must be *rationally* justifiable. Secondly, the rules, requirements and procedures should constitute a *suitable* measure to realise the rational intention behind them. Thirdly, rules, requirements and procedures must be *necessary* for realising the intention. In other words, there should not exist any alternative procedural method for realising the intention in question. See also Göransson and Karlsson, above, n 11, at 64–66.

(hereafter the DO) and the board against Ethnic Discrimination are appointed. The DO is charged with the task of ensuring compliance with the AED and informing public opinion, while the board decides on civil fines and reviews appeal cases. Under certain circumstances the DO can provide legal representation for individual employees and job applicants. This right of representation is, as in the EWMA, secondary to the rights of the unions to represent their members. The DO may apply to the board for an order — the non-compliance of which is subject to a civil fine — concerning employers who fail in their duties to implement the active measures described in the Act.

The AED in Action

It is somewhat more difficult to assess the impact of the AED on discrimination than it was to assess the efficacy of the EWMA, which has not been amended in a fundamental way since 1991. It would perhaps be more instructive to take a brief look at how the AED has developed to become the law that it is today before attempting to form an opinion regarding its efficacy.

The first AED was enacted in 1986.[22] This original legislation did not contain provisions prohibiting ethnic discrimination in recruitment and/or employment. Instead it created the Office of the Ombudsman against Ethnic Discrimination and charged the DO with the task of counteracting discrimination by informing public opinion of discrimination, and further, by scrutinising the actions of employers. The law gave the DO the necessary legal power to demand from employers, against whom a complaint was lodged, explanation for their alleged discriminatory treatment of job seekers or employees. The AED (1986) was heavily criticised, as a result of which it was revised and amended after eight years.[23] The new law[24] gave the DO greater powers to legally counteract ethnic discrimination and became Sweden's first anti-discrimination legislation to protect ethnic minorities (consisting essentially of those of immigrant background) in the labour market. The AED (1994) did not, however, cover the entire recruitment process. The employers could simply evade short listing applicants with foreign names or accents, and in this way exclude them from being considered seriously for a job opening, without the risk of being sued. Also, the Act fell short of making any impact on indirect discrimination, which meant that employers could use certain seemingly objective procedures to

[22] See Swedish Legislation SFS 1986:442.
[23] In 1992 I conducted a study of the AED (1986) which was published in R Banakar, *The Dilemma of Law: On Conflict Management in a Multicultural Society* [original title: Rättens Dilemma: Om konflikthantering i ett mångkulturellt samhälle] (Lund, Bokbox, 1994).
[24] See Swedish Legislation SFS 1994:134.

exclude certain ethnic groups from participation, like demanding proof of proficiency in the Swedish language for jobs which required limited verbal or written skills, which would exclude some immigrant groups. Finally, the AED placed the burden of proof on the claimant, making it extremely difficult to demonstrate that a direct discrimination had actually taken place. As a result, and despite the fact that the necessary legal powers to take cases to the labour court were conferred on the DO by the AED (1994), the ombudsman only succeeded in taking one case to court. This case, incidentally, was lost by the DO.[25]

At the same time the plight of certain immigrant groups in the Swedish labour market was highlighted in the mass media and public political debates. Various studies also showed that many immigrants felt that they were being discriminated against.[26] A range of factors gave empirical weight to immigrants' claims regarding relatively widespread ethnic discrimination in Sweden. Previous studies demonstrated that immigrants had *significantly* higher unemployment rates, *significantly* lower incomes and inferior working conditions compared with a comparable Swedish group.[27] Their mobility in the labour market, and consequently their upward mobility, was considerably less than native Swedes.[28] Among certain immigrant groups, such as Latin Americans and second-generation immigrants, even a downward mobility in the labour market had been observed.[29] Social scientists who had studied the relationship between immigration, the economic development of Sweden and the status of immigrants in the Swedish

[25] For a study of the efficacy of the AED (1994) see R Banakar, *The Doorkeepers of the Law* (Aldershot, Ashgate, 1998).

[26] See, eg, A Lange, *Invandrare om etnisk diskriminering* (Stockholm Universitet, CEIFO, 1996). In this study, which was conducted on behalf of the DO in order to highlight the relation between immigrants and Swedes, it was shown that a large portion of Sweden's immigrant population had been subjected to discriminatory, degrading and threatening or violent behaviour during their stay in Sweden. The investigation was carried out by the Swedish Bureau of Official Statistics (SCB) and was based on interviews with 1008 African, Arab, Latin American and Polish immigrants who had come to Sweden between 1971 and 1991. One of the questions asked was if they had applied for a job over the last five years for which they were qualified, but failed to obtain the position in question because of their ethnic, national or religious background. Among those who responded to this question, 33.7% of Africans, 38.5% of Arabs, 24.8% of Latin Americans and 24.8% of Poles reported being discriminated against in their search for employment. A considerably larger percentage reported encountering threatening behaviour in public places. Fifty-one per cent of all Africans queried, 45.5% of Arabs, 45% of Latin Americans and 12% of Poles reported that they had been threatened or insulted because of their ethnic origin.

[27] Source: Swedish Immigration Authorities, *På tal om invandrare* (Regarding the Immigrants), SIV, 1994.

[28] J Ekberg, *Yrkeskarriärer under 1970-talet* (Stockholms läns landsting, Regionplanekontoret, Rapport, 1985: 9); Swedish Official Investigation (SOU 1989: 111) *Invandrare i storstad.* Underlagsrapport från Storstadsutredningen, 1989) 38.

[29] W Knocke, *Invandrare möter facket–Betydelsen av hemlandsbakgrund och hemvist i arbetslivet* (Stockholm, Arbetslivscentrum, 1982) 66 and J Ekberg, *Inkomsteffekter av invandring* (Högskolan i Växjö, Centrum för arbetsmarknadspolitisk forskning, 1983).

labour market pointed out that two separate labour markets, one for ethnic Swedes and one for immigrants, existed in Sweden. The latter consisted mainly of low-paid jobs that require working in shifts or in unhealthy working environments with no prospect for career advancement.[30]

Not surprisingly, the criticism against the AED (1994) soon mounted and a proposal for a new law containing the basis of the AED (1999), which was briefly described in the previous section, was submitted to Parliament. The AED has, therefore, gone through three distinct stages in its transition from an anti-discrimination law without specific provisions prohibiting unlawful discrimination in working life to a law with sanctions against direct and indirect discrimination. It would be of general interest to consider each of these stages separately. However, this task falls outside the present undertaking.

Let us now consider the flow of cases through the offices of the DO and the EO and compare the ombudsman's impact on resolving discrimination cases. (See Table 1 on p 171)

Not all the complaints lodged with the DO (or with the EO for that matter) pass through the system. Many of them, in fact 84 per cent of all the complaints between 1998 and 2001, were dismissed by the DO at an early stage as they were not within the jurisdiction of the ombudsman or did not fall under any of the rules constituting the AED. This should be compared with the EO's rate of dismissals which is well below 60 per cent during the same period. Assuming that ethnic minority groups do not have a tendency to register bogus complaints with the DO (see the concluding discussions) this means that the DO's rate of success in processing cases — which can indicate the DO's success in the application of the AED — is significantly smaller than that of the EO's. Expressed differently, the chance that a complaint is dismissed is greater when it is lodged as an ethnic discrimination complaint than when it is lodged as a gender discrimination complaint.

Focusing on the performance of the DO and the impact of the AED, four significant observations can be made on the basis of the flow of cases as reported by the ombudsman:

1 The volume of cases has been steadily rising.

2 The DO (not unlike the EO) is still unable to bring a significant number of cases to the Labour Court.

3 The DO shows that it can resolve cases more effectively through ADR than by litigation (the same hypothesis which explained the tendency of the EO to employ ADR can be used to explain the DO's application of non-adversarial methods).

[30] C-U Schierup and S Paulson, *Arbetets etniska delning* (Stockholm, Carlsson, 1994).

4 the number of cases which have been settled out of court has, however, increased significantly (in the previous years of 1997, 1996 and 1995 the number of cases settled was also steadily increasing, although this number constituted only a small portion of discrimination cases as a whole).

Some of the conclusions to be drawn here are similar to those already formulated with regard to the EWMA, namely that the efficacy of the AED is not to be sought in its ability to enforce sanctions prescribed by law against ethnic discrimination but in its ability to function as a means of dispute resolution, ie its impact on social relations are through its mediatory role rather than through litigation.

SOCIAL SOURCES OF THE ANTI-DISCRIMINATION ACTS

To understand why the EWMA functions as it does one needs to place it in a historical context which goes back at least to the turn of the nineteenth century. Compared with many other European countries, women in Sweden have had a strong socio-political position. Swedish women with property, for example, could vote in city elections from 1862. Although this voting right was granted only to a very specific category of women and despite the fact that it can be described as a function of property rights rather than a recognition of the political rights of women, it nonetheless remains one of the earliest voting rights ever won by women. Regardless of its intentions, this right provided women with a port of entry into the otherwise male-dominated public life in Sweden. This development received further impetus by the establishment of the Swedish Association for Women's Suffrage (*Landsföreningen för kvinnlig rösträtt*) in 1903 and led to women's attainment of national suffrage and the right to hold office at the national level in 1921.[31] The following year, in 1922, the first five women were elected to the *Riksdag* (the Swedish Parliament). This was soon followed by women obtaining a number of other rights ranging from a general right (with certain exceptions) to hold governmental offices (1925), to maternity insurance benefits (1931), equal basic pensions (1935) and legal safeguards against dismissal due to pregnancy, childbirth or marriage (1939). Karin Kock was the first woman to become a Cabinet minister in 1947. That same year there were two more important rights introduced: equal pay for equal work for state employees and also child allowance. This development

[31] In Britain, the suffrage movement began in the 1860s, though women did not gain full voting rights until 1928. In the United States women won the right to vote in 1920 although they had actually secured full voting rights by constitutional action in individual states much earlier, starting with Colorado in 1893.

continued into the 1950s, 1960s and 1970s, during which time women constantly strove towards, and succeeded in, obtaining new social, economic and political rights which helped them to redress the power imbalance which existed between women and men to some extent.[32]

This study argues that the 1980 EWMA needs to be viewed as a continuation of, and an integral part of this ongoing process. The introduction of the EWMA and its limits of efficacy cannot be evaluated independently of the struggle of the women's movement to gain equal rights in general, and equal wages and other opportunities in working life in particular. In this sense the social source of the EWMA is the Swedish women's movement which, not unlike similar social movements elsewhere, did not consist of a socially or politically homogeneous group and was, in fact, divided into various groups reflecting the diversity of women's experiences. Yet a number of factors, such as the right to vote, the right to equal pay for equal work, equality between the sexes and 'a focus on the peace issue' has bridged the differences between Swedish women and enabled their organisations to build coalitions with a common objective.[33] The EWMA represents, in a sense, a very important legal manifestation of some of the values which made it possible to mobilise women to act collectively towards a new form of social organisation. How successful have women been in their struggle? Most women would agree that despite all the rights they have gained,[34] much work remains and needs to be done, and many battles will continue to be fought before a complete equality between women and men can finally be achieved.

The significance of the social sources of the EWMA becomes apparent when we compare it with the way the AED was introduced and established. In section two, *The AED in Action*, we briefly described the three stages of development of the Act against ethnic discrimination. We are now going to focus on the socio-political background of this development. From the 1960s onwards Swedish law came under international pressure to satisfy the legal standards set by various conventions, such as the ILO and UN Conventions. In response to this pressure the Swedish government routinely set up commissions to investigate the need to amend the anti-discrimination laws. For example, in 1968 the Committee for the Inquiry into the

[32] For a complete list of gender-related legal progress see *Women and Men in Sweden, Facts and Figures* published by the Swedish Official Bureau of Statistics (SCB) 2000. For an account of the Swedish women's political struggle at the turn of the nineteenth century see U Wikander 'Sekelskiftet 1900: konstruktion av nygammal kvinnlighet' in U Wikander and U Manns (eds) *Det eviga kvinnliga: En historia om förändring* (Lund, Studnetlitteratur, 2001).

[33] A Peterson, *Women as Collective Actors: A Case Study of the Swedish Women's Peace Movement 1898–1990* (Göteborg, Research Report from the Department of Sociology, 1992).

[34] For example, in 2002, women constituted over 42% of the members of Parliament in Sweden, which can be compared with 38% in Denmark and 36% in Norway. Women's life expectancy, educational attainment, and income are highest in Sweden, Canada, Norway, the USA and Finland.

Prohibition of Racial Discrimination, which was created in response to international criticism, found that Swedish law did not conform to Article 5 of the Convention on the Elimination of All Forms of RacialDiscrimination. However, the Committee maintained that there was no evidence of the existence of ethnic discrimination in the labour market and expressed its misgivings in principle about legal intervention in the labour market. In 1983 the government formed a new committee: The Commission on Ethnic Prejudice and Discrimination. The Commission argued in its report that according to the Convention on the Elimination of All Forms of Racial Discrimination, Sweden had an obligation to legislate against ethnic discrimination in the labour market. Furthermore, the Commission found that extensive ethnic discrimination was practised in the Swedish labour market, and consequently presented proposals — modelled on an existing Equality between Women and Men Act — to counteract such discrimination. The proposals included the prohibition of discrimination on ethnic grounds by employers against job applicants and employees, and proposed the awarding of monetary compensation. However, the Commission's legislation proposals were critically received and the Swedish government simply postponed all such decisions regarding legislation to a later date. In 1986, however, the government agreed to introduce the first AED (which as mentioned above did not have proper sanctions against unlawful discrimination in working life) and to set up the first office of the Ombudsman against Ethnic Discrimination, charged with the task of counteracting ethnic discrimination and reporting to Parliament on the ethnic situation in the country.[35] In 1989 a newly formed Special Commission against Racism and Xenophobia argued once again that Sweden needed to take additional measures to fulfil the provisions of the Convention on the Elimination of All Forms of Racial Discrimination. The Commission failed however, to establish that discrimination constituted a real problem in Sweden. It did, nevertheless, argue that further legislation was justified since immigrants, even after the establishment of the Ombudsman Against Ethnic Discrimination (hereafter the DO), still felt as if they were objects of discrimination, and were still, in fact, a vulnerable group in the labour market. Furthermore, the Commission argued that the effectiveness of action on the part of the DO would increase if such legislation became a reality. In December of that same year the DO also presented a proposal to the government for legislation against ethnic discrimination in the labour market. Yet none of these proposals and reports, which were submitted by different commissions and the DO, succeeded in persuading the government

[35] For studies of ethnic discrimination in Sweden at the beginning of 1980s see C Westin, *Majoritet om minoritet: En studie i etnisk tolerans i 80-talets Sverige: En rapport från Diskrimineringsutredningen* (Stockholm, Publica, 1984) and E Bergman and B Swedin, *Vittnesmål — Invandrares syn på diskriminering i Sverige* (Stockholm, Publica, 1982).

to alter its perception of ethnic discrimination in Sweden. The official line remained unchanged in its approach to the problems of racism and ethnic discrimination and the authorities defined these problems in terms of individual psychology and attitudes, which could best be 'informed' or 'reasoned' away through governmental consultations with employers' organisations and unions.[36]

According to Carl-Ulrik Schierup, the Swedish government's unwillingness to legislate is linked to the nature of the corporate political process in Sweden, which combines capitalist economy with widespread state intervention and economic planning. He writes:

> Before becoming a serious object of discourse for the parliamentary political process, any major policy issue has to pass through the 'iron triangle' of the central unions, the central association of employers and concerned state agencies. And neither the unions nor the central association have shown any interest in anti-discrimination legislation.[37]

Schierup emphasises the effect of political and economic structures on the process of legislation. However, besides the ideological power of economic interests in society, there are other factors such as *values* that shape ethno-cultural relations. These values are reflected in public opinion and the way discourses on ethno-cultural issues in a society are conducted.[38] These values, which are not necessarily a function of economic structures and interests, exert an impact on the introduction of new legislation through public discourse. At the same time the law, both as legislation and as legal practice, contributes to the moulding of these public opinions and discourses on different matters and therefore even helps to reproduce certain values related to social, cultural and political issues. In the context of this study, legislation and legal practice should be seen as both a cause and an effect with relation to public opinion, public discourse and socio-cultural values. Law is subsequently viewed here as an integral part of the ongoing process of social change in a modern society.

However, when it is introduced by the state from above, law is not necessarily a reflection of public opinion and might in fact challenge the dominant attitudes and values in society. This type of legislation can prove to be highly ineffective. Public opinion against ethnic discrimination and its underlying basic values did not exist in Sweden until the early 1990s. Therefore the need for anti-discrimination legislation which would protect the entire sphere of public life had failed to make itself felt within the ethni-

[36] Cf E Bergman (ed), *Solidaritet och konflikt–Etniska relationer i Sverige* (Stockholm, Carlssons, 1989).
[37] C-U Schierup in A Ålund and C-U Schierup, *Paradoxes of Multiculturalism* (Aldershot, Avebury, 1991) 128.
[38] See Banakar, above n 24.

cally homogeneous Swedish state administration. The first proper Swedish Act against Ethnic Discrimination in working life was enacted in 1993 after many years of intense critical discussion at the national level and extensive international critique of the Swedish position on racial discrimination. Sweden's move to join the EU, which required that it harmonised its laws on many civil rights issues within the EU, might have also contributed to its sudden change of mind on this issue (as mentioned above the EWMA had been amended and harmonised with European legislation a few years earlier).

The AED was imposed on Sweden mainly as a result of political pressure exerted at the level of state administration by human rights agencies and commissions against racism. Thus, in Sweden the basic motivation for a law to curb ethnic discrimination was shared only by a handful of immigrant and human rights organisations. The EWMA, on the other hand, emerged out of the political movement of a large section of Swedish society and, therefore, had its underlying values already established to a degree among ordinary Swedes. In short, unlike the AED, it enjoyed popular support of a section of the people of Sweden.

CONCLUSION

The recognition that the two anti-discrimination laws discussed above have different social sources is instructive in evaluating their potential impact on social conditions. Since the underlying values of the EWMA were already partially rooted among a large section of the Swedish population and, thus, enjoyed some support, it was only to be expected that it would function more effectively than the AED, which was introduced 'top down' by political pressure. For the same reason, the AED remains more dependent on the state for its existence than the EWMA, whose fundamental values were regarded as rights by a section of society even before it was posited as valid law. Despite the similarities between these two laws, ie that both are expressed in legislative form to curb unfair discriminatory practices in working life, one emerges from below out of a political movement of a section of society, the other is introduced from above through political pressure. The former is geared, in the first place, to the everyday culture and custom of ordinary people, while the latter is primarily, though not exclusively, a function of state administration. Subsequently, the communicative structures facilitating their enactment and their potential to influence behaviour are very different. In the case of the EWMA, the law and its object of regulation were already set in relation to each other through an ongoing discourse on the desirability and necessity of establishing equality between women and men in working life, embracing both the grass-roots level and the political system (as mentioned above, women carrying such values entered the political life of Sweden at the turn of the nineteenth century).

In the case of the AED, no such similar discourse on the rights of minorities existed prior to its introduction. In fact, far from being concerned with the natural right of immigrant groups to protection against ethnic discrimination, the Swedish public discourse constructed the immigrant groups in Sweden as social and economic problems.[39] Understandably, many employers and even agencies within the public sector regarded ethnic discrimination as an unproblematic form of practice. In 1996, after the introduction of the first anti-discrimination Act containing a ban on discrimination in working life, it was, for example, disclosed that many public and private job centres automatically excluded immigrants from their list of applicants to certain job openings when requested to do so by the employers.[40] This disclosure supported a previous investigation conducted by Ylve Brune on behalf of the Swedish immigration authorities on the situation of immigrants in the labour market, which illustrated widespread discrimination in the labour market. Many of the employers interviewed by Brune openly admitted that, whenever possible, they avoided recruiting immigrants.[41] The AED, therefore, had to construct its object of regulation by redefining ethnic discrimination as a socially undesirable practice with detrimental effects. It had to problematise ethnic discrimination for native Swedes — who constitute the overwhelming majority of the population — as *de facto* existing and undesirable behaviour in a way that EWMA did not need to do.

A further point to be made here is that in both cases the anti-discrimination laws need to be understood in relation to their objects of regulation and not as legal instruments existing apart from what they were set to regulate. The EWMA emerged at the same time as the need to guarantee equality between women and men consolidated itself as a specific right through a political discourse in the grassroots. The AED, on the other hand, had to initiate such a rights discourse, a fact that is reflected in the process of developing the legislation against ethnic discrimination, which began with the appointment of an ombudsman against ethnic discrimination, who was primarily to improve ethnic relations by extra-legal means and to report to Parliament.

The volume of complaints received by each of these ombudsmen is also linked to the degree to which the rights represented by the two anti-discrimination laws are already rooted in the mainstream culture of the

[39] See R Banakar, 'Det offentliga samtalet om ethnokulturella frågor' (Public Discourse on Ethno-Cultural Issues) *Häften för kritiska studier* ((1993) The Swedish Critical Studies Review) 2–21.

[40] This became public knowledge when some journalists, pretending to be recruiting manpower for fictitious firms, contacted a number of employment centres. The manpower they were looking for did not have to possess any particular skills and did not need to be competent in the Swedish language. The journalists requested that immigrants were to be excluded from the shortlist prepared by the job centre. No fewer than 14 of the 24 job centres that were contacted accepted this discriminatory procedure without any question. Source: D Nyheter, 'Dyr diskriminering av invandrare', 8 January 1996.

[41] See Y Brune, *Invandrare i svenskt arbetsliv* (Norrköping, Statens Invandrarverk, 1993).

Swedish society. When considering that the population of women is approximately three times larger than the population of ethnic minorities, the number of cases lodged with the DO becomes, relatively speaking, five times larger than those lodged with the EO. One possible explanation is that ethnic discrimination is considerably more widespread in society. This explanation is supported by a recent study conducted by the DO which demonstrates that both employers and unions have a poor knowledge of the AED. Notwithstanding the DO's campaigns to inform the public and private sectors about the law against ethnic discrimination, according to this study, one third of all employers in Sweden have no knowledge of the AED and of those who are acquainted with the AED only a fraction have a detailed knowledge of the law. Also, some 65 per cent of employers have not fulfilled the 'active measures' required of them by the AED. At the same time, studies conducted by the DO indicate that a majority of the immigrant population feel that they are being discriminated against in the labour market. Although the experience of being discriminated against is not necessarily a proof of the existence of actual discriminatory treatment, yet the fact that a significant section of the immigrant population in Sweden shares this experience, indicates a serious problem, one of the causes of which might very well be the existence of widespread ethnic discrimination.[42] All this points to the fact that the values of non-discrimination in relation to ethnically different groups and its corresponding right of ethnic minorities to equal treatment are far from established in Sweden.

To sum up, although it is essential to critically scrutinise the technical elements of any legislation and when possible to eliminate their shortcomings, no amount of legal/technical improvements and sophistication necessarily bring us any closer to the policy goals envisaged by the legislature or to the realisation of rights which do not already enjoy some form of popular support. Thus, the two Swedish anti-discrimination laws and their corresponding rights to equal treatment produce different results, not because they operate differently from a point of view internal to the law, or because they prescribe different sanctions and employ different procedures, or because one is enforced more rigorously than the other, but because they constitute two different forms of legislation, the one emerging from below as a result of an ongoing rights discourse and acting bottom up, the other being imposed from above to introduce a rights discourse and acting top down.

[42] See the DO's Final Report on *Immigrants' Experiences of Discrimination* (Slutreport om invandrares diskriminering) from 1999. According to this study, 1/3 of the 3,338 immigrant respondents who had applied for job openings during the last 5 years maintained that they were refused employment because of their foreign background. A quarter of the respondents reported that they had been subjected to ethnic harassment in their workplace.

8

Human Rights and French Criminal Justice: Opening the Door to Pre-Trial Defence Rights

JACQUELINE HODGSON

INTRODUCTION

THE PASSING OF the Human Rights Act 1998 has been celebrated by many as the dawning of a new era, in which human rights will now become a natural part of UK legal discourse, upheld by the courts, asserted by lawyers and legislated by Parliament. More cautious observers will want to wait a little before proclaiming the legislation an unqualified success. What I seek to do in this chapter is to offer some observations upon another jurisdiction, France, where the European Convention on Human Rights (ECHR) has been incorporated into domestic law for nearly thirty years.[1] Drawing upon my own qualitative empirical work,[2] as well as case law and recent legislation, I consider some of the ways in which

[1] Though the right of individual petition to the European Court was only agreed in 1981.

[2] I am grateful to the British Academy and the Nuffield Foundation for supporting early fieldwork (1993–94) and to the Leverhulme Trust for funding the subsequent larger study (1997–99). A total of 18 months observational fieldwork was conducted in the period 1993–94 and 1997–98 by me and two French colleagues (to whom I am greatly indebted), Ms Geneviève Rich and Ms Brigitte Perroud. The sites of research were Paris, two large urban centres, a medium sized town and a small area of 170,000 inhabitants, referred to as sites A–F (in site B, interviews only were conducted). We spent between one and four months at each site, located in the offices of *procureurs*, *juges d'instruction*, police and *gendarmes*, where we were able to observe the ways in which criminal investigations are directed and supervised on a daily basis, as well as the conduct of pre-trial hearings and the questioning of suspects and witnesses. By being placed in the office of the group being observed, we were able to follow cases through the process and to supplement our observations with discussion of particular cases or decisions and the wider issues which arose out of them. We were also allowed access to case dossiers at each stage of the process. At the end of the observation period we

the ECHR has impacted upon the French criminal justice process and the legal actors working within it. An examination of the legal, political and structural contexts that both influence and constrain the reception of Convention rights, illustrates the complexity of operationalising and making effective, even rights which are, in theory, fully incorporated into the domestic legal system. It also poses questions about the nature and scope of Convention rights and the extent to which we can legitimately expect them to provide 'universal' guarantees which are understood and applied consistently across jurisdictions.[3]

The French example provides an interesting point of comparison for a number of reasons. First, the UK operates a dualist constitutional system which requires the express enactment of parliamentary legislation in order to incorporate international law, treaties or conventions into domestic law. Thus, it was necessary to pass the European Communities Act 1972 in order that European law could be relied upon and applied directly in the domestic courts. The Human Rights Act 1998 achieves a similar (though not identical) objective in relation to the ECHR. France, on the other hand, has a monist constitutional system and under Article 55 of the Constitution, ratified conventions such as the ECHR are automatically incorporated into French law[4] without the need for further legislation. Free from the shackles of parliamentary supremacy, the Convention can be relied upon directly at all levels.[5] As the UK grapples with the impact of its own version of near-incorporation (which leaves the principle of parliamentary supremacy intact), it is instructive to consider the outcomes of a different approach, where incorporation (in theory at least)

conducted 20 interviews (primarily with *magistrats*) and received 37 questionnaire responses from *procureurs* and 12 from police. While the process of comparative research can be a difficult one and in particular, understanding subjects in their own terms, the methodology adopted has a number of strengths. The qualitative data gathered over a relatively long time period provides a detailed and intricate account of the daily workings of the criminal process and the practices of key actors within it — across different locations and different time periods. In order to avoid the premature narrowing of research issues and an excessively ethnocentric approach, data was cross-checked and challenged contemporaneously within the field (with the actors observed and on occasions, with the other fieldworker) and then subsequently across sites, as well as through interviews and questionnaires. The input of three different field workers (an English lawyer, a French lawyer and a French social scientist) also ensured that a variety of perspectives contributed to the development of the study.

[3] The extent to which rights are universally understood and applied is also an important issue in the debate around the EU Charter of Fundamental Rights and its role in promoting a more integrated Europe.

[4] In the hierarchy of norms, they are considered below constitutional law but above domestic legislation.

[5] While the Declaration of the Rights of Man and the Citizen has existed since 1789, the ECHR provides additional guarantees, especially in the area of criminal procedure (eg Arts 5 and 6) and so is to be preferred. In addition, the Declaration is a constitutional norm and so cannot be used by the ordinary courts in reviewing the proper scope and interpretation of a statute.

is both total and constitutionally guaranteed. Secondly, while the UK is in its infancy in the direct enforcement of the ECHR, France ratified the Convention in 1974 and therefore exemplifies a jurisdiction with a much longer experience of negotiating human rights within criminal justice, experience on which it is useful to draw. In particular, it is useful to examine the factors which contribute to (non) compliance and to the development (or not) of a wider legal culture in which notions of human rights are easily accommodated. Thirdly, French criminal procedure is largely inquisitorial, which has an important bearing on the way in which notions such as 'defence rights' and 'equality of arms' are understood, interpreted and applied within this different structural and procedural context.

Beginning with a brief overview of the incorporation of the ECHR and the changing ways in which the Convention has influenced the courts and the legislature, I will then focus upon the recent reform of June 2000, which seeks to 'reinforce the protection of the presumption of innocence and the rights of victims.' The promotion of ECHR guarantees forms an important part of this reform and discussion will centre upon the context in which this legislation was necessary and an empirical account of the ways in which certain Convention rights and guarantees are understood and applied in practice.

The thrust of my argument is that despite its monist system (which should make incorporation and application less problematic), France exhibits many of the same anxieties as the UK in terms of judicial autonomy and national sovereignty. Furthermore, the translation of Convention guarantees into the French inquisitorial context has been problematic, creating tensions with prevailing legal cultures at both the macro level of the courts and legislature and at the micro level of police, lawyers and judges.

INCORPORATING THE CONVENTION

Incorporation of the ECHR was initially resisted for several decades and it was only after many years of debate that France finally ratified the Convention in 1974. This reluctance arose out of fears that incorporation would result in a loss of sovereignty[6] and that it would interfere unduly with France's domestic law in sensitive areas such as the president's powers in times of war, the funding of religious schools and the treatment of people detained by the police.[7] Once ratified, enforcing the superiority of this and

[6] This was a politically sensitive issue given the involvement of the French government in the Algerian conflict in the 1950s.

[7] At that time, six days (now reduced to four) for those suspected of offences against the state and terrorism.

other treaties under Article 55 of the Constitution also proved problematic and the issue was litigated in each of the supreme judicial bodies in France.[8] Concern to avoid exposing France to the close scrutiny of an international organisation meant that the right to individual petition was yet further delayed until 1981.[9]

In other countries with a monist system, such as The Netherlands, incorporation has resulted in the Convention being used in the domestic courts on a regular basis and the evolution of a developed human rights jurisprudence.[10] The same has not been true of France, which has a high rate of condemnation by the European Court, around half of them relating to criminal procedure.[11] Furthermore, the condemnations relate not simply to one-off cases, but to faults which are endemic to the French system, such as police brutality, the non-respect of defence rights and excessive periods of detention before trial, suggesting that incorporation has had little impact on many important areas of criminal procedure and justice. Before examining recent legislation passed in France relating to criminal procedure, I will look briefly at some of the preceding case law relating to Convention guarantees and the response of the French courts and legislature.

FRANCE CONDEMNED

Once individual petition to the European Court was allowed and applicants in France were no longer dependent upon the domestic courts to uphold their Convention rights, there followed a string of cases in which the European Court condemned practices such as the procedure for setting up telephone taps;[12] the absence of legal aid provision to instruct a

[8] Primarily concerning EC law, the point was litigated in the Conseil Constitutionnel, the Cour de cassation and the Conseil d'Etat. See E Steiner in C A Gearty (ed), *European Civil Liberties and the European Convention on Human Rights: A Comparative Study* (The Hague, Kluwer, 1997), 267–305, 278–80. These concerns were also apparent in France's initial reluctance to embrace the superiority of EC law. See eg, discussion in AZ Drzemczewski, *European Human Rights Convention in Domestic Law: A Comparative Study* (Oxford, Clarendon Press, 1983).

[9] Successive governments claimed (i) that human rights were already adequately protected by French domestic law and (ii) that the application of the Convention should be tested by the national courts before making available international remedies. See further Steiner, above n 8, at 276–8.

[10] See, eg Y Klerk and E Janse de Jorg in CA Gearty (ed), above n 8.

[11] On a year on year basis, only Italy and Turkey have more cases decided against them (though the nature of those against Turkey are generally of the most serious nature and the majority of those against Italy relate to delay). The figures for the last few years are: 1999 Italy (44), Turkey (18), France (16); 2000 Italy (233), France (49), Turkey (23); 2001 Italy (359), Turkey (169), France (32); 2002 Italy (325), France (61), Turkey (54). Denmark, Germany and The Netherlands all have comparatively low numbers of cases decided against them.

[12] *Kruslin & Huvig*, ECHR 24/04/90.

defence lawyer;[13] the length of detention awaiting trial;[14] and the violent treatment of those detained in police custody (*garde à vue*, GAV).[15] France duly responded with legislation[16] and the Cour de cassation took note of the European Court decisions in the development of its own jurisprudence.[17] A 'high point' in this positive reception of the Convention was reached in 1993, when legislation was passed[18] which put in place, among other things, a legal framework to regulate the period of police detention of suspects and the amount of time suspects could be detained during investigation under the *instruction* procedure.[19] However, the tide changed with the new political administration and a number of provisions were repealed or never implemented.[20] There then followed a period of retrenchment, leading to what Marguénaud describes as a 'disaster', where criminal procedure went adrift from the Convention and the attitude of the courts and legislators became increasingly one of 'arrogance'.[21] The Cour

[13] *Pham Hoang,* ECHR 25/09/92.
[14] *Letellier,* ECHR 26/06/91, *Kemmache,* ECHR 27/11/91.
[15] *Tomasi,* ECHR 27/08/92.
[16] Eg Following *Kruslin & Huvig,* ECHR 24/04/90, a law was passed regulating telephone tapping (loi No 91–646). Anticipating the decision on *Pham Hoang,* ECHR 25/09/92, loi No 91–647 reformed legal aid provision.
[17] Following a Ministry of Justice circular issued immediately after the *Huvig* and *Kruslin* cases, emphasising the conditions under which telephone taps should be ordered, the Cour de cassation enforced this through its case law. It was criticised in this, as usurping the legislative function by adding conditions to Art 81 CPP, the authority under which the *juge d'instruction* may order a telephone tap to be set up.
[18] This legislation was preceded by a commission whose task was to examine the extent to which French criminal procedure was in conformity with the ECHR: chaired by Mireille Delmas-Marty, *La mise en état des affaires pénales: Rapport de la Commission Justice pénale et Droits de l'homme* (Paris, La Documentation Française, 1991). For discussion of this legislation see H Trouille, 'A Look at French Criminal Procedure' [1994] *Criminal Law Review* 735–44 and J Hodgson and G Rich, 'A Criminal Defence for the French?' (1993) 143 *New Law Journal* 414ff.
[19] This procedure refers to the investigation undertaken by the *juge d'instruction*, which occurs in some 7% of all criminal cases. It is mandatory for the most serious offences, *crimes*, but otherwise, within the discretion of the public prosecutor, the *procureur* whether to refer lesser offences. Given the lack of resources, in practice, it will only be the more serious or complex *délits* that are referred, or cases where the police require wider powers which can only be authorised by the *juge d'instruction*. Of the 37,000 cases referred to the *juge d'instruction* in 2001, around 7,000 related to *crimes* and 30,000 to *délits*.
[20] Eg the *juge délegué* had been introduced in Spring 1993, responsible for determining whether or not to detain those investigated by the *juge d'instruction*. This was promptly repealed in August of the same year and the decision returned to the *juge d'instruction*. In a process of staged implementation, lawyers were allowed access to suspects held in police custody, 20 hours after the start of detention. The plan had been to extend the arrangement, allowing access from the start of detention, but this also was abandoned by the new government. Interestingly, both of these reforms were finally legislated in the June 2000 Act, discussed below. The shift from Jospin's socialist government to the rightwing Raffarin administration is again impacting on criminal justice legislation, the Interior Minister, Nicolas Sarkozy being very active in this respect. See also n 35 below.
[21] J-P Marguénaud, 'La dérive de la procédure pénale française au regard des exigences européennes' [2000] *Dalloz (Chroniques)* 249–55.

de cassation,[22] instead of incorporating the jurisprudence of the European Court within its own, contrived to limit the applicability of the Convention, either by distinguishing cases on tenuous and cynical grounds,[23] or holding that decisions which allowed the appellant to claim reparation had no effect upon the domestic law, so accentuating the 'declaratory' nature of European Court decisions.[24] Thus, France continued to apply practices and procedures which had been clearly condemned by the European Court and unsurprisingly, this led to further findings against France. For example, despite the well known case of *Poitrimol,*[25] where the European Court held that denial of appeal was an excessive penalty for the non-appearance of the appellant in the Cour de cassation, there followed three more cases in which the French courts continued with this practice — *Guérin, Omar* and *Coquin.*[26] The legislature, for its part, was also indifferent to the rulings from Strasbourg. It failed to address the excessive delays which continued to blight the criminal justice process, resulting in a further three condemnations in October 1999.[27] The defiance of the French judges and legislators on the one hand, and the increasingly broad interpretation of the Convention developed by the new permanent European Court on the other, came to a spectacular head in July 1999, dealing a serious blow to France. In the case of *Selmouni*,[28] the Court unanimously held that France had violated Article 3 of the ECHR, not only on account of inhuman and degrading treatment, but more significantly on the more serious ground of torture.[29] This makes

[22] The highest criminal court, which does not make a decision on the facts of the case, but on whether the law has been applied correctly.

[23] Resulting in another European Court condemnation, *Lambert,* ECHR 24/08/98.

[24] Despite the European Court's decision that there had been an unreasonable delay contrary to Art 6(1) ECHR in *Kemmache* 27/11/91, the Cour de cassation (03/02/93) held that the provision for reparation meant that the decision did not affect the validity of any of the procedures of the domestic law.

[25] ECHR 23/11/93.

[26] 19/01/94, 07/02/94 and 15/02/94 respectively. This, of course, resulted in further condemnations by the European Court — *Omar & Guérin*, ECHR 29/07/98.

[27] In *Djaïd*, ECHR 29/09/99 the Cour de cassation had taken more than two years to decide an appeal on a point of law; in *Donsimoni*, ECHR 05/10/99 it took over five years to bring to trial an accomplice to fraud in the Tribunal Correctionnel (this court hears the majority of criminal cases); and in *Maini*, ECHR 26/10/99 the *instruction* took over four and a half years. Further condemnations have followed: In *PB,* ECHR 01/11/00, *Gombert & Gochgarian*, ECHR 13/05/01 and *Richet*, ECHR 13/05/01, the delay was some four years and nine months; in *Zannouti*, ECHR 31/07/01 it was nearly six years, of which five and a half were spent in custody.

[28] ECHR 28/07/99. The applicant claimed that the police beat him, assaulted him with objects, urinated on him, dragged him by the hair, sexually assaulted him (although this part of the claim was not proved) and threatened him with a blow torch.

[29] Although the Court found that the pain and suffering experienced by the applicant was sufficiently severe to constitute torture, they also noted the higher standards which were now applied. The Court also noted that because: 'the Convention is a living instrument and must be interpreted in the light of present day conditions, certain acts which were classified in the

France only the second country (Turkey being the first) to have such a finding against it.[30]

With the socialist administration of the late 1990s, legislation following the Truche Commission report (1997)[31] and some Cour de cassation decisions[32] seemed to be indicative of a possible change in approach, which is more receptive to the need for conformity with the Convention.[33] While the Cour de cassation appears to be continuing this trajectory,[34] it is unlikely to be mirrored by the legislature in the present political climate and it is unclear whether or not it will be maintained, or whether we will see the Cour retreat to the position adopted in the mid-1990s. Jospin's government diluted some of the provisions of the 2000 project (described below) in the 'petite loi' of March 2002 and the optimism surrounding the original reform had already evaporated by that time, as rising crime figures and presidential election concerns with law and order took centre stage.[35] Under the new rightwing Raffarin administration which took office in 2002, a range of authoritarian measures were proposed by the Minister of the Interior, Nicholas Sarkozy (who has been criticised as dominating the justice agenda) and the justice minister, Dominique Perben

past as "inhuman and degrading treatment" as opposed to "torture" could be classified differently in future. It takes the view that the increasingly high standard being required in the area of the protection of human rights and fundamental liberties correspondingly and inevitable requires greater firmness in assessing breaches of the fundamental values of democratic societies' (para 101). Knowing that the same case, if brought ten years earlier, would have been unlikely to result in a finding of torture was doubtless of little consolation to France.

[30] *Aksoy v Turkey* (1996) 23 EHRR 553. Concern over the treatment of political detainees in Greece led to a Commission finding of torture against Greece, confirmed by the Committee of Ministers — *Greek case* (1969) 12 YB 170.

[31] Chaired by the president of the Cour de cassation, Pierre Truche, *Rapport de la commission de réflexion sur la Justice* (Paris, La documentation Française, 1997).

[32] Eg *Dentico* (02/03/01) where the Cour de cassation held that there was a breach of Art 6 (1) ECHR. Reversing a long line of decisions where the defendant had been convicted in her absence, the Court held that denying legal representation to absent defendants breached their right to fair trial and to defence representation.

[33] There is still criticism of what some see as the increasingly interventionist approach of the European Court. One commentator responded to a recent European Court decision, *Dulaurans*, ECHR 21/03/00 (where the decision, not simply the procedure of the Cour de cassation was condemned) by questioning whether, just as the Franc has surrendered to the Euro, the Cour de cassation will have to make way for the European Court as the ultimate appeal court. J-F Burgelin, 'La Cour de cassation en question' (2001) 12 *Dalloz* 932–34.

[34] See, eg the important decision 02/03/01 which, following *Poitrimol*, ECHR 23/11/93 and *Van Pelt*, 23/05/00 (and contradicting earlier case law, see above n 26) reinterpreted Arts 410, 411 and 417 CPP, holding that it would be contrary to the right to a fair trial and to defence assistance to judge a person in their absence, without hearing their defence lawyer. Note also the change in practice, excluding the *Parquet général* from the decision making process of the Cour de cassation, described in the Court's 2001 annual report.

[35] Note also the passing of Loi No 2001–1062 *relative à la sécurité quotidienne* in November 2001, which included controversial anti-terrorism measures, added to the Bill at the last moment.

followed suit.[36] Predictably, there has been a shift to more repressive legislation (notably in relation to the treatment of juvenile offenders) with aspects of the June 2000 already modified[37] and strengthening the fair trial rights of the accused is not a priority on the current government's legislative agenda.[38] There are a variety of factors which have influenced the legal landscape — notably changes of government, but also the defence of national sovereignty from the encroachment of an international body, wider considerations of the national *politique pénale*, concerns as to how France is regarded within the international community (notably following the shame of the *Selmouni* decision) and the European Court's more robust interpretation of the Convention. Whatever the explanations, the fact remains that incorporation of the ECHR represents only one stage towards bringing Convention rights into French criminal procedure. The courts and Parliament may act to hinder, as much as to help this process.

Having outlined the broader picture, I now turn to an important recent piece of criminal justice legislation, the June 2000 project,[39] which has been presented as an important advance in strengthening the rights of both suspects and victims, ensuring that criminal procedure reflects better the ECHR and so avoids continued condemnations from Strasbourg.[40] As well as considering the context of the reform and why it was necessary, I will also examine the ways in which defence rights in particular are understood by those responsible for operationalising the new procedures and the consequences this might have for the success of both the legislation and a wider rights culture.

LEGISLATING THE ECHR GUARANTEES: THE JUNE 2000 REFORM

The June 2000 law is an important reform which has attracted much debate both before and since its arrival on the statute book[41] and it has already

[36] See, eg the 2004 legislation, which doubles the length of time suspects in some cases might be detained in GAV, with access to custodial legal advice denied until 36 hours into the detention period.

[37] See, eg Loi No 2002–1138 *d'orientation et de programmation pour la justice*, 9 September 2002. The *loi pour la sécurité intérieure* in March 2003 repealed the provision put in place in 2000, which required the police to inform the suspect of her right to silence.

[38] See, eg *Le Monde*, 10 January 2003, p 10.

[39] This legislation is part of a wider reform package legislated after the Truche Commission report in 1997. For a more detailed discussion of the reform, see J Hodgson, 'Suspects, Defendants and Victims in French Criminal Justice: The Context of Recent Reform' (2002) 51 (4) *International and Comparative Law Quarterly* 781–816.

[40] See, eg the speeches to the Sénat of the then Minister of Justice Mme Guigou, 15 June 1999, 29 March 2000.

[41] Loi No 2000–516 *du 15 juin 2000 renforçant la protection de la présomption d'innocence et les droits des victimes*.

been amended in a small, but arguably significant, 'reform of the reform',[42] which takes account of the views and experiences of practitioners. It seeks to 'strengthen the protection of the presumption of innocence and the rights of victims,' and it does this in a number of ways: by reinforcing some of the guarantees established in the 1993 reforms; by responding to specific condemnations by the European Court; and by enacting some basic ECHR requirements. What is of particular interest to the outside observer, is the extent to which it has been felt necessary to enact legislation in order to ensure conformity with basic Convention rights: as the case law discussed above demonstrates, reliance upon the monist system of incorporation alone appears to have failed to incorporate ECHR guarantees sufficiently into French criminal procedure. This is not wholly surprising. Even in a monist constitutional system, it would be unrealistic to expect incorporation alone to transform sufficiently the legal landscape. There will inevitably be some aspects of domestic law which will need revising through legislation and France provides an interesting case study of how and in what circumstances this is effected and the interplay with existing domestic legal cultures. In some instances, existing legal provisions have been amplified and interpreted by the courts in a way that ensures conformity. But in other cases, even where there is clear conflict between the French conception of due process rights at a systemic level and the standards developed by the ECHR, these differences have been allowed to stand, leaving case law and legislation defiantly out of step with the Convention. The June 2000 legislation is an example of a reform which seeks explicitly to bring French criminal procedure into line with the ECHR.

Many of the European Court decisions against France concern Article 5(3) ECHR and the length of time suspects spend on remand in prison while the investigation is ongoing, before any decision to prosecute has been taken. While long periods of detention were in accordance with French law, they were held to breach the Convention. Famously, in the case of *Tomasi*[43] a detention period of over five and a half years before the accused was finally tried and acquitted, was held to be unjustified.[44] This led to some changes in the 1993 reform (including the short-lived *juge délegué*) but the huge numbers of people in pre-trial custody continued to be a thorn in the side of justice ministers.[45] The current reform transfers the power to detain a person under investigation during *instruction* from the *juge d'instruction* to

[42] The 'petite loi' of March 2002 is officially described as a law complementing that of June 2000. Further changes have been made under the new Raffarin administration and a reform in March 2003, sponsored by the Interior Minister, Nicolas Sarkozy, removed the obligation (introduced in the 2000 reform) upon the police to inform the suspect of her right to silence.
[43] ECHR 27/08/92. See also *Kemmache*, ECHR 27/11/91 and *Letellier*, ECHR 26/06/91.
[44] It should be noted, that suspects detained in custody who are eventually acquitted at trial or against whom no prosecution is ever brought, can claim compensation from the state.
[45] See also *Muller* (17/03/97).

the newly created *juge des libertés et de la detention*, in the hope that this will reduce the number of those detained.[46]

Another area in which France has failed to respond to decisions of the European Court is in the treatment of those appealing to the Cour de cassation. Under Article 583 *Code de procédure pénale* (CPP), unless special dispensation had been granted, appellants to the Cour de cassation were obliged to surrender themselves into custody the day before their hearing took place. Failure to do so resulted in the automatic rejection of the appeal. Despite repeated condemnations by the European Court, on the grounds that this was an excessive penalty to impose upon appellants and in breach of Article 6 ECHR, the French courts continued to apply the rule.[47] The legislature has now intervened and Article 583 has been amended accordingly.

Provisions are also finally in place for the re-examination of cases successfully brought to the European Court by individuals who claim that they were treated unfairly in some way. France was heavily criticised for its refusal to reopen a case after it had been condemned by the European Court in 1997 for failing to respect the rights of the defence: Abdelhamid Hakkar was convicted in his absence and without defence representation, of murdering a police officer.[48] The only other European country failing to reopen a case considered unfair under the ECHR (and the only other to be convicted of torture) is Turkey. The June reform amended Article 626 CPP to ensure that in future, such cases can be reopened at the request of any of the parties involved.

Other aspects of the reform, while not relating to specific condemnations by the European Court, address important Convention requirements more generally. For example, the reform of Article 63–1 CPP requiring the police to inform the suspect of the reasons for her detention in police custody is necessary in order to comply with Article 5(2) ECHR which states that: 'Everyone who is arrested shall be informed promptly, in a language which he understands, of the reasons for his arrest and of any charge against him.' Similarly, the provision of translators at all stages of the criminal process is a basic ECHR requirement. The reform also removed the power of the police to detain in GAV witnesses against whom there was no suspicion of having committed an offence.[49] Other significant changes

[46] Although the wish of the *juge d'instruction* to remand a suspect in custody is followed in the majority of cases, the reform appears to have been successful in reducing the numbers of people detained. See, eg *le Monde*, 10/05/01 and the *chiffres-clés de la justice* published by the Ministry of Justice which show an annual fall from around 22,500 for the years preceding the reform, to 16,700 in 2001.

[47] *Poitrimol*, ECHR 23/11/93; *Omar and Guérin*, ECHR 29/7/98; *Khalfaoui*, ECHR 14/12/99.

[48] See, eg discussion in *Le Monde*, 16/02/00.

[49] This power was removed in 1993 in the case of ordinary investigations (*enquêtes préliminaires*) and the 2000 legislation does the same for *enquêtes flagrantes* — the 85% of

include allowing the suspect access to her defence lawyer at the start of the GAV (rather than after 20 hours, as was previously the case) and the obligation upon the police, for the first time, to inform the suspect of her right to silence (though this has subsequently been repealed).

It is apparent, even from this brief sketch of some of the most salient provisions, that the reform makes important changes to the administration of French criminal justice, plugging significant gaps in the protection of the accused which have persisted (many of them never litigated) despite incorporation of the ECHR — and this is to be welcomed. However, even taking into account the different historical roots and legal culture of French criminal justice as an inquisitorial/mixed procedure, with a different structure of safeguards based around a judicial supervision model, there were (and arguably, still are) significant deficiencies to be addressed. This was a criminal process, where until the passing of these reforms, the police were not obliged to tell the suspect either of her right to silence (though this is again the case) or of the nature of the enquiry in connection with which she was being held; where the suspect held in police custody had access to a defence lawyer only after 20 hours of detention and then, for only half an hour (an arrangement which meant that in practice, less than 10 per cent of people held in GAV were able to consult with their lawyer); where witnesses could be held in GAV; and where there was no appeal against conviction for the most serious offences, *crimes*, tried in the *cour d'assises*.

AVOIDING ADVERSARIALISM

The reform is a significant step forward in developing the due process protections of those accused and convicted in the criminal courts and in changing the rhetoric of criminal justice to a discourse which is more influenced by and which now takes more seriously, the jurisprudence of the ECHR. There is greater talk of 'defence rights' of 'participation rights' and of 'equality of arms'. However, behind the optimistic rhetoric of universal norms and standards, there remains a sense of unease about just how far such changes in criminal procedure might legitimately go. In particular, while seeing itself as the 'homeland of rights' and a faithful adherent to the ECHR, France is also deeply sceptical of invoking concepts such as 'equality of arms' in a way which might be regarded as moving away from the inquisitorial or mixed system to which France is committed, and towards an adversarial procedure — a move which is to be avoided at all costs. During the passage of the Bill through Parliament, the then justice minister

investigations which relate to recently committed offences. The original power was considered to be in conformity with the Convention under Art 5(1)(b) 'in order to secure the fulfilment of any obligation prescribed by law.'

used every available opportunity in Parliament and in the media, to affirm her resistance to things adversarial. For example, in addressing the *Sénat* (15 June 1999), Madame Guigou said:

> The adversarial system of justice is by nature unfair and unjust. It favours the strong over the weak. It accentuates social and cultural differences, favouring the rich who are able to engage and pay for the services of one or more lawyers. Our own system is better, both in terms of efficiency and of the rights of the individual ... I prefer, and I want to make this quite plain, an independent judge who investigates evidence both for and against the suspect, to police officers who carry out large parts of the criminal investigation without any judicial supervision.

In an interview with *Le Monde* (15 December, 1999), she rejected the idea of the defence lawyer playing a greater role in the process:

> Lawyers are there to help their clients and to ensure the proper conduct of the *garde à vue*, but not to start getting involved in the case. I have chosen not to adopt the adversarial procedure because it reinforces the inequalities of access to the law. It would lead ultimately, for example, to the use of private investigators in order to verify the investigation led by the police.

As a consequence of this tension, those sponsoring the reform have had to tread a fine line, introducing changes that will ensure ECHR compliance, yet doing this in a way which does not challenge the basic structures and procedures of the existing legal process. The strengthening of defence rights in particular, is seen as being at odds with the judicial supervision model which is at the heart of French pre-trial procedure. Despite the optimistic rights-based rhetoric surrounding its introduction, the result is a relatively cautious piece of legislation which, in many instances, makes only the minimum changes necessary to ensure compliance with the Convention.[50] In particular, while the statute establishes protections such as the right to silence and the need for reasonable suspicion before placing a person in GAV, the official Ministry of Justice circulars, in many instances, act as a kind of counter current to the legislation, undercutting the effectiveness of the legislative provisions. For example, the principle that the suspect should not be required to incriminate herself is intimately linked to the presumption of innocence and to the fair trial guarantees under Article 6 ECHR. Although the right to silence existed for the suspect held in GAV prior to June 2000, it was not until this reform that the

[50] Eg, while suspects may now have access to custodial legal advice at the start of the *garde à vue*, consultation is limited to 30 minutes and the lawyer may not be present during the interrogation. The Truche Commission's recommendation that interrogations be tape recorded was rejected.

police were legally obliged to inform her of the right. However, this advance was undercut somewhat by the terms of the accompanying circular. While officers were reminded that the law required them to inform the suspect of her right to silence at the start of the GAV, the circular pointed out that there was no obligation beyond this. Officers were instructed not to remind the suspect of her right to silence at the start of interrogations, on the grounds that it was neither desirable nor legally required; to do so would be 'pointless'; and it would encourage the suspect to say nothing, which would be against her own interests.[51] In essence, the suspect was informed of her right, but there was a concern that she should be dissuaded from exercising it. The Raffarin administration has now gone further in repealing this provision altogether.

DEFENCE RIGHTS AND THE CULTURE OF JUDICIAL SUPERVISION

It is in the treatment of pre-trial defence rights in particular that we see demonstrated most clearly the tensions between the development of ECHR guarantees and those contained within domestic French criminal procedure.

Although expressed as the right to a fair trial, Article 6 guarantees apply well before the accused ever reaches the courtroom. The jurisprudence of the European Court recognises that the trial cannot be treated as a discrete phase in the criminal process, unaffected by the processes which precede it. A denial of defence rights at the pre-trial stage is likely to prejudice the preparation of the defence case and so the fairness of the trial. Thus, Article 6 guarantees have been held to apply to the individual from the point of charge. This has been interpreted in a substantive rather than formal way, looking at the realities of the procedure rather than the appearance or official terminology.[52] Once the individual is under investigation, her position has been substantially affected[53] and she is, at that point, in need of and entitled to the protection of Article 6 — even if a formal charge or indictment is never brought.[54] This protection includes access to custodial legal advice as it is 'fundamental to the preparation of [an accused person's] defence'[55] which in turn forms part of the fair trial requirements which are

[51] It is interesting that a right which is generally regarded as being for the protection of the suspect, is seen in the reverse way in France, as being contrary to her interests.
[52] *Adolf v Austria* 1982 4 EHRR 313 para 30.
[53] This may be at the point of arrest (*Foti v Italy* 1983 5 EHRR 313 para 52) or formal police charge (*X v UK* 1979) 14 DR 26.
[54] As in *Allenet de Ribemont v France* 1995 20 EHRR 557 where the Court held that the person was charged at the point of arrest.
[55] *Bonzi v Switzerland* (1978) 12 DR 185 at 190.

relevant before trial 'in so far as the fairness of the trial is likely to be prejudiced by an initial failure to comply with them.'[56]

For many French practitioners, however, the development of pre-trial defence rights is regarded negatively, as undermining the existing structure of legal protections effected through the prevailing model of judicial supervision — and the professional and ideological distance between the *magistrat* who represents the public interest and the *avocat* who represents the interests of the suspect/accused, contributes further to this polarisation of approaches.[57] The extent to which such personnel consider pre-trial defence rights necessary or appropriate is significant in assessing the ways in which Convention rights are understood and received by legal actors, as well as the likely impact which reforms such as the 2000 legislation will have on their daily practices. For this reason, the nature and consequences of the judicial supervision model and the ways in which it functions in practice merit closer examination.

The French criminal justice process, though properly described as mixed (defence lawyers have access to the dossier in serious cases and there is open debate around decisions such as pre-trial detention) retains important inquisitorial elements. Most notably, the regime for pre-trial investigation still has at its heart the model of judicial investigation. An independent judicial officer, a *magistrat,* is responsible for investigating the offence, gathering both incriminating and exculpatory evidence in the search for the truth. The idea is that this is not a pitched battle between the police or prosecution and the suspect, but that there is one neutral investigator, investigating all aspects of the case and acting in the public interest. In the most serious or complex cases, this will be the *juge d'instruction*, but in the majority of cases (over 90 per cent) it will be the *procureur*. These judicial officers are responsible for ensuring the proper treatment of the suspect during the investigation including the respect of the rights of the defence. During the *instruction*, the defence is able to consult the dossier of evidence, suggest lines of enquiry and request that certain investigations are carried out. In the majority of cases, however, where the investigation is complete by the end of the GAV (during which time the defence lawyer has no access to the case dossier), the defence has no such opportunity and her role remains limited to the trial stage.

There are several observations that can be made about this model and the way in which it is able to accommodate ECHR notions of defence

[56] *Imbroscia v Switzerland* (1994) 17 EHRR 441 at para 36.

[57] *Magistrats* are the career trained judiciary and include the *procureur* (the public prosecutor), the *juge d'instruction* and the trial judge. The defence lawyer, as an *avocat*, undergoes different professional training. For discussion of the place of the defence lawyer in France, see further Hodgson above n 39; J Hodgson, 'Constructing the pre-trial role of the defence in French criminal procedure: An adversarial outsider in an inquisitorial process?' (2002a) 6(1) *International Journal of Evidence and Proof* 1–16.

rights and equality of arms. First, the centrality of the *magistrat* and in particular, her involvement in the investigative process while the suspect is in police detention, is held to obviate the need for anything more than cursory defence assistance,[58] militating against the strengthening of pre-trial defence rights. Yet, the nature of this judicial involvement is distant and characterised generally (both in practice and in the text of the law) as a form of (largely retrospective) legal bureaucratic review.[59] In the majority of investigations (some 93 per cent), it is the *procureur* who directs the police investigation and who is responsible for the conduct of the GAV. Supervision in these instances is a form of accountability at a distance, conducted by telephone or fax, or in some cases, with no police-*procureur* contact until the end of the detention period.[60] It would be unthinkable for a *procureur* to be present during the interrogation of a suspect:

> There used to be a woman in the *permanence* who did go down to the police station and it caused a terrible rumpus. The police were furious that she just turned up. You have to be careful when you go down — so that the police don't think it's because you're suspicious of them. [*Procureur*, Area D]

Her role is not to 'check up' on the police, so much as to ensure that the investigation appears to be legally justified and conducted according to the rules. A central feature of the police-*magistrat* relationship (and so, of judicial supervision) is trust: the police are not regarded in oppositional terms, but rather, as working alongside the *procureur*.[61] In this way, the *procureur* is unable to offer any real guarantees as to the treatment of the suspect and the process of her investigation and interrogation. Moreover, even if the *procureur* wished to play a greater part in supervising the conduct of the enquiry, the volume of work makes impossible any closer involvement except in the most serious cases.[62] This is not a model of supervision in which direct personal intervention is either required by the law or made possible by the limited resources available. The protection of defence rights is instead assured through documented compliance with

[58] That is, a 30 minute consultation, which until recently, took place 20 hours into the detention period.
[59] The *instruction* procedure represents the purest model of judicial supervision, but even there, the bulk of the investigation is assigned to the police through the legal procedure of issuing *commissions rogatoires*.
[60] See generally, J Hodgson, 'Hierarchy, Bureaucracy, and Ideology in French Criminal Justice: Some Empirical Observations' (2002b) 29(2) *Journal of Law and Society* 227–57.
[61] See further J Hodgson, 'The police, the prosecutor and the *juge d'instruction*: Judicial Supervision in France, Theory and Practice' (2001) 41 *British Journal of Criminology* 342–61.
[62] In urban areas, the *procureur* is responsible for tens of police stations and *gendarmeries* and hundreds of officers.

legal procedures — through a review concerned with the official form of the investigation, rather than the process. Neither in theory nor in practice, does judicial supervision provide the kind of protection for defence rights which is contemplated by the ECHR or which renders unnecessary the pre-trial participation of the defence lawyer.[63]

Secondly, where pre-trial defence rights have been introduced, the way in which they and the role of the defence lawyer are understood in the context of the judicial supervision model, is not in terms of assisting the suspect in the preparation of her case, as interpretations of the Article 6 guarantee might suggest.[64] Rather her role is to act as part of the wider procedural guarantees which are the concern of judicial supervision and ultimately, to legitimate the GAV process:

> In France, the lawyer is not there to advise the person, but to signal any problems in the conditions of the *garde à vue*; not so much to provide legal advice as moral support. [*Procureur*, D3].[65]
>
> This is not a time set aside specifically for preparing the defence but for the lawyer to have a first look at the events and to check the conditions of detention, to protect the suspect from abuse, but essentially, to protect the police from false accusations. There is no longer any violence — in 1970, yes — but not now. [Police officer, area D].

Anything that goes beyond replication of the *procureur*'s role is seen as inappropriate and as benefiting the suspect unfairly. The whole dynamic of the investigation in an inquisitorial process is (theoretically) configured quite differently from the model generally assumed by the ECHR. It is not viewed in a dichotomous way with the police and suspect as the two main players. Instead, the judicial officer is at the centre of the enquiry, assisted by the police. The suspect, victim and other witnesses have only walk-on parts. Thus, for the suspect to be legally represented during the interrogation is seen as privileging her interests over those of the victim and the need to conduct an effective investigation. However, this model ignores the reality of criminal investigations in France and the extent to which they are dominated by the police, rather than by *magistrats*, whether through

[63] For a more detailed comparative account of the detention and questioning of suspects, see J Hodgson, 'The detention and interrogation of suspects detained in police custody in France: a comparative account' (2004) 1(2) *European Journal of Criminology* 166–99.

[64] Note the criticism of the Documentation and Research Department of the *Cour de cassation*, who criticise the limited access to custodial legal advice available to suspects in France, which 'in no way enables them to exercise genuine rights to defence'. Response to the 2003 European Commission Green Paper, 'Procedural Safeguards for Suspects and Defendants in Criminal Proceedings throughout the European Union'.

[65] Quotations from interviews are referenced by the area (letter) and respondent (number). Extracts from the fieldnotes reference the status of the person and the area.

the wholesale assignment of investigative tasks to officers through *commission rogatoire* or the absence of any real control over the GAV and its importance in obtaining confession evidence.[66]

Interestingly, *procureurs* we observed did not regard the nature of their relationship with the police or the distant way in which supervision was conducted as problematic. Indeed, they had a strong sense of their role in ensuring the protection of defence rights, and were at home with notions of ECHR guarantees. But, in the procedural context of judicial supervision, these guarantees were understood in quite dilute terms. For them, much of this protection is provided through signed statements and a dossier constructed according to proper legal form. The process of interrogation and evidence gathering is less of a concern and the psychology of false confessions is a virtually unknown concept. Notions of equality of arms and defence rights take on a rather different meaning when viewed within an inquisitorial context.

CHARACTERISING THE ROLE OF THE DEFENCE

Paradoxically, although the defence lawyer has been involved in the pretrial stage during the *instruction* since 1897 (being present in interviews and having access to the dossier),[67] it is only since 1993 that suspects have been allowed any contact with their lawyer during the more hostile and coercive environment of the *garde à vue*. The 1993 reform permitted suspects held in *garde à vue* to consult their lawyer for 30 minutes, 20 hours after the start of detention. Under the June 2000 legislation, this has now been changed to immediate access, but still for 30 minutes and there is no access to the dossier, no right to be present during police-suspect interrogation and, despite the strong recommendation of the Truche Commission, interrogations are not taperecorded. It is the *procureur* as the judicial supervisor who remains responsible for the proper conduct of the *garde à vue* and for the treatment of the suspect.

The centrality of judicial supervision in the pre-trial phase means that the presence of the defence is not considered conducive to 'equality of arms', but rather, an imbalance which would privilege the interests of the suspect over those of the victim. Above all, the defence role is not seen as something which would strengthen the integrity of the process, but which would undermine it and benefit only the accused. Lawyers are portrayed as tending towards corruption:

> A lawyer lives from his clients and in the past, we have often observed that the deontology of the lawyer comes after his own interests and those of

[66] See further Hodgson (2001) above n 61.
[67] This was fiercely criticised at the time, as likely to frustrate the *juge's* investigation.

> his client. [There would be a] risk of accomplices fleeing, of searches rendered useless after friends had been informed. [Police questionnaire respondent, commenting on the proposal that lawyers gain access to their clients at the start of police detention].
>
> Some lawyers don't want to be searched. They are searched when they go to prison, but they don't want to be searched by the police ... There are a minority of bad lawyers who will alert the family and friends. I have proof that that has happened [Senior police officer, area C].
>
> We don't like lawyers, because they are hooligans too. A lawyer in Paris stole a piece of evidence from the file. He was paid 33,000 francs to do that. Some people pay each month so that when they are in trouble and need a lawyer ... [Police officer, area C].

As the justice minister has frequently argued, as benefiting the wealthy,

> To systematically have lawyers present during the *garde à vue* is to privilege the most intelligent and the most wealthy criminals. If the Mafia have the chance to have a lawyer during *garde à vue*, they will get one immediately and he will be the best, because he will be paid ... On the other hand, the poor boy who has never been in trouble before will ask for a lawyer immediately — will he come? Not necessarily. If he comes, will he have the necessary ability? By no means sure [D3].
>
> The lawyer, he works as a liar, to see how far he can distort the law ... The latest problem we have is the criminality of politicians and public figures ... Those who make the law protect themselves ... These 'Anglomaniacs' claim that equality of objectives is the same as equality of arms. But lawyers and judges are not the same. The lawyer wants to acquit the person who pays him. The judge wants to deliver justice to protect society [*Juge d'instruction*, area F].
>
> All the changes in terms of rights for the suspect are a cover for manipulating the system to the advantage of the few — the elite and the well-to-do [Police officer, area A].
>
> [The introduction of lawyers at the police station] is done for two reasons. To protect criminals and to help lawyers earn more money! ... They will always warn the other people that we are looking for, or at least the family ... Those who have more money can get a better lawyer and be better protected [Police officer, area C].

Despite the increasing reference to ECHR concepts of defence rights and equality of arms, these notions continue to be regarded in negative terms if they are invoked during the police investigation. Any pre-trial engagement on the part of the defence is considered inappropriate and unfair. Thus, their presence was opposed by *magistrats*, police and many commentators in 1993, and although it has not proved to hinder the enquiry, there was again resistance to allowing earlier access to custodial legal advice in 2000. The unwelcome introduction of an adversarial element, as the defence lawyer is perceived to be, undermines the structure and ideology of judicial supervision conducted by a public interest oriented *magistrat*:

> Only the *parquet*[68] should be able to check on the dossier of evidence and have access to it. Only the *parquet* should have access to the suspect if necessary [Police questionnaire respondent].
>
> 'Supervision of the *garde à vue* is the job of the *parquet* and not of the lawyer' [Police questionnaire respondent].
>
> 'I do not expect [lawyers] to participate in the search for the truth, because the truth can be terrible for their client. They are not paid to condemn their client. It is the lawyer's role to search for what is most useful to his client, against the interests of society, the interests which the *procureur* protects.' [*Procureur*, E4]

Even respected commentators, such as Jean Pradel have reacted strongly. He has recently argued that the expanded role of the defence lawyer will tempt the police to engage in a form of 'noble cause corruption' in order to ensure investigations are conducted effectively.[69] In many ways, this response is unsurprising, given the negative ways in which defence lawyers have been characterised in England and Wales, where they might properly be expected to play an adversarial role.[70] Yet, the more serious objection to pre-trial defence involvement in France is its potential to undermine the existing legal structure of judicial supervision, as understood in ideal terms.

Thus, to positively encourage the exercise of rights rather than simply informing the suspect of their existence was criticised, as was the proactive assembling of the defence case or the adoption of a posture benefiting the suspect rather than the inquiry. As one *procureur* in area D explained:

> *Procureur*: 'I would not be happy with [the lawyer's] presence in more serious matters. They will tell the suspect to say nothing because people will feel better if they say nothing, than if they confess.'
> Researcher: 'But people have the right to remain silent?'
> *Procureur*: 'Why yes! Of course!'

These accounts of the proper role of the defence are phrased in the neutral language of the professional ideology of the *magistrat*, appealing to

[68] Also known as the *ministère public*, this is the collective term for *procureurs*.
[69] J Pradel, 'Les personnes suspectes ou poursuivies après la loi du 15 juin 2000: Evolution ou révolution?' (2001) (13) *Dalloz, Doctrine* 1039–47, 1042. Pradel also argues (at 1041) that in regarding the suspect as vulnerable, the reform has perhaps gone too far in multiplying the number of measures for her protection.
[70] See discussion in M McConville, J Hodgson, L Bridges and A Pavlovic, *Standing Accused: The Organisation and Practices of Criminal Defence Lawyers in Britain* (Oxford, Clarendon, 1994).

concerns of 'public interest' and the need to avoid any hindrance to the conduct of an 'effective investigation'. Yet, the open hostility to any active defence participation is also indicative of the contradiction between the interests that the *procureur* is required to protect in theory (those of the victim and the suspect; the search for the truth and the rights of the defence) and her preoccupation in practice, with obtaining a confession in her search for the 'truth'. When asked about the possibility of the defence lawyer being present during the police interrogation of the suspect, *procureurs* responded in the following terms:

> It's true that the *garde à vue* exerts a certain psychological pressure and for some people that pressure may lead to slightly ill-considered admissions ... But that is not the point of view of a *procureur* — there are no innocents in *garde à vue* ... The *juge d'instruction* is not going to interview the suspect three or four times, sit across the table from him and say 'Are you going to admit this?' The police station is a hostile environment. It's unpleasant and the police will use more pressure. And that does not make it unlawful — sometimes you need some pressure [D3].
>
> There are two things which do not seem to me to go in the same direction. On the one hand, the need to protect the rights of the defence of the accused, his access to the dossier. On the other hand, the effectiveness of the police investigation. Sometimes, the measures taken [for the defence] can seem to go against this concern with effectiveness. For example, I am totally hostile to the lawyer being present at the start of the *garde à vue* ... a lawyer who tells his client 'you will be in *garde à vue* for 24 or 48 hours, in your own interest, try and say nothing' — from the start, that defeats the whole object and the effectiveness of the *garde à vue* is no longer important .... We know full well that if someone does not admit their guilt in *garde à vue*, they never will do after that [*Procureur*, E3].
>
> Unless they are caught red-handed, people deny everything, even in the face of witnesses and evidence. They hide behind the presumption of innocence more and more. If a man does not speak, it is justifiable to place him in custody. The search for the truth is fairly easy, but they just refuse to confess [*Juge d'instruction*, area F].

The extended presence of a lawyer was disliked because of the constraints it placed upon police methods of investigation and interrogation and the pressures that were considered necessary to 'get to the truth'. This is perhaps surprising given the relatively high number of *procureur* questionnaire respondents (40 per cent) who reported suspecting that violence or excessive pressure was sometimes used against the suspect during the *garde à vue*. Far from usurping the role of the *parquet*, the presence of the defence lawyer threatened to expose the weaknesses of judicial supervision and the nature of police practices which remain conveniently concealed. For example, an officer in area C explained how he had falsely claimed to have a signed statement incriminating a suspect in order to make him confess:

> If a lawyer had been there I couldn't have done that, 'playing' with non-existent admissions. But you have to do that, to get to the truth. We don't have many resources. And the people who are here are not honest, are not responsible people. They wouldn't be at the police station if there wasn't some evidence against them ... We just want to get to the truth.

And an officer in area D expressed the same concern:

> No, that's no good. You have to leave the police to do their job ... If you think the guy did it, you try and get him to talk. You use blackmail, put the pressure on — it's not very moral, but they haven't got any morals either. If there was a witness, we certainly couldn't do that ... In short, we need to be left to do our job, because these are not angels we are dealing with.

The tape recording of police interrogations was opposed for the same reason, as one *juge d'instruction* in area C explained to us on hearing that this was standard procedure in England and Wales:

> It's unbelievable! And to think that we might end up doing that here ... You should just leave the police to do their job. When you're dealing with difficult people like drug addicts and hooligans, you need to put the pressure on. I don't mean hitting them, but you have to make them talk [*Juge d'instruction*, Area C].

While resistance to the extended entrenchment of pre-trial defence rights (by both the legislature and practitioners) is premised upon notions of retaining inquisitorial procedural consistency, empirical evidence (and that of outside bodies)[71] suggests that the safeguards currently in place are inadequate. Furthermore, closer inspection of the rhetoric of legal actors themselves reveals their clear crime control (rather than neutral, public interest) orientation and their preoccupation with the obtaining of confessions — something which the presence of a lawyer may hinder. Legal requirements to direct and supervise the police have been interpreted very broadly and the guarantees of the neutral judicial officer searching for the truth in the public interest, while in theory justifying the awesome concentration of power in the hands of one person, in practice, provide inadequate protection and offer no real guarantee of equality of arms or the protection of defence rights.

[71] Eg successive reports of the European Committee for the Prevention of Torture and Inhuman or Degrading Treatment or Punishment, 1998, 2001.

SOME CONCLUSIONS

More than three years after the 2000 reform project became law, we see more clearly than ever, the two faces of French criminal justice. On the one hand, there is the public and international face which claims to embrace the ECHR and to incorporate it through formal legal mechanisms — constitutional incorporation, application in the courts, additional legislative guarantees where required. But there also seems to be a parallel domestic discourse which recognises the strength of the existing legal culture and which seeks to downplay the impact upon criminal procedure of the European Convention, reassuring those responsible for its implementation on a daily basis that the inquisitorial process remains intact, police powers are not significantly curbed and any change in procedure is only minimal. Some of what is given with one hand is subtly taken away with the other.

Despite the apparently universal guarantees of 'equality of arms' offered by the ECHR and France's monist system of incorporating the Convention, its criminal procedure has until recently lacked many of the most basic safeguards — informing the suspect of the charges for which she is being detained; allowing her prompt access to legal advice; providing a translator; and the right of appeal from the trial court, the cour d'assises. Furthermore, many of these deficiencies had not been litigated. Cases brought before the European Court relating to defence rights and equality of arms concern the stages of trial and appeal. The pre-trial stage has been relatively neglected — other than one or two infamous cases of police brutality and the longstanding problem of excessive periods of pre-trial detention.[72] The concept of equality of arms and defence rights in the pre-trial stage is underdeveloped, with the focus on police brutality, rather than on other measures which might avoid this and offer better protection to the suspect. The assumption on the part of legislators, the courts and legal actors themselves (including, it would seem, many defence lawyers) is that judicial supervision affords these guarantees and that the really important stage, where the defence requires protection, is the trial. It is for this reason that both legislation and accompanying circulars set a fairly low threshold of compliance and that a more sustained framework of defence rights would be considered contrary to the inquisitorial procedure in place. However, this assumption is not supported empirically. Only 7 per cent of investigations are handled through the *instruction* procedure, leaving the vast majority to the supervision of the *procureur*, where accountability is more distant. The resulting dossier,

[72] Steiner (1997) above n 8 at 282–83 discusses the narrow interpretation given to Article 6(1) ECHR, in order that the *instruction* phase was held not to be covered by the Article.

nevertheless, is treated as the product of a judicially supervised enquiry, even though it lacks the defence and procedural safeguards of *instruction*. This is particularly significant given the absence of live evidence in most cases. Witness statements are accepted on paper, with no opportunity for live questioning by the judge or lawyers. In short, there is a considerable gap between inquisitorial theory, which justifies the relatively minimalist interpretation of ECHR requirements, and practice, which suggests that the accused remains unprotected. In addition, the European Court has acknowledged the importance of pre-trial defence rights as part of the accused's fair trial protections. The Committee for the Prevention of Torture and Inhuman or Degrading Treatment or Punishment (2001) has also expressed grave concern at the *garde à vue* regime, in particular the evidence of police violence and systematic maltreatment of suspects, recommending that a code of conduct for police interrogation be produced and that lawyers be present during interviews, which should also be tape recorded.[73] The French government has rejected these recommendations as unnecessary. The Committee also expressed the hope that good use would be made of the *procureur*'s power to visit the police station. The government response was that such visits would ensure that detention was conducted according to law (even though they are clearly aimed at monitoring the material conditions, not the procedures) but 18 months later, the visiting requirements have been reduced from four times a year to only once.[74]

It would seem that the French monist approach, while able to effect minor adjustments through the decisions of the Cour de cassation, is unable to ensure the kind of structural and systematic changes which ECHR jurisprudence now demands and which the June 2000 project has sought to achieve. In this way, it is not so very different from the experience in England and Wales, where we have witnessed government hostility to European Court decisions (notably those relating to Northern Ireland)[75] and the law has only gradually been changed where required.[76] The cultures and practices of legal actors and the shield provided by the

[73] The Truche Commission (above n 31, at 64) also recommended as essential the tape recording of interrogations.

[74] Debates in Parliament and the Ministry of Justice circular make it clear that visits are to inspect the material conditions in which people are held, as there has been concern that suspects have been detained in cells which are without adequate heating, lighting and ventilation.

[75] Notably *McCann v UK* (1995) 21 EHRR 97. In response to the Court's condemnation under Art 5(3) of the detention of a terrorist suspect for four days and six hours (*Brogan v UK* (1989) 11 EHRR 117) the government did not alter the law, but simply re-entered a derogation from Art 5(3) under Art 15. This derogation was upheld in *Brannigan & McBride v UK* (1993) 17 EHRR 594.

[76] Eg the Interception of Communications Act 1985 followed from the decision in *Malone v UK* (1984) 7 EHRR 14, where the Court found a breach of Art 8.

apparently public interest orientation of the *magistrat* are also an important feature of the success of legislation which seeks to reinforce these ECHR guarantees.

The tension inherent in making these changes stems from the different ways in which Article 6 guarantees are interpreted and understood in a different legal procedural context. It may be appropriate that there is a degree of local interpretation in implementing Convention guarantees and the ways in which rights and guarantees are afforded may differ. However, the problem comes when the legislature is proceeding on the basis of a procedural model that has little foundation in reality. 'Equality of arms' in France has focused on the trial and the pre-trial stage during *instruction*; it is understood in a way which is very much bound up with the model of judicial supervision, which casts the suspect as a witness in the investigation rather than a party whose interests require protection. The distant, legal bureaucratic way in which this supervision is effected in practice, however, including the crime control orientation of the *procureur* in particular, suggests that additional protection is required to give proper effect to the notion of 'equality of arms'.[77] In addition, the cultures and practices of legal actors, together with the approach of the higher courts create tensions in the translation of the Convention into the French inquisitorial context.

[77] Two recent miscarriages of justice in France demonstrate further the vulnerable position of suspects, even before the *juge d'instruction*. Interrogated by *gendarmes* in April 1987, Patrick Dils initially denied any involvement in the offence, but after spending the night in custody, he finally admitted to the grotesque murder of two eight-year-old boys in Montigny-lès-Metz. He maintained his admissions before the *juge d'instruction*, retracting them one month later in a letter to his lawyer. It was 15 years before his conviction was finally overturned in April 2002. Joël Pierrot also maintained his false admissions before the trial judge, before having his conviction for armed robbery overturned in May 2002 when it was discovered that two other men had confessed to the robbery and been convicted and sentenced.

9

The Millennium Blip: The Human Rights Act 1998 and Local Government

LUKE CLEMENTS AND RACHEL MORRIS

THE LAST FIVE years have been marked by a rare period of substantial and planned constitutional adjustment in the UK. The government's professed purpose in driving through these changes has been to 'nurture a culture of understanding of rights and responsibilities at all levels in our society.'[1] A major and underpinning part of this programme has been the enactment of the Human Rights Act 1998 (HRA). The Act, releasing into the rich ecosystem of the UK's common law a new breed of rights — human rather than property based — and in many respects positive and energetic compared with those that have come to characterise the somewhat torpid and largely negative native system. The incorporation of convention rights into our domestic law has prompted dramatic comparisons; parallels with Magna Carta; the Bill of Rights and to a radical new Equity. If mere weight of reportage is the appropriate measure, then it would seem that it has opened a new dimension of legal opportunity and conception — in architectural terms, an ogive to the Saxon mason.

Coinciding with and tracking these fundamental changes, has been a shift in the process by which the effectiveness of local government performance is measured. The Local Government Act 1999 replaced the previous largely monetarist based mechanism, 'Compulsory Competitive Tendering', with a new regime — 'Best Value'.[2] Best Value's stated aim is to secure

[1] Labour Party, *Bringing Rights Home* (London, Labour Party, December 1996).
[2] The duty came into force from 1 April 2000.

continuous improvement in the exercise of all local authority functions[3]; it creates 'a demanding new performance framework for local authorities that ... challenge[s] them to re-assess their aims and objectives.'[4] These ambitions are to be achieved by a complex array of administrative mechanisms — national standards, centrally set performance measures and targets, and the imposition of a comprehensive inspection regime. The new administrative regime, of which Best Value is an example, arguably reflects the more complex social and cultural environment envisaged by the government's constitutional reforms — and its much vaunted 'third way' — interlinking radical 'new' principles of citizenship with tough 'new' business models of process and performance. As the minister responsible for implementing the programme in England said of the scheme: 'good local services are an essential part of [the] drive for a fairer, more decent society.'[5]

THE RESEARCH STUDY (METHODOLOGY)

While a number of studies have considered the judiciary's response to the challenges of the HRA[6] there have been few that have assessed the effectiveness of local government's response. As a consequence and with the support of the Economic and Social Research Council[7] a research study was undertaken to explore this issue.

The study sought to better understand the social reality of local authority behaviour in the face of such a momentous legislation. In pursing this objective it endeavoured to address a number of questions, including the extent of local authority awareness of the HRA, the extent (and nature) of their preparations for its implementation, its impact on policy and their perceptions about its practical implications. The chosen research method consisted of a questionnaire sent to all local authorities in the UK followed up by selected personal interviews of local authority officers. In order to assess the validity and relevance of the survey's general questions it was decided to seek information from the authorities in relation to one specific subject area. For the reasons outlined below, it was decided that this should

[3] Explanatory Notes to the 1999 Local Government Act, para 3.
[4] Audit Commission, *Better by Far: Preparing for Best Value* (London, Audit Commission, 1998) 5.
[5] 'Best Value' conference speech by Hilary Armstrong, Minister for Housing, 12 February 1998.
[6] The Lord Chancellor's Department publishes quarterly reports of the HRA's impact on the Courts at http://www.lcd.gov.uk/hract/hrimpact3.htm and statistical information concerning the Act's impact on the courts is published by the Human Rights Act Research Project, at http://www.doughtystreet.co.uk/data/h_rights/data/hr_hrar_stats.htm; and see also Public Law Project, 2003).
[7] Reference no R000239238.

relate to their responsibilities in relation to gypsies and other travellers (hereafter referred to simply as 'travelling people').

The research commenced with the piloting of a questionnaire[8] which, through closed format and fixed response questions, generally explored local authority awareness and understanding of the Act, and whether and how this had altered the ways in which they provided services generally and, more specifically, related to travelling people in their area (including the context of Best Value). The revised questionnaire was then sent in a single mailing for the attention of the chief executive within all local authorities in the UK (to ensure freedom from geographic and temporal biases), for self-completion and return. With such a large survey, a degree of methodological compromise was considered inevitable. The study suggests that in approximately one third of the cases the questionnaires were completed in their entirety by an officer from within the chief executive's department and in the remainder, by a chief executive's delegate in combination with the authority's officer with general responsibility for travelling people. The questionnaire consisted of two parts. The first sought responses on the general impact of the Human Rights Act 1998 and the second sought specific responses in relation to the Act's impact upon the travelling people who resided in or resorted to its area. The mailing took place at the beginning of October 2001 and responses were collated until the survey concluded at the end of March 2002: the overall response rate being 30.47 per cent (142 of 466).

Officers in twelve authorities — selected by sampling stratified only to reflect the divisions listed above — were subsequently visited or telephoned to explore through interviews the knowledge of and issues around the implementation of human rights and Best Value principles into authority policy and practice. The quotations in this paper derive either from these interviews or from written comments made in the questionnaire responses.

TRAVELLING PEOPLE AS A CASE STUDY

Research of this nature benefits from having a case study group or function area with which to compare and evaluate the data derived from the general survey. Various groups / function areas could have fulfilled this role — for instance the use of one area of service delivery through which authorities interact with the entire local population (ie, education). Drawbacks with

[8] The questionnaire was piloted with one established (ie pre-existing) contact in each of five types of local authority — county, unitary, district, metropolitan borough and London borough.

such an approach included the limited scope of such a review, in that it would involve many classes of people and needs and only one human right. This would result in analysis of the impact of one right specifically, rather than the impact of new rights-based thinking. It was therefore considered preferable to focus upon one population that makes clearly defined, but diverse, demands on local authorities.

Travelling people appeared to fulfil this role, being a small societal group coming into regular contact with a range of local government departments. The fact that they are generally an economically deprived, socially excluded and unpopular minority for which the purported 'cultural' element of the HRA appeared to have particular relevance, made them particularly suitable. Additionally it was widely predicted (as discussed below) that the Act would induce a significant number of legal and administrative challenges to the way local authorities dealt with their travelling people.

LEGAL IMPLICATIONS FOR LOCAL AUTHORITY RESPONSIBILITIES TO TRAVELLING PEOPLE

Section 6 HRA has enormous reach — making it unlawful for any public authority to act in a way which is incompatible with a 'Convention right'; an 'act' for this purpose includes a failure to act (section 6(6)). Given the substantial implications for local authorities of this section it was not surprising that local authority journals carried significant numbers of articles which endeavoured to anticipate the likely areas from which challenges might emerge.[9] Many of these articles identified a number of legal issues relating to the local authority / travelling people interface as likely to be problematical. Additionally it appears that informal local authority lawyer networks/discussion groups arose to explore the potential impact of the legislation.[10]

Travelling people actively interact with the law in many ways. Many of these concern (directly or indirectly) the use of land: for example, the planning regime, trespass, the statutory eviction powers of the police and other public authorities, access to social accommodation and the security of tenure available on public authority gypsy sites.

It is however too simplistic to restrict analysis to the issue of land use alone. Many Romany gypsies and Irish travellers, for instance, live in

[9] See, eg L Clements, 'The Human Rights Bill' (1998) *Journal of Local Government Law* 4–7; N Dobson, 'Work in progress — Human Rights' (2000) 73 *Journal of Local Government Law* and F Klug, 'The Human Rights Act: Basic Principles and Values' (2001) *Journal of Local Government Law*, 41ff.

[10] K Meechan, 'The Human Rights Act — Public Authority Preparations' (2001) *Journal of Local Government Law* 56–60.

houses or on permanent sites. Many travelling people are more concerned about other potential Convention issues such as access to education[11] and health services.[12] For many the issue finds expression in terms of as 'systematic denial of a traditional way of life' or of being 'treated as inferior.'[13]

Much recent public law litigation concerning travelling people has been articulated in terms of their fundamental human rights — both before domestic courts and the court in Strasbourg. Although the cases have ranged against a variety of targets, a common theme has frequently been the issue of discrimination and social exclusion. Thus, complaints concerning inadequate access to educational facilities,[14] have emphasised the extraordinarily high rates of illiteracy among travelling people.[15] Likewise, cases challenging the refusal of planning permission have highlighted the marked disparity between the grant rate of planning permissions for gypsy sites contrasted with the general grant rate.[16] Several commentators on the potential impact of the HRA on local authority functions not unnaturally therefore highlighted the planning development and control system as being a likely 'hotspot' for challenge.[17] Local authority planning enforcement and eviction action against travelling people has also been the subject of challenge — both on the basis of the severe accommodation problems experienced by travelling people of which almost 30 per cent have nowhere legal to site their caravans[18] and on the basis that the enforcement processes constitute a disproportionate interference with their Article 8 Convention rights (right to respect for private and family life and home).[19]

[11] Office for Standards in Education (OFSTED), *The Education of Travelling Children: A Report from the Office of Her Majesty's Chief Inspector of Schools* (HMR/12/96/NS, London, OFSTED, 1996).

[12] R Morris and L Clements, *Disability, Social Care, Health and Travelling People* (Cardiff, Traveller Law Research Unit, Cardiff Law School, 2001).

[13] See, eg J-P Liégeois, *Gypsies and Travellers* (Strasbourg, Council of Europe, 1987); D Hawes and B Perez, *The Gypsy and the State* (Bristol, The Policy Press, 1996) and D Kenrick and C Clark, *Moving On: The Gypsies and Travellers of Britain* (Hatfield, University of Hertfordshire Press, 1999).

[14] *Coster v UK* 24876/94: 4 March 1998: one of six gypsy cases declared admissible on this date: the lead case being *Chapman v UK* (2001) 33 EHRR 399. *Coster v UK* being finally determined on 18 January 2001; 33 EHRR 479.

[15] Above, n 11.

[16] The grant rate for gypsies is (it appears) approximately 10%, in contrast to the equivalent rate for all applications of over 90% — Lord Irvine of Lairg LC, *Hansard*, HL Deb, vol 555, 7 June 1994, col 1132.

[17] See, eg T Jones, 'Property Rights, Planning Law and the European Convention'(1996) 3 *European Human Rights Law Review* 233ff and Advisory Council for the Education of Romany and other Travellers (ACERT), *Directory of Planning Policies for Gypsy Site Provision in England* (Bristol, The Policy Press, 1997).

[18] Above, n 12.

[19] See, eg H Barnett, 'The rights of gypsies — landmark or signpost?' (1996) 146 (6767) *New Law Journal*, 1628–30; T Corner, 'Planning, Environment and the European Convention on

IMPLEMENTATION OF THE ACT AT LOCAL AUTHORITY LEVEL

In its consultation paper, *Bringing Rights Home,* the Labour Party argued that the incorporation of the ECHR into domestic law would bring about a new rights awareness and the re-establishment of a balanced relationship of rights and responsibilities.[20] The passing of the Act does not in itself achieve this ambition, nor does it change 'the relationship between the state and citizen' nor indeed, does it in itself redress 'the dilution of individual rights by an over-centralising government that has taken place over the past two decades.'[21] Change of this nature requires more. Theoretically this could be achieved either through purposeful proactive measures (such as officer training, policy reviews and general 'awareness raising') or as a consequence of reactive change — where the pace of reform is dictated by external measures (such as an auditing regime or via a Human Rights Commission with standard setting and enforcement powers).

Given that the HRA has (as yet) no external enforcement apparatus — no Commission and no auditing/reporting mechanisms — an assessment of the effectiveness of the quality of local authority training programmes, policy reviews and general 'awareness raising' has particular relevance.

HUMAN RIGHTS TRAINING WITHIN LOCAL AUTHORITIES

Although the Act received Royal Assent on 9 November 1998 its commencement was delayed until October 2000[22] to enable the implementation of proactive measures of the type described above. These included substantial policy reviews within central government departments[23] and an equally extensive programme of training[24] — including judicial training.[25] At the same time, the Home Office took lead responsibility for disseminating information on the Act to local authorities; principally through the medium of leaflets, posters, guidance booklets, a newsletter and an internet

Human Rights' (April 1998), *Journal of Public Law* 301–14; I Cameron, 'Respect for the Home: Treatment of Gypsies' (1998) 4(2) *European Public Law* 153–54 and J Ross, 'Uncommon Humanity: Travellers, Ethnicity and Discrimination' (1999) 4(1), *Contemporary Issues in Law* 1–30.

[20] Above, n 1.
[21] *Ibid.*
[22] So far as it related to UK local authorities; the devolved institutions in Wales and Scotland were effectively bound by the Act from July 1999.
[23] Home Office, *Human Rights News* 1 (July 1999), 4.
[24] A Hammond, 'The Human Rights Act and the Government Legal Service' (1999) 20 (3) *Statute Law Review* 230–37.
[25] Lord Chancellor's Department, *News Releases,* 12 July October 2000.

web site.[26] The unit's guidance to local authorities 'Putting Rights into Public Service' advised:

> No one should be complacent. Prepare carefully, checking in advance that your arrangements are compatible with the Human Rights Act. And even if you are satisfied about compliance, think about what you can do to foster human rights in your workplace.

A recurrent message in all subsequent publications — notably the newsletter 'Human Rights News' was that 'staff training is vital.'[27] Local authorities were notified of external training events[28] and the message regularly reinforced that 'training and awareness raising [are] just as important as the review process' and that it was their role to 'make awareness of the Convention a core professional competence.'[29]

Parallel with this strong instruction from the centre, general and specialist local government journals carried ever increasing comment upon the impact of the legislation (and advertisements for training courses). The Local Government Association heavily promoted awareness of the legislation stating on its website immediately prior to the Act's commencement on the 2 October 2000 'Authorities should by now be preparing for implementation, and building the cultural and legal requirements of the Act into their policies and decisions.'[30] This message was reinforced by a 1998 Institute for Public Policy Research (IPPR) study that drew attention to the poor state of local authority HRA preparedness. The report stressed the need for comprehensive training on the Act, warning that a failure to address this need could result in a 'plethora of litigation.'[31]

The timing and quality of the training commissioned by local authorities gives some indication of their approach to the Act. Broadly speaking there are three potential categories of response. The first is that little or nothing is done. The second, that training of a Strasbourg-proofing kind is undertaken. By this we mean that the purpose of the training is to enable staff to maintain the administrative status quo by anticipating the likely challenges and then adapting their bureaucratic processes to neutralise this threat. This is essentially protectionist — in that it seeks to preserve the pre-existing organisational culture and outcomes. The third response would be to aim to incorporate the constitutional and cultural content of the legislation into

[26] www.homeoffice.gov.uk/hract — that subsequently moved to the Lord Chancellors Department — www.lcd.gov.uk/hract

[27] Above, n 23, at 2.

[28] Home Office, *Human Rights News* 2 (November 1999), 3.

[29] Home Office, *Human Rights News* 3 (October 2000) 1, 3.

[30] www.lga.gov.uk on 6 June 2000.

[31] S Spencer and I Bynoe, *A UK Human Rights Commission — the Options* (London, IPPR, 1998).

the way the organisation functions — effectively a qualitative response that seeks to promote genuine institutional change — or in the words of the government — to 'nurture a culture of understanding of rights and responsibilities at all levels.'[32]

By October 2001, the survey indicates that three quarters (78 per cent)[33] of local authorities had undertaken a general programme of staff training / awareness raising in relation to the legislation. A significant majority of these programmes commenced in 2000 (62 per cent)[34] the year the Act came into force, and well over a year after its Royal Assent.

Sixty-five per cent (90) of respondents who had had training expressed satisfaction with it — training that for just under a half (45 per cent) consisted of a single event and for the other half, was part of an ongoing programme.[35] The responses to follow up personal interviews however suggested a degree of inconsistency in these programmes:

> The Act is still very much on the agenda within the Council. There is no rolling programme of training but it is on the agenda.
> The HRA training ... could be characterised as 'patchy'.
> Received no training on the HRA — passed me by.

Most local authorities did not therefore fully utilise the two-year period between Royal Assent and the Act's commencement but concentrated their training programmes into the period immediately before or in the year after its commencement and for more than half the training was a one-off event. Accordingly the survey indicates that of the three potential categories of local authority training response (outlined above) that approximately:[36]

— 20 per cent did little or nothing;
— 35 per cent undertook a Strasbourg proofing exercise (at best); and
— 45 per cent may have endeavoured to incorporate the qualitative aspects of the legislation in their programme.

If this assessment is correct (and further findings discussed below suggest that the real situation may have been even less promising) it is a cause for

[32] Above, n 1.
[33] In answer to the question '*Has your authority undertaken a general programme of staff training / awareness raising in relation to the Human Rights Act 1998?*', 78.8% (115) stated that they had; 18.5% (27) had not; 2.7% (4) did not know — indicating that at the very least the authority officer completing the questionnaire had not received such training.
[34] Of the 94 responses to this question, 18% had their training in 1998/9 and 18% in 2001.
[35] Sixty-four authorities (45%) had ongoing programmes; 44 (31%) had not; 9 (6%) did not know and 25 (18%) could not answer the question as they had not yet had any training.
[36] See n 14 above.

concern. As already noted the Act is not self implementing. If local authority training and awareness raising measures are as 'patchy' as the research suggests, then they are unlikely to be an effective method of delivering the qualitative aspects of the legislation.

One possible reason for the inadequate preparations by over half of all local authorities may be attributable to external constraints, namely an inadequate supply of training materials. A 2000 IPPR report suggested that, apart from the Home Office guidance,[37] there was a lack of information provided by central government.[38] Levels of concern about the adequacy of these materials appeared to have reduced by the time of the present survey — albeit that they remained appreciable with almost 40 per cent expressing dissatisfaction.[39] This matches the district audit findings in its 2002 report,[40] which also found significant levels of local authority concern about the level of support they received, observing:

> Despite general guidance being available, the most common complaint was that there was a lack of good practice guidance in this area. As a result, some staff felt that they were operating in a vacuum and/or trying to reinvent the wheel. (District Audit 2002: 4)

Whether the slow and inconsistent roll out of training programmes can be attributed to the failings of central government, is uncertain. There is no doubt that after the initially critical report of the IPPR in 1998, substantial materials were made available by the Home Office — although it perhaps unlikely that the one prompted the other. It is also far from clear that local authorities would have initiated their training programmes earlier if the Home Office materials had been available sooner. It is at least arguable that the defining factor was the publication of the Act's commencement date: local authorities having a number of other initiatives to digest in the period 1997–2000, not least the advent of the Best Value regime resulting from the Local Government Act 1999 (LGA).

[37] Home Office, *Putting Rights into Public Service: The Human Rights Act 1998: An Introduction for Public Authorities* (London, Home Office, 1999).

[38] Institute of Public Policy Research (IPPR), *Report on IPPR Survey onto whether Public Authorities are Preparing for Implementation of the Human Rights Act 1998* (unpublished. London, IPPR, 2000).

[39] Of 142 respondents to the question, 74 (52%) considered the materials to be about the right amount; 56 (39%) insufficient level; 1 (0.7%) more than enough; 4 (3%) didn't know and 8 ticked 'other' — comments including 'more than enough information but insufficient support and guidance' and 'OK, but we need codes of practice.'

[40] An assessment by the auditing agency of the Audit Commission of the 'Human Rights Act 1998 compliance arrangements' of 88 local government and health bodies in England and Wales.

With the benefit of hindsight the materials provided by the Home Office appear to be of at least adequate scope and quality. The 2000 IPPR study reported that those authorities with an existing knowledge of the Act were enthusiastic about the Home Office materials[41]; materials elsewhere described as 'praised and appreciated' by local authorities. The IPPR study however considered that local authorities had legitimate grievance in relation to the lack of materials provided by other government departments: whether this is a valid criticism, and whether it could be sustained by the time of the present survey (carried out 18 months later than that by the IPPR) is however questionable. It is the case that the guidance issued by individual departments of state (other then the Home Office) was notable either by its brevity or indeed by its absence. However the Home Office materials were clearly designed (and expressed to be) of relevance to all local authority departments and functions. The Home Office was merely the designated lead authority and its guidance was intended to apply to 'all aspects of [local authority] work'[42] and its advice ranged across the full range of local authority functions.

In addition, as noted above the LGA and many other independent and professional organisations provided training and consultancy assistance with the legislation. The question therefore arises as to whether local authority expectations of central government support were unrealistic and if so, why?

The Act, if not complex, is undoubtedly unusual, not least because of its cross-cutting impact — affecting as it does virtually every facet of local authority activity. However, in this respect it is not unique. The 'Best Value' obligations created by the Local Government Act 1999, for instance, also have a very wide ranging impact on almost all local authority functions. No one, however, could complain of a lack of materials in relation to the implementation of the 1999 legislation — adding another mechanism to the pre-existing stable of local audits, such as the OFSTED regime in education and the joint inspections of social services departments. Indeed it is arguable that local authorities have become so sensitised to legislation being accompanied by the familiar paraphernalia of prescriptive performance measures, audits and inspections that they are either losing the ability to take initiative themselves to implement — audit free — cross cutting legislation, or that in an environment dominated by measured outcomes, frameworks, league tables and the like, legislation that has none of these trappings is considered of low importance or at least low priority.

[41] Above, n 38, at 8.
[42] Above, n 29.

POLICY REVIEW IN THE LIGHT OF THE HUMAN RIGHTS ACT 1998

The government's encouragement to local authorities to conduct proactive across the board policy reviews[43] was reinforced by Home Office guidance which stressed the need for local authorities to:

> Think about how, and the extent to which, the laws underpinning your policies and procedures could help you do more to build a culture of rights and responsibilities.[44]

Three-quarters (77 per cent) of respondents to the survey reported that their authority had taken steps to ensure that the Act was taken into account in decision making by their executive or regulatory committee. A smaller number (61 per cent) however were able confirm that they had taken the additional step of undertaking a general 'Strasbourg' testing of their policies.[45] A quarter of respondents (26 per cent) stated that that their authority had not undertaken such a review and although half of these expected such a review to take place within the coming year, approximately half did not.

This finding is again in line with that of other researchers. Coope and Lane found that by 2001 only four of their sample of 11 core public authorities were in a state of preparedness. The remaining seven authorities, were at best 'in the process of seeing their plans through,' but in the main could be described as having 'taken little action other than to "cast an eye" over' the implications of the legislation.[46] Likewise, the 2002 District Audit report concluded that a number authorities were adopting a 'wait and see' approach to the legislation and that '45 out of 88 local authorities and health bodies had not reviewed their policies and procedures for compliance.'[47]

[43] J Wadham and H Mountfield, *Blackstones Guide to the Human Rights Act 1998* (London, Blackstone Press, 1999) iv.

[44] Above, n 37 at 12.

[45] Respondents were asked whether there had 'been a general review of their authorities' policies in light of the coming into force of the Act' and, if not, whether such a review was planned to take place in the following 12 months. Eighty-nine authorities (61%) stated that such a review had taken place; 26% of respondent authorities (38) had not undertaken such a review; (19–13% were unable to answer the question, and 9 did not answer it). Of the 38 which said 'no', 20 stated that such a review was due to take place some time in the coming year, and 18 that it was not planned.

[46] S Coope and L Lane, *Public Authorities and the Human Rights Act: An Explanatory Study* (Scottish Executive Central Research Unit; Edinburgh: Stationery Office, 2001) 16.

[47] District Audit, *The Human Rights Act: a Bulletin for Public Bodies* (London, District Audit, 2002), 2.

On one level of course, it is positive that a majority of authorities had undertaken such a review, however it must be a matter of concern, that three years after the Act received Royal Assent, and one year after its enactment, a significant number of authorities (possibly 40 per cent in total) have still not undertaken a general 'Strasbourg' testing policy review — and that an appreciable minority (possibly 12 per cent) had no intention of doing so. This, again is of concern given that the absence of external implementation mechanisms in the legislation.

The present survey did not seek to assess the quality of the general policy reviews or the reasons for inaction by the minority of councils. However the District Audit report found that 56 per cent of the public authorities it surveyed had no clear corporate approach to this issue and attributed this failure to prioritise to 'resource pressures, large-scale change agendas and competing priorities.'[48] If this is explanation for the minority failure it would suggest a general perception that it would not be unduly risky to adopt a reactive approach (of only amending policies as and when challenged). Again it could be argued that the absence of any 'follow-up' mechanisms encouraged this view; 'risk' must undoubtedly include not only expensive litigation, but also damaging inspection reports and attendant poor publicity, reduced grants and the implementation of 'special measures' and so on.

The present survey sought to contrast the general policy review activity with the level of review councils had undertaken in relation to travelling people specific policies.

Accordingly authorities were asked whether, as a result of the Act, they had reviewed the development of their policies in relation to travelling people in the function areas of education, eviction, planning and site management. On the basis of the above analysis, it would be reasonable to predict that approximately 61 per cent would have undertaken such reviews. However the responses were in every case lower, averaging only 36 per cent. Only 25 per cent of respondents were able to confirm that their authority had undertaken a policy review in relation to the issue of planning and travelling people — despite it being generally (and correctly[49]) predicted to have been one of the key risk areas.

[48] *Ibid*, at 3.

[49] A substantial number of travelling people related planning cases have resulted see for instance *South Buckinghamshire District Council v Porter (and others)* [2003] UKHL 26; *R v Carmarthenshire County Council, ex p Price* [2003] EWHC 42 (Admin) and *Wrexham County Borough Council v National Assembly for Wales & Berry* [2002] EWHC Admin 2414. In research undertaken by the Public Law project analysing all judicial review applications to the High Court in first 3 months of 2002 it found that 100% of travelling people cases raised human rights arguments both at leave and at substantive hearings — Public Law Project, *The Impact of the Human Rights Act on Judicial Review* (London, Public Law Project, 2003) 11, 13.

Table 1: Local Authority Policy Reviews ~ Travelling People Policies

Policy area	Yes	No	Don't know
Education (n81)	32%	38%	30%
Eviction (n131)	54%	35%	11%
Planning (n100)	25%	40%	35%
Site management (n105)	33%	42%	25%

Approximately one third of respondents were able to confirm that their authority had undertaken a policy review in the equivalent areas of education and/or site management policies. It was only in relation to the issue of evictions that the policy review statistic approached the predicted figure, with 54 per cent of respondents stating that their authority had undertaken such a review. Accordingly actual local authority policy review performance — consequent upon the Act — was materially less for traveller specific policies than the general rate for all local authority policies.

There are a number of possible explanations for this marked difference. It may be, for instance, that traveller policies are considered to be of such marginal relevance that they have fallen outside the general policy review process. Alternatively, it may be that the respondents had overestimated their authorities' general Strasbourg policy testing performance. The former possibility appears improbable, given the extent to which briefings, articles and courses have accentuated the potential risk of HRA challenge from this sector. Although the latter possibility is difficult to conclusively discount, it also seems that so large a discrepancy cannot be attributed solely to this factor; furthermore, this would not explain the difference between the eviction policy review rate and that for the other function areas (see Table 1 above). A further potential explanation, that the non-reviewing authorities had no significant history of travelling people in their area, also appears on analysis (by cross reference to the bi-annual gypsy counts issued by the Office of the Deputy Prime Minister — and its predecessor departments) not to account for the discrepancy.

A persuasive explanation for this disparity of result appears to be that there is something in the nature of traveller related issues that militate against effective *a priori* policy review. Most obviously this can be attributed to the politically controversial nature of traveller related matters. A proposal to review (say) traveller's rights in accessing the planning system would in itself be contentious, if that review anticipated adapting the local system to increase the likelihood of gypsy caravan sites obtaining planning permission or resisting enforcement action. It takes little imagination to envisage the resulting potential for controversy. In such a situation, political prudence might well dictate the adoption of a wait and see policy: a policy that not only conserved officer time and avoided the risk of adverse publicity, but also enabled the elected local politicians to pass the HRA implementation buck to the courts and planning inspectorate.

In relation to certain local authority responsibilities, not being proactive may indeed be the most attractive political option. A recognition of this factor also brings into view the powerful role played by elected members in many authorities. Put simply, there are few votes to be gained by elected members actively promoting policies on behalf of unpopular causes. In such cases it is arguably easier to have these policies imposed in response to external factors, for instance a House of Lords judgement, as indeed occurred in relation to planning enforcement policies in *South Bucks District Council v Porter* (2001).[50]

District Audit highlighted this factor, stating that 'within local government, an obstacle to adopting a corporate approach for reviewing policies has been a lack of member interest and engagement. This has resulted in a lack of support for front-line staff and inertia as far as taking the human rights agenda forward was concerned.'[51] As one respondent to the survey commented:

> Elected members are still the biggest obstacle; still boys' club culture / village pump politics.

If this is the explanation for the unexpectedly low local authority activity in reviewing their traveller specific policies, then this could also explain why the responses relating to 'eviction' policies were markedly different. Significantly, over 56 per cent of authorities had reviewed their traveller specific eviction policies. Unlike the other areas (education, planning and site management) which could be viewed as providing potential benefits to the travelling minority, robust eviction policies tend to command majority support. It logically follows that their continued vigour is likely to be of considerable interest to elected members — and therefore suited to proactive review — but only of the Strasbourg proofing kind.

One could abstract from this specific example, the general principle, expressed in Table 2 below. The determinant appears to be local authority perception of what the impact of the HRA provoked outcome is likely to be.

[50] Above, n 49.
[51] Above, n 47, at 3.

Table 2: Theoretical Policy Review Outcomes

Implementation of the measure is perceived as	Predicted outcome
Benefiting an unpopular minority	No policy review
Impairing the interests of the majority or an influential minority	Policy review limited to Strasbourg proofing exercise
Benefiting the interests of the majority or an influential minority	Full policy review

Tentative as these conclusions are — they again give cause for concern. The justification for fundamental human rights legislation invariably includes reference to the need for safeguards for unpopular minorities — not least Travelling People — as Sieghart has remarked 'all human rights exist for the protection of minorities.'[52] If, however, the legislation has no Commission or other enforcement regime — then given the imperfect nature of the training and the picture of highly selective policy review that emerges, then all that can be relied upon is for reactive change. However, there is very little evidence to suggest that local government anxiously adheres to the spirit and letter of each judicial pronouncement — as Epp has observed 'judicial declarations of individual rights often find only pale reflections in practice.'[53] Indeed the evidence points in the opposite direction.[54] Halliday's research in particular demonstrates the failure of judicial review to control local authority bureaucratic cultures — indeed he goes further, persuasively arguing that '*even if* the structural conditions in which the administration of law in government took place were conducive to the flourishing of legal conscientiousness, judicial review may still be a largely ineffective means of regulating the administrative process.'[55]

EXTERNAL EVALUATION MEASURES

The need for authority wide policy reviews to assess the impact of the Act, and from an insurance perspective, to identify high risk areas, is only one aspect of an implementation strategy. Additionally, sound administrative practice requires some mechanism that is capable of assessing the effectiveness of its response to the new legislative environment; some means

[52] P Sieghart, *The Lawful Rights of Mankind* (Oxford, Oxford University Press, 1985) 168.
[53] CR Epp, *The Rights Revolution* (Chicago, University of Chicago, 1998).
[54] See, eg GR Rosenberg, *The Hollow Hope: Can Courts Bring About Social Change?* (London, University of Chicago Press, 1991) and M Sunken, L Bridges and G Mazeros, *Judicial Review in Perspective* (London, Public Law Project, 1993).
[55] S Halliday, 'The Influence of Judicial Review on Bureaucratic Decision-Making' (2000) *Public Law* 110–22, 117.

of evaluating the outcomes; its successes, failures and omissions. Given that such an appraisal tool was available — 'Best Value' — and that this tool had been amended to incorporate sïmilar rights based legislation' eg, race equality standards,[56] respondents were asked whether they had taken any steps to incorporate Human Rights Act considerations within their Best Value regime. Additionally they were asked to express their view as to the relationship between their human rights and Best Value strategies.

Best Value is a sophisticated programme backed up by a substantial body of duties, targets, audits and guidance.[57] This level of sophistication has meant that some commentators, for instance the IPPR, have suggested it as an appropriate mechanism for measuring the effectiveness of local authority HRA implementation.[58] Sixty-five per cent of respondents[59] considered that HRA principles were broadly complementary with the Best Value agenda as opposed to 25 per cent who considered that the two strategies had little in common. However, only 51 per cent of the respondents could report that their authorities had taken the step of incorporating human rights considerations into their Best Value regimes, albeit that over 28 per cent of respondents did not know if they had or had not.

Although the survey produced no further quantitative data on the relevance and impact of the Best Value regime — its importance was volunteered in a number of questionnaire responses and in five of the twelve personal interviews. It appears therefore that Best Value and other auditing regimes have relevance to local authority implementation of the HRA in two distinct ways. The first could summarised as the 'coincident impact': namely that the implementation of the HRA coincided with the implementation of the Best Value regime — which for a variety of reasons proved to more compelling. The explanation for this is probably self evident. Best Value is highly prescriptive, requires the development by the local authority of detailed plans and is accompanied by an array of performance targets, voluminous guidance and a rigorous auditing regime. For all its emphasis on the concept of 'value' its evaluation methods are based upon a host of quantative measures. The local authority imperative of developing and maintaining internal systems so as to meet these external targets and not fail the highly public auditing process means that legislation of this type is far more likely to concentrate the minds of local councils than open textured rights based 'stand alone' legislation.

[56] L Clements and J Read, *Disabled People and European Human Rights* (Bristol, Policy Press, 2003) 93.
[57] University of Warwick (Local Government Centre), *Improving Public Services: Evaluation of the Best Value Pilot Programme — Final Report* (London, Department of the Environment, Transport and the Regions, 2001).
[58] Above, n 38, at 13.
[59] 81 from a total of 145 who responded to this question.

The second relevant feature of Best Value, from the perspective of the implementation of the Human Rights Act 1998, could be summarised as the 'cumulative impact'. This arises from the fact that Best Value is but one example of a host of such performance measurement regimes — present and past. Concern about the impact such programmes have on the culture and governance of local councils is not new. Lipsky observed that such measures can not only have negative consequences for competing demands,[60] but can interfere with the quality of public services, since in his view the 'most important dimensions of service performance defy calibration.'[61] Some commentators have gone further and implied that the new accountability culture is itself inimical to a human rights culture. O'Neill, for instance observes that '[c]entral planning may have failed in the Soviet Union but it is alive and well in Britain today.'[62] Power's critique of the 'audit explosion'[63] is adopted by Harris in his analysis of its cultural impact on local authorities, stating that '[a]ssumptions of distrust become self-fulfilling as auditees adapt their behaviour to the audit process, distorting reality so that it conforms to an auditable reality and becoming less trustworthy as a result of a process designed to make them more trust worthy.'[64] Clements and Read also question the usefulness of Best Value audits as a way of measuring the effectiveness of HRA implementation, arguing that 'the fact that virtual human rights safeguards have been put in place, may make an organisation less responsive in reality.'[65]

It is not only, therefore, the alleged cultural distortions introduced by the Best Value regime that are of relevance in suggesting that the programme has had a materially negative impact on local authority implementation of the HRA. It is at least arguable that the very prescriptiveness of programmes of this nature stifles initiative in other fields — fixating local government officers with the sole objective of satisfying centrally generated targets and auditing regimes.

The two distinct problems associated with the Best Value regime — one short term — its coincident impact and the other long term — its cumulative impact could be part of the explanation for apparent marginalisation by local authorities of the HRA: an Act that lacks an effective engine (eg a Commission or detailed educational programme) that would enable it make headway against the relentless flow of highly prescriptive legislation that has come to so dominate the officers working in this sector.

[60] M Lipsky, *Street-Level Bureaucracy (*New York, Russell Sage Foundation, 1980) 170.
[61] *Ibid,* at 168.
[62] O O'Neill, *A Question of Trust* (Cambridge, Cambridge University Press, 2002) 46.
[63] M Power, *The Audit Society: Rituals of Verification* (Oxford, Oxford University Press 1997) 135–36.
[64] J Harris, *The Social Work Business* (London, Routledge, 2003) 94–95.
[65] Above, n 56, at 95.

LOCAL AUTHORITY PERCEPTIONS OF THE IMPLICATIONS OF THE HRA FOR THEIR PRACTICES

Part one of the survey (addressing the authority-wide impact of the Act) concluded with questions that sought to ascertain, in broad terms, whether the council had a predominantly positive or negative perception of the legislation. One of these addressed the general impact of the Act, asking 'in your authority, is the impact of the Human Rights Act likely to result in' — there then being six suggested consequences. The results are as follows:

Table 3: Likely General Impact of the HRA

Act will result in	More	Less	Same
Bureaucratic obligations (137)	51%	1%	48%
Discretion in decision making (139)	24%	32%	44%
Efficiency of service delivery (135)	14%	23%	63%
Equality of opportunity (140)	48%	2%	50%
Legal challenges (140)	63%	3%	34%

The most striking result is the large group of respondents who thought that the Act would make no difference to the aspects listed. Striking also is the fact that 52 (37 per cent) of the respondents thought that the HRA would result in the same amount or fewer legal challenges and that 106 (76 per cent) considered that it would make no change or indeed restrict discretion in decision making. Both these results would tend to suggest that the respondents had a less than perfect understanding of the legislation — particularly in relation to the issue of discretion.[66] The respondent's assessment that the Act would have a significant impact on equality of opportunity (the term used by many local authorities for anti-discriminatory policies) also calls into question their understanding of the legislation — since many legal commentators believe that the Act's contribution in this field will be limited (when compared with domestic and EU legislation).[67]

The survey tested these general responses with travelling people specific questions, including 'does your authority consider that the Human Rights Act will increase or decrease the probable risk of legal challenge by travelling people?'

[66] Many commentators on the Act have considered that its proportionality requirements would increase the level of discretion in decision making — a prediction born out by subsequent judgements, see for instance *R v SS Home Department ex Mahmood* [2001] 1 WLR 840 and *R v SS Home Department, ex p Daly* (2001) [2001] 2 WLR 1622: [2001] 3 All ER 433.

[67] See, eg S Fredman, 'Equality Issues' in Markesinis (ed), *The Impact of the Human Rights Bill on English Law* (Oxford, Clarendon, 1998) and G Gilbert, 'The Protection of Minorities under the European Convention on Human Rights' in J Dine and B Watt (eds), *Discrimination Law* (London, Longman, 1996).

Table 4: Likely Travelling People Related Litigation Resulting from the HRA

Act will result in	More	Less	Same	Don't know
Legal challenges (144)	75%	1%	5%	19%

As will be seen from the above table a significant majority of the respondents considered that the Act would increase the risk of legal challenge by travelling people. This finding suggests that local authorities considered travelling people related litigation more likely to be generated by the Act, than general litigation (the 63 per cent result detailed in Table 3 above). It also supports the view expressed above — that it was not ignorance of the threat of litigation from travelling people that caused many local authorities not to review their travelling people related policies — but political calculation.

A concluding question in the travelling people specific section of the survey asked 'do you believe that the Human Rights Act has made it more or less likely that the following will occur in relation to travelling people in your area?'

Table 5: Likely General Policy Impact of the HRA on Travelling People

	More	Less	Same
Availability of conventional housing (n118)	9%	3%	88%
Evictions of unauthorised campers (n133)	2%	34%	64%
Flexibility of planning policies (n114)	23%	4%	73%
Provision of public sites (n130)	18%	5%	77%
Toleration of unauthorised camping (n135)	33%	6%	61%

The number of respondents who thought that the Act would have little practical effect in these key areas clearly dwarf those who thought otherwise — albeit that the minority generally viewed the Act as providing benefits for travelling people. However, the powerful message conveyed by these results is that most local authorities consider that the HRA was likely to be only marginally beneficial in the lives of one of one of the UK's most socially excluded and deprived minorities. It indicates that little progress has been made in nurturing a human rights culture at local authority level — and that Sir Stephen Sedley was prescient to warn (prior to the implementation of the Act) of the risk that society's losers and winners would merely become the same losers and winners under the HRA.[68]

[68] S Sedley, 'First Steps Towards a Constitutional Bill of Rights' (1997) 5 *European Human Rights Law Review* 458ff, 463.

CONCLUSIONS

The research suggests that although awareness of the HRA was high, and although anxiety about the implications of it for local authority practice may also have been high, now that the Act is in force, a significant proportion of the respondents regard it as being a non-event. This finding is particularly strong in relation to the specific questions about the implications for the position of travelling people. It is striking that so many respondents thought the Act would make no difference to the various aspects (general and specific) of local authority practice. This finding stands in great contrast to the constitutional implications of the HRA, and to the predictions concerning the impact of the HRA for local authorities in general and for travelling people in particular.

It appears that the hype surrounding the Act's introduction may have contributed to this problem. The post-October 2000 sense of 'let down' or 'let off' — likened by a number of respondents to the millennium blip — has tended to obscure the important cultural content of the legislation and at present there appears little evidence that this aspect being addressed. The Act is at risk of being viewed as yesterday's event (a 'damp squib', to quote another respondent), and this danger is being reinforced by the dearth of central government materials, case law updates and specific local government targeted training initiatives.

This is not to say that such an outcome does not go with the grain of the prevailing organisational culture of many authorities. This aspect of the constitutional reform agenda appears to have been frustrated, or at the very least been distorted, to conform with the pre-existing organisational norms of local authority work. Although the survey encountered a number of officers who were endeavouring to bring about a 'rights based cultural' change — these could perhaps be characterised as those engaged in 'subversive decision making' that in effect undermines their authority's dominant agendas.[69]

In such an environment there is clearly a need for some external initiative to ensure that regression to the established organisational routine does not suffocate the qualitative aspect of this constitutional measure. Whether this impetus comes from a human rights commission or sustained educational measures (or a combination of the two) is outside the scope of the present paper. However, it does appear reasonably clear that the nature of the legislation does not readily lend itself to auditing, at least of the Best Value type. Indeed it is probable that the shadow cast by these auditing exercises may have materially suppressed local authority efforts to implement the Act.

[69] Above, n 55, at 118.

This is particularly so, in relation to the Best Value regime, whose 'roll out' coincided with, overshadowed and arguably frustrated that of the HRA.

The research provides persuasive evidence that in relation to travelling people, a passive non-implementation policy has very many attractions for local government. This finding may have general application for other minority rights or 'unpopular causes' and is perhaps the message emerging from the research of greatest importance.

In May 2003, when this chapter was being finalised, the House of Lords gave judgment in four consolidated cases — generally referred to as *South Bucks District Council v Porter* (2003).[70] The cases involved applications by the four local authorities for injunctions against gypsy families who were camping on land in breach of planning controls. The law lords set aside the long established precedent that in such matters the court's role was merely to act as a rubber stamp and in so doing rejected the local authorities' argument that the *status quo* had not been affected by the HRA. Lord Clyde referred to the respondents' problems of health and lack of alternative accommodation 'made more problematic as [they] ... are Gypsies where considerations of humanity may be particularly acute', and Lord Bingham of Cornhill justified the court's change of approach by quoting Vaclav Havel: 'The Gypsies are a litmus test not of democracy but of civil society.'

The judgment encapsulates many of the themes that emerge from the present research. Over the last five years the judiciary have not only got to grips with the fundamental implications of the HRA, they have also absorbed its cultural and constitutional significance. This has been achieved by a substantial, possibly unprecedented, educational programme backed by the energetic and eloquent support of the senior judges — not least Lord Bingham himself. However, during this period, the present research suggests that the response of local authorities has been muted — and in respect of the rights of minorities (such as travelling people) it has been profoundly disappointing. If the treatment of minorities is the acid test of whether a culture of understanding of rights and responsibilities has been nurtured in local government — then by any objective measure, this test has been failed.

[70] See n 49 above.

10

Empowering Children? Legal Understandings and Experiences of Rights in the Scottish Children's Hearings System

ANNE GRIFFITHS AND RANDY FRANCES KANDEL[1]

INTRODUCTION

OUR CHAPTER EXPLORES the legal understandings and experiences of young people who come before the children's hearings system in Glasgow. Since 1971 the children's hearing system has been based on a welfare approach to children's rights promoted by a user-friendly environment, often including an informal roundtable discussion of the issues. Recently, in response to developments taking place in the broader international arena, including international conventions such as the United Nations Convention on the Rights of the Child (UNCRC) and the European Convention on Human Rights and Fundamental Freedoms (ECHR) that has now been partially incorporated into UK law by the Human Rights Act 1998, due process concerns at the hearing have become subject to greater scrutiny. In particular, the human rights challenges raised by the Scottish case of *S v Miller*[2] have led to the introduction of legal representation for children at a hearing. The case highlights the tensions that

[1] The authors wish to thank Claire McDiarmid, Kay Tisdall and Janice McGhee for their insightful comments on a draft version of this chapter. The text as it stands, however, is the authors' sole responsibility. We would also like to thanks the editors for their support and assistance and the Annenberg Foundation for funding the field research on which this chapter is based.

[2] 2001 SLT 531.

arise in upholding an informal, welfare-based perspective while promoting a more formalist due process approach to children's rights. These tensions arise because the informal welfare-based perspective and the formalist due process perspectives represent very different ways of thinking about children's rights. Another important dimension, which is often ignored in legal discourse, is the way in which children themselves experience and perceive of their rights for they may differ considerably from both the welfare and formalist approaches to such rights. It is essential to take their perspectives into account when working with these models if international human rights for children are to have any meaning.

Our discussion contrasts the legal and institutional understandings of children's rights with the views of young people who have been involved with the children's hearings system. We first discuss the classic Kilbrandon approach to the system, followed by the human rights challenge posed by *S v Miller.* Finally, we focus on the views of young people based on our study,[3] which was conducted between 1997–2000. This involved extensive interviews with 40 children's panel members, 25 safeguarders, 25 social workers, 25 parents and 132 children, as well as attendance at 34 hearings. Of the 132 children and young persons, 65 had some experience of the hearings system and 67 did not. They were drawn from a range of sources including four Glasgow secondary schools.[4] In this chapter our data derive from panel members' observations and those of 65 young people who had some experience of the system, 50 of whom were interviewed individually,[5] and 15 of whom were interviewed in three focus groups.[6] This research highlights the tensions between institutional and legal interpretations of human rights and the young people's ideas about participation, empowerment and the role of lawyers in children's hearings.

[3] Forms part of a comparative research project on 'The Child's Voice in Legal Proceedings' funded by the Annenberg foundation in the USA. It contrasts the differing approached to juvenile justice displayed by the lay-based, relatively informal setting of children's hearings in Glasgow, with the more formal proceedings in a New York State Family Court. See A Griffiths and RF Kandel, 'Legislating for the Child's Voice: Perspectives from Comparative Ethnography of Proceedings Involving Children' in M Maclean (ed), *Making Law for Families* (Oxford, Hart Publishing, 2000).

[4] These were Govan High, John Paul Academy, Holyrood and Whitehill.

[5] These consisted of 20 girls (aged 11, 13, 5x 14, 8x 15, 2x 16, 17, 2 no age) and 30 boys (aged, 11, 5x 12, 7x 13, 8x 14, 6x 15, 27, 2 no age). Interviewees were recruited as follows: 23 from the Glasgow secondary schools listed above; 22 from residential schools including the Good Shepherd (girls only), St Philips (boys only), Ballykinrain (boys only) and the secure unit at Kerelaw(mixed); three from Drumchapel and Easterhouse social work departments; and two from City Centre Initiative which deals with homelessness among young people.

[6] These young people were recruited by *Who Cares*? (an organisation specialising in advocacy for children in residential care run by adults who have been in care) and interviewed at their Glasgow office.

A NATIONAL CONCEPTION OF JUSTICE: A SCOTTISH PERSPECTIVE

The first of its kind in both Europe and the UK, the children's hearing system represented a radical move away from courts towards a more informal system of justice. Implemented in 1971[7] and now regulated by Part II of the Children (Scotland) Act 1995,[8] it focuses on children as vulnerable beings in need of assistance.[9] It is based on the philosophy of the Kilbrandon Committee[10] which led to the creation of the hearings system, that where children have difficulties their best interests are served by working with them and their families to alter their situation so that state intervention is rendered unnecessary. In pursuing this aim no distinction was drawn between children as offenders and children who had been offended against, as both required care and protection because their 'normal upbringing process' had 'fallen short'.

Children's hearings take the form of panels that deal with children under 16 who are in need of compulsory measures of supervision.[11] Reasons for state intervention in this context cover a wide range of circumstances[12] including the neglect and abuse of children, or the commission of offences by children, as well as dealing with children who are 'beyond the control of a relevant person' or who fail 'to attend school regularly without reasonable excuse.' The children and their families are referred by the reporter[13] to a lay panel of three members[14] who do not require legal training,

[7] Under the Social Work (Scotland) Act 1968.

[8] Along with the Children's Hearings (Scotland) Rules 1996 (SI 1996/3261), hereafter referred to as the 1996 Rules and the Children's Hearings (Legal Representation) (Scotland) Rules 2002 SSI 2002 No 63. For details concerning changes brought about by the 1995 Act see A Lockyer and FH Stone, *Juvenile Justice in Scotland Twenty Five Years of the Welfare Approach* (Edinburgh, T & T Clark, 1998) 104–22.

[9] For detailed information on children's hearings see L Edwards and A Griffiths, *Family Law* (Edinburgh, WGreen/Sweet & Maxwell, 1997); B Kearney, *Children's hearings and the Sheriff Court* (Edinburgh, Butterworths, 2000); Lockyer and Stone, above n 8; C McDiarmid, 'Perspectives on the Children's Hearings System' in J Scoular (ed), *Family Dynamics: Contemporary Issues in Family Law* (Edinburgh and London, Butterworths/ LexisNexis, 2001); KMcK Norrie, *Children's Hearing in Scotland* (Edinburgh, W Green, 1997); E Sutherland, *Child and Family Law (*Edinburgh, T & T Clark, 1999).

[10] *Report on Children and Young Persons, Scotland,* Cmnd 2306 (1964).

[11] See s 56(6) and s 65(1). Children over 16 but under 18 in respect of whom a supervision requirement remains in force may also come before a hearing under s93(2)(b) of the 1995 Act.

[12] Under s 52(2).

[13] It is the reporter, who may or may not be legally qualified, who draws up the grounds for referral and who is employed by the Scottish Children's Reporter Administration (SCRA), a national body charged with the management and deployment of reporters throughout Scotland. This is under the Local Government etc (Scotland) Act 1994, s 128(4) and (5). The term 'reporter' means the Principal Reporter and any officer of SCRA to whom he has delegated any of his functions under s 131 (1) of the 1994 Act.

[14] One of whom must be male, one of whom must be female, and one of whom acts as the chair. See s 39(3) and (5).

who are unpaid, and who are drawn from all walks of life. Panel members receive training before they serve and are required to attend further in-service training sessions to extend their knowledge and skills. When a hearing is held it is the panel members who must decide whether to discharge the referral, or whether a child is in need of compulsory measures of supervision, and if so, what conditions if any should be imposed.[15]

In reaching their decision panel members must adhere to three overriding principles. These are that:

1. The welfare of the child is paramount (s 16 (1)).
2. Children must be able to express their views and have them taken into account, where sufficiently mature, (s 16 (2)) with a presumption in favour of children aged 12 or over having such maturity (s 11 (10)).
3. There should be minimum intervention, that is, that a hearing should only make an order if it is better for the child that such an order is made than to make no order at all (s 16(3)).

KEY FEATURES OF THE SYSTEM

Although a legal forum, every effort is made in a hearing to encourage children and families to participate in proceedings by dispensing with the kind of legal formalities associated with courts. Thus, in keeping with Kilbrandon's recommendations, a determination of the facts is separated out from a disposal of the case by the requirement that no hearing can proceed unless the child and family accept the grounds for referral.[16] In this way the demands of formal legality — requiring determination of the facts with regard to due process — are kept distinct from a disposal of the case. In cases of dispute, the hearing can either discharge the referral or refer the matter to the sheriff court for a finding as to whether the disputed grounds are established.[17]

This approach, premised on consensus as the starting point for discussion, seeks to avoid the adversarial nature of legal proceedings. It is one that has traditionally minimised the role of lawyers so that children and families are not subject to confrontation with and intimidation by the kind

[15] Under s 70 the hearing has a wide range of powers including the power to make a supervision requirement with a condition of residence placing the child in a foster or local authority home, or even, in secure accommodation.

[16] Under s 65(9) where a child is too young to understand the grounds for referral, or has not in fact understood them after an explanation has been given, the hearing can either discharge the referral or direct the reporter to apply to the sheriff for a finding as to whether the grounds of referral are established.

[17] Section 65(7)(a).

of legal process that operates in ordinary law courts. Rules of evidence and procedure are much less stringent than in a court, and while lawyers may be present at a hearing they rarely appear. Panel members work hard at speaking directly with children and their families because they believe this promotes a more open and frank discussion of the issues. Efforts have been made to foster this type of communication by creating a more informal setting for discussion, around a table, instead of adhering to the more formal layout of a court. Typically present at the hearing are the child, the parents or persons with care, the child's social worker and any other person working with the child, the reporter and the panel members. At the end of the hearing panel members reach their decision which is based on a majority vote[18] and inform the child and any relevant person[19] that, if dissatisfied with the decision, they have three weeks to lodge an appeal with the sheriff.[20]

These aspects of the system are aimed at making the hearing more user friendly than courts by promoting transparency and a more informal environment. Yet the more 'informal' features of the system that are said to promote enhanced communication and participation have come under attack for failing to take adequate account of the 'rights' of those engaged in the process.

HUMAN RIGHTS CHALLENGES AND LEGAL PERSPECTIVES: *S V MILLER*

More recently, in the case of *S v Miller*[21] which was heard in Scotland's highest ranking civil court, the Court of Session, the hearings system has been charged with infringing children's human rights, especially with regard to Articles 5 (right to liberty and security) and 6 (the right to a fair trial) of the ECHR. Our chapter focuses on Article 6 in the context of a right to a fair hearing in civil proceedings.[22]

Article 6 provides that in determining civil rights and obligations or any criminal charge, everyone is entitled to a fair and public hearing within a reasonable time by an independent and impartial tribunal established by law. The Court held that referral to a hearing on the ground that a child has

[18] There is no statutory provision to this effect but it has been the universal and accepted practice since 1971.

[19] Defined as being the child's parent or any person having parental rights in respect of the child under s 86(4).

[20] Under s 51(1)(a) this period commences from the date of the hearing.

[21] 2001 SLT 531. As a result of this case SCRA has agreed to make their reports available to children, who were not previously entitled to them, except where this would be detrimental to their interests.

[22] For discussion of some of the other issues raised by this case see L Edwards, '*S v Miller*, The End of the Children's Hearings System As We Know It?' [2001] *SLT* 187ff.

committed an offence did not amount to criminal proceedings triggering the specific rights to legal representation guaranteed by Article 6. However, all parties accepted that Article 6 applied in respect of determining the child's civil rights and obligations because Article 8 rights constituted a 'civil right' for the purposes of Article 6. This is because a hearing may determine issues as to whether or not the child should live with his/her parent or parents, or whether or not there should be contact between parent and child and on what conditions, affecting the child's right to family life under Article 8.[23] Thus the issue was one of,

> whether the non-availability of free legal assistance in the referral proceedings before the children's hearing is incompatible with the right to a fair hearing in the determination of [S's] civil rights and obligations (Lord Macfadyn at p 577C).

While legal aid, in the form of advice and assistance, is available for children such as S prior to a hearing, and legal representation is available in any hearing in the sheriff court to determine whether the grounds for referral are established, or on appeal, it is not available in proceedings *before* a children's hearing.

The key consideration for the court was whether or not a young person at a hearing could effectively conduct his or her own case. The Lord President accepted that in some cases the issues are so straightforward and the child so mature and capable that s/he can indeed conduct his or her own case quite satisfactorily, but he also observed that,

> On the other hand, it is important to bear in mind that many of the children who appear before hearings will be young, unable to read well and unused to expressing themselves beyond the circle of their family and friends, especially to adults whom they do not know. I find it quite impossible to conclude that all the children appearing before a hearing would be able to understand, far less to criticise or to elucidate, all the reports and other documents and all the factors which the hearing may be called upon to consider when deciding what measures are most appropriate to deal with their case. The present case is itself by no means straightforward, involving, as it does, an incident where S may claim to have acted in defence of his father.[24] In these circumstances, it cannot be assumed.....that the lay representative will always be able to provide the kind of skilled assistance that may be required if the child's case is to be presented effectively (at p 544 K-L).

[23] Alternatively, the right to liberty is a civil right. Therefore proceedings before a children's hearing in which the hearing could make a supervision requirement specifying secure accommodation are proceedings for the determination of the child's civil rights.

[24] S had come before the hearing for assault because he and his father, who died of his injuries, had become involved in a fight with another man.

On this basis the court held that the right to a fair trial under Article 6(1) required that legal representation be made available to children in proceedings before a children's hearing. However, the decision did not mean that *all* children attending a hearing would automatically be entitled to such representation, but only those where the interests of justice so require, in order for their case to be presented effectively. The new Children's Hearings (Legal Representation) (Scotland) Rules 2002[25] now provide for such representation, not by ordinary solicitors using civil legal aid funds, but by 'legal representatives' to be drawn from the new panels of safeguarders and curators *ad litem* who must hold a current solicitor's practising certificate.[26] The tests for appointment of a legal representative are taken from *S v Miller* namely, if it is required to allow the child to 'effectively participate', or if there is a possibility that the child may be placed in secure accommodation.[27] The decision to appoint can be made prior to the hearing[28] or later by the children's panel itself.[29] Still left unanswered, however, is the question of when legal representation for children is required on a day-to-day basis.

CHILDREN'S PERCEPTIONS OF HEARINGS

Fear

The first serious hurdle to overcome with respect to participation is fear. Children under five play happily on laps and around or under tables. However, almost everyone older who had some experience of panels found them 'scary' because

- 'It's frightening to have to go and talk in front of lots of people' (13-year-old boy).
- 'They're all strangers. I don't know them. But they know all about you' (13-year-old girl).

Over time with exposure to the system it becomes less nerve wracking. As one 14-year-old boy explained 'the first and second time I found it hard to speak. Then I found it easier [at panels after that].'

[25] SSI 2002 No 63. These rules came into force on 23 February 2002 replacing an earlier version, SSI 2001 No 478.
[26] See r 5. Appointment of a 'legal representative' will not preclude appointment of a safeguarder under s 41 of the 1995 Act.
[27] 2002 Rules, r 3(1).
[28] At a s 64 business meeting, 2002 Rules, r 4.
[29] 2002 Rules, r 4.

Understanding the Panel's Purpose

Despite assurances from panel members that they are there to help, young people do not necessarily comprehend this. Of the 38 who expressly commented on the panel's purpose,

- Seven saw it as having some sort of regulatory/punitive role — 'Tae deal with those in the wrong' (14-year-old boy).
- Two viewed it as having the role of a court — 'A court for young people' (15-year-old girl).
- Three viewed it as deciding whether or not to remove you from home — 'They're just there tae put you in a residential home' (14-year-old boy).
- Two saw the panel as an extension of the social work department — as being 'just there to agree with social work' (16-year-old girl).
- Six did not know why panels existed (three girls and three boys).
- One 11-year-old boy living in a residential home declared that the panel's purpose was 'shit'.

However, there were 17 who saw the panel as there to fulfil a protective role or provide some kind of help to young people:

- To 'make sure you're in no danger' (12-year-old boy).
- 'To look after you [and] make sure you go to school' (15-year-old girl).
- 'Tae find the best situation for the child' (14-year-old girl).

Even where young people understand that the panel is there to help them, apart from the stress induced by the power imbalance of being brought before three adult strangers to engage in a dialogue about their future development, they still face obstacles that must be overcome if they are to participate effectively in the children's hearings process.[30]

Understanding Language, Grounds and the Decision-Making Process

Only four out of the fifty young people individually interviewed observed that they had had no difficulty in understanding the language that was used, and in one case of a 15-year-old girl, this was due to her parents' assistance.

[30] These include conflicting loyalties, presenting family in a bad light, technicalities and formal procedures, and lack of communication with panel members. See A Griffiths and RF Kandel, 'Hearing Children at Children's Hearings' (2000) 3 *Child and Family Law Quarterly* p 283ff.

In contrast, 17 out of 50 stated that they had difficulties in understanding the language of referral and that used by panel members during the hearing.[31] Another eight noted that, while they had learned to understand what was being said, they still encountered difficulties sometimes.[32] In six of these cases the young people attributed the understanding they had acquired to help given by parents, relatives and social or care workers. The following observations represent some of the young people's comments:

— 'They use too big words I think. When you're only young, I mean 12 or 13 I would sit and go through my report, I would be sitting in the children's panel and I would say what does that mean. What did this mean. I didnae have a clue what half the words meant cause its social work language' (16-year-old girl).
— 'I didn't really understand what panels were about when first started going' (girl, no age available). She would advise panel members to 'break all their big long words down into their [young persons] kind of speech so that young people can understand it better.'
— 'I only understood a wee bit' but 'didnae ask them [panel members] nuthin' 'cos 'yer shy when yer talking tae other people' (12-year-old boy).'
— 'I wisnae listening when they read out the Acts and all that rubbish I didnae have a clue' (16-year-old girl).

Comprehension depended to a large extent on the person's age, whether or not this was his/her first time before a panel, and panel members' abilities to translate from technical legal language (which forms the basis for the remit) or on social workers' interventions (or in one case that of a lawyer) to get panel members to translate grounds into ordinary age appropriate language. For example, in one case a 13-year-old girl found her social worker intervening to get the panel chair to explain what they meant when they referred to an 'interdict'.[33] Almost all the young people interviewed, aged between 11 and 27, found the language very hard to follow at times because of its formality. Those with the greatest comprehension tended to be those who had been through the system for years, usually ending up in residential homes or in a secure unit. By 15 they had acquired an understanding of the system through experience. Ironically, the formal legal language of referral was introduced to bolster the rights component of the system to protect children and families from the dangers of 'informalism' that may lead to coercive state intervention and social control under the guise of welfare. The use of formal, technical language is especially prevalent

[31] Nine girls (3x 14, 3x 15, 16, 2x no age) and 8 boys (12, 3x 13, 2x 14, 14, 27).
[32] Four girls (2x 14, 2x 15) and 4 boys (2x 12, 2x no age).
[33] An interdict is the Scottish equivalent to an English injunction.

at the start of the hearing where the grounds for referral are read out and at the end of the hearing when the child or young person is made aware of his or her right to appeal.

The use of language directly correlates with an understanding of the grounds of referral that are central to the hearing's process, for unless the grounds are accepted the hearing cannot proceed. Twenty-one out of the fifty interviewed expressly stated that they had had some difficulty in understanding the grounds presented to them. These broke down as follows:

— Four stated that they did not understand the grounds.[34]
— Thirteen stated that they generally understood the basis for their referral but sometimes did not.[35]
— Four stated that they did not initially understand the grounds but had come to do so as they gained more experience of the system.[36]

Sixteen expressly stated that they did understand the grounds as presented to them, but in five cases this was only through the intervention of a third party, such as a parent or social worker, who was not a panel member. Sixteen[37] reported accepting grounds that were unclear to them or that they did not understand or that they disagreed with, while only 14[38] stated that they had never accepted grounds in these circumstances. While some young people (especially those with experience of the hearings system) felt they could ask for an explanation where they were unclear about the grounds for referral, they were in the minority. Most of the others felt that they should just let matters ride:

— because they had a general idea why they were there (often because their social worker had discussed the panel with them beforehand)[39]
— because they felt asking for an explanation was not worth the effort — three had views like 'I could'nae be bothered ' (14-year-old boy)
— because they were afraid of appearing stupid — two had views like 'I just said aye to everything they [panel members] said because I didn't know what they were talking about so I thought if I just said "aye" they wouldn't think I was stupid or something' (15-year-old girl)

[34] One girl (no age) and 3 boys (12, 15, 27).
[35] Five girls (2 x 14, 3x 15) and 8 boys (12, 2x 13, 2x 14, 3x 15).
[36] One girl (no age) and 3 boys (12, 14, no age).
[37] Ten girls (2x 14, 4x 15, 16, 17, 2x no age) and 6 boys (2x 12, 14, 2x 15, no age).
[38] Three girls (13, 14, 15) and 11 boys (2x 13, 2x 13, 4x 14, 2x 15, no age).
[39] Those in focus groups strongly expressed this view.

— because they wanted to get the panel over with as quickly as possible — five had views like 'to make it quicker' (15-year-old boy)
— because they felt if most of the grounds were applicable it was easier to admit to them all and get on with the hearing,[40] or
— because I was embarrassed — 'I couldn't do that [ask what it meant and show ignorance]' (14-year-old girl).
— I wanted to say as little as possible — 'cos if I said no I would have to speak more [and hates to talk]' (15-year-old girl), or
— I didn't understand — 'The first time it took me about four different panels to understand the words they were telling me about [was 13 at first panel]. They came oot with all big fancy words and I'm like, I mean I'm only a wee boy, what does it mean?' (27-year-old man).[41]

Even those who understood noted that others may have difficulty. One 14-year-old girl understood the process,

> because I'm dead bright. Just because I'm in a place like this [residential school] doesn't mean I'm not bright.' However, she acknowledges that other young people may need help because 'They [panel members] use all these big words and all that and a lot of people can't understand them and you're like 'Oh god, what's going to happen at the panel' and you're too scared to ask anybody.

However, most young people understood the panels' decisions and for the few who had some doubt this tended to be cleared up in a discussion with the social worker after the panel. Only four out of 50 young people said that they did not understand the hearing's decision.[42] This was in contrast with 27[43] who acknowledged understanding and 12[44] who claimed they generally understood, but sometimes had not, especially when younger. Young people did generally know what a right of appeal was, so that there were only eight who claimed lack of knowledge[45] Twenty-four generally understood what it meant (but not the technicalities of it)[46] and six[47] who

[40] This reasoning that one should accept all the grounds if most of them applied was most strongly expressed in focus groups.
[41] Our data included an interview with a man who had had extensive experience of the hearing's system as a child in order to acquire a perspective on how the system appeared to a young person as an adult.
[42] Three girls (2x 14, no age) and 1 male (13).
[43] Seven girls (13, 3x 14, 2x 15, 16) and 20 boys (4x 12, 5x 13, 5 x 14, no age).
[44] Six girls (3x 15, 16, 17, no age) and 6 boys (13, 2x 14, 15, 27 no age).
[45] Two girls (14, 15) and 6 boys (2x 12, 2x 13, 15, no age).
[46] Two girls (14, 15) and 6 boys (2x12, 2x 13, 15, no age).
[47] Four girls (15, 16, 17, no age) and 2 boys (15, 27).

had not known when they first came into the system (aged five or six) but had learned from experience.[48]

None of the 50 interviewed individually had ever appealed. Panel members expressed the view that this was because of a high degree of consensus reached in the panel and acceptance of the panel's decision. While eight[49] young people had not appealed because they were satisfied with the panel's decision a number put forward other reasons such as it was not worth the effort or that it was pointless,[50] so that, as one 16-year-old girl observed 'Most times I just can't be bothered appealing because I don't think I'd get anything out of it anyway.' In two cases their social worker advised against it.[51] These views were based on perceptions that adults don't really listen or pay attention to young people.[52] Although a number of young people acknowledged that panel members try their best they may not succeed because of the language, generation and/or class barrier (which prevents them from understanding where the young person is coming from).[53]

Participation

Effective representation involves having the power to participate. All young people observed that they had been very frightened at their first hearing and that this had affected their ability to participate.[54] Six commented that while they had had difficulty speaking initially they had learned to do so over time.[55] They explained:

— 'When I first went [to a hearing] I never spoke, Now, I just talk straight away' [but doesn't have any sense of whether adults listen] (15-year-old boy).

[48] Of the remaining 12, 5 never got as far as a hearing (3 girls and 2 boys) and 7 for whom have no express information (3 girls and 4 boys).
[49] Four girls (13, 2x 14, 15) and 4 boys (2x 13, 14, 15).
[50] Fifteen expressed this view, (6 girls, 2x 14, 2x 15, 16, no age) and 9 boys (13, 4x 14, 3x 15, no age).
[51] Two made this observation one 15-year-old girl and one 27-year-old man.
[52] See following discussion below on young people's views on participation in the hearing especially those of young people who say little or nothing.
[53] A study of 1,155 children referred to the hearings system in Scotland in 1995 found that children primarily came from households characterised by social and economic disadvantage. See L Waterhouse and J McGhee, 'Children's Hearings in Scotland: Compulsion and Disadvantage' (2002) 24(3) *Journal of Social Welfare and Family Law* 279ff. Of the 40 panel members interviewed in our study out of around 400 members serving Glasgow in 1997–98, nearly all came from professional/management backgrounds. Only one panel member was a taxi driver (who owned his own business) and one was a secretary.
[54] Lack of participation in hearings was also found in a field study conducted by researchers at the University of Stirling. See C Hallett et al, *The Evaluation of Children's Hearings in Scotland (*Scottish Office Central Research Unit, 1998*)*, vol 1. See also K Marshall, *Children's Rights in the Balance* (The Stationery Office, 1997), 50.
[55] Two girls (14, no age) and 4 boys (2x 13, 2x 15).

— 'The first time I didnae speak 'cos I was scared. The second time I was a bit shy and then I started talking' (15-year-old boy).
— 'Initially I just didnae care about the panel, I just agreed with them and aw that but see now I've realised that ye canny just sit, ye need to ask questions an aw that' (14-year-old girl).

In some cases the young person had not only declined to participate but had been openly hostile. One 14-year-old girl in a residential home explained '[I used to say] fuck the system before it fucks you, but now I'm saying you've got to work with the system or your're not going to get anywhere.' However, although she speaks up now 'there are times when I've just sat and shut my gob.'

However, some still say as little as possible. Fifteen young people tended to keep quiet for the following reasons:[56]

— 'I hardly talk at panels. I get a wee bit nervous' (14-year-old girl).
— 'I'm worried what is gonnae happen to me' (12-year-old boy).
— Depends 'a lot on what kind of panel it is and who's on the panel. I prefer to just get it done quick, get it over as quick as I can so I can get hame' (14 year-old-boy).
— 'Too many strangers in the room' (14-year-old girl).

Whatever the level of verbal participation, only nine young people felt that panel members listened or paid attention to what they had to say at hearings.[57] Fifteen[58] were of the view that they did not and eleven[59] observed that while panel members listened to them sometimes at other times they did not. They expressed the following views:

— 'Panel members don't really listen to you anyway 'cos they just agree with social work' (15-year-old boy).[60]
— 'Ah didnae have any say in it [because panel had already made up its mind]' (14-year-old girl).[61]
— 'They just talk tae you and don't listen to you.' Doesn't think it matters much when young person is called on to speak 'cos it does naw matter much. They are gonnae say you are going here anyway' (14-year-old boy).

[56] Seven girls (3x 14, 3x 15,16) 8 boys (11, 2x 12, 2x 14, 3x 15).
[57] Three girls (15, 16, 17) and 6 boys (11, 12, 2x 14, 15, 27).
[58] Four girls (13, 3x 15) and 11 boys (4x 12, 4x 13, 2x 15, no age).
[59] Six girls (2x 14, 2x 15, 2 no age) and 5 boys (3x 14, 2x 15).
[60] Three other young people expressed this view, 2 girls (16, 17) and one 14-year-old boy.
[61] Two other young people expressed this view, one 14-year-old girl and one 14-year-old boy.

One 10-year-old boy from a residential school commented that panel members did not listen to him because 'they already had their minds made up.' When asked why he thought this was the case he explained 'they didn't even leave the room ... they just came straight out with the decision in front of you.' Ironically, while this boy considered failure to adjourn indicated a failure to take his views seriously, panel members consider that their decision-making on the spot demonstrates transparency, openness, and independence precisely because there is no conferring with colleagues prior to giving a decision.

In some cases young people acknowledged that failure to listen to them might be the result of aggressive or abusive behaviour towards panel members:

— 'If you start shouting and swearing, you know they just don't listen at all. Unless you put it across in the right manner they'll not listen to you' (15-year-old boy).
— 'I've freaked at them a few times and geed them abuse and I dinnae think they listen to you if you dae that' (14-year-old boy).

Young people know if panel members are listening or not because,

— 'When I say stuff they answer what I say. And they tell me what I'm wanting and all that' (12-year-old boy).
— 'They join the conversation' they don't listen 'when they sit there reading' (15-year-old girl).
— 'They just, well, looked at me and concentrated on like what ah wiz saying' (boy no age).
— 'They speak about things you've been saying earlier on' (13-year-old boy).

When asked whether they felt they could participate in their hearings, 15 said yes,[62] 13 said sometimes yes but sometimes no,[63] and 10 said no.[64] Those that experienced difficulty in participating did so for some of the following reasons:

— 'One of the things I dinnae like about the panel, they think that they're better than you and they don't talk to you they talk right through you' (15-year-old girl).
— 'Some panel members don't listen at all they just keep writing.' Considers those ones 'awfully rude. It's good when they give advice rather than being critical' (14-year-old girl).

[62] Four girls (13, 3x 15) and 11 boys (4x 12, 4x 13, 2x 15, no age).
[63] Six girls (2x 14, 2x 15, 2 no age) and 7 boys (4x 14, 3x 15).
[64] Five girls (2x 14, 15, 16, 17) and 5 boys (11, 2x 14, 15, 27).

— 'Sometimes they just sit and read all the paper work. You cannie listen and read at the same time' (girl, no age available).
— Some panel members 'just sit and write and all that and that's dead distracting for me' (15-year-old girl).
— 'You can get some of them that will lecture yi and frighten yi right aff' (15-year-old boy)
— 'They sit and look at you and talk to as if you's that height and you're a wee bit of dirt or something' (15-year-old girl)
— 'You can tell when panel members are against you "the way they look at yi man" and also "the way they talk to yi. Look you up and doon an' that." As a result "when a panel [member] talks tae me ah don't [say anything] ah just listen, and ah talk tae them when ah'm spoken tae. Never considered appealing. Ah woudnae appeal, cause yi couldnae win against it. It's like the polis, yi couldnae win"' (14-year-old boy).

On the other hand those who felt they could participate made the following observations:

— 'A good panel is one where they talk to you like a normal person. People that go to panels are all about thirteen, fourteen now and they're not wains [kids], they're not babies, we just, we want to be spoken to as say people would speak to you like' (15-year-old girl)
— 'Maest of them [panel members] listen to you' (15-year-old boy)
— 'Panel members were "nice". They "explained things an' didnae just like rush through things" "they talked to me like a person"' (13-year-old girl)

Knowledge of Writing and Confidentiality

Provisions exist to encourage participation. Young people have the option to write to panel members expressing their views and the chair may clear the hearing to talk to the child alone where this must be done to obtain the child's views or because the presence of a relevant person or persons is causing or is likely to cause the child significant distress.[65] Thirty interviewees, however, had no knowledge that they could write to the panel.[66] Of the 20 who had such knowledge, the majority did not write[67]on the basis that they

[65] Section 46(1) of the 1995 Act.
[66] These included 11 girls and 19 boys.
[67] Only 8 wrote to the panel (5 girls and 3 boys) while 12 (4 girls and 8 boys) did not do so.

saw no point, couldn't be bothered or never thought it necessary.[68] Thus, knowledge does not necessarily lead to action. Literary skills may be an issue here as many of the young people have been out of the school system for years. Those who do write are in the minority and often live in a residential home or secure unit where they are assisted by members of staff if writing letters. However, the general view of 24 young people who commented on whether writing was useful (whether or not they had previous knowledge about writing) was either a negative one or that it was unnecessary[69] because:

— '[I] dinnae see the point' (12-year-old boy)
— '[I] never considered it because "I just go in and say what I'm going to say"' (14-year-old boy)
— 'Aye, I've wrote [but] it had no effect.' 'They would say right we've listened to what you've had to say what you've wrote down but the decision is you're back in care. That was always the decision. So I would get to the point where I didnae bother writing in,' (16-year-old girl)

Only four out of the fifty interviewed had experienced the room being cleared to talk to them or their parents on their own.[70] All four found that it made it easier for them to speak. However, an obstacle exists in that in order to promote an open process the substance of what is said in private must be revealed to those who have been excluded on their return.[71] Panel members fear this inhibits discussion but one of the four, a 14-year-old girl, when asked if this inhibited her stated 'no really'. Out of 24 young people who had never experienced the room being cleared but who commented on whether they thought this might make it easier for a young person to participate, nine said 'yes',[72] eight said 'no',[73] and seven said 'maybe'.[74] When asked if they would change their minds if the substance would have to be revealed on the absent parties' return, three of those who said they would speak if the room was cleared changed their minds and said they would not speak in these circumstances,[75] five said it would make no difference as they wouldn't speak anyway (because of the difficulties outlined earlier),[76]

[68] In one case, that of a 14-year-old girl, this was because of disability.
[69] There were 16 comments to this effect compared with 8 positive views, like '[I've] never done it but it could make it easier for young people' (15-year-old boy).
[70] Two girls (14,15) and 2 boys (13, 14).
[71] Section 46(2) 1995 Act.
[72] Four girls (2x 14, 2x 15) and 5 boys (13, 2x14, 15, 27).
[73] Four girls (2x 15, 16, 17) and 4 boys (2x12, 14, 15).
[74] Three girls (14, 16, and no age) and 4 boys (12, 13, 14, no age).
[75] One girl (15) and 2 boys (14, 27).
[76] One girl (16) and 4 boys (2x 12, 2x 14).

and six said it would make no difference and would not put them off speaking.[77]

Representation

The power to participate not only involves an understanding of the language and process of decision-making but may be enhanced through representation. In *S v Miller* it was argued that where a child's interests were in need of protection a safeguarder could be appointed under section 41 of the 1995 Act.[78] However, the court did not consider that this was adequate since the decision to appoint a safeguarder lies with the hearing and not with the child. As the Lord President pointed out the appointment is made only to safeguard 'the interests' of the child and not to vindicate his or her rights. Our interviews with 25 safeguarders uphold the Lord President's observations for they all viewed themselves as an independent third party appointed by a children's panel to report back to the panel on what they considered to be in the child's best interests. While the child's views were important they did not consider themselves to be acting as the child's advocate where their view of what was in the child's best interests differed from that of the child or his or her parents.

However, children's hearing regulations do provide that, even at the disposal stage, a child and any relevant person attending the hearing may be accompanied by a person who may assist them in their representation.[79] Only ten[80] of those interviewed knew this compared with nineteen who had no knowledge.[81] Six out of the ten with knowledge took someone with them. Among those persons were a grandmother, a priest, an older sibling, a guidance teacher from school and a befriender. Those who had no knowledge, when asked if they would have taken someone with them if they had known replied as follows:

— Ten said yes[82]
— One said probably (15-year-old girl)
— Two said didn't know[83]
— Four said no[84]

[77] Five girls (2x 14, 15, 16, no age) and 1 boy (15).
[78] A safeguarder is a person who carries out an independent investigation into what is 'in the best interests of the child,' by speaking to the child and family and any other relevant persons who may have information, and then reports back to the panel.
[79] 1996 Rules, r11 paras 1 and 2.
[80] Five girls (14, 2x15, 16, 17) and 5 boys (12, 3x13, 14).
[81] Eight girls (3x 14, 4x 15, 1 no age) and 11 boys (12, 3x13, 14, 4x 15, 27, no age).
[82] Four girls (13, 3x 14) and 6 boys (12, 2x 13, 2x 15, 27).
[83] Two girls (15, no age).
[84] Four boys (2x 13m 2x 15).

When asked if they thought it would be useful for a young person to have someone to assist them, sixteen said yes,[85] ten said no or that it would make no difference,[86] and three stated that they did not know.[87] Those in favour took the view:

— 'it would be helpful to have somebody that was a similar age to you and you could tell them and they could speak up for you at the panel' (15-year-old girl).
— 'it would make it a lot easier to say what you think' (15-year-old girl).
— 'Aye, that would be good [to have someone to say] I'm here to speak up for you and if you've got any questions ask me and then I'll put it forward to them [the panel]. If you don't understand the answers just say and I'll explain better. That would be helpful. It all depends on the person. It depends on what they are like' (27-year-old man).

However, even those in favour expressed certain caveats,[88] such as providing a young person with a choice and with making sure that this person did not appropriate the young person's voice, eg, it would be good 'but not if that person said it the wrong way' (13-year-old boy) or if they ended up 'mixing your story up and getting it wrang' (15-year-old boy).

When asked about what kind of person should assist young people, one 15-year-old girl took the view that this person should be of a similar age because otherwise he or she would be out of touch with young people's perspectives. One 14-year-old boy thought the representative should be a 'relative, parent or friend.' However, another 14-year-old boy was adamant that this person 'should not be a friend or your Mum or Dad' but liked having a lawyer because 'if yi get stuck for words an' that and don't know what tae say and you start to get embarrassed, they just like pit in for yi.'

Those who considered representation not generally useful did so because they felt it was important for the young people to speak for themselves or because they felt it would make no difference as the panel had already reached a decision. They made statements like:

— 'no [to representation] because every time people speak for you it's just like you can't get it across yourself. But I think if you put it to the panel yourself, your own opinion of it and what you felt

[85] Ten girls (3x 14, 6x 15, 17) and 6 boys (12, 13, 14, 2x 15, 27).
[86] Three girls (2x 14, 15) and 7 boys (2x 12, 2x 13, 3x 14).
[87] One girl (no age) and 2 boys (2x 15). In 21 cases (6 girls and 15 boys) no information was forthcoming on this issue.
[88] That is 5 out of 10 ten including 3 girls and 2 boys.

and think should happen to you, I think they'll listen to you because it's you that's telling them and it's not somebody [else] saying it for you' (14-year-old girl).

— 'no really because the panel have already made up their minds' (14-year-old boy).
— 'children should "speik up for theirsel". But does recognise 'if I wiz havin' difficulty ah would tell someone to speak for us, aye' and that person would be "a person that knows us and knows about us" ' (14-year-old boy).

Those who were doubtful about representation expressed views like 'I don't know. Some folk would think it's a good idea but other people have got a different opinion. You've got to learn to speak for yourself I think.' (15-year-old boy).

When asked if they thought they would have benefited in their own hearing from having a representative, twelve[89] said yes, thirteen[90] said it was unnecessary, and five didn't know.[91] Five considered it unnecessary because they preferred to speak for themselves even if they had difficulty in speaking to panel members. One 15-year-old girl explained, 'I mean I change my mind quite a lot so I'd be more wanting to speak myself. They could interview me and I could say a total different thing, well you know what you say at the panel then I could think a total different thing when I wake up the next morning.' Another 14-year-old girl said 'I do it all for myself because I know I can do it for myself. And I've had too many people telling me "No, you need help. You can't do it for yourself." I'm going to prove them wrong. That's the goal for me.' On the other hand, one 16-year-old girl said it would have been useless because 'you cannie win either way. You cannie, that's a fact. I'm just glad they [the panel] cannie tell me what to do anymore.'

Representation by a Lawyer

Only five of those interviewed had been represented by a lawyer.[92] In one case a 14-year-old girl had had legal representation at a panel three times on the advice of her social worker. On one occasion the panel had asked her if she wanted a lawyer 'and I said naw but in some situations I think you should have a lawyer present.' She did not expand on this. In general

[89] Seven girls (2x 14, 4x 14, 17) and 5 boys (12, 13, 14, 2x15).
[90] Five girls (13, 2x 14, 15, 16)and 8 boys (12, 3x 13, 4x 14).
[91] Two girls (15, no age) and 3 boys (12, 13, 14).
[92] One girl (14) and 4 boys (2x 12, 2x 14).

those interviewed had only a vague idea of what a lawyer does. Ten[93] expressly stated that they had never had any experience of a lawyer and had no idea what s/he does, in one case venturing the view 'I think a lawyer's really just the same as a social worker' (15-year-old girl). In seven[94] cases there were strong views that lawyers were inappropriate:

— 'Ah wouldnae like lawyer' (15-year-old boy).
— 'Naw, I don't think they're appropriate at all' (13-year-old boy).
— Unnecessary 'because I don't need one' (13-year-old boy).
— 'Naw, [should not have representation by a lawyer] no for a children's panel. It's no aboot tae dae wi' evidence, it's aboot the moral issue init, whats happening an' a' that.' (14-year-old boy).

In most of these cases, although strong feelings were expressed, no reason was given why lawyers were considered unsuitable for representing young people at a hearing. Whatever the difficulties young people encounter with the hearings system, eighteen[95] out of fifty stated that they considered that the panel had tried to help them, even when they disagreed with the decisions reached by the panel, compared with only eight[96] who expressed a negative view. As one 15-year-old girl put it, although she had disagreed with the outcome of her panel 'they does their best for ya.' However, almost half of those interviewed also expressed the view that there was a real need for those involved in the hearings system to work on improving young people's knowledge and understanding of it.[97]

Legal Understandings and Rights to Lawyers

In consequence of *S v Miller* and the regulations that followed from it, the right to a fair hearing embodied in Article 6 of the ECHR now includes the young person's right to legal representation at a children's hearing where required to 'effectively participate' or if there is a possibility of being placed in secure accommodation. However, the young people who come before the panels find themselves caught in a socio-legal construction of childhood that balances their autonomy rights to participate in decisions affecting their welfare[98] with their best interests (welfare rights)[99] which are the paramount consideration under Scots law.

[93] Three girls (13, 14, 15) and 7 boys (3x 13, 2x 14, 15, no age).
[94] One girl (14) and 6 boys (3x 13 2x 14, 15).
[95] Six girls (13, 2x 14, 2x 15, no age) and 12 boys (3x 12, 3x 13, 14, 4x 15, no age).
[96] Two girls (16, no age) and 6 boys (11, 13, 2x 15, 14, 27).
[97] Twenty-four expressed this view including 14 girls (13, 4x 14, 5x 15, 16, 17 2 no age) and 10 boys (12, 3x 13, 14, 3x 15, 27, no age).
[98] UNCRC Art 12(1) and (2).
[99] UNCRC Art 3(1) and (2).

While Article 5 of the UNCRC implicitly recognises that the balance should be assessed in the light of a child's evolving capacities, it is adults (the reporters and panel members) and not children who make the final judgment as to their ability to understand, criticise, and elucidate their cases.[100] According to the rules promulgated pursuant to *S v Miller*, the reporter or the panel members can assign legal representation to the child at a business meeting prior to the hearing (business meetings are relatively rare) or the panel members can assign legal representation to the child at the hearing itself.

The new rules raise several unusual issues. Although the rules are intended to empower children at hearings, the procedure is entirely best interests based. The decision to have or not have a lawyer is not in the hands of the child, and there appears to be no rule permitting a child to make such a request. It is not even certain that every child might have a right to waive legal representation. Given the language of *S v Miller*, finding ineffective participation where a child cannot understand, criticise, or elucidate the case, it is likely that a child may be assigned legal representation particularly because he or she is not mature enough to understand the process. This is quite the opposite approach from the roughly similar situation of an interparental residence and contact dispute in a Scottish divorce, where a child can be sisted into the action provided he or she can 'demonstrate to their solicitor a general understanding of what it means to instruct the solicitor.'[101] If the child is considered too immature to understand, or to give a directive to a solicitor, it is questionable whether the child can waive legal representation. This brings to the foreground of interest children's legal understandings,[102] especially about lawyers and the children's hearings process.

The data above show clearly that virtually all children are aware that their participation at the panels is not as effective as it could be. All young people said they had been very frightened at their first hearing and this had

[100] Art 5 provides 'States parties shall respect the responsibilities, rights and duties of parents or ... other persons legally responsible for the child, to provide in a manner consistent with the evolving capacities of the child, appropriate directions and guidance in the exercise by the child of the rights recognised in the present Convention.'

[101] A Cleland, 'Children's Voices' in J Scoular (ed), *Family Dynamics: Contemporary Issues in Family Law* (Edinburgh and London, Butterworths/Lexis Nexis, 2001) 7ff, 21. 'Scots law makes it clear that the judging of a child's capacity to instruct a solicitor is a matter for the solicitor alone. Legislation provides that a child under 16 'shall have legal capacity to instruct a solicitor, in connection with any civil matter, where that person has a general understanding of what it means to do so.' The presumption of maturity at age 12 applies. This has meant that the courts have been unable to intervene to stop the separate representation of a child, once the child has been sisted as a third party'.

[102] We use the term 'legal understanding' rather than the grander term 'legal consciousness', as the latter implies an overarching orientation towards the law. Our interviewees and ethnography were limited to what children did and felt and said about the children's hearings. We think it is unfair to them to extrapolate their views in such a way.

affected their participation. When asked if they could participate in their hearings, 15 said yes, 13 said sometimes yes but sometimes no, and ten said no. Effective participation involves informed participation and as the Glasgow research demonstrates young people have difficulty in understanding the purpose of a children's panel and the language in which the decision-making process is conducted. They also lack knowledge about rights to representation and other aspects of the hearings system including the more technical details such as invoking a right of appeal.[103]

However, even where they know their participation may be impaired by a sense of powerlessness engendered by perceptions that what they have to say carries little weight with panel members when measured against other professionals' opinions, such as social workers' recommendations, many of the young people we interviewed preferred to speak for themsleves. Other attitudes, such as diffidence, a sense of futility at a seeming fait accompli, or mouthing off, hamper forthright communication. Underlying this all, is their knowledge that their lives are in the hands of the children's hearings system, that is much more powerful than they, and the individual panel members who look down, or seem to look down on them, from the majesty of higher social class and age.[104]

While, from the perspective of the legal system, legal representation might seem the obvious, if incomplete, remedy, most of the children we interviewed did not necessarily understand it that way.[105] Our interviews, conducted prior to the *S v Miller* case, broadly covered the children's views on assistance and representation. The interviewees made it clear that they regarded representation as a choice that a young person should be free to adopt or reject on one's own terms.

A number of young people preferred to represent themselves, even if they say very little, rather than cede control to another person, especially an adult, over what is presented in their name. Autonomy as well as narrative authenticity was important to them.

When asked if it would be useful to have someone to assist them, 16 said yes, 10 said no or that it would make no difference, and 3 stated they did not know. Of the ten interviewees who knew they could be accompanied by a person to assist them in representation,[106] 6 in fact did bring people. Their

[103] These issues also form part of the findings of recent study carried out by K Marshall, K Tisdall and A Clelland, on the '*Voice of the Child' Under the Children (Scotland) Act 1995* vols 1 and 2 (Scottish Executive, 2002), vol 2, 33–50.

[104] Above, n 53.

[105] The study by K Marshall, K Tisdall and A Clelland noted that in contrast to the largely negative opinions of lawyers held by children who had not had independent representation 'those who have been legally represented have very positive views' (above n 103, vol 2, at 44). However, the authors acknowledge that given the limited number of and selection biases of children interviewed 'further research is required to explore how lawyers and other representatives can effectively engage with children' (vol 1, at 3).

[106] 1996 Rules, r 11 paras 1 and 2.

choices, discussed earlier, suggest they were chosen for emotional support and personal relationship to the child — not technical know how or speaking ability.

Interestingly enough, when the interviewees were asked specifically whether they would have benefited from having a representative at their own hearing, 12 said it would have been helpful, 13 that it was unnecessary, and five had no opinion. The slight change in the majority opinion from the general to the specific question again indicates the importance of autonomy. Several interviewees stressed their desire to do it and say it for themselves at the panel, even if it was hard work and not entirely successful.

Even where they acknowledged the value of assistance, they were concerned with having choice, and at pains to establish that this should not be at the expense of appropriating the young person's voice or view of proceedings. To some it was especially important to have a person of similar age who was in touch with young people's perspectives. For others, the best choice of representative, if any, would be an articulate peer, emotionally uninvolved, but culturally and contextually related to their life experience and able to narrate without mixing up the meanings.

Reading between the lines of the young people's comments is the sense that they want their individual identities to be recognised and to be respected for who they are. By speaking to the panel members in their own voices, and telling so much of the narratives of their lives as they wish, they can be understood as a distinct individual. At the same time, other interviewees stated that assistance and representation would make no difference, largely because everything is a done deal, or 'you cannie win either way.' These two poles of 'I can do it myself,' and 'Nothing can be done,' also influenced the way the children reacted to the idea of representation by a lawyer.

The interviewees had scant knowledge of lawyers or what they did. But some had strong, largely negative views about being represented by them, which they could not back up with reasons. While lawyers may or may not be the best choice for assisting in the telling of narrative tales, the young people's dislike may be born of ignorance. The comment of one interviewee, that the hearing is not about evidence but about the moral issues, also suggests that the young people may have absorbed the anti-legalistic ethos of the children's hearings system, which is now inevitably undergoing change.

Most interviewees were hazy about the technicalities of their legal rights, and could not understand what lawyers might do that social workers or safeguarders do not. Perhaps they perceived them as just more posh talking engines of the elite bureaucracy because they are unaware of the possibilities of advocacy. Their instincts may not be off the mark. It is possible that more legalism may prove an intrusion in the children's hearings system.

However, there are a number of advocacy skills that lawyers can provide that the majority of interviewees had no knowledge of. These include helping to write a letter to the panel members, determining whether or not to plead to grounds, narrating a client's story, changing the nature of a panel conversation by either using probing questions to get information, or closing off avenues of talk, and negotiating in ways that may get a child a specific placement or order that he or she wants.

In sum, there are four possible reasons that the young people we interviewed were largely not in favour of lawyers. First is the attitude that 'I don't need what I don't know about,' especially in regard to service professionals. Similar views were expressed during our research regarding other professions. For example, in contrast to our New York research, where counselling and therapy are par for the course for families in family court, mention of a psychologist or psychiatrist brought out the comment 'I don't need that. I'm not crazy.'[107] Second is the very serious concern that lawyers may mangle or change their narratives. Third is the attitude of the children's hearings system itself that discourages legalism. Fourth is the young people's ignorance of the due process technicalities, the social welfare and criminal laws, and the human rights that underpin the best interests conversation during the panel sessions. These reasons are interrelated. Without awareness of technical pitfalls, they don't feel a lack of legal technicians.

The fact that the interviewees do not want something that they know nothing about is not a reason to stop the process. However, the strong views of the young people we interviewed ought to be considered in developing the style of lawyering in the children's hearings system. What panel members will want to know remains to be seen. But the interviews strongly suggest that if lawyers are assigned, the young people would prefer a staunch advocacy model, with an educative component that would enhance their options and understanding,[108] and a thorough enough dialogue with their lawyers for them to understand and negotiate upon their real life narratives, not mere normative models.[109] It is yet to be seen whether the lawyers will steer the young people's authentic narratives through the minefield of a blurred law and welfare discourse[110] to help them get what they

[107] See generally RF Kandel and A Griffiths, 'Reconfiguring Personhood: From Ungovernability to Parent Adolescent Autonomy Conflict Actions' (2003) 53(3) *Syracuse Law Review* 995ff.

[108] See J Cherry, 'Note: The Child as Apprentice: Enhancing the Child's Ability to Participate in Custody Decision Making by Providing Scaffolding Instruction' (2003) 72 *S Cal L Rev* 811ff (discussing a model to break down issues and concerns in ways that children can understand and help them be engaged in cases concerning them).

[109] See J A Chaplan, 'Youth Perspectives on Lawyers' Ethics: A Report on Seven Interviews' (1996) 64 *Fordham L Rev* 1763ff (explaining that youths appreciated their attorneys when they used postmodern narrative analysis rather than normative analysis in deciding to represent their young clients).

[110] See, generally RT Lakoff, *Talking Power: The Politics of Language in Our Lives* (New York, Basic Books, 1990).

want or impose another professional discourse with its own power and knowledge,[111] that young people will find still another distortion.

Young people's fear and anxiety about what is in store for them at a hearing is something that will always be present at any type of proceedings regardless of how formal or informal they may be. What can be done is to ensure that all young people who are brought before a hearing receive adequate support and information about the process including assisting a young person to participate in ways that they feel are appropriate for them. Although social workers claim to fulfil this role, their success in doing so varies enormously and depends to a large extent on the kind of rapport that they establish with the child or young person. Specific proposals for enhancing children's understanding and participation have been detailed elsewhere and include the provision of user-friendly leaflets or videos (especially important where young people have learning disabilities), discussion and debate in schools, or the use of children's rights officers.[112]

Although *S v Miller* seeks to enhance children's rights by providing for legal representation in children's hearings, its remit and that of subsequent regulations is far from clear. Having rejected that legal representation should be mandatory in all cases (which was the solution adopted in by the United States Supreme Court in delinquency proceedings in the case of *In Re Gault*)[113] it leaves open the question of when it is necessary to enable a child or young person to 'effectively participate' in a hearing. It also raises questions about what effective participation entails, for it raises issues about whether children necessarily acquire a better understanding of the process through legal representation and whether they in fact have more power to make their voices heard and acted upon. These issues must be more cogently addressed if international human rights for children are to have any meaning.

[111] See, generally M Foucault, *Discipline and Punish: The Birth of the Prison* (2nd edn., New York, Alan Sheridan trans, Vintage Books, 1995); M Foucault, *Birth of the Clinic: An Archaeology of Medical Perception* (New York, AL Sheridan Smith trans, Pantheon Books, 1973) (expounding of the ways that professional discourses of law, psychology and medicine create their own kinds of knowledge that are diffused forms of power, or, as Foucault dubs it 'power knowledge').

[112] See Griffiths and Kandel, above n 30.

[113] 387 US 1 (1967).

Bibliography

ABEL-SMITH, B and STEVENS, R *Lawyers and the Courts: A Sociological Study of the English Legal System 1750–1965* (London, Heinemann, 1967) Advisory Council for the Education of Romany and other Travellers (ACERT), *Directory of Planning Policies for Gypsy Site Provision in England* (Bristol, The Policy Press, 1997)

AGI, M *René Cassin: Père de la Déclaration universelle des droits de l'homme* (Paris, LAP, 1998)

AGRIKOLIANSKY, É *La ligue française des droits de l'Homme et du citoyen depuis 1945: Sociologie d'un engagement civique* (Paris, l'Harmattan, 2002a)

—— ' "Liberté, liberté chérie": La gauche et les libertés publiques dans les années 1970. Usages politiques d'une catégoric juridique,' Presentation at l'Université de Picardic, Curapp, 14–15 November 2002

ALLMAND, W 'The International Criminal Court and the Human Rights Revolution', (2000–01) 46 *McGill Law Journal*

ALSTON, P (ed), *Promoting Human Rights Through Bills of Rights: Comparative Perspectives* (Oxford, Oxford University Press, 1999)

—— and CRAWFORD, J (eds), *The Future of UN Human Rights Treaty Monitoring* (Cambridge, Cambridge University Press, 2000)

AN-NAIM, A *Human Rights in Cross-Cultural Perspectives — A Quest for Consensus* (Philadelphia, University of Pennsylvania Press, 1992)

ARKINSTALL, J and O'BRIEN, C 'Table of Cases under the Human Rights Act' [2002] *European Human Rights Law Review*

Audit Commission, *Better by Far: Preparing for Best Value*, (London, Audit Commission, 1998)

Audit Commission, *Human Rights: Improving Public Services,* (London, Audit Commission, 2003)

AYRES, I and BRAITHWAITE, J *Responsive Regulation: Transcending the Deregulation Debate* (Oxford, Oxford University Press, 1992)

BAMFORTH, N 'Parliamentary sovereignty and the Human Rights Act 1998 [1998] *Public Law* (1998)

—— 'The True "Horizontal Effect" of the Human Rights Act 1998' (2001) 117 *Law Quarterly Review*

BANAKAR, R 'Det offentliga samtalet om ethnokulturella frågor' (Public Discourse on Ethno-Cultural Issues) *Häften för kritiska studier* ((1993) The Swedish Critical Studies Review 1–2)

—— *The Dilemma of Law: On Conflict Management in a Multicultural Society* [original title: Rättens Dilemma: Om konflikthantering i ett mångkulturellt samhälle] (Lund, Bokbox, 1994)

—— *The Doorkeepers of the Law* (Aldershot: Ashgate, 1998)

—— *Merging Law and Sociology* (Berlin, Galda & Wilch, 2003)

—— and TRAVERS, M *An Introduction to Law and Social Theory* (Oxford, Hart Publishing, 2002)

BANCAUD, A *Une exception ordinaire: La magistrature en France (1930–1950)* (Paris, Gallimard, 2002)

BARKER, L 'Third Parties in Litigation: A Systematic View of the Judicial Function' (1967) 29, *Journal of Politics*

BARNETT, H 'The rights of gypsies — landmark or signpost?' (1996) 146 (6767) *New Law Journal*

BARTOLOMEI, M-L and HYDEN, H (eds), *The Implementation of Human Rights in a Global World, Lund Studies in Sociology of Law* (Lund, Lund Studies in Sociology of Law, 1999)

BELL, DA, BROWN, D, JAYASURIYA, K and JONES, DM *Towards Illiberal Democracy in Pacific Asia* (New York, St Martin's Press, 1995)

BELOFF, MJ and MOUNTFIELD, H 'Unconventional Behaviour? Judicial uses of the European Convention in England and Wales' [1996] *European Human Rights Law Review*

BENTLEY, A *The Process of Government* (Chicago, University of Chicago Press, 1908)

BERGMAN, E (ed), *Solidaritet och konflikt–Etniska relationer i Sverige* (Stockholm, Carlssons, 1989)

—— and SWEDIN, B *Vittnesmål – Invandrares syn på diskriminering i Sverige* (Stockholm, Publica, 1982)

BERK, RA and ROSSI, PH *Thinking about Program Evaluation*, (Newbury Park, CA, Sage, 1990)

BERRY, J *Lobbying for the People: The Political Behavior of Public Interest Groups* (Princeton, NJ, Princeton University Press, 1977)

BETTATI, M *Le droit d'ingérence. La mutation de l'ordre mondial* (Paris, Odile Jacob, 1996)

BIRNBAUM, P *l'Afaire Dreyfus: La République en péril* (Paris, Gallimard, 1994)

BLACK-BRANCH, JL 'Observing and Enforcing Human Rights under the Council of Europe: The Creation of a Permanent European Court of Human Rights' (1996–97) 3:1 *Buffalo Journal of International Law*

BOEREFIJN, I *The Reporting Procedure under the Covenant on Civil and Political Rights: Practice and Procedures of the Human Rights Committee* (Oxford, Hart Publishing, 1999)

BOURDIEU, P and WACQUANT, L *An Invitation to Reflexive Sociology* (Chicago, University of Chicago Press, 1992)

BRAITHWAITE, J *To Punish or Persuade: Enforcement of Coal Mine Safety* (Albany, State University of New York Press, 1985)

BRUNE, Y *Invandrare i svenskt arbetsliv* (Norrköping, Statens Invandrarverk, 1993)

BUCHANAN, T 'Amnesty International in Crisis, 1966–7', forthcoming in *Twentieth Century British History* (2004)

—— '"The Truth Will Set You Free": The Making of Amnesty International' (2002) 37(4) *Journal of Contemporary History*

BURGELIN, JF 'La Cour de cassation en question' (2001) 12 *Dalloz*

BUXTON, R 'The Human Rights Act and Private Law' (2000) 116 *Law Quarterly Review* 48ff

BYERS, M *Custom, Power and the Power of Rules: International Relations and Customary International Law* (Cambridge, Cambridge University Press, 1999)

BYNOE, I and SPENCER, S *Mainstreaming Human Rights in Whitehall and Westminster* (London, IPPR, 1999)

CALDEIRA, GA and WRIGHT, JR 'Amicus Curiae Briefs before the Court: Who Participates, When, and How Much?' (1990) 52 *Journal of Politics*

CAMERON, I 'Respect for the Home: Treatment of Gypsies' (1998) 4(2) *European Public Law*

CAMP KEITH, L 'The United Nations International Covenant on Civil and Political Rights: Does It Make a Difference in Human Rights Behavior?' (1999) 36 *Journal of Peace Research*

CARDENAS, S 'Transgovernmental Activism: Canada's Role in Promoting National Human Rights Commissions' (2003) 25 *Human Rights Quarterly*

—— 'Emerging Global Actors: The United Nations and National Human Rights Institutions' (2003) 9 *Global Governance*

CASSESSE, A *Human Rights in a Changing World* (Cambridge, Polity Press, 1990)

——, GAETA, P, JONES, JRWD (eds), *The Rome Statute of the International Criminal Court: A Commentary* (Oxford, Oxford University Press, 2002)

CHAMBERS, G *Practising Human Rights* (London, Report 28, RPPU, Law Society, 1998)

CHAPLAN, JA 'Youth Perspectives on Lawyers' Ethics: A Report on Seven Interviews' (1996) 64 *Fordham L Rev*

CHARLE, C *La crise des sociétés impériales: Allemagne, France, Grande-Bretagne 1900–1940* (Paris, Éditions du Seuil, 2001)

CHAYES, A and CHAYES, AH *The new sovereignty: compliance with international regulatory agreements* (Cambridge, Mass Harvard University Press, 1995)

CHELIMSKY, E 'Thoughts for a New Evaluation Society' (1997) 3 *Evaluation*

—— and SHADISH, W (eds), *Evaluation for the 21st* Century (Thousand Oaks, CA, Sage, 1997)

CHERRY, J 'Note: The Child as Apprentice: Enhancing the Child's Ability to Participate in Custody Decision Making by Providing Scaffolding Instruction', *S Cal L Rev,* 72 (2003), p.811ff

CHRISTENSEN, A 'Strukturella aspekter på diskrimineringslagstiftning och normative förändringsprocesser' in A Numhauser-Henning (ed), *Perspektiv på likabehandling och diskriminering* (Lund, Juristförlaget, 2000)

CHRISTIE, K 'Regime Change and Human Rights in Southeast Asia' (1995) 43 *Political Studies*

CLELAND, A 'Children's Voices' in Scoular, J (ed), *Family Dynamics: Contemporary Issues in Family Law* (Edinburgh and London: Butterworths/Lexis Nexis, 2001) 7ff

CLEMENTS, L 'The Human Rights Bill' (1998) *Journal of Local Government Law* 4–7

CLEMENTS and READ, J *Disabled People and European Human Rights* (Bristol, Policy Press, 2003)

COBBAN, A *A History of Modern France. Volume 3: 1871–1962* (Middlesex, Penguin, 1965)

COHEN, B and STAUNTON, M 'In Pursuit of a Legal Strategy: The National Council for Civil Liberties' in Cooper, J and Dhavan, R (eds), *Public Interest Law* (London, Blackwell Publishers, 1986)

COMMAILLE, J 'La juridicisation du politique. Entre réalité et connaissance de la réalité' in Commaille, J Dumoulin, L and Robert, C (eds), *La juridicisation du politique. Leçons scientifiques* (Paris, LGDJ, 2000) 241–51

COOPE, S and LANE, L *Public Authorities and the Human Rights Act: An Explanatory Study* (Edinburgh, Scottish Executive Central Research Unit Stationery Office, 2001)

COOPER, J and DHAVAN, R (eds), *Public Interest Law* (London, Blackwell Publishers, 1986)

CORNER, T 'Planning, Environment and the European Convention on Human Rights' (April 1998) *Journal of Public Law* 301–14

CORTNER, RC 'Strategies and Tactics of Litigants in Constitutional Cases' (1968) 17 *Journal of Public Law* 17

COWAN, RB 'Women's Rights Through Litigation: An Examination of the American Civil Liberties Union Women's Rights Project, 1971–1976' (1976) 8 *Columbia Human Rights Law Review*

CROFT, J 'Whitehall and the Human Rights Act 1998' (2000) *European Human Rights Law Review* 392ff

—— *Whitehall and the Human Rights Act 1998* (London, The Constitution Unit, University College London, 2000)

CROW, I 'Evaluating Initiatives in the Community' in Jupp, V Davies, P and Francis, P (eds), *Doing Criminological Research* (London, Sage, 2000)

DAVIDSON, S *The Inter-American Human Rights System* (Aldershot, UK, Ashgate Publishing Company, 1997)

DE LA MARE, T and GALLIFANT, K 'The Horizontal Effect of the Human Rights Act 1998' [2001] *Juridical Review*

DEZALAY, Y and GARTH, BG *The Internationalization of Palace Wars: Lawyers, Economists, and the Contest to Transform Latin American States* (Chicago, University of Chicago Press, 2002)
DICKSON, B 'The Contribution of Human Rights Commissions to the Protection of Human Rights' [2003] *Public Law*
District Audit, *The Human Rights Act: A Bulletin for Public Bodies* (London, District Audit, 2002)
DOBSON, N 'Work in progress — Human Rights' (2000) 73 *Journal of Local Government Law*
DONNELLY, J *Universal Human Rights in Theory and Practice* (Ithaca, NY, Cornell University Press, 2003)
DOUZINAS, C *The End of Human Rights: Critical Legal Thought at the Turn of the Century* (Oxford, Hart Publishing, 2000)
DRZEMCZEWSKI, AZ *European Human Rights Convention in Domestic Law: A Comparative Study* (Oxford, Clarendon Press, 1983)
EASTMAN, N and PEAY, J (eds), *Law Without Enforcement: integrating mental health and justice* (Oxford, Portland, Oregon, Hart, 1999)
EDELMAN, 'Legal Environments and Organisational Governance: The Expansion of Due Process in the American Workplace' (1990) 95 *American Journal of Sociology*
EDWARDS, L '*S v Miller* The End of the Children's Hearings System As We Know It?' [2001] *SLT* (2001)
—— and GRIFFITHS, A *Family Law* (Edinburgh, W Green/Sweet & Maxwell, 1997)
EKBERG, J *Inkomsteffekter av invandring* (Högskolan i Växjö, Centrum för arbetsmarknadspolitisk forskning, 1983)
ENGEL, D and Frank Munger, *Rights of Inclusion: Law and Identity in the Life Stories of Americans with Disabilities* (Chicago, University of Chicago Press, 2003)
EPP, CR *The Rights Revolution: Lawyers, Activists, and Supreme Courts in Comparative Perspective* (Chicago, The University of Chicago Press, 1998)
EPSTEIN, L *Conservatives in Court* (Knoxville, Tenn, University of Tennessee Press, 1985)
—— and Kobylka, JF *The Supreme Court and Legal Change* (Chapel Hill, NC, University of North Carolina Press, 1992)
ETZIONI, A 'Social Norms: Internalization, Persuasion and History' (2000) 34, *Law and Society Review*
SIR EVANS, V 'The European Court of Human Rights: A Time for Appraisal', in Robert Blackburn and JJ Busuttil (eds), *Human Right for the 21st*. Century (London, Pinter, 1997)
EWICK, P and SILBEY, S *The Common Place of Law: Stories from Everyday Life* (Chicago, University of Chicago Press, 1998)
EWING, KD 'The Human Rights Act and Parliamentary Democracy' (1999) 62 *Modern Law Review* 75ff

FALK, R *Human Rights Horizons: The Pursuit of Justice in a Globalizing World* (London, Routledge, 2000)

FARRAN, S *The UK before the European Court of Human Rights: Case Law and Commentary* (London, Blackstone, 1996)

FELDMAN, D 'The Human Rights Act 1998 and Constitutional Principles' (1999) 19 *Legal Studies*

—— 'Public Interest Litigation and Constitutional Theory in Comparative Perspective' (1992) 52 *The Modern Law Review*

FELICE, WF *The Global New Deal: Economic and Social Human Rights in World Politics* (Maryland, Rowman Littlefield, 2003)

FINLAY, A 'The Human Rights Act: The Lord Chancellor's Department's Preparations For Implementation' [1999] *European Human Rights Law Review*

FOUCAULT, M *Discipline and Punish: The Birth of the Prison* (2nd edn, New York, Alan Sheridan trans, Vintage Books, 1995)

—— *Birth of the Clinic: An Archaeology of Medical Perception* (New York, AL Sheridan Smith trans, Pantheon Books, 1973)

FREDMAN, S *Discrimination and Human Rights: The Case of Racism* (Oxford, Oxford University Press, 2002)

—— 'Equality Issues' in Markesinis (ed), *The Impact of the Human Rights Bill on English Law* (Oxford, Clarendon, 1998)

FREEMAN, M *Human Rights: An Interdisciplinary Approach* (Cambridge, Polity Press, 2002)

FRIEDMAN, LM *The Legal System: A Social Science Perspective* (New York, Russell Sage Foundation, 1975)

FRIEND, JW *The Long Presidency: France in the Mitterrand Years 1981–1995* (Colorado, Westview Press, 1998)

GALANTER, M 'Why the 'Haves' Come Out Ahead: Speculation on the Limits of Legal Change' (1974) 9 *Law & Society Review*

GALLIGAN, DJ 'Authoritarianism in Law and Government: The Promise of Administrative Justice, (2001) 54 *Current Legal Problems*

—— 'Public Administration and the Tendency to Authoritarianism' in Sajo, A (ed), *Out of and Into Authoritarian Laws* (Klauser, 2002)

GALLIGAN, D and KURKCHIYAN, M (eds), *Law and Informal Practices: The Post-Communist Experience* (Oxford, Oxford University Press, 2003)

GARTH, BG and SARAT, A (eds), *How Does Law Matter?* (Evanston, IL, Northeastern University Press, American Bar Association, 1998)

—— (eds), *Justice and power in sociolegal studies* (Evanston, IL, Northwestern University Press, American Bar Foundation, 1998)

GAUDEMENT, YH *Les Juristes et la vie politique de la IIIè République* (Paris, PUF, 1970)

GIBNEY, MJ 'Introduction' in MJ Gibney (ed), *Globalizing Rights* (Oxford, Oxford University Press, 2003)

GILBERT, G 'The Protection of Minorities under the European Convention on Human Rights' in Dine, J and Watt, B (eds), *Discrimination Law* (London, Longman, 1996)
GÖRANSSON, H and KARLSSON, A *Diskrimineringslagarna: En praktisk kommentar* (Stockholm, Norstedts Juridik, 2000)
—— *Supplement till 'Diskrimineringslagarna'* (Stockholm, Norstedts Juridik, 2001)
GOSTIN, L *Human Rights and Public Health in the Aids Pandemic* (Oxford, Oxford University Press, 1997)
GREEN, M 'What do we talk about when we talk about Indicators: Current Approaches to Human Rights Measurement' (2001) 23 *HRQ*
GRIFFITHS, A and KANDEL, RF 'Hearing Children at Children's Hearings' (2000) 3 *Child and Family Law Quarterly*
—— 'Legislating for the Child's Voice: Perspectives from Comparative Ethnography of Proceedings Involving Children' in M Maclean, (ed), *Making Law for Families* (Oxford/Portland, Hart Publishing, 2000)
GROSZ, S and HULTON, S 'Using the European Convention on Human Rights' in Cooper, J and Dhavan, R (eds), *Public Interest Law* (London, Blackwell Publishers, 1986)
GURR, TR *Peoples Versus States: Minorities at Risk in the New Century* (Washington, DC, US Institute of Peace Press, 2000)
HALLETT, C et al, *The Evaluation of Children's Hearings in Scotland* (Scottish Office Central Research Unit, 1998)
HALLIDAY, S 'The Influence of Judicial Review on Bureaucratic Decision-Making' [2000] *Public Law* 110–22
—— *Judicial Review and Compliance with Administrative Law* (Oxford, Hart Publishing, 2004).
HALPERN, SC 'Assessing the Litigative Role of ACLU Chapters' in SL Wasby (ed), *Civil Liberties: Policy and Policy Making* (Lexington, Mass, Lexington Press, 1976)
HAMMOND, A 'The Human Rights Act and the Government Legal Service' (1999) 20(3) *Statute Law Review*
HANDLER, J Hollingsworth, E and Ehrlanger, H *Social Movements and the Legal System* (New York, Academic Press, 1978)
HANDY, C *Understanding Organisations* (Penguin, 1997)
VOGEL, H-H 'The Sources of Swedish Law, in M Bogdan (ed), *Swedish Law* (Stockholm, Norstedts Juridik, 2000)
HARE, I 'Vertically Challenged: Private Parties and the Human Rights Act' [2001] *European Human Rights Law Review*
HARLOW, C 'Public Law and Popular Justice' (2002) 65 *The Modern Law Review*, 65 (2002)
—— and RAWLINGS, R *Pressure Through Law* (London, Routledge, 1992)
HARRIS, J *The Social Work Business* (London, Routledge, 2003)
HART, HLA *The Concept of Law* (Oxford, Clarendon, 1961).

HARTMAN, JF 'Derogation from Human Rights Treaties in Public Emergencies — A Critique of Implementation by the European Commission and Court of Human Rights and the Human Rights Committee of the United Nations' (1981) 22:1, *Harvard Journal of International Law*

HATHAWAY, OA 'Do Human Rights Treaties Make a Difference?' (2002) 111 *Yale Law Journal*

HAWES, D and PEREZ, B *The Gypsy and the State* (Bristol, The Policy Press, 1996)

HAWKINS, K 'Compliance Strategy, Prosecution Policy and Aunt Sally' (1990) 30 *British Journal of Criminology*

HEINZ, JP, PAIK, A and SOUTHWORTH, A 'Lawyers for Conservative Causes: Clients, Ideology, and Social Distance' (2003) 37 *Law & Society Review*

HENDERSON, CW 'Conditions Affecting the Use of Political Repression' (1991) 35(1) *The Journal of Conflict Resolution* and UNDP, *Human Development Report 2002*

HENKIN, L and HOLGROVE, J (eds), *Human Rights: An Agenda for the Century* (Washington DC, American Society of International Law, 1994)

HEPPLE, B 'Have Twenty Years of Race Relations Act in Britain Been a Failure?' in B Hepple and EM Szyszczak (eds), *Discrimination: The Limits of Law* (London, Mansell, 1992)

HERTOGH, M and HALLIDAY, S 'Judicial Review and Bureaucratic Impact in Future Research' in M Hertogh, and S Halliday, (eds), *Judicial Review and Bureaucratic Impact: International and Interdisciplinary Perspectives* (Cambridge, Cambridge University Press, 2004)

HEWITT, P 'The NCCL Fifty Years On' in P Wallington, (ed), *Civil Liberties 1984* (Oxford, Martin Robertson & Co, 1984)

HEYNS, C and VILJOEN, F *The Impact of the United National Human Rights Treaties on the Domestic Level* (The Hague/London/New York, Kluwer Law International, 2002)

HODGE, H 'A Test Case Strategy' in Partington, M and Jowell, J (eds), *Welfare Law and Policy* (London, Frances Pinter Ltd, 1979)

HODGSON, J 'Constructing the pre-trial role of the defence in French criminal procedure: An adversarial outsider in an inquisitorial process?' (2002) 6(1) *International Journal of Evidence and Proof*

—— 'The detention and interrogation of suspects detained in police custody in France: a comparative account' (2004) 1(2) *European Journal of Criminology*

—— 'Hierarchy, Bureaucracy, and Ideology in French Criminal Justice: Some Empirical Observations' (2002) 29(2) *Journal of Law and Society*

—— 'The police, the prosecutor and the *juge d'instruction*: Judicial Supervision in France, Theory and Practice' (2001) 41 *British Journal of Criminology*

—— 'Suspects, defendants and victims in french criminal justice: The context of recent reform' (2002) 51(4) *International and Comparative Law Quarterly*

—— and RICH, G 'A Criminal Defence for the French?' (1993) 143 *New Law Journal*

HOJNACKI, M 'Interest Groups' Decisions to Join Alliances or Work Alone' (1997) 41 *American Journal of Political Science*

HOLMES, S 'Constitutionalism, Democracy, and State Decay' in Koh, H and Slye, K (eds), *Deliberative Democracy and Human Rights* (London: Yale University Press, 1999)

Home Office, *Putting Rights into Public Service: The Human Rights Act 1998: An Introduction for Public Authorities* (London, Home Office, 1999)

Human Rights Watch, *Protectors or Pretenders? Government Human Rights Commissions in Africa* (New York, Human Rights Watch, 2001)

HUNT, M 'The Human Rights Act and Legal Culture: The Judiciary and the Legal Profession' ( ) 26(1), *Journal of Law and Society*

—— *Using Human Rights Law in English Courts* (London, Hart Publishing, 1997)

IGNATIEF, M *Isaiah Berlin: a life* (London, Chatto & Winden, 1998)

International Council on Human Rights Policy, *Performance and Legitimacy: National Human Rights Institutions* (Switzerland, IPPR, 2000)

LORD IRVINE, 'Activism and Restraint' [1999], *European Human Rights Law Review*

IVERS, G and O'CONNOR, K 'Friends as Foes: The Amicus Curiae Participation and Effectiveness of the American Civil Liberties Union and Americans for Effective Law Enforcement in Criminal Cases, 1969–1982' (1987) 9, *Law and Policy*

JACOB, H *Justice in America* (Boston, Little Brown, 1978)

JENSEN, EG and HELLER, TC *Beyond Common Knowledge Empirical Approaches to the Rule of Law* (Palo Alto, Stanford University Press, forthcoming)

JONES, T 'Property Rights, Planning Law and the European Convention' (1996) 3, *European Human Rights Law Review*

KAGAN, R and SCHOLZ, J 'The "Criminology of the Corporation" and Regulatory Enforcement Strategies' in Hawkins, K and Thomas, J (eds), *Enforcing Regulation* (Boston, Mass., Kluwer-Nijhoff, 1984)

KANDEL, RF and GRIFFITHS, A 'Reconfiguring Personhood: From Ungovernability to Parent Adolescent Autonomy Conflict Actions' (2003) 53(3), *Syracuse Law Review*

KARPIK, L *Les avocats: Entre l'état, le public et le marché XIIIè-XXè siècle* (Paris, Gallimard, 1995)

KATZ, J *Poor People's Lawyers in Transition* (New Brunswick, NJ, Rutgers University Press, 1982)

KEARNEY, B *Children's hearings and the Sheriff Court* (Edinburgh, Butterworths, 2000)
KEARNEY, JD and MERRILL, TW 'The Influence of Amicus Curiae Briefs on the Supreme Court' (2000) 148 *University of Pennsylvania Law Review*
KECK, ME and SIKKINK, K *Activists Beyond Borders: Advocacy Networks in International Politics* (Ithaca, NY, Cornell University Press, 1998)
KENRICK, D and CLARK, C *Moving On: The Gypsies and Travellers of Britain* (Hatfield, University of Hertfordshire Press, 1999)
KEY, VO *Politics, Parties and Pressure Groups* (New York, Crowell, 1964)
KIRSCH, P 'Negotiating an Institution for the Twenty-First Century: Multilateral Diplomacy and the International Criminal Court' (2000–01) 46 *McGill Law Journal*
KLUG, F 'The Human Rights Act: Basic Principles and Values' [2001] *Journal of Local Government Law*
—— *Values for a Godless Age: The Story of the United Kingdom's New Bill of Rights* (London, Penguin Books, 2000)
—— and Starmer, K 'Incorporation through the "front door": the first year of the Human Rights Act', *Public Law*
KLUGER, R *Simple Justice,* (New York, Alfred E Knopf, Inc, 1975)
KNOCKE, W *Invandrare möter facket–Betydelsen av hemlandsbakgrund och hemvist i arbetslivet* (Stockholm, Arbetslivscentrum, 1982)
KOSHNER, AJ *Solving the Puzzle of Interest Group Litigation* (Westport, Conn, Greenwood Press, 1998)
KOTTER, J and HESKETT, J *Corporate Culture and Performance* (Simon and Schuster Free Press, 1992)
KRASNER, SD 'Sovereignty, Regimes and Human Rights' in V Rittberger, and P Mayer, (eds), *Regime Theory and International Relations* (Oxford, Oxford University Press, 1993)
KRISLOV, S 'The Amicus Curiae Brief: From Friendship to Advocacy' (1963) 72 *Yale Law Journal*
LABOUR PARTY, *Bringing Rights Home: Labour's Plans to Incorporate the European Convention on Human Rights into UK Law* (London, Labour Party, 1996)
LAKOFF, RT *Talking Power: The Politics of Language in Our Lives* (New York, Basic Books, 1990).
LANGE, A *Invandrare om etnisk diskriminering* (Stockholm Universitet, CEIFO, 1996)
LAWRENCE, SE *The Poor in Court: The Legal Services Program and Supreme Court Decision Making* (Princeton, NJ, Princeton University Press, 1990)
LAZARUS, L *Contrasting Prisoners' Rights* (Oxford, Oxford University Press, 2004)
LECLERC, H *Un combat pour la justice. Entretiens avec Marc Heurgon* (Paris, Éditions la Découverte, 1994)

LE SUEUR, A 'Access to Justice Rights in the United Kingdom' [2000] *European Human Rights Law Review*

LESTER, A 'Amici Curiae: Third Party Interventions Before the European Court of Human Rights' in F Matscher, and H Petzold, (eds), *Protecting Human Rights: The European Dimension* (Koln, Carl Heymanns Verlag KG, 1988)

—— and PANNICK, D 'The Impact of the Human Rights Act on Private Law' (2000) 116 *Law Quarterly Review*

LIÉGEOIS, J-P *Gypsies and Travellers* (Strasbourg, Council of Europe, 1987)

H and LINDHOLT, L *Human Rights Indicators. Country and Regional Database* (Copenhagen, Danish Institute for Human Rights, 2000)

LIPSKY, M *Street-Level Bureaucracy (*New York, Russell Sage Foundation, 1980)

LIVINGSTONE, S 'The Northern Ireland Human Rights Commission' (1999) 22 *Fordham International Law Journal*

LOCHAK, D *Les droits de l'homme* (Paris, La Découverte, 2002)

LOCKWOOD, B 'The United Nations Charter and United States Civil Rights Litigation 1946–1955' (1984) 69 *Iowa State Law Review*

LOCKYER, A and Stone, FH *Juvenile Justice in Scotland Twenty Five Years of the Welfare Approach* (Edinburgh, T & T Clark, 1998)

LOUX, A 'Losing the Battle, Winning the War: Litigation Strategy and Pressure Group Organisation in the Era of Incorporation' (2000) 11 *Kings College Law Journal*

LUHMANN, N *A Sociological Theory of Law*; translated by King, E and M Albrow, ed M Albrow, (London, Routledge & Kegan Paul, 1985)

—— *Closure and openness: on reality in the world of law* (Florence, European University Institute, 1986)

LYELL, N 'Whither Strasbourg?' [1997] *European Human Rights Law Review*

MCCANN, M 'Reform Litigation on Trial' (1992) 17 *Law and Social Inquiry*

—— *Rights at Work: Pay Equity Reform and the Politics of Legal Mobilization* (London, University of Chicago Press, 1994)

MCCONVILLE, M, HODGSON, J, BRIDGES, L and PAVLOVIC, A *Standing Accused: The Organisation and Practices of Criminal Defence Lawyers in Britain* (Oxford, Clarendon, 1994)

MCCRUDDEN, C *Anti-discrimination Law* (Aldershot, Dartmouth, 1991)

MCDIARMID, C 'Perspectives on the Children's Hearings System' in J Scoular, (ed), *Family Dynamics: Contemporary Issues in Family Law* (Edinburgh and London, Butterworths/LexisNexis, 2001)

MADSEN, MR, 'Virtecl legalitet ogeller 'pidgin law'? En Præliminær analyse of menneskereHigheder som transnational ret', in Petersen, H (ed), *Globaliseringer, ret og retsfilosofi* (Copenhagen, ΔJØF, 2002)

MARGUÉNAUD, J-P 'La dérive de la procédure pénale française au regard des exigences européennes' [2000] *Dalloz (Chroniques)*

MARGUENAUD, JP 'l'Effectivité des arrêts de la Cour européenne des droits de l'Homme en France' (2001) 24 *Journal des droits de l'Homme*

MARKMANN, C *The Noblest Cry* (New York, St Martin's Press, 1965)

MARKS, S 'Civil liberties at the margin: The UK derogation and the European Court of Human Rights' (1995) 15(1), *Oxford Journal of Legal Studies*

MARSHALL, K *Children's Rights in the Balance* (The Stationery Office, 1997)

MARSHALL, K, TISDALL, K and CLELLAND, A '*Voice of the Child' Under the Children (Scotland) Act 1995* (Scottish Executive, 2002)

MEDINA, C 'The Inter-American Commission on Human Rights and the Inter-American Court of Human Rights: Reflections on a joint venture' (1990) 12 *Human Rights Quarterly*

MEECHAN, K 'The Human Rights Act: Public Authority Preparations' [2001] *Journal of Local Government Law*

MELTSNER, M *Cruel and Unusual: The Supreme Court and Capital Punishment* (New York, Random House, 1973)

MERON, T 'Norm Making and Supervision in International Human Rights: Reflections on Institutional Order' (1982) 76(4) *American Journal of International Law*

MERRILS, JG and ROBERTSON, AH *Human Rights in Europe: A Study of the European Convention on Human Rights* (Manchester, Manchester University Press, 2001)

MNOOKIN, RH *Bargaining in the Shadow of the Law: the case of divorce* (Oxford, Social Science Research Council, 1979)

MORAG-LEVINE, N 'Partners No More: Relational Transformation and the Turn to Litigation in Two Conservationist Organizations' (2003) 37 *Law & Society Review*

MORRIS, R and CLEMENTS, L *Disability, Social Care, Health and Travelling People* (Cardiff, Traveller Law Research Unit, Cardiff Law School, 2001)

MORRIS, M and JACOBS, LR 'You Got a Problem with That? Exploring Evaluators' Disagreements about Ethics' (2000) 24(4) *Evaluation Review*

MUGWANYA, GW 'Realizing Universal Human Rights Norms Through Regional Human Rights Mechanisms: Reinvigorating the African System' (1999) 10(1) *Indiana International and Comparative Law Review*

MULLINS, *Management and Organisational Behaviour* (6th edn, FT Prentice Hall, 2001)

NEIER, A *Taking Liberties* (New York, Public Affairs, 2003)

NEWBURN, T 'What Do We Mean by Evaluation? (2001) 15 *Children and Society*

NEWBY, H *Social Science and Public Policy* (Swindon, Economic and Social Research Council, 1993)

NORDMANN, J and BRUNEL, A, *Aux Vents de L'histoire* (Arles, Actes Sud, 1996)

KMcK Norrie, *Children's Hearing in Scotland* (Edinburgh, W Green, 1997)

Numhauser-Henning, A 'Labour Law' in Bogdan, M (ed), *Swedish Law: In the New Millennium* (Stockholm, Norstedts Juridik, 2000)

O'Connor, K *Women's Organizations' Use of the Courts* (Lexington, Mass, Lexington Books, 1980)

O'Connor, K and Epstein, L 'The Rise of Conservative Interest Group Litigation' (1983) 45 *Journal of Politics*

Odinkalu, C 'The Individual Complaints Procedures of the African Commission on Human and Peoples' Rights: A Preliminary Assessment' (1998) 8 *Transnational Law and Contemporary Problems*

Olson, SM 'Interest Group Litigation in Federal District Court, Beyond the Political Disadvantage Theory' (1990) 52 *Journal of Politics*

Olson, M *The Logic of Collective Action* (Cambridge, Harvard University Press, 1965)

O'Neill, A 'The European Convention and the Independence of the Judiciary' (2000) 63 *Modern Law Review*

O'Neill, O *A Question of Trust* (Cambridge, Cambridge University Press, 2002)

Ornstein, NJ and Elder, S *Interest Group Lobbying and Policy Making* (Washington, DC, Congressional Quarterly Press, 1978)

Owen, JM and Rogers, PJ *Program Evaluation: Forms and Approaches* (St Leonards, New South Wales, Allen and Unwin, 1999)

Parsons, T *Action theory and the human condition* (New York, Free Press, 1978)

—— *Social systems and the evolution of action theory* (New York; London, Free Press; Collier Macmillan, 1977)

Pateyron, É *La contribution française à la rédaction de la Déclaration universelle des droits de l'homme* (Paris, La Documentation française, 1998)

Patton, MQ *Utilization-Focused Evaluation*, (Thousand Oaks, CA, Sage, 1997)

Pawson, R and Tilley, N 'What Works in Evaluation Research?' (1994) 34 *British Journal of Criminology*

Pearce, F and Tombs, S 'Ideology, Hegemony, and Empiricism: Compliance Theories of Regulation' (1990) 30 *British Journal of Criminology*

Pecheul, A *Les dates-clefs de la protection des droits de l'homme en France* (Paris, Ellipses, 2001)

Peterson, A *Women as Collective Actors: A Case Study of the Swedish Women's Peace Movement 1898–1990* (Göteborg, Research Report from the Department of Sociology, 1992)

Pityana, B `National Institutions at Work: The Case of South Africa' in K Hossain, L Besselink, H Selaisse, and E Volker, (eds), *Human Rights Commissions and Ombudsman Offices: National Experiences Throughout the World* (Kluwer, 2001)

PLEMING, N 'Assessing the Act: A Firm Foundation or a False Start?' [2000] *European Human Rights Law Review*

POE, SC and TATE, CN 'Repression of Human Rights to Personal Integrity in the 1980s: A Global Analysis' (1994) 88(4) *American Political Science Review*

POWER, M *The Audit Society: Rituals of Verification* (Oxford, Oxford University Press, 1997)

PRADEL, J 'Les personnes suspectes ou poursuivies après la loi du 15 juin 2000: Evolution ou révolution?' (2001) 13 *Dalloz, Doctrine,*

PROSSER, T *Test Cases for the Poor* (London, Child Poverty Action Group, 1983)

PRURO, S 'The Role of Amicus Curiae in the United States Supreme Court: 1920–1966' (PhD Dissertation, State University of New York at Buffalo, 1971)

Public Law Project, *The Impact of the Human Rights Act on Judicial Review* (London, Public Law Project, 2003)

PUTMAN, RD with LEONARDI, R and NANETTI, RY *Making Democracy Work: Civic Traditions in Modern Italy* (Princeton, Princeton University Press, 1993)

RABIN, RL 'Lawyers for Social Change: Perspectives on Public Interest Law' (1976) 28 *Stanford Law Review* 207ff

RAINE, JW and Walker, CP *The Impact on Courts and the Administration of Justice of the Human Rights Act 1998* (London, LCD Research Series 9/02, 2002)

RAPHAEL, T 'The Problem of the Horizontal Effect' [2000] *European Human Rights Law Review* 393ff

RAZ, J 'On the Nature of Rights' (1984) 93 *Mind* 194–214

RICHARDSON, G *Policing Pollution* (Oxford, Clarendon Press, 1983)

RICHARDSON, G and MACHIN, D 'Judicial Review and Tribunal Decision-Making, [2000] Public Law, 494

RIGGS, S, FULLER, EDELMAN, LB, MATUSIK, SF 'Legal readings: Employee interpretation and mobilization of law' (2000) 25(1) *The Academy of Management Review* 200–16

RISSE, T, ROPP, SC and SIKKINK, K (eds) *The Power of Human Rights: International Norms and Domestic Change* (Cambridge, Cambridge University Press, 1999)

RISSEE-KAPPEN, T *Bringing Transnational Relations Back In* (Cambridge, Cambridge University Press, 1995)

ROBERTSON, G *Crimes Against Humanity* (London, Penguin Books, 1999)

—— *The Justice Game* (London, Vintage, 1999)

ROSE, N 'Crime cases dominate ECHR bids' (1998) 95(07) *Law Society's Gazette*

ROSENBAUM, S 'Lawyers *Pro Bono Publico*: Using International Human Rights Law on Behalf of the Poor' in Lutz, EL Hannum, H and Burke, K (eds), *New Directions in Human Rights* (Philadelphia, University of Pennsylvania Press, 1989)
ROSENBERG, G *The Hollow Hope: Can Courts Bring About Social Change?* (London, University of Chicago Press, 1991)
ROSS, J 'Uncommon humanity: travellers, ethnicity and discrimination' (1999) 4(1) *Contemporary Issues in Law*
ROTH, A-K *Nya jämställdhetsboken: från teori till praktik* (Stockholm, Norstedts Juridik, 2002)
RUBENSTEIN, WB 'Divided We Litigate: Addressing Disputes Among Group Members and Lawyers in Civil Rights Campaigns' (1997) 106 *The Yale Law Journal* 1623ff
RUBIN, E *Abortion, Politics and the Court* (Westport, Conn, Greenwood Press, 1982)
SALGADO, EM and O'BRIEN, C 'Table of cases under the Human Rights Act', [2001] *European Human Rights Law Review*
SANDLER, D *International Treaty Institutions And State Compliance: Rules Processes And Practices* (forthcoming)
SANDLER, DJ et al (eds) *Protecting the Gulf of Aqaba: a regional environmental challenge* (Washington, DC, Environmental Law Institute, 1993)
SANKEY, J 'Decolonisation: Cooperation and Confrontation at the United Nations' in E Jensen, and T Fisher, (eds), *The United Kingdom — The United Nations* (London, Macmillan, 1990)
SARAT, A and KEARNS, T 'Beyond the great divide: forms of legal scholarship and everyday life' in A Sarat, and T Kearns, (eds), *Law in Everyday Life* (Ann Arbor, University of Michigan Press, 1993)
SARD, B 'The Role of the Courts in Welfare Reform' (1988) 22 *Clearinghouse Review* 367ff
SCHATTSCHNEIDER, EE *The Semi-Sovereign People* (New York, Holt, Rinehart and Winston, 1960)
SCHEINGOLD, S *The Politics of Rights: Lawyers, Public Policy, and Political Change* (New Haven, Yale University Press, 1974)
SCHEPELLE, KL and WALKER, JL Jr, 'The Litigation Stratgies of Interest Groups' in JL Walker, Jr (ed), *Mobilizing Interest Groups in America: Patrons, Professions, and Social Movements* (Ann Arbor, University of Michigan Press, 1991), p.183ff
SCHIERUP, C-U and PAULSON, S *Arbetets etniska delning* (Stockholm, Carlsson, 1994)
—— in ÅLUND, A and SCHIERUP, C-U *Paradoxes of Multiculturalism* (Aldershot, Avebury, 1991)
SCHLOZMAN, KL and TIERNEY, JT *Organized Interests and American Democracy* (New York, Harper and Row, 1986).

SCHULZ, D (ed), *Leveraging the Law: Using the Courts to Achieve Social Change* (New York, Peter Lang, 1998)
SEDLEY, S 'First Steps Towards a Constitutional Bill of Rights' (1997) 5 *European Human Rights Law Review*
SEDLEY, S 'Human Rights: A Twenty-First Century Agenda' (1995) *Public Law*
SIEGHART, P *The Lawful Rights of Mankind* (Oxford, Oxford University Press, 1985)
SIKKINK, K 'The Emergence, Evolution and Effectiveness of the Latin American Human Rights Network', in E Jelin, and E Hershverg, (eds), *Constructing Democracy, Human Rights, Citizenship and Society in Latin America* (Colorado, Westview Press, 1996)
SILBEY, S 'Cultural Analyses of Law' (1992) 17(1) Law and Social Inquiry
SINGH, R *The Future of Human Rights in the United Kingdom* (Oxford, Hart Publishing, 1997)
SLAPPER, G 'Impact on the legal system of the European Court of Human Rights' (1997) 20 *Student Law Review*
SMITH, R 'How Good Are Test Cases?' in J Cooper and R Dhavan (eds), *Public Interest Law* (London, Blackwell Publishers,1986)
SOROUSH, A Reason, Freedom, and Democracy in Islam: Essential Writings of *by Abd Al-Karim Surush*, Mahmoud Sadri (Translator), Ahmad Sadri (ed) (Oxford, Oxford University Press, 2000)
SOUTHWORTH, A 'Lawyer-Client Decision-Making in Civil Rights and Poverty Practice: An Empirical Study of Lawyers' Norms' (1996) 9 *Georgetown Journal of Legal Ethics*
SPARER, EV 'The Right to Welfare' in N Dorsen (ed), *The Rights of Americans* (New York, Random House, 1970)
SPENCER, S and BYNOE, I *A UK Human Rights Commission: The Options* (London, IPPR, 1998)
STAMMERS, N 'Social Movements and the Social Construction of Human Rights' (1999) 21 *Human Rights Quarterly*
STEINER, HJ and ALSTON, P *International Human Rights in Context: Law, Politics, Morals* (2nd edn, Oxford, Oxford University Press, 2000)
STEINER, E in Gearty, CA (ed), *European Civil Liberties and the European Convention on Human Rights: A Comparative Study* (The Hague, Kluwer, 1997)
STONE SWEET, A *Governing With Judges: Constitutional Politics in Europe* (Oxford, Oxford University Press, 2000)
STREET, H *Freedom, the Individual and the Law* (3rd edn, Harmondsworth, Pelican, 1975)
SUNKIN, M, BRIDGES, L and MAZEROS, G *Judicial Review in Perspective* (London, Public Law Project, 1993)
SUTHERLAND, E *Child and Family Law* (Edinburgh, T&T Clark, 1999)

TEUBNER, G (ed), *Autopoietic law: A new approach to law and society* (Berlin, Walter de Gruyter, 1988)

TEUBNER, G and FEBBRAJO, A (eds), *State, law, and economy as autopoietic systems: regulation and autonomy in a new perspective* (Milano, Giuffrè, 1992)

THOMAS, DC *The Helsinki Effect: International Norms, Human Rights, and the Demise of Communism* (Princeton, Princeton University Press, 2001)

TOLLEY, H Jr, 'Interest Group Litigation to Enforce Human Rights' (1990) 105 *Political Science Quarterly*

—— *The International Commission of Jurists: Global Advocates of Human Rights* (Philadelphia, University of Pennsylvania Press, 1994)

TROUILLE, H 'A Look at French Criminal Procedure' [1994] *Criminal Law Review*

TRUMAN, D *The Governmental Process* (New York, Alfred E Knopf, Inc, 1951)

TUSHNET, M *The NAACP's Legal Strategy Against Segregated Education, 1925–1950* (Chapel Hill, NC, University of North Carolina Press, 1987)

University of Warwick (Local Government Centre), *Improving Public Services: Evaluation of the Best Value Pilot Programme — Final Report* (London, Department of the Environment, Transport and the Regions, 2001)

VILLIGER, ME 'The European Court of Human Rights' (2001) 95 *American Society of International Legal Proceedings*

VOSE, CE *Caucasians Only* (Berkeley, University of California Press, 1959)

WADE, HWR 'Human rights and the judiciary' (1998) 520 *European Human Rights Law Review*

WADE, W 'Horizons of horizontality (2000) 116 *Law Quarterly Review*

WADHAM, J 'Human Rights on Test' (15 April 1997) *Solicitors' Journal*

WADHAM, J and MOUNTFIELD, H *The Human Rights Act 1998* (London, Blackstone Press Ltd, 1999)

WALKER, S *In Defense of American Liberties: A History of the ACLU* (New York, Oxford University Press, 1990)

WATERHOUSE, L and MCGHEE, J 'Children's Hearings in Scotland: Compulsion and Disadvantage' (2002) 24(3) *Journal of Social Welfare and Family Law*

WESTIN, C *Majoritet om minoritet: En studie i etnisk tolerans i 80-talets Sverige: En rapport från Diskrimineringsutredningen* (Stockholm, Publica, 1984)

WIKANDER, U "Sekelskiftet 1900: konstruktion av nygammal kvinnlighet" in Wikander, U and Manns, U (eds) *Det eviga kvinnliga: En historia om förändring* (Lund, Studnetlitteratur, 2001)

WINCH, P *The Idea of a Social Science and its Relation to Philosophy* (2nd edn, London, Routledge, 1990)

Index